DESSERTS

The Ultimate Cookbook

DESSERTS

The Ultimate Cookbook

CIDER MILL PRESS

BOOK
PUBLISHERS
KENNEBUNKPORT, MAINE

CONTENTS

THE MIGRATION OF DESSERTS

*I*f you've ever experienced the "clack, clack, crack!" of your spoon hitting the top of a crème brûlée, you know it is one of the most satisfying dessert experiences, not only in sound and taste, but in memory as well. Perhaps you had your first crème brûlée in a dimly lit restaurant celebrating a Valentine's Day with a loved one, or in a busy and bustling brasserie on a corner in Paris. It is this kind of sensory experience that creates dessert memories, which remind us of life's beautiful, sweet moments. Nostalgia and dessert seem to go hand-in-hand. Take for instance award-winning pastry chef, author, and TV personality Christina Tosi, who has achieved success thanks to her ability to elevate the flavors and textures of her childhood to match a more refined palate. Taking all the food experiences and collecting them into one memory shapes your palate and ultimately your identity, a big piece of who you are and the way you experience sweet things.

A certain smell, sound, or sight will open the file cabinets of our mind, where we thumb through our memories to recall the last time we smelled, heard, or saw something similar. For instance, when a chocolate soufflé is rising in the oven and the smell hits your nostrils, the amygdala kicks into gear, reminding your brain of the last time you had a chocolate soufflé, and all the surrounding layers of that experience. Perhaps you've baked cookies alongside your Nana, have the same birthday cake year in and year out, or remember the smells wafting from a neighborhood bakery while walking home from church on a Sunday. All of these dessert memories and moments become a part of your individual life story. If you're a sweet tooth, like me, most of your fondest memories are associated with dessert. I promised myself that if I ever did have to choose a "last meal," it would definitely be the flakiest pain au chocolat aux amandes and foamy cappuccino, because one sunny day in Paris I had this exact breakfast, and have never felt happier in my life.

In his book *In the Name of Identity* Amin Maalouf defines identity as one entity composed of many parts. One person can be shaped by multiple experiences: in travel, in the cross-

ing of a country's border into a new culture, and in the passing-on of tradition. Identity not only shapes each individual story but also ties us all together into the larger human narrative. Maalouf asserts that "identity can't be compartmentalized. You can't divide it up into halves or thirds or any other separate segments. I haven't got several identities: I've got just one, made up of many components in a mixture that is unique to me, just as other people's identity is

unique to them as individuals." Whether you grew-up making patczki on Fat Tuesday, kubbuz flatbreads over a hot stove, tiramisu, or layered mille-feuille, I am convinced that desserts also carry their own unique identities made up of many elements. They have been passed down from generation to generation, kitchen to kitchen, plate to plate. Desserts have crossed borders, through monarchs and empires and chefs, and have trickled down to the masses, reminding us that history, power, economics, and the movement of humans have defined cultural norms around the table. "But croissants are assuredly French!" one could argue. But are they really?

Growing-up in a Lebanese American family, it was a rite of passage to make the crêpe paper–thin sheets of pastry that would eventually become baklawah, a Lebanese sweet composed of phyllo, walnuts, and rosewater syrup. The recipe was passed down from my sithu, to my mom and aunts, and eventually to all of us cousins. Every year we would all gather with our bandanas and aprons, and report for duty to make baklawah from scratch—a two-day task—starting with that finicky phyllo. Anytime in my childhood if I ever let the word "baklava" slip from my mouth, my aunt would chide me and say, "bak-la-wah," which is the Lebanese version of its better-known Greek and Turkish cousins. Like the movement of humans and the lines that divide us, desserts have traveled many miles, crossing and re-crossing borders. They have been adapted and claimed by countries, cultures, and individual families, each offering a unique touch, whether in nomenclature or preparation. For all of us, desserts are a memory, a tradition, an homage to a place, person, community, or culture.

The origins of dessert can be traced back to the Greco-Roman era of classical antiquity when people made a basic pastry dough from flour mixed with water (around 1300 BCE). Meanwhile, in the Mesoamerican region, the Mayans, too, were using cocoa beans to make the world's first hot chocolate: xocolatl (or bitter water) made with crushed cocoa, cornmeal, and chili pepper. Later on, in the 1400s, Spanish conquistadors (most notably Hernán Cortés) not only conquered the Aztecs of Mexico, but took hold of their cocoa, bringing it back to Europe. From there, sugar was added to cut the drink's bitterness, and it spread throughout the continent. According to Bizma Turzmizi in the article "Food Stories: Cake Rusk," sugar itself became a commodity as expansion, wars, and the slave trade made it accessible to multiple nations, "spread[ing] to Persia and then to the

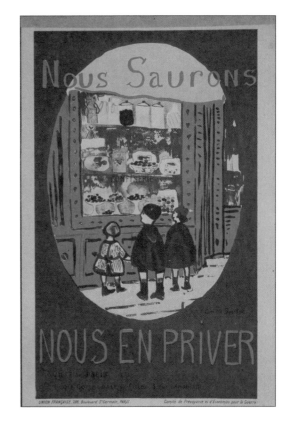

Eastern Mediterranean and Arabia, and with the Muslim invasion of Spain, and the Crusades saw the advent of the developing spice trade. The cooking techniques and ingredients of India, Arabia, and Persia spread into North-

ern Europe. So, modern day cakes traveled to Europe from Asia, and then back to Asia, as if it was an import from Europe." Before then, sugar was a commodity reserved only for the elite, and was mixed into savory dishes as a sign of status.

It wasn't until the 16th century that the word "dessert" ("desservir" in French, meaning to "clear-out, clear the table" [for sweets]) came to be a common term and a stand-alone staple on the table at the end of a meal. This was also when recipes for pastry dough started to appear in European cookbooks. *A Peopre New Booke of Cokery*, published in London in 1545, included the following recipe: "To make a short paest for tarte – Take fyne floure and a cursey of fayre water and a dyshe of swete butter and a lyttel saffron, and the yolckes of two eggs and make it thyne and tender as ye maye."

It was common practice in Europe during this time for royalty and monarchs to marry other monarchs, as a way to unite a kingdom or consolidate power. For instance, Catherine de Medici of Italy married Henry II in France, shifting religious and political power of the region. As these royal elite crossed borders, they either traveled with their chefs from country to country, or persons followed, exposing new culinary techniques between countries. This was especially evident at coronation ceremonies and feasts of the time. Pastries and sweets from Venice (an influential Renaissance city filled with wealthy merchants), eventually found their way to Versailles. According to the Brooklyn's Museum accounts, Catherine's cousin, Marie de Medici, was the daughter of a Tuscan grand duke and a Habsburg archduchess who married King Henry IV of France. La Varenne, author of *Le Cuisinier françois* (1652) and *Le Pâtissier françois* (1653), was said to have worked in her kitchens before compiling these influential cookbooks. The Portuguese and Spanish monarchs, too, were sending ships to new lands for colonization and ultimately

exploitation of local indigenous populations during the age of conquistadors, discovering whole new worlds of flavor and tradition.

It is important to also mention the role convents and monasteries played in the development of pastry throughout the Middle Ages and onward. As wars and conflicts were happening all around Europe, these holy habitations became cultivators of creativity, safe havens from the outside world. Danielle Oteri recalls in *The Holy History of Italian Pastries* that nuns in particular "baked elaborate, labor-intensive pastries from ancient recipes that they sold to the public to support themselves." The sfogliatella is one such delicacy that came about during the period: "The story goes that a nun was experimenting with a bit of leftover semolina flour soaked in milk. She added candied fruit, wrapped it all between two pieces of flaky pastry softened with lard, and formed it into the shape of a monk's hood." This santarosa pastry (named after the convent of Santa Rosa in Conca dei Marini along the Almafi Coast in Italy where the nun had first created it) would later become sfogliatella, named by Neapolitan pastry chef Pasquala Pintauro after remaining a convent recipe secret for over 150 years.

Desserts continued to develop in the 17th and 18th centuries, mainly in the empires of Austria and Prussia, as well as the Ottoman Empire in what is now primarily the Middle East. The British Empire very soon started colonizing new lands, amassing new claims all over the globe and establishing extensive trade networks. India was the jewel in the crown of the British Empire. Called the "British Raj," Britain ruled over India for its spices, textiles, and manpower from 1858 to 1947. In 1947, the British Raj was divided into two sovereign dominion states, India and Pakistan. Pakistanis still enjoy teatime and British treats such as sliced pound cake, or "cake rusk." Rusks are twice-baked breads, similar to biscotti, "a legacy of

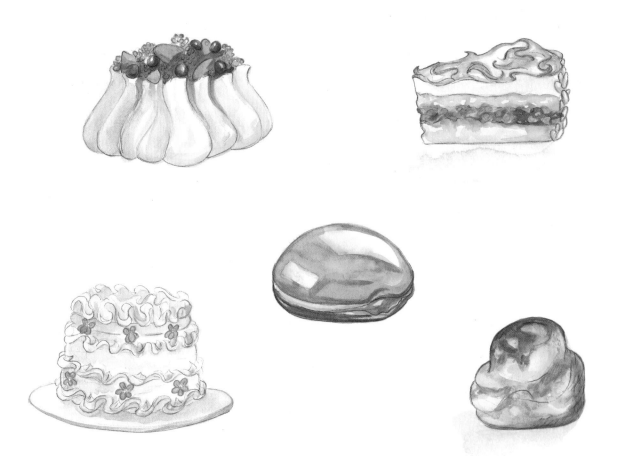

Elizabethan naval provisions . . . indestructible enough to last out a long voyage at sea," is how Alex Testere described them in "Who Came Up with the Modern Dessert Course?" Soetbeskuit ("sweet rusks") are also widespread in South Africa today, a legacy of the Dutch East India Company, which brought them along the spice route in the 1600s.

Every dessert has a full, rich history behind it, and over the years desserts have been adapted by certain countries as a matter of national pride. Perhaps the most told example is the pavlova, a baked meringue with cream and berries, named after dancer Anna Pavlova. In the 1920s she toured Australia and New Zealand, and today the dessert has planted itself in the food memories of both Aussies and Kiwis. Both countries claim to have invented the dessert and named it after this famous ballerina. New Zealander Dr. Andrew Paul Wood and Australian Annabelle Utrecht met debating the pavlova's origins and eventually wrote a book on its his-

tory entitled *Beat Until Stiff: The Secret History of the Pavlova and a Social History of Meringue Desserts*. What they found was there were meringues with cream and fruit elements dating back at least an entire century in aristocratic kitchens across German-speaking lands during the reign of the Habsburg monarchy. The pavlova even pre-dated that, possibly originating in Africa and finding its way to central Europe via the Portuguese. As power shifted between empires and kingdoms, the meringue went with it. German-speaking immigrants to the United States and Australia brought meringue-based desserts such as the baiser torte and the spanische windtorte. Pavlova settled itself in Australia and New Zealand as part of the identity of the country, and yet its identity is in reality "composed of many parts" in the same way Maalouf believes individual identities form.

France is a country marked by many traditions, and its pastry might very well be one of its best known. It is hard to differentiate pastry from France because it is such an important part of daily life. In "The History of Pastry" Clare Gazzard explains how "Marie-Antoine Carême is widely considered to be the first 'celebrity pastry chef,' bringing pastry into the world of grande cuisine. His elaborate creations graced the windows of his Paris pâtisserie before he went on to cook for European leaders, including George IV. The glamor and splendor associated with these rich, buttery confections helped grow the popularity of French pastry desserts as the epitome." There are countless French pastries that have made their way around the world, such as pâte à choux (the base pastry that constitutes eclairs and cream puffs), macarons, mousse au chocolat, tarte tatins, and crêpes. But the reverse is true too. Desserts have traveled to France from elsewhere and become symbols of regional French identity, such as la tropézienne. Saint-Tropez is located along the French

Côte d'Azur, known for its stunning blue waters and exclusive coastal enclaves that today draw film stars and the social elite from around the world. In 1955, a Polish immigrant named Alexandre Micka settled in Saint-Tropez, and opened a pastry shop where, as Alex Ledsom tells it, "he sold one of his grandmother's recipes, a rich round and flat brioche split in half, filled with an unctuous combination of two different creams, and studded with pearl sugar." It was recorded that the French actress Brigitte Bardot was filming a movie in that area, fell in love with the dessert, and came up with the idea of naming it after the town.

World War I marked the dissolution of both the Hapsburg monarchy and the Ottoman Empire, and immigrants continued to settle in America, creating an entirely new expanse of desserts as an established part of American identity. "Before becoming an immigrant one is

Woellert's history of the nutty, dry fruit custard known as Ozark pudding: "The grandmother of the Ozark pudding is the French Huguenot cake gâteau aux noisettes ("cake with hazelnuts"), which French Protestants brought to South Carolina after escaping religious persecution in Europe. Because hazelnuts were not prevalent, the nut was replaced with pecans and called Huguenot torte. When it finally made it to Missouri and Arkansas, the pecan was replaced by the local black walnut and it was renamed for the third time. The pecan pie, therefore, is a close first cousin of Ozark pudding."

Scandinavian and Central European desserts also rose in prominence on the American dessert scene as larger influxes of immigrants came through Ellis Island, bringing recipes and traditions along with them. Danish kringle found its flaky origins in monasteries in Denmark, and in the 1800s traveled to the United States. This filled and iced ring officially became Wisconsin's State Pastry on June 30, 2013, with Racine named "Kringle Capital of the World" according to State Symbols USA. Hungarian kiffle cookies are delightful, crumbly bites typically filled with apricot, poppy seeds, prune (lekvar), nuts, or raspberry. The Butter Maid Bakery explains, too, that there are many variations of recipes and spellings of this crescent cookie made with sour cream or cream cheese, such as: kolachky (Polish), kifla (Romanian and Serbian), and kipfel (Austrian). Kifli refers to

a migrant, an émigré," writes Maalouf. "Before coming to one country one has had to leave another. And a person's feelings about the country he has left are never simple . . . and some ties linger on: those of language, religion, music; those with your companions in exile; those celebrated special holidays; those connected with cooking and food." As humans crossed borders into unknown lands and encountered new territory, beginning a new way of life and discovering a new culture, desserts morphed into something new entirely. Take, for instance, Dan

the crescent shape of the cookie and dates back to pagan traditions involving offerings to the moon goddess Selene. These cookies are fondly remembered in Midwestern homes in particular, as recipes have been passed down between generations after immigrants settled in areas such as Cleveland and Chicago.

The Great Depression changed the eating habits of Americans, because of the lack of specialty goods during this period. Specialty sweets simply were not widely available because the economy had tanked. However, it is interesting to note that common desserts we eat today came out of this period of scarcity, such as the red velvet cake. In "The Truth About Red Velvet Cake," Debra Kelly writes: "The fact that the recipe called for cocoa powder instead of chocolate bars made this dessert much more affordable . . . at the time, butter was being rationed thanks to World War II, but since their recipe called for bottles of red dye, vanilla, and artificial butter flavoring, it was a way for people to get just a little bit of decadence while still doing their part on the home front."

Post-war America challenged dessert norms of the past as newer, faster ways of processing became available. High-fructose corn syrup was one such invention during this time period, making processed desserts more popular, such as the notorious Twinkie and boxed cake mixes. As American desserts continued to gain popu-

larity, each decade saw its own sweets correspond with the trends of its time: trifles, icebox cakes and cookies (as "ice boxes" evolved into refrigerators), puddings, jellos, and layered ice cream treats such as the Baked Alaska.

The agricultural landscape and climate of a specific region have also shaped dessert experiences. In the Middle East, nuts and dried fruits are readily available because the arid air lends itself well to growing almonds, dates, figs, and apricots. Even today, if you step into a Turkish bazaar, you will witness countless stalls of dried nuts and fruits, all neatly organized in drawers

and large bags, ready for purchase.

The popular tres leches cake was developed in Central America due to a lack of availability of perishable milk, so canned sweetened condensed milk, evaporated milk, and cream were used instead. Brazil's most popular sweet, brigadeiros, also use sweetened condensed milk as the main

ingredient. These chocolatey truffles were sold by women along the campaign route of the "cute and single" Eduardo Gomes, an Air Force brigader running for president in 1946.

Daifuku is a chewy mochi filled with anko (red bean paste made from the adzuki bean), a popular dessert option in Japan. Similarly, taiyaki is made from a light batter exterior and filled with red bean paste and recognizable by its fish-shape ("tai" is sea bream and "yaki" means grilled or baked). Rice and adzuki beans are commonly grown in Asia, making for a readily available sweet. In India, ghee ("sacred fat") has found its way into desserts not only because Hindus consider cows to be a sacred animal, but also because of the hot climate. Rendering the butter to a clarified state allows the ghee to be stored more easily in the heat. Popular desserts like gulab jamun, ladoo, and barfi are all made using ghee. When my sister lived in Tanzania teaching English to grade schoolers, I was constantly asking, "What are you having for dessert?" and she would simply reply, "Grilled plantain," commonly grown in that region.

Similarly, when I took a trip to Costa Rica, I could hardly get enough of fresh fruits like papaya as the perfect after-dinner treat.

The kouign-amann ("butter cake") is a staple and regional specialty of Brittany, the butter region of France, known for its prized cows. At Food52, Caitlin Raux Gunther explains how "Brittany is a verdant, hilly region that contains several microclimates, among them prime land for agriculture and expansive green pastures for well-fed cows. Those Breton cows make some of the country's finest dairy products . . . And, as any baker will tell you, exceptional butter makes for exceptional baked goods." Although the kouign-amann was created in the 1800s from leftover dough scraps, pâtissiers from Douarnenez in Brittany eventually registered only "authentic" versions of this buttery sweet as an Indication Géographique Protégée or IGP (Indication of Geographic Protection) food label, indicating a food product's geographic origins, marking this dessert in relation to its surrounding environment.

Some desserts just seemed to have come about almost by accident. What a happy surprise!

There are countless examples of specific dessert preparations that carry a story. These shared stories changed me and inspired me to start The C. Love Cookie Project, a reminder that we all share this life experience as a collective

whole. In his book *A Baker's Odyssey: Celebrating Time-Honored Recipes from America's Rich Immigrant Heritage* Greg Patent writes: "Food is like language. You grow up learning to speak your mother tongue, and at the same time you develop tastes for specific foods. If you move to a new country, you yearn for connection to the place you left, and food is the magical link."

Minutas in El Salvador is shaved ice in the US and nam khaeng sai in Thailand. New sweet experiences have been carried from one place to another, but all share a common bond. It is the story of humanity—dessert is an element that connects us, prompting our senses toward familiarity—it is the hope of connection. I trust that this book will bring you closer together, as you pore over recipes, test the limits of taste, and, ultimately, your worldview. Perhaps you'll create something you can carry with you to far-off lands, and share the experience with a new friend. It is the connection and the carrying over that has always defined dessert, and our human experience.

KATHERINE J. SLEVIN

Katherine J. Slevin has been in the baking and pastry industry for over 16 years. Born in Illinois, she was surrounded by lots of love and taste-testers throughout her childhood. She worked in the pastry kitchens of luxury hotels, cake shops, family-owned boulangerie-pâtisseries, Parisian pastry giant Pierre Hermé, and finally James Beard Award nominee Standard Baking Co. in Portland, Maine, before striking out on her own to start the C. Love Cookie Project and C. Love Baking Academy. Her goal with C. Love is to encourage and empower immigrant women to join the baking community in Portland, and beyond. Her lifelong commitment to pastry and serving others continues to propel her work, highlighting immigration through the art of pastry. When she's not creating desserts or welcoming women into the kitchen space, Slevin enjoys riding around Portland on her bike, learning new languages, and getting lost in foreign cities, always with a pastry in hand.

THE FUNDAMENTALS
OF FLAVOR:
Flour, Salt, Eggs & Sugar

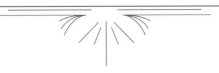

FLOUR

For most people, flour is just a powdery substance that is sold in a paper bag and stored in a cabinet.

But once you start getting serious about baking, you will quickly realize that the type of flour you use is a big part of both successes and failures. In no time, hunting for flours will become as natural as hunting for the freshest and plumpest fruits at the grocery store.

Technically, flour derives from the grinding of seeds, nuts, or roots. The most commonly used flour comes from wheat, but flours from other grains, or cereals, are also very common.

Hearty and able to be processed into an affordable staple that can then be made into a dizzying variety of foodstuffs, wheat is the world's most widely grown cereal, accounting for nearly one-third of the global cereal harvest as of 2017.

Wheat seeds consist of a large, starchy endosperm and an oily germ, which are enclosed in an outer layer of bran. The fibers are primarily in the bran, while the endosperm is where the starches and most of the proteins are stored. Fats are stocked in the germ of the wheat kernel.

Wheat and other cereals can be ground into flours featuring varying degrees of fineness. Coarse flours, like semolina, are best suited for pasta making. Fine flours, like the widely used all-purpose flour, are ideal for baking. If you want to make a pastry with a feathery texture, look for superfine flour, which is silky to the touch and confers that elegant feel to the baked goods it produces.

Research shows that wheat flour's ability to absorb water increases with a reduction in particle size. Dough development time and stability also grow as the flour increases in fineness. This is due to the tendency of flour proteins to be more readily available in the finest fractions of milled flour. A dough made with finer flour is also more extensible, allowing for easier shaping. In all, this results in baked goods with higher volumes, lighter textures, and better colors compared to those made with coarser flours.

In order to obtain an even lighter and airier consistency in baked goods made from wheat flour, the bran is either partially or totally eliminated, or sifted out. Bran removal, which has been done since antiquity, now relies on

increasingly sophisticated milling and sifting techniques.

Based on the amount of bran present in wheat flour, different labels are applied, such as: whole wheat, sifted, unbleached white, and white (i.e. bleached).

Whole wheat flour is obtained when all the bran contained in the wheat kernel is included in the milled flour. However, not all whole wheat flours are the same. Most whole wheat flours available at the store are not made by grinding the whole seed at once. Instead, the bran, which was previously removed, is added back to the refined flour. The resulting flour, which is called whole wheat, will not truly include the whole ground wheat kernel, but only the endosperm and bran fractions. In fact, the vitamin-rich wheat germ is not included in most industrially produced whole wheat flours.

Sifting flour aims to remove the bran and leave the endosperm and wheat germ. Different methods and degrees of sifting are used to create flours with different percentages of bran content, also known as "ashes."

Unbleached white flour is obtained via roller mill technology. This sophisticated method involves mechanically isolating the endosperm from the bran and the wheat germ and milling only the endosperm. This results in a flour that is lighter and whiter than flour produced by sifting. Unbleached white flour is extremely versatile and has a long shelf life, but the term does not mean that the flour is necessarily free from chemical additives. A very common additive in unbleached white flour is potassium bromate, which improves performance in the oven by strengthening the dough and allowing it to rise higher. However, this additive has been cited as a possible carcinogen, and is banned in the United Kingdom, Canada, and the European Union. Because of this, you may want to seek out unbleached white flour that is also unbromated.

If you see flour that is identified as "white flour," and does not specify being unbleached, this might mean that the flour has been bleached. Bleaching is done to increase white-ness and improve performance in the oven. Through bleaching, the flour is oxidized, which can mimic the natural aging of flour.

FLOURS USED IN BAKING

All-purpose flour: A versatile white flour that can be relied upon to produce outstanding results in nearly every baking preparation. It is generally a combination of flour from hard (bronze-colored wheat that has a higher protein, and thus higher gluten, content) and soft wheat (wheat with a light golden color; also referred to as "white wheat"). It is the most frequently recommended flour in this book.

Pastry flour: Superfine white wheat flour with relatively low protein content (around 9 percent) that is ideal for light, flaky baked goods. It is not a must, and the results it achieves can be duplicated with an all-purpose flour with a protein content on the lower end of the spectrum, but some baking enthusiasts swear by it for piecrusts and croissants.

Cake flour: Another smooth, superfine white wheat flour, and its protein content is even lower (ranging from 6 to 8 percent) than pastry flour. It lends baked goods the tender texture and high rise that is particularly desirable for cakes and biscuits.

Bread flour: White flour with a high protein content, which is ideal for bread baking, since the extra-elastic dough it produces can capture and hold more carbon dioxide than recipes using cake or pastry flour. Generally obtained from hard wheat, it is to be avoided when making desserts, as its high-protein content will result in tough and dense cakes and cookies.

LOCAL OR COMMERCIAL?

Not so long ago, there were thousands of mills in the United States. But, with the advent of modern milling techniques in the 19th century, large mills reduced the need for smaller, less technologically advanced gristmills. By the turn of the last century, mass-produced flour was the norm across the globe.

But the locavore movement has ushered in a revival of local, artisan milling, and the availability of flour that has been milled without the use of industrial technology is on the rise. How-

ever, local mills are still too few and too scattered to provide a significant proportion of our flour. And, as distribution channels are limited for artisan mills, the best way for most people to buy small-batch flour is online.

Most contemporary artisan mills use the ancient technique of stone milling. This technology is as old as farming, although important developments have since occurred, with stone mills powered by electricity now in operation.

Most flours produced by an authentic stone mill will not be the superfine, powdery, white substance that is fundamental to turning out quality desserts. Artisan mills can utilize more advanced technology to produce flours that are better suited to baking than what is traditionally produced by a stone mill, but the main point of artisan mills is to provide a more wholesome flour, not mimic the products of industrial giants.

SALT

Contrary to what most non-bakers think, the primary reason to add salt to a dough is not for taste. Although salt does improve the taste, the other functions it serves are far more important.

Baking without salt will result in flat baked goods that in no way resemble the airy delight you were envisioning when you set out. The presence of salt in dough also slows down the activity of yeasts, bacteria, and enzymes, reducing acidity and allowing more time for the sweet, flavorful sugars to develop.

Salt also helps the dough create a better structure by making gluten (the protein that holds together baked goods) more robust and more effective at keeping the gasses in, producing results that are higher in volume and feature a more open crumb.

Salt absorbs water; thus, a dough containing salt will be drier and more elastic, and less difficult to work with during handling and shaping.

Keep in mind that salt stiffens the dough, which is why you should generally try to add it during the last phases of mixing/kneading rather than at the beginning, so as not to make the dough too tough too early.

In this book, fine sea salt and kosher salt are called for. Fine sea salt should be used in any baking recipe that does not specify a kind of salt. Where kosher salt is suggested, the Diamond Crystal brand should be used.

EGGS

For the purpose of making glorious desserts, it is best to secure the highest-quality eggs available.

Eggs provide more protein, which, when combined with the gluten, enhances the structure of a dough, making it elastic, soft, and easier to roll out without tearing.

It is important to use eggs that have a vibrantly orange yolk, as it is a sign of a healthy, happy, and well-fed chicken. Egg yolks get their color from carotenoids, which are also responsible for strengthening the chicken's immune system. Because chickens only hatch eggs if they have sufficient levels of carotenoids, the yolks possess hues of dark gold and orange. Paler yolks are often a result of chickens feeding on barley or white cornmeal, which don't nourish them as well as a diet based on yellow corn and marigold petals.

Using brown or white eggs is up to personal preference, since they have the same nutritional profiles and taste. However, there are good arguments for buying brown eggs. First, brown eggs come from larger breeds that eat more, take longer to produce their eggs, and produce eggs with thicker protective shells, which prevents internal moisture loss over time and helps them maintain their freshness.

Eggs in the United States are graded according to the thickness of their shell and the firmness of their whites. Large egg producers can assess the quality of each individual egg and efficiently sort them by size, weight, and quality. With almost scientific precision, eggs are graded AA (top quality), A (good quality found in most supermarkets), and B (substandard eggs with thin shells and watery whites that don't reach consumers but are used commercially and industrially). They are also further categorized by size: medium, large (the most common size), and extra-large.

The past decade or so has seen a rise in the popularity of free-range and organic eggs. The chickens that produce these eggs are fed organic feed and are caged with slightly more space at their disposal than those raised at conventional chicken farms. The jury is still out on whether free-range eggs taste better, but they constitute an additional, and perhaps politically oriented, option for aspiring bakers.

SUGAR

The standards—granulated sugar (which is referred to, simply, as "sugar" in the recipes), confectioners' sugar (which is the same as powdered sugar), and brown sugar—will be what are required in almost all of the recipes in this book. But in your endeavors you may come across a recipe that calls for one of these sugars, which are less common.

Caster sugar: A superfine sugar with a consistency that sits somewhere between granulated sugar and confectioners' sugar. Since it can

dissolve without heat, unlike granulated sugar, it is most commonly called for in recipes where the sugar needs to melt or dissolve quickly, as in meringues. This ease can come with a hefty price tag that scares some people off, but you can easily make caster sugar at home with nothing more than a food processor or a blender and some granulated sugar. Place the granulated sugar in the food processor or blender and pulse until the consistency is superfine, but short of powdery. Let the sugar settle in the food processor, transfer it to a container, and label to avoid future confusion.

Demerara sugar: A large-grained raw sugar that originated in Guyana and is now produced in a number of countries around the globe. It is commonly referred to as a "brown sugar" due to its color, but brown sugar is refined white sugar that has been bathed in molasses. Demer-ara has a natural caramel flavor that comes through in any dish it is added to. Famous for the depth and complexity it can lend to recipes, it is worth experimenting with if a certain recipe is falling short of your ideal flavor. Demerara's large grains also pack a pleasant crunchy quality, making it perfect for sprinkling on muffins, cakes, and cookies.

Turbinado sugar: Very similar to demerara sugar, possessing the large, crunchy grains and rich flavor that has made demerara fashionable of late. If you're going to give either of these sugars a try, keep in mind that they contain more moisture than granulated sugar. This probably won't be a problem in preparations featuring a moist batter, such as brownies. But in recipes that are on the arid side, like pastry and cookie doughs, substituting demerara or turbinado might take you wide of the mark.

Muscovado sugar: A cane sugar with a very moist texture and a molasses-forward flavor. It is best suited to savory dishes, but may be worth incorporating into preparations where you're after something other than standard sweetness. As with demerara and turbinado, you want to keep moisture in mind whenever you're thinking of utilizing it in a recipe.

Sanding sugar: A larger-crystal sugar used for decorating and finishing baked goods. Due to the larger size of its grains, sanding sugar will not fully melt in the oven, giving cookies and piecrusts a shiny and slightly crusty topping.

SUGAR SUBSTITUTES

As far as sugar alternatives go, substituting an equivalent amount of a combination of maple syrup and honey is probably the easiest route when baking. Agave nectar is another option, but it will affect the tenderness and flavor of baked goods. If you want to use agave nectar, swap it in for the suggested amount of sugar and add ¼ cup of flour to your preparation.

For those who have blood sugar concerns, stevia is the best bet to approximate the effect sugar would provide. Avoid saccharin (which will leave a strong aftertaste) and aspartame.

CARAMELIZING SUGAR

Caramelizing sugar is a key weapon in any confectioner's arsenal, as it lends desserts rich aromas and deep, complex flavors. Often perceived to be daunting and a little dangerous, here's what you need to stick the landing the next time you're asked to make caramel.

Like many aspects of desserts, caramelizing sugar is a matter of basic chemistry. Applying heat to the combination of water and sugar leads us to a simple syrup. Continuing to heat the syrup causes the evaporation of water, which leads to a higher concentration of sugar in the solution. That higher concentration causes a more intricate structure as the mixture cools. There is a range of caramel, from the weakest stage at 235°F to full caramelization at 338°F.

When cooking or caramelizing sugar, the "wet" method is strongly preferred, as it slows

down the speed the sugar cooks and minimizes the chance that the caramel will burn. To employ this method, combine water and sugar in a saucepan and bring to a boil. When the sugar and water are combined, swirl the pan to distribute the water, run your finger under cold water, and wipe the sides of the pot clean of any granules of sugar. This prevents the sugar that has not been incorporated from cooking too quickly and burning on the side of the pot. It is also recommended that you keep a pastry brush and a bowl of cold water nearby when making caramel, so that you can carefully brush the sides of the pot with the cold water and control the speed at which the sugar cooks, maintaining the proper balance needed to make caramel.

BUTTER

In this book, the majority of the recipes call for unsalted butter. Salted butter is not the preferred choice because the salt content in each stick of butter varies, making it hard to exercise the necessary control over the amount of salt in your desserts.

For a few preparations, cultured butter is called for. Widely available in Europe and something of a specialty item in the United States, its higher percentage of butterfat is essential to those light but rich pastries like the croissant. Made from fresh pasteurized cream instead of sweet cream like most butters in the US, cultured butter also has live bacterial cultures added to it after it has been pasteurized, lending the final product a unique tang. Despite being a less common ingredient in American kitchens, cultured butter can be found in many large supermarkets.

CHOCOLATE

Whether it be milk or dark, sweet, bitter, or white, the array of flavors that chocolate provides, and the number of desserts this versatility can carry, causes people all across the globe to be powerless against its sweet song.

The rare ingredient that is as comfortable playing with others as it is standing on its own, it's quite possible that chocolate is responsible for putting more smiles on people's faces than any other food.

No one is certain exactly when chocolate started to be a crave-worthy ingredient the world over, but it is believed that the Olmec civilization, which inhabited present-day Mexico, used cacao in a bitter, ceremonial drink, a hypothesis borne out by traces of theobromine—a stimulant that is found in chocolate and tea—being found on ancient Olmec pots and vessels.

While the exact role of chocolate in Olmec culture is impossible to pin down because they kept no written history, it appears that they passed their reverence for it onto the Mayans, who valued chocolate to the point that cocoa beans were used as currency in certain transactions. It is interesting that access to this precious resource wasn't restricted to the wealthy among the Mayans, but was available enough that a beverage consisting of chocolate mixed with honey or chili peppers could be enjoyed with every meal in a majority of Mayan households.

The next great Mexican civilization, the Aztecs, carried things even further. They saw cocoa as more valuable than gold, and the mighty Aztec ruler Montezuma II supposedly drank gallons of chocolate each day, believing that it provided him with considerable energy and also served as a potent aphrodisiac.

No one is certain exactly which explorer brought this New World tradition back

to Europe, with some crediting Christopher Columbus and others Hernan Cortes. Whoever is responsible, they created a sensation on the continent. Chocolate-based beverages that were sweetened with cane sugar or spruced up with spices such as cinnamon became all the rage, and fashionable houses where the wealthy congregated and indulged began popping up all over Europe by the early 17th century.

Chocolate remained in the hands of Europe's elite until a Dutch chemist named Coenraad Johannes van Houten discovered how to treat cacao beans with alkaline salts to produce a powdered chocolate that was more soluble. This "Dutch cocoa" made cocoa affordable for all, and opened the door for mass production.

The first chocolate bar was produced by the British chocolatier J. S. Fry and Sons, though the amalgamation of sugar, chocolate liqueur, and cocoa butter was far chewier, and less sweet, than the bars turned out for the modern palate.

Swiss chocolatier Daniel Peter is widely credited as the individual who added dried milk powder to chocolate to create milk chocolate in 1876. Peter then teamed with his friend Henri Nestlé to create the company that brought milk chocolate to the masses.

In order to produce chocolate, the seeds of the cacao tree are harvested, heaped into piles to ferment, dried in the sun, and roasted at low temperatures to develop the beguiling flavors. The shells of the beans are then removed and the resulting nibs are ground into cocoa mass (which is also called cocoa liquor) and placed under extremely high pressure to produce cocoa powder and cocoa butter. From there, the cocoa powder and cocoa butter are partnered with sugar to produce dark chocolate, and sugar and milk powder to produce milk chocolate.

Dark chocolate has a minimum of 55 percent cocoa and can go all the way to 100 percent, which is extremely bitter, though it carries an extremely complex flavor. The dark chocolate you'll use in your desserts will tend to land in the 55 to 70 percent range.

Milk chocolate tends to range from 38 to 42 percent cocoa and contains milk or heavy cream along with cocoa beans and sugar. The lower cocoa content creates a creamier and silkier chocolate that is preferred by many.

Now for the question that continues to burn hotly in the minds of many: Is white chocolate chocolate? It depends. It does not contain the cocoa mass that is produced by grinding the roasted nibs of the cacao bean finely, so some do not consider white chocolate to be a true chocolate. Some apocryphal tales assert that white chocolate is the result of cocoa beans that have not been roasted, that is far from the case. White chocolate is instead made with cocoa butter (a product resulting from roasted cocoa beans), sugar, and milk powder.

Cocoa powder is pulverized, unsweetened cocoa mass that provides any dessert an intense injection of chocolatey flavor. The amount of cocoa liquor in cocoa powder varies from 88 to 100 percent, with the remainder being supplied by dried cocoa butter.

VANILLA

While it is synonymous with the bland and flavorless, for a large group of people, vanilla is anything but boring. Equal parts smooth and sweet, its ability to both soothe and dazzle the taste buds is unmatched. Any skeptics out there should talk to their favorite baker about the crucial role vanilla plays in a number of desserts, adding a luscious aroma and lightness whose absence would be glaring, rendering the finished confection unacceptable to anyone who had experienced it previously.

Vanilla is typically categorized according to where the orchid that produces the bean is grown, and, as those who are devotees of the vanilla bean know, there is plenty of variation in its flavor across the globe. Madagascar Bour-

bon vanilla has nothing to do with American whiskey—though, to be fair, it's an understandable mistake given that many bourbons do carry strong notes of vanilla. Instead, it refers to Bourbon Island (now known as Reunion), an island east of Madagascar in the Indian Ocean, after which the vanilla that grows in the region was named. The sweet, creamy flavor of these beans is what comes to mind when most think of vanilla, as its incredible versatility has made it ubiquitous. Mexican vanilla adds a bit of nutmeg-y spice to vanilla's famously sweet and creamy quality, which makes it a wonderful addition to those cinnamon- and nutmeg-heavy desserts that show up around the holidays, and it can also be used to dress up a barbecue sauce. Indonesian vanilla beans carry a smoky, woody flavor and aroma that is particularly welcome in cookies and chocolate-rich desserts. Tahitian vanilla possesses floral flavor that carries hints of stone fruit and anise, making Tahitian vanilla a perfect match for fruit-based desserts, as well as ice creams and custards. It is interesting to note that Tahitian vanilla is a different species of orchid than the one that produces the other three, and its beans are noticeably plumper.

However, this appellation tendency does not apply to French vanilla. Instead, this appellation refers to the traditional French method for making ice cream, which utilizes a rich egg custard base. Those eggs, some claim, give vanilla a richness and depth that the bean can't attain on its own, forming such a memorable match that the flavor, which carries caramel and floral notes, resides in a category all its own. This classification begs the question: What of vanilla ice cream made without eggs? Ice cream prepared in this manner is referred to as "Philadelphia-style."

Using pure vanilla extract as opposed to the seeds of a vanilla bean will not affect the taste of your preparation, so don't be wary of any recipe that recommends the former. Ultimately, vanilla extract is made by macerating vanilla beans in a combination of water and alcohol. It is the more common recommendation due to its lower price and the ease of selling larger amounts. While using vanilla bean in place of extract won't do much to the taste, those dark little flecks do add an aesthetic element that the extract cannot, giving any dessert that utilizes the seeds an air of sophistication. If you want to take advantage of this in any recipe that recommends vanilla extract, simply substitute the seeds of 1 vanilla bean for every 1 tablespoon of extract.

TIPS & TECHNIQUES

ACCURACY IS THE NAME OF THE SWEETS GAME

Precision is important in all forms of cooking, but it is crucial when it comes to making desserts, and baking in particular. The beloved taste and texture of your favorite confection hinge on a delicate balance of flavors and interactions between ingredients, meaning that, most often, getting the results you desire means a commitment to measuring the components by weight, especially for ingredients such as flour.

If you and a friend were both to measure a cup of flour and place the flour on a scale, the weights would be different. This discrepancy occurs because of inconsistencies that arise when packing and filling a cup of flour. This goes for any ingredient measured using spoons or cups. These dry measuring cups and measuring spoons do not have a universal standard and can vary from brand to brand. But, no matter where you are or what you are measuring on, weight is weight. Four ounces for one person in France will be four ounces for another in Wichita, Kansas.

Throughout this book, weights will be given for a number of ingredients, particularly in the recipes that will be baked. A liquid in ounces should be measured by volume unless otherwise specified. Liquids such as water that have a density of 1, which means they have a 1:1 ratio of weight to volume—i.e., they can be weighed on a scale or measured by volume and produce the same result. Dry ingredients labeled by ounce should be measured on a scale.

Aside from assuring consistency and quality, weighing ingredients also saves time. Instead of readying an array of measuring cups that will all have to be cleaned afterward, you simply place a bowl on the scale, tare it, and begin adding ingredients. Another benefit of weighing ingredients is that it becomes easier to double or halve a recipe.

TAKE YOUR TEMPERATURE

Temperature is very important for certain ingredients, as most recipes call for you to emulsify items with different densities and structures. Having these various items at a similar temperature allows them to come together in a smooth and cohesive manner. Let us take butter that has softened at room temperature, for example.

The creaming method is the process of combining butter and sugar until airy, light, and fluffy. This process is only possible when the butter is warm enough that the friction from beating it opens up small pockets, which trap air as the sugar is being incorporated. As more air enters the mixture, it grows lighter, almost fluffy.

Eggs are another ingredient where various temperatures make a big difference in the final product. As a general rule, take your eggs out of

the refrigerator at least one hour before starting your preparation.

You want everything to be at room temperature for baked goods that intend to have a lighter, more delicate texture. Any dough or batter that must rest at room temperature or be refrigerated before going in the oven does not need to be made with room-temperature ingredients.

If you're short on time, there are a few things that can be done to warm up said ingredients. Butter, milk, water, and sour cream can be gradually heated in a microwave until they reach room temperature. Conversely, if your kitchen is cold and your metal mixing bowl is chilling your product too quickly, you can lightly run the flame of a kitchen torch over the outside of the bowl to help maintain the higher temperature of the mixture inside.

SIFTING

Sifting is another important step in many recipes. This process allows one to separate the flour particles, which lightens the mix and allows other ingredients to be evenly distributed, resulting in baked goods with a lighter, fluffier texture. It's wise to have a small and a large sifter on hand. A small sifter is good for dusting and decorating. A larger sifter is best for aerating mixes that use cake flour, baking powder, baking soda, and cocoa powder.

READ THE RECIPE. THEN READ IT AGAIN.

One of the most common and detrimental mistakes in cooking is starting preparations without reading the recipe all the way through. Take the time to read the recipe so you can see how much time you will need, what ingredients are required, what items need to be at room tem-

perature, etc. Reading the recipe carefully allows you to get organized so that you can focus on executing it properly when the time comes. It's easy to leave something out or miss a key step when you're rushing to grab items and containers as you go. It's also much harder to pay attention to how a certain batter feels, or how a cookie smells as it turns toward the last minute of baking, hindering the sixth sense that is key for overcoming the inevitable changes in conditions and ingredients.

PREPARE BAKING PANS

Getting your baking pans ready before starting a particular preparation is another good habit to develop, as it enables you to save time between finishing mixing a dough or batter and putting it in the oven. Baking is all about timing—just consider that most leavening agents, especially when used in a cake batter, start to lose their power the moment they are moistened and mixed. Reducing the amount of time a leavening agent has to work without the aid of heat will pay off big in the final result.

DO NOT OPEN THE OVEN!

The temptation to open the oven and take a closer look to ensure that whatever's in there is baking properly is overwhelming. Resist the temptation, especially when there's a cake in the oven, for at least three-quarters of the suggested baking time. A drop in temperature could cause the final product to deflate slightly, nullifying all the work you did to mix the dough or batter properly.

BUILDING BLOCKS

*G*etting serious about your sweet tooth means getting ready to make the foundational pieces from scratch. Yes, you can easily purchase each of the following cornerstones at your local grocery store, but we're certain you'll feel better tackling tough preparations and serving them to your loved ones if you get in the habit of whipping them up yourself.

While these recipes are meant to be added to, a number of them—such as the Pound Cake (see page 62), Butterscotch Pastry Cream (see page 84), and Milk Chocolate Crémeux (see page 95)—are treats in their own right, able to delight with nothing further required.

PERFECT PIECRUSTS

YIELD: 2 (9-INCH) PIECRUSTS / **ACTIVE TIME:** 15 MINUTES / **TOTAL TIME:** 2 HOURS AND 15 MINUTES

Perfect buttery, flaky crusts that will serve you well no matter how you use them.

1. Transfer the butter to a small bowl and place it in the freezer.

2. Place the flour, salt, and sugar in a food processor and pulse a few times until combined.

3. Add the chilled butter and pulse until the mixture is crumbly, consisting of pea-sized clumps.

4. Add the water and pulse until the mixture comes together as a dough.

5. Place the dough on a flour-dusted work surface and fold it over itself until it is a ball. Divide the dough in two and flatten each piece into a 1-inch-thick disc. Cover each piece completely with plastic wrap and place in the refrigerator for at least 2 hours before rolling it out to fit your pie plate.

INGREDIENTS:

8	OZ. UNSALTED BUTTER, CUBED
12.5	OZ. ALL-PURPOSE FLOUR, PLUS MORE AS NEEDED
½	TEASPOON KOSHER SALT
4	TEASPOONS SUGAR
½	CUP ICE WATER

CRIMPING A PIECRUST

Crimping creates a decorative edge on your piecrust. It also defines it, keeping it from folding over in the oven. To crimp a piecrust, place your left thumb and left index finger approximately 1 inch from each other. Crook your right index finger and work your way around the pie plate, pressing your right index finger into that 1-inch space and against the inside edge of the piecrust.

PÂTÉ SUCRÉE

YIELD: 2 (9-INCH) CRUSTS / **ACTIVE TIME:** 15 MINUTES / **TOTAL TIME:** 2 HOURS AND 15 MINUTES

If you want a sweet piecrust, this is your best bet. It also makes for a wonderful tart shell.

1. In the work bowl of a stand mixer fitted with the paddle attachment, cream the butter, sugar, and salt on medium speed until the mixture is creamy, light, and fluffy, about 5 minutes.

2. Add the egg and egg yolks and beat until incorporated. Add the flour and beat until the mixture comes together as a dough.

3. Place the dough on a flour-dusted work surface and fold it over itself until it is a ball. Divide the dough in two and flatten each piece into a 1-inch-thick disc. Cover each piece completely with plastic wrap and place in the refrigerator for at least 2 hours before rolling it out to fit your pie plate.

INGREDIENTS:

8	OZ. UNSALTED BUTTER, SOFTENED
8	OZ. SUGAR
¼	TEASPOON KOSHER SALT
1	EGG
2	EGG YOLKS
1	LB. ALL-PURPOSE FLOUR

GRAHAM CRACKER CRUST

YIELD: 1 (9-INCH) CRUST / **ACTIVE TIME:** 10 MINUTES / **TOTAL TIME:** 1 HOUR

Whether you're intent on making a cheesecake to remember or putting a twist on your favorite pie, your quest starts here.

1. Preheat the oven to 375°F. Place the graham cracker crumbs and sugar in a large mixing bowl and stir to combine. Add the maple syrup and 5 tablespoons of the melted butter and stir until thoroughly combined.

2. Grease a 9-inch pie plate with the remaining butter. Pour the dough into the pie plate and gently press into shape. Line the crust with aluminum paper, fill with uncooked rice, dried beans, or pie weights, and bake for about 10 minutes, until the crust is firm.

3. Remove from the oven, discard the aluminum foil and weights, and allow the crust to cool completely before filling.

INGREDIENTS:

1½ CUPS GRAHAM CRACKER CRUMBS

2 TABLESPOONS SUGAR

1 TABLESPOON REAL MAPLE SYRUP

3 OZ. UNSALTED BUTTER, MELTED

BLIND BAKING

The technique of baking a piecrust before filling it is also known as "blind baking." When working with a custard filling, as in a lemon meringue or pumpkin pie, baking the crust ahead of time has several advantages. It prevents pockets of steam from forming in the crust once it is filled, which can cause the crust to become puffy and uneven. Blind baking also keeps the bottom of the crust from becoming soggy, and allows the edge of the pie to be sturdy. Uncooked rice is the most typical weight when blind baking a pie, though dried beans and weights designed specifically for the task can also be utilized. To blind bake a crust, prick it with a fork, line it with aluminum foil, and fill with your chosen weight. Place the crust in a 350°F oven and bake for 15 to 20 minutes, until it is golden brown and firm. Remove, remove the weight, and let the crust cool completely before filling.

COOKIE CRUST

YIELD: 1 (9-INCH) CRUST / **ACTIVE TIME:** 20 MINUTES / **TOTAL TIME:** 1 HOUR AND 15 MINUTES

Fill this with ice cream or pudding and you've got a decadent dessert in minutes.

1. Preheat the oven to 300°F and grease an 18 x 13–inch baking sheet with nonstick cooking spray. Place three-quarters of the butter and the sugars in the work bowl of a standing mixer fitted with the paddle attachment and beat the mixture until it is light and fluffy, about 5 minutes. Add the vanilla and melted chocolate and beat to combine, scraping down the work bowl as needed.

2. Sift the cocoa powder, baking soda, salt, and flour into a separate mixing bowl. Add the dry mixture to the wet mixture and beat until just combined. Place the dough on a flour-dusted work surface and roll it out so that it will fit the baking sheet and is approximately ⅛ inch thick.

3. Place in the oven and bake until firm, about 20 minutes. Check the crust after 15 minutes to make sure you don't overcook it—it is ready when you don't leave an impression while gently pressing down in the middle. Remove and let cool. While the crust is cooling, place the remaining butter in a saucepan and melt over medium-low heat. Leave the oven at 300°F.

4. Use a rolling pin or a food processor to break the crust into crumbs. Place the crumbs in a mixing bowl, add the melted butter and egg white, and work the mixture with your hands until it becomes sticky.

5. Press the crumbs into a greased 9-inch pie plate and bake for 5 to 6 minutes, until the crust is firm. Remove from the oven and let cool before filling.

INGREDIENTS:

8	OZ. UNSALTED BUTTER, AT ROOM TEMPERATURE
5.3	OZ. LIGHT BROWN SUGAR
5.3	OZ. SUGAR
1	TABLESPOON PURE VANILLA EXTRACT
¾	CUP SEMISWEET CHOCOLATE CHIPS, MELTED
½	CUP COCOA POWDER
1	TEASPOON BAKING SODA
½	TEASPOON KOSHER SALT
8.75	OZ. ALL-PURPOSE FLOUR, PLUS MORE AS NEEDED
½	EGG WHITE

COCOA CRUST

YIELD: 1 (9-INCH) CRUST / **ACTIVE TIME:** 20 MINUTES / **TOTAL TIME:** 2 HOURS

A crust for those who feel there's no such thing as too much chocolate when it comes time to satisfy their sweet tooth.

1. Place the flour, cocoa powder, sugar, and salt in a food processor and pulse until combined. Add the butter and shortening and pulse until the mixture resembles coarse crumbs. Add the egg yolk and water and pulse until the mixture comes together as a dough.

2. Form the dough into a disc, cover it completely with plastic wrap, and refrigerate for 1 hour.

3. Preheat the oven to 350°F. Remove the dough from the refrigerator and let it rest at room temperature for 5 to 10 minutes. Place the dough on a flour-dusted work surface and roll it out to ¼ inch thick. Place the crust in a greased 9-inch pie plate, line it with aluminum foil, and fill it with uncooked rice, dried beans, or pie weights. Place in the oven and bake for 15 to 20 minutes, until firm.

4. Remove from the oven, discard the weights and aluminum foil, and let the crust cool completely before filling it.

INGREDIENTS:

5	OZ. ALL-PURPOSE FLOUR, PLUS MORE AS NEEDED
2	TABLESPOONS COCOA POWDER
2	TABLESPOONS SUGAR
½	TEASPOON FINE SEA SALT
2	OZ. UNSALTED BUTTER
2	TABLESPOONS SHORTENING
1	LARGE EGG YOLK
2-3	TABLESPOONS ICE WATER

MERINGUE SHELL

YIELD: 1 (9-INCH) SHELL / **ACTIVE TIME:** 20 MINUTES / **TOTAL TIME:** 2 HOURS AND 45 MINUTES

The best landing spot for berries handpicked at the height of summer.

1. Preheat the oven to 225°F and grease a 9-inch pie plate with butter. Place the egg whites and cream of tartar in the work bowl of a stand mixer fitted with the whisk attachment and beat on high until foamy. With the mixer running, incorporate the sugar 2 tablespoons at a time, waiting until the sugar has dissolved before adding the next increment. Beat until the mixture is glossy and holds stiff peaks.

2. Add the vanilla, beat to incorporate, and spread the meringue over the pie plate, making sure to extend it all the way up the sides. Place in the oven and bake for about 1 hour, until the meringue is firm and a toothpick inserted into the center comes out clean. Turn off the oven and allow the shell to rest in the oven for 1 hour.

3. Remove from the oven, transfer the pie plate to a wire rack, and let cool completely before filling.

INGREDIENTS:

	UNSALTED BUTTER, AS NEEDED
3	EGG WHITES, AT ROOM TEMPERATURE
¼	TEASPOON CREAM OF TARTAR
5.25	OZ. SUGAR
½	TEASPOON PURE VANILLA EXTRACT

NUTTY CRUST

YIELD: 1 (9-INCH) CRUST / **ACTIVE TIME:** 10 MINUTES / **TOTAL TIME:** 45 MINUTES

Any nut can be used to make this crust, but pecans and almonds produce the best results. Going with one of those and mixing in ¼ to ½ cup hazelnuts is another great option.

1. Preheat the oven to 400°F and generously grease a 9-inch pie plate with butter. Place the nuts in a food processor and pulse until a coarse meal forms.

2. Transfer the nuts to a bowl and add the honey and butter. Work the mixture with a pastry blender or your hands until combined. Press the mixture into the pie plate, place it in the oven, and bake for about 10 minutes, until the nuts look browned and smell toasted. Remove from the oven, transfer to a wire rack, and let the crust cool completely before filling.

INGREDIENTS:

1 OZ. UNSALTED BUTTER, CHILLED AND CHOPPED, PLUS MORE AS NEEDED

1½ CUPS NUTS

1½ TABLESPOONS HONEY

GLUTEN-FREE CRUST

YIELD: 1 (9-INCH) CRUST / **ACTIVE TIME:** 15 MINUTES / **TOTAL TIME:** 1 HOUR

Getting a flaky crust that is also gluten-free has been impossible—until now.

1. Place the flour, sugar, xanthan gum, and salt in a large mixing bowl. Add the butter and work the mixture with a pastry blender until it is a coarse meal.

2. Place the egg and lemon juice in a separate bowl and whisk until the mixture is very foamy. Add it to the dry mixture and stir until the mixture just comes together as a dough.

3. If the dough isn't quite holding together, add the water in 1-tablespoon increments until it does. Form the dough into a disc, cover it completely with plastic wrap, and refrigerate for 30 minutes.

4. Remove the dough from the refrigerator and let it rest at room temperature for 10 minutes. Place it on a flour-dusted work surface, roll it out to ¼ inch thick, and place it in a greased 9-inch pie plate. Fill as desired.

INGREDIENTS:

5.3   OZ. GLUTEN-FREE FLOUR, PLUS MORE AS NEEDED

1   TABLESPOON SUGAR

½   TEASPOON XANTHAN GUM

½   TEASPOON FINE SEA SALT

3   OZ. UNSALTED BUTTER, CHILLED AND CUT INTO SMALL PIECES

1   LARGE EGG

2   TEASPOONS FRESH LEMON JUICE

ICE WATER, AS NEEDED

POUND CAKE

YIELD: 1 CAKE / **ACTIVE TIME:** 20 MINUTES / **TOTAL TIME:** 2 HOURS AND 15 MINUTES

t's good on its own, piled with berries, drizzled with ganache, as part of a trifle, folded into ice cream—in other words, just about anything you can think of.

1. Place the butter in the work bowl of a stand mixer and let it stand until it is room temperature, about 25 minutes.

2. Place the eggs, egg yolks, and vanilla in a mixing bowl and beat until combined. Set the mixture aside.

3. Preheat the oven to 325°F and generously butter a 9 x 5–inch loaf pan, dust it with flour, and knock out any excess.

4. Attach the paddle attachment to the stand mixer. Add the salt to the butter and beat on medium until the mixture is smooth and creamy, 2 to 3 minutes. Gradually add the sugar and beat until the mixture is fluffy and almost white, 5 to 8 minutes. Scrape down the bowl as needed while mixing the batter.

5. Gradually add the egg mixture in a steady stream and beat mixture until light and fluffy, 3 to 4 minutes. Remove work bowl from the mixer and scrape it down with a rubber spatula.

6. Working in three or four increments, sift the cake flour over the mixture and use a rubber spatula to fold the mixture and thoroughly incorporate the flour before adding the next increment.

7. Transfer the batter to the prepared loaf pan and smooth the top with a rubber spatula. Place the cake in the oven and bake until golden brown and a toothpick inserted in the center of the cake comes out clean, about 1 hour and 15 minutes.

8. Remove the pan from the oven and let the cake cool in the pan on a wire rack for 15 minutes. Invert the cake onto wire rack and let it cool completely before serving.

INGREDIENTS:

8   OZ. UNSALTED BUTTER, CHILLED AND DIVIDED INTO TABLESPOONS, PLUS MORE FOR GREASING

3   LARGE EGGS

3   LARGE EGG YOLKS

2   TEASPOONS PURE VANILLA EXTRACT

7   OZ. CAKE FLOUR, PLUS MORE AS NEEDED

½   TEASPOON FINE SEA SALT

8.75   OZ. SUGAR

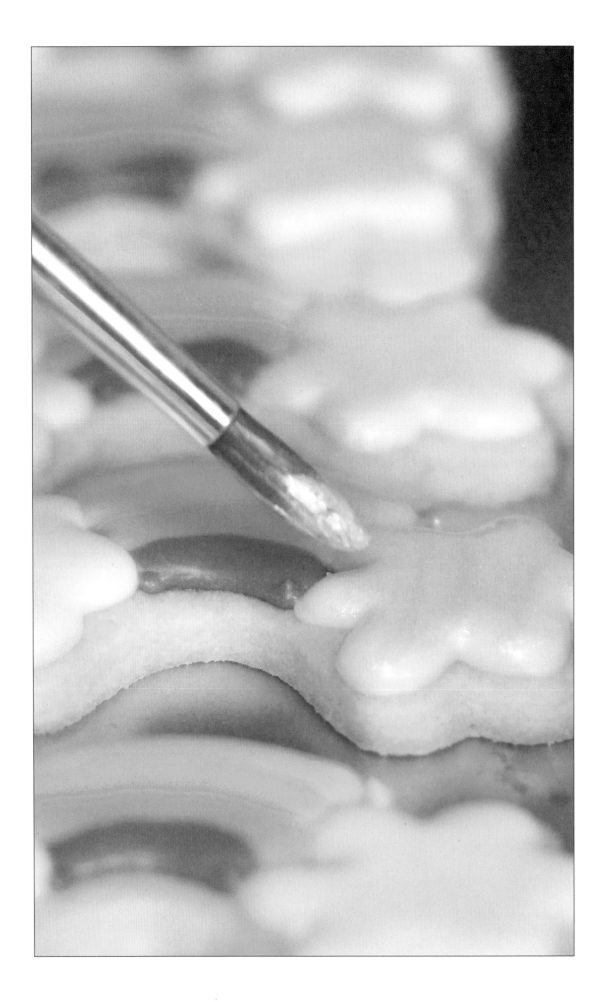

ROYAL ICING

YIELD: 3 CUPS / **ACTIVE TIME:** 5 MINUTES / **TOTAL TIME:** 5 MINUTES

The beautiful and rich icing that is attached to so many warm memories around the holidays.

1. Place the egg whites, vanilla, and confectioners' sugar in a mixing bowl and whisk until the mixture is smooth.

2. If desired, add food coloring. If using immediately, place the icing in a piping bag. If making ahead of time, store in the refrigerator, where it will keep for 5 days.

INGREDIENTS:

6	EGG WHITES
1	TEASPOON PURE VANILLA EXTRACT
2	LBS. CONFECTIONERS' SUGAR
1-2	DROPS OF GEL FOOD COLORING (OPTIONAL)

FRANGIPANE

YIELD: 4 CUPS / **ACTIVE TIME:** 10 MINUTES / **TOTAL TIME:** 10 MINUTES

A sweet almond concoction that serves as the filling for almond croissants, and also finds its way into many fruit tarts.

1. In the work bowl of a stand mixer fitted with the paddle attachment, cream the almond paste, butter, and salt on medium speed until the mixture is light and fluffy, about 5 minutes.

2. Reduce the speed to low, add the eggs one at a time, and beat until incorporated, again scraping the work bowl as needed. Add the flour and beat until incorporated. Use immediately or store in the refrigerator for up to 2 weeks.

INGREDIENTS:

12   OZ. ALMOND PASTE

4   OZ. UNSALTED BUTTER, SOFTENED

¼   TEASPOON KOSHER SALT

4   EGGS

1.75 OZ. ALL-PURPOSE FLOUR

FRENCH MERINGUE

YIELD: 4 CUPS / **ACTIVE TIME:** 10 MINUTES / **TOTAL TIME:** 10 MINUTES

The lightest and fastest of the three types of meringues, but also the least stable.

1. In the work bowl of a stand mixer fitted with the whisk attachment, whip the egg whites and salt on medium until soft peaks form.

2. Add the sugar 1 tablespoon at a time and whisk to incorporate. Wait about 10 seconds between additions.

3. When all of the sugar has been incorporated, whip until the mixture holds stiff peaks. Use immediately.

INGREDIENTS:

4   EGG WHITES

      PINCH OF KOSHER SALT

½   CUP SUGAR

SWISS MERINGUE

YIELD: 3 CUPS / **ACTIVE TIME:** 20 MINUTES / **TOTAL TIME:** 20 MINUTES

This meringue is fluffy, shiny, and almost cloudlike, making it good for topping cakes and pies, and also as a filling for macarons.

1. Fill a small saucepan halfway with water and bring it to a gentle simmer.

2. Place the egg whites, sugar, and salt in the work bowl of a stand mixer. Place the bowl over the simmering water and whisk until the mixture reaches 115°F.

3. Return the bowl to the stand mixer and fit it with the whisk attachment. Whip on high until the meringue is shiny, glossy, and holds stiff peaks, about 5 minutes. For best results, use the meringue the day you make it.

INGREDIENTS:

4   EGG WHITES

       PINCH OF KOSHER SALT

1   CUP SUGAR

ITALIAN MERINGUE

YIELD: 3 CUPS / **ACTIVE TIME:** 15 MINUTES / **TOTAL TIME:** 30 MINUTES

The most involved of all the meringues, but also the most versatile and reliable.

1. Place the sugar and water in a small saucepan that is fit with a candy thermometer and bring the mixture to a boil.

2. While the syrup is coming to a boil, place the egg whites and salt in the work bowl of a stand mixer fitted with the whisk attachment and whip on medium speed until the mixture holds stiff peaks.

3. Cook the syrup until the thermometer reads 245°F. Immediately remove the pan from the heat once the syrup stops bubbling and let it sit for 30 seconds.

4. Reduce the speed of the mixer to medium-low and slowly pour the syrup down the side of the mixing bowl until all of it has been incorporated. Raise the speed to high and whip until the meringue is glossy and holds stiff peaks.

INGREDIENTS:

1	CUP SUGAR
¼	CUP WATER
4	EGG WHITES
	PINCH OF KOSHER SALT

AMERICAN BUTTERCREAM

YIELD: 3 CUPS / **ACTIVE TIME:** 10 MINUTES / **TOTAL TIME:** 10 MINUTES

A simple but delicious frosting that will soon become your go-to.

1. In the work bowl of a stand mixer fitted with the paddle attachment, combine the butter, confectioners' sugar, and salt and beat on low speed until the sugar starts to be incorporated into the butter. Raise the speed to high and beat until the mixture is smooth and fluffy, about 5 minutes.

2. Reduce the speed to low, add the heavy cream and vanilla, and beat until incorporated. Use immediately, or store in the refrigerator for up to 2 weeks. If refrigerating, return to room temperature before using.

INGREDIENTS:

1	LB. UNSALTED BUTTER, SOFTENED
2	LBS. CONFECTIONERS' SUGAR
⅛	TEASPOON KOSHER SALT
¼	CUP HEAVY CREAM
½	TEASPOON PURE VANILLA EXTRACT

ITALIAN BUTTERCREAM

YIELD: 3 CUPS / **ACTIVE TIME:** 20 MINUTES / **TOTAL TIME:** 30 MINUTES

A more elegant frosting—not as sweet as the American iteration, quite versatile, and absolutely gorgeous.

1. Place the sugar and water in a small saucepan, fit it with a candy thermometer, and bring the mixture to a boil.

2. While the syrup is coming to a boil, place the egg whites and salt in the work bowl of a stand mixer fitted with the whisk attachment and whip on medium speed until the mixture holds stiff peaks.

3. Cook the syrup until the thermometer reads 245°F. Immediately remove the pan from the heat and once the syrup stops bubbling let it stand for an additional 30 seconds.

4. Reduce the speed of the mixer to medium-low and slowly pour the syrup down the side of the mixing bowl until all of it has been incorporated. Raise the speed to high and whip until the meringue is glossy and holds stiff peaks.

5. Add the butter 4 oz. at a time and whip until the mixture has thickened.

6. Reduce the speed to medium, add the vanilla, and beat until incorporated.

7. Use immediately, or store in the refrigerator for up to 2 weeks. If refrigerating, return to room temperature before using.

INGREDIENTS:

2	CUPS SUGAR
½	CUP WATER
8	EGG WHITES
¼	TEASPOON FINE SEA SALT
1.5	LBS. UNSALTED BUTTER, SOFTENED
1	TEASPOON PURE VANILLA EXTRACT

CREAM CHEESE FROSTING

YIELD: 3 CUPS / **ACTIVE TIME:** 10 MINUTES / **TOTAL TIME:** 10 MINUTES

The quintessential frosting for carrot and red velvet cakes, as well as any confection where you're looking to add creaminess.

1. In the work bowl of a stand mixer fitted with the paddle attachment, combine the butter, cream cheese, confectioners' sugar, and salt and beat on low speed until the sugar starts to be incorporated into the butter. Raise the speed to high and beat until the mixture is smooth and fluffy, about 5 minutes.

2. Reduce the speed to low, add the heavy cream and vanilla extract, and beat until incorporated. Use immediately, or store in the refrigerator for up to 2 weeks. If refrigerating, return to room temperature before using.

INGREDIENTS:

8	OZ. UNSALTED BUTTER, SOFTENED
8	OZ. CREAM CHEESE SOFTENED
2	LBS. CONFECTIONERS' SUGAR
⅛	TEASPOON KOSHER SALT
¼	CUP HEAVY CREAM
½	TEASPOON PURE VANILLA EXTRACT

CLASSIC CHOCOLATE FROSTING

YIELD: 1½ CUPS / **ACTIVE TIME:** 15 MINUTES / **TOTAL TIME:** 1 HOUR AND 30 MINUTES

There's considerable disagreement on whether it is OK to melt the chocolate in the microwave, but there's no doubt the double boiler will produce better, and more consistent, results.

1. Fill a small saucepan halfway with water and bring it to a simmer over medium heat.

2. Place the chocolate and cream in a large heatproof bowl and place it over the simmering water. Stir occasionally until the mixture is smooth and glossy.

3. Remove the bowl from heat, add the butter, and stir briefly. Let mixture stand until the butter is melted, about 5 minutes, and then stir until the mixture is smooth.

4. Place the frosting in the refrigerator until it has cooled and thickened, 30 minutes to 1 hour.

INGREDIENTS:

1 LB. MILK CHOCOLATE, CHOPPED

⅔ CUP HEAVY CREAM

8 OZ. UNSALTED BUTTER, SOFTENED AND DIVIDED INTO TABLESPOONS

PASTRY CREAM

YIELD: 2½ CUPS / **ACTIVE TIME**: 15 MINUTES / **TOTAL TIME**: 2 HOURS AND 15 MINUTES

A delightful, straightforward custard that can be used to fill cream puffs, doughnuts, or eclairs.

1. Place the milk and butter in a saucepan and bring to a simmer over medium heat.

2. As the milk mixture is coming to a simmer, place the sugar and cornstarch in a small bowl and whisk to combine. Add the eggs and whisk until the mixture is smooth and creamy.

3. Slowly pour half of the hot milk mixture into the egg mixture and stir until incorporated. Add the salt and vanilla, stir to incorporate, and pour the tempered egg mixture into the saucepan. Cook, while stirring constantly, until the mixture is very thick and about to come to a boil.

4. Remove from heat and pour the pastry cream into a bowl. Place plastic wrap directly on the surface to prevent a skin from forming. Refrigerate and chill for about 2 hours.

INGREDIENTS:

2 CUPS WHOLE MILK

1 TABLESPOON UNSALTED BUTTER

½ CUP SUGAR

3 TABLESPOONS CORNSTARCH

2 LARGE EGGS

 PINCH OF SEA SALT

½ TEASPOON PURE VANILLA EXTRACT

AUTUMN-SPICED PASTRY CREAM

YIELD: 2½ CUPS / **ACTIVE TIME:** 30 MINUTES / **TOTAL TIME:** 2 HOURS AND 30 MINUTES

A spiced, creamy custard that provides the finishing touch to any holiday dessert.

1. In a mixing bowl, combine the sugar, cornstarch, and egg yolks and whisk until combined, about 2 minutes. Set the mixture aside.

2. Place the milk, cinnamon, nutmeg, ginger, and cloves in a saucepan and bring to a simmer over medium heat. Remove the pan from heat.

3. Slowly pour half of the hot milk mixture into the egg mixture and stir until incorporated. Add the salt and vanilla, stir to incorporate, and pour the tempered egg mixture into the saucepan. Cook, while stirring constantly, until the mixture is very thick and about to come to a boil.

4. Remove the pan from heat, add the butter, and stir until thoroughly incorporated.

5. Strain the pastry cream through a fine-mesh strainer into a small bowl.

6. Place plastic wrap directly on the surface to prevent a skin from forming. Refrigerate for about 2 hours. This will keep in the refrigerator for up to 5 days.

INGREDIENTS:

½	CUP SUGAR
3	TABLESPOONS CORNSTARCH
6	EGG YOLKS
2	CUPS WHOLE MILK
1½	TEASPOONS CINNAMON
1	TEASPOON FRESHLY GRATED NUTMEG
½	TEASPOON GROUND GINGER
⅛	TEASPOON GROUND CLOVES
¼	TEASPOON KOSHER SALT
1½	TEASPOONS PURE VANILLA EXTRACT
2	OZ. UNSALTED BUTTER, SOFTENED

BUTTERSCOTCH PASTRY CREAM

YIELD: 2½ CUPS / **ACTIVE TIME:** 30 MINUTES / **TOTAL TIME:** 2 HOURS AND 30 MINUTES

A rich custard with deep notes of caramelized sugar and butter. This can be used as a filling, or stand on its own as butterscotch pudding.

1. In a small bowl, combine the cornstarch and egg yolks and whisk for 2 minutes. Set the mixture aside.

2. Place the light brown sugar and water in a saucepan, fit the pan with a candy thermometer, and cook over high heat until the thermometer reads 290°F.

3. Remove the pan from the heat. While whisking, slowly add the milk to the sugar. Be careful, as the mixture will most likely splatter. Place the pan over high heat and bring the mix back to a simmer. Remove the pan from heat.

4. Slowly pour half of the hot milk mixture into the egg mixture and stir until incorporated. Add the salt and vanilla extract, stir to incorporate, and pour the tempered egg mixture into the saucepan. Cook, while stirring constantly, until the mixture is very thick and about to come to a boil. Remove the pan from heat.

5. Add the salt, vanilla, and butter and whisk until fully incorporated.

6. Strain the pastry cream through a fine-mesh strainer into a small bowl.

7. Place plastic wrap directly on the surface to prevent a skin from forming. Refrigerate for about 2 hours. This will keep in the refrigerator for up to 5 days.

INGREDIENTS:

3	TABLESPOONS CORNSTARCH
6	EGG YOLKS
½	CUP LIGHT BROWN SUGAR
2	TABLESPOONS WATER
2	CUPS MILK
¼	TEASPOON KOSHER SALT
1½	TEASPOONS PURE VANILLA EXTRACT
2	OZ. UNSALTED BUTTER, SOFTENED

CARAMELIZED WHITE CHOCOLATE

YIELD: 1 CUP / **ACTIVE TIME:** 25 MINUTES / **TOTAL TIME:** 1 HOUR AND 30 MINUTES

This is a game-changer. Caramelizing the milk solids in white chocolate yields an incredibly aromatic and caramel-flavored chocolate.

1. Preheat the oven to 250°F.

2. Line a rimmed 18 x 13–inch baking sheet with a silicone baking mat.

3. Chop the white chocolate into small pieces and spread them over the baking sheet. Add the salt and oil and stir to coat the chocolate pieces.

4. Place the baking sheet in the oven and bake for 10 minutes.

5. Use a rubber spatula to spread the chocolate until it covers the entire silpat mat. Place back in the oven and bake until the white chocolate has caramelized to a deep golden brown, about 30 to 50 minutes, removing to stir every 10 minutes.

6. Carefully pour the caramelized white chocolate into a heatproof container. Store at room temperature for up to 1 month.

INGREDIENTS:

1   LB. WHITE CHOCOLATE

     PINCH OF FINE SEA SALT

2   TABLESPOONS CANOLA OIL

BUTTERFLUFF FILLING

YIELD: 4 CUPS / **ACTIVE TIME:** 10 MINUTES / **TOTAL TIME:** 10 MINUTES

A go-to filling for cakes, whoopie pies, and cookie sandwiches.

1. In the work bowl of a stand mixer fitted with the paddle attachment, cream the marshmallow creme and butter on medium speed until the mixture is light and fluffy, about 5 minutes.

2. Add the confectioners' sugar, vanilla, and salt, reduce the speed to low, and beat for 2 minutes. Use immediately, or store in the refrigerator for up to 1 month.

INGREDIENTS:

8   OZ. MARSHMALLOW
     CREME

10   OZ. UNSALTED BUTTER,
     SOFTENED

11   OZ. CONFECTIONERS'
     SUGAR

1½   TEASPOONS PURE VANILLA
     EXTRACT

¾   TEASPOON KOSHER SALT

CHANTILLY CREAM

YIELD: 2 CUPS / **ACTIVE TIME:** 5 MINUTES / **TOTAL TIME:** 5 MINUTES

Chantilly Cream is a sweet, vanilla-infused whipped cream that transforms a simple dessert into an event.

1. In the work bowl of a stand mixer fitted with the whisk attachment, whip the heavy cream, sugar, and vanilla on high until the mixture holds soft peaks.

2. Use immediately, or store in the refrigerator for up to 3 days.

INGREDIENTS:

2   CUPS HEAVY CREAM

3   TABLESPOONS SUGAR

1   TEASPOON PURE VANILLA EXTRACT

CINNAMON CHANTILLY CREAM

YIELD: 2 CUPS / **ACTIVE TIME:** 5 MINUTES / **TOTAL TIME:** 5 MINUTES

Use this spiced whipped cream to add a bit of flair to any autumn-inclined dessert.

1. In the work bowl of a stand mixer fitted with the whisk attachment, whip the heavy cream, sugar, cinnamon, and vanilla on high until the mixture holds soft peaks.

2. Use immediately, or store in the refrigerator for up to 3 days.

INGREDIENTS:

2   CUPS HEAVY CREAM

¼   CUP CONFECTIONERS' SUGAR

1   TABLESPOON CINNAMON

1   TEASPOON PURE VANILLA EXTRACT

VANILLA GLAZE

YIELD: 1½ CUPS / **ACTIVE TIME:** 5 MINUTES / **TOTAL TIME:** 5 MINUTES

This is intended for the doughnuts in this book, but it's equally delightful on cakes and cookies.

1. In a mixing bowl, whisk all of the ingredients until combined.

2. If the glaze is too thick, incorporate tablespoons of milk until it reaches the desired consistency. If too thin, incorporate tablespoons of confectioners' sugar. Use immediately, or store in the refrigerator for up to 5 days.

INGREDIENTS:

½   CUP MILK, PLUS MORE AS NEEDED

¼   TEASPOON PURE VANILLA EXTRACT

1   LB. CONFECTIONERS' SUGAR, PLUS MORE AS NEEDED

HONEY GLAZE

YIELD: 1½ CUPS / **ACTIVE TIME:** 5 MINUTES / **TOTAL TIME:** 5 MINUTES

That sweet taste of Sunday mornings that we all remember from childhood.

1. In a mixing bowl, whisk all of the ingredients until combined.

2. If the glaze is too thick, incorporate tablespoons of milk until it reaches the desired consistency. If too thin, incorporate tablespoons of confectioners' sugar. Use immediately, or store in the refrigerator for up to 5 days.

INGREDIENTS:

½ CUP MILK, PLUS MORE AS NEEDED

1 TABLESPOON HONEY

¼ TEASPOON KOSHER SALT

1 LB. CONFECTIONERS' SUGAR, PLUS MORE AS NEEDED

MILK CHOCOLATE CRÉMEUX

YIELD: 4 CUPS / **ACTIVE TIME:** 30 MINUTES / **TOTAL TIME:** 24 HOURS

Meaning "creamy" and "mousse-like" a crémeux is incredibly versatile, and can be used as a cake filling, spread on scones, or enjoyed on its own.

1. Place the gelatin sheets in a small bowl and add 1 cup of ice and enough cold water that the sheets are completely covered. Set aside.

2. Place the chocolate in a heatproof mixing bowl.

3. Place half of sugar and the egg yolks in a small bowl and whisk for 2 minutes. Set the mixture aside.

4. In a small saucepan, combine the milk, heavy cream, and remaining sugar and bring to a simmer over medium heat.

5. Slowly pour half of the hot milk mixture into the egg mixture and stir until incorporated. Add the salt and vanilla extract, stir to incorporate, and pour the tempered egg mixture into the saucepan. Cook, while stirring constantly, until the mixture thickens and is about to come to a full simmer (if you have an instant-read thermometer, 175°F). Remove the pan from heat.

6. Remove the bloomed gelatin from the ice water. Squeeze to remove as much water as possible from the sheets. Add the sheets to the hot milk mixture and whisk until they have completely dissolved.

7. Pour the hot milk mixture over the chocolate and let the mixture sit for 1 minute. Whisk to combine, transfer to a heatproof container, and let it cool to room temperature.

8. Refrigerate overnight before using.

INGREDIENTS:

2	SHEETS OF SILVER GELATIN
10.7	OZ. MILK CHOCOLATE
¼	CUP SUGAR
4	EGG YOLKS
¾	CUP MILK
¾	CUP HEAVY CREAM

GIANDUJA CRÉMEUX

YIELD: 1 QUART / **ACTIVE TIME:** 30 MINUTES / **TOTAL TIME:** 24 HOURS

Gianduja is a sweet chocolate that contains 30 percent hazelnut paste. If it proves difficult to find in stores, turn to the internet.

1. Place the gelatin sheets in a small bowl and add 1 cup of ice and enough cold water that the sheets are completely covered. Set aside.

2. Place the chocolate in a heatproof mixing bowl.

3. Place half of sugar and the egg yolks in a small bowl and whisk for 2 minutes. Set the mixture aside.

4. In a small saucepan, combine the milk, heavy cream, and remaining sugar and bring to a simmer over medium heat.

5. Slowly pour half of the hot milk mixture into the egg mixture and stir until incorporated. Add the salt and vanilla extract, stir to incorporate, and pour the tempered egg mixture into the saucepan. Cook, while stirring constantly, until the mixture thickens and is about to come to a full simmer (if you have an instant-read thermometer, 175°F). Remove the pan from heat.

6. Remove the bloomed gelatin from the ice water. Squeeze to remove as much water as possible from the sheets. Add the sheets to the hot milk mixture and whisk until they have completely dissolved.

7. Pour the hot milk mixture over the chocolate and let the mixture sit for 1 minute. Whisk to combine, transfer to a heatproof container, and let it cool to room temperature.

8. Refrigerate overnight before using.

INGREDIENTS:

2	SHEETS OF SILVER GELATIN
12	OZ. GIANDUJA CHOCOLATE, CHOPPED
¼	CUP SUGAR
4	EGG YOLKS
¾	CUP MILK
¾	CUP HEAVY CREAM

CHOCOLATE GANACHE

YIELD: 1½ CUPS / **ACTIVE TIME:** 10 MINUTES / **TOTAL TIME:** 15 MINUTES

The key to adding a bit of chocolate and beauty to your cakes and pies. This preparation will work with any chocolate—dark, milk, or white.

1. Place the chocolate in a heatproof mixing bowl and set aside.

2. Place the heavy cream in a small saucepan and bring to a simmer over medium heat.

3. Pour the cream over the chocolate and let the mixture rest for 1 minute.

4. Gently whisk the mixture until thoroughly combined. Use immediately if drizzling over a cake or serving with fruit. Let the ganache cool for 2 hours if piping. The ganache will keep in the refrigerator for up to 5 days.

INGREDIENTS:

8 OZ. CHOCOLATE

1 CUP HEAVY CREAM

HOT FUDGE

YIELD: 2 CUPS / **ACTIVE TIME:** 15 MINUTES / **TOTAL TIME:** 15 MINUTES

A must for anyone whose sweet tooth fixates on frozen treats.

1. Place the cream, corn syrup, brown sugar, cocoa powder, salt, half of the chocolate, and the espresso powder in a saucepan and cook over medium heat until the chocolate is melted.

2. Reduce the heat and simmer for 5 minutes. Remove the pan from heat and whisk in the remaining chocolate, the butter, and the vanilla. Serve immediately.

INGREDIENTS:

⅔	CUP HEAVY CREAM
½	CUP LIGHT CORN SYRUP
⅓	CUP DARK BROWN SUGAR
¼	CUP COCOA POWDER
½	TEASPOON FINE SEA SALT
8	OZ. BITTERSWEET CHOCOLATE, CHOPPED
½	TEASPOON ESPRESSO POWDER
1	OZ. UNSALTED BUTTER
1	TEASPOON PURE VANILLA EXTRACT

CARAMEL SAUCE

YIELD: 2 CUPS / **ACTIVE TIME:** 15 MINUTES / **TOTAL TIME:** 1 HOUR AND 30 MINUTES

The perfect caramel sauce for cakes, topping ice cream, or just dipping.

1. Place the sugar and water in a small saucepan and bring to a boil over high heat. Resist the urge to whisk the mixture; instead, swirl the pan occasionally.

2. Once the mixture turns a dark amber, turn off the heat and, whisking slowly, drizzle in the heavy cream. Be careful, as the mixture may splatter.

3. When all of the cream has been incorporated, add the butter, salt, and vanilla and whisk until smooth. Pour the hot caramel into mason jars to cool. The caramel sauce can be stored for 1 week at room temperature.

INGREDIENTS:

1	CUP SUGAR
¼	CUP WATER
½	CUP HEAVY CREAM
3	OZ. UNSALTED BUTTER, SOFTENED
½	TEASPOON KOSHER SALT
½	TEASPOON PURE VANILLA EXTRACT

CAJETA

YIELD: 1½ CUPS / **ACTIVE TIME:** 1 HOUR / **TOTAL TIME:** 5 HOURS

The Mexican version of dulce de leche, but it's made with goats' milk, which gives it a slightly tangy finish. Traditionally, cajeta is served over ice cream or fried dough, but it's pretty dang good on anything.

1. Place the goats' milk, sugar, cinnamon stick, and salt in a medium saucepan and bring to a simmer over medium-low heat.

2. In a small bowl, combine the baking soda and water. Whisk the mixture into the saucepan.

3. Continue to simmer for 1 to 2 hours, stirring frequently.

4. When the mixture turns a caramel color and is thick enough to coat the back of a wooden spoon, remove the pan from heat and let the cajeta cool for 1 hour.

5. Transfer to mason jars and refrigerate until set. This will keep in the refrigerator for up to 1 month.

INGREDIENTS:

4	CUPS GOATS' MILK
1	CUP SUGAR
1	CINNAMON STICK
⅛	TEASPOON KOSHER SALT
1½	TEASPOONS WATER
¼	TEASPOON BAKING SODA

BOURBON TOFFEE SAUCE

YIELD: 4 CUPS / **ACTIVE TIME:** 10 MINUTES / **TOTAL TIME:** 20 MINUTES

This uber-sweet, velvety sauce is unbeatable on a warm cobbler made from fresh summer fruit, on your favorite ice cream.

1. Place the butter, light brown sugar, maple syrup, heavy cream, and salt in a medium saucepan and bring the mixture to a boil over medium heat.

2. Let the mixture boil for 30 seconds, while continually whisking.

3. Remove the pan from heat and whisk in the bourbon.

4. Use immediately, or store in the refrigerator for up to 1 month. If storing in the refrigerator, reheat before using.

INGREDIENTS:

7	OZ. UNSALTED BUTTER
¾	CUP PACKED LIGHT BROWN SUGAR
¾	CUP MAPLE SYRUP
¼	CUP HEAVY CREAM
¼	TEASPOON KOSHER SALT
2	TABLESPOONS BOURBON

COATING CHOCOLATE

YIELD: 1 CUP / **ACTIVE TIME:** 10 MINUTES / **TOTAL TIME:** 10 MINUTES

Coating chocolate is a quick and simple way to add a crackly layer of chocolate to ice cream or a chocolate-dipped dessert.

1. Combine all of the ingredients in a small saucepan and place it over low heat.

2. Stir constantly until the chocolate has melted and the mixture is smooth. Use immediately.

INGREDIENTS:

8	OZ. DARK CHOCOLATE (55 TO 65 PERCENT)
4	OZ. COCONUT OIL
½	TEASPOON PURE VANILLA EXTRACT
⅛	TEASPOON KOSHER SALT

SUMMER BERRY COMPOTE

YIELD: 2 CUPS / **ACTIVE TIME:** 20 MINUTES / **TOTAL TIME:** 1 HOUR

Use this as a filling in fruit tarts, or to top parfaits and cakes.

1. Place the berries, lemon juice, lemon zest, and sugar in a medium saucepan and cook over medium heat until the berries begin to burst and release their liquid, about 10 minutes.

2. Stir in the cornstarch, salt, and vanilla and reduce the heat to medium-low. Cook, stirring occasionally, until the mixture thickens slightly.

3. Remove the pan from heat and let the compote cool completely before storing in an airtight container. The compote can be served warm or chilled. It will keep in the refrigerator for up to 1 week.

INGREDIENTS:

4	PINTS OF ASSORTED BERRIES
	ZEST AND JUICE OF 1 LEMON
1	CUP SUGAR
3	TABLESPOONS CORNSTARCH
¼	TEASPOON KOSHER SALT
2	TEASPOONS PURE VANILLA EXTRACT

STREUSEL TOPPING

YIELD: 3 CUPS / **ACTIVE TIME**: 10 MINUTES / **TOTAL TIME**: 10 MINUTES

Great on top of pies, fruit bars, a crumble, or muffins.

1. In the work bowl of a stand mixer fitted with the paddle attachment, beat the flour, sugar, brown sugar, oats, cinnamon, and salt on low speed until combined.

2. Turn off the mixer and add the butter.

3. Raise the speed to medium and beat the mixture until the mixture is crumbly and the butter has been absorbed by the dry ingredients. Make sure not to overwork the mixture.

4. Store in the refrigerator for a week and place on muffins before baking.

INGREDIENTS:

9	OZ. ALL-PURPOSE FLOUR
6	OZ. SUGAR
6	OZ. LIGHT BROWN SUGAR
4	OZ. ROLLED OATS
2¼	TEASPOONS CINNAMON
¾	TEASPOON KOSHER SALT
8	OZ. UNSALTED BUTTER, CHILLED AND DIVIDED INTO TABLESPOONS

COOKIES

As Marcel Proust showed with the world-shaking brilliance that issued from that bite of a madeleine, cookies reside in the memory, in the mind. The sight of them on a tiered stand around the holidays, piled high with the bounty of a recent cookie swap. An afternoon spent making drop cookies with a loved one, trading turns licking the spoon. Sneaking into a kitchen to grab a chocolate chip cookie just out of the oven to savor its pillowy warmth at its peak.

This magic that lingers is due in some part to the cookie's unique ability to be crisp but still moist, rich without also being heavy. But there's also plenty of room for mystery within that mystique, which makes sense to those who have experienced the alchemy that takes place when an unbelievably simple to prepare dough is put in the oven.

CHOCOLATE CHIP COOKIES

YIELD: 16 COOKIES / **ACTIVE TIME**: 15 MINUTES / **TOTAL TIME**: 45 MINUTES

You will not believe the difference browning the butter makes to this classic preparation.

1. Preheat the oven to 350°F. Place the butter in a saucepan and cook over medium-high heat until it starts to brown and gives off a nutty aroma (let your nose guide you here, making sure you frequently waft the steam toward you). Transfer to a heatproof mixing bowl.

2. Place the flour and baking soda in a bowl and whisk until combined.

3. Add the sugars, salt, and vanilla to the bowl containing the melted butter and whisk until combined. Add the egg and egg yolk and whisk until mixture is smooth and thick. Add the flour-and-baking soda mixture and stir until incorporated. Add the chocolate chips and stir until evenly distributed. Form the mixture into 16 balls and place on parchment-lined baking sheets, leaving about 2 inches between each ball.

4. Working with 1 baking sheet at a time, place it in the oven and bake until golden brown, 12 to 16 minutes, rotating the sheet halfway through the bake time. Remove from the oven and let cool to room temperature before serving.

INGREDIENTS:

7	OZ. UNSALTED BUTTER
8.75	OZ. ALL-PURPOSE FLOUR
½	TEASPOON BAKING SODA
3.5	OZ. SUGAR
5.3	OZ. DARK BROWN SUGAR
1	TEASPOON FINE SEA SALT
2	TEASPOONS PURE VANILLA EXTRACT
1	LARGE EGG
1	LARGE EGG YOLK
1¼	CUPS SEMISWEET CHOCOLATE CHIPS

CLASSIC SUGAR COOKIES

YIELD: 48 COOKIES / **ACTIVE TIME:** 40 MINUTES / **TOTAL TIME:** 3 HOURS

These seem to abound around the holidays, but are wonderful any time of year—particularly when made with a loved one.

1. In the work bowl of a stand mixer fitted with the paddle attachment, cream the butter and brown sugar on medium speed until the mixture is very light and fluffy, about 5 minutes. Scrape down the work bowl and then beat the mixture for another 5 minutes.

2. Reduce the speed to low, add the egg, and beat until incorporated. Scrape down the work bowl and beat the mixture for 1 minute on medium.

3. Add the remaining ingredients, reduce the speed to low, and beat until the mixture comes together as a dough. Form the dough into a ball and then flatten it into a disc. Cover the dough completely with plastic wrap and refrigerate for 2 hours.

4. Preheat the oven to 350°F and line two baking sheets with parchment paper.

5. Remove the dough from the refrigerator and let it sit on the counter for 5 minutes.

6. Place the dough on a flour-dusted work surface and roll it out until it is approximately ¼ inch thick. Use a cookie cutters to cut the dough into the desired shapes and place them on the baking sheets. Form any scraps into a ball, roll it out, and cut into cookies. If the dough becomes too sticky or warm, place it back in the refrigerator for 15 minutes to firm up.

7. Place the cookies in the oven and bake until lightly golden brown at their edges, 8 to 10 minutes. Remove from the oven, transfer to a wire rack, and let cool for 10 minutes before enjoying or decorating.

INGREDIENTS:

8	OZ. UNSALTED BUTTER, SOFTENED
7	OZ. LIGHT BROWN SUGAR
1	EGG
12	OZ. ALL-PURPOSE FLOUR, PLUS MORE AS NEEDED
1	TEASPOON BAKING POWDER
½	TEASPOON KOSHER SALT

SNICKERDOODLES

YIELD: 24 COOKIES / **ACTIVE TIME:** 25 MINUTES / **TOTAL TIME:** 1 HOUR

It's well known that the cream of tartar is essential in these classic cookies. But the cinnamon is just as important, so make sure you use a top-quality offering.

1. Preheat the oven to 375°F and line two baking sheets with parchment paper. Whisk together the flour, cream of tartar, baking soda, 1½ teaspoons of the cinnamon, and the salt in a mixing bowl.

2. In the work bowl of a stand mixer fitted with the paddle attachment, cream the butter and all but 2 oz. of the sugar on medium speed until light and fluffy. Add the egg and vanilla and beat until combined, scraping down the work bowl as needed. With the mixer running on low, add the dry mixture in three increments, waiting until each portion has been incorporated until adding the next. A thick dough will form.

3. Roll 1-tablespoon portions of the dough into balls. Place the remaining cinnamon and sugar in a mixing bowl and stir to combine. Roll the balls in the mixture until coated and place them on the baking sheets.

4. Place in the oven and bake for 10 minutes, until puffy and very soft. Remove from the oven, press down with a spatula to flatten them, and let cool on the baking sheets for 10 minutes before transferring to a wire rack to cool completely.

INGREDIENTS:

15	OZ. ALL-PURPOSE FLOUR
2	TEASPOONS CREAM OF TARTAR
1	TEASPOON BAKING SODA
2½	TEASPOONS CINNAMON
½	TEASPOON KOSHER SALT
8	OZ. UNSALTED BUTTER, SOFTENED
11.6	OZ. SUGAR
1	LARGE EGG, AT ROOM TEMPERATURE
2	TEASPOONS PURE VANILLA EXTRACT

MACARONS

YIELD: 30 MACARONS / ACTIVE TIME: 1 HOUR / TOTAL TIME: 4 HOURS

Featuring a crispy outside and a cloudlike center, these confections are, for once, entirely worth the hype. For ideas on what to fill them with, see the Building Blocks chapter.

1. Place the almond flour and confectioners' sugar in a food processor and blitz for about 1 minute, until the mixture is thoroughly combined and has a fine texture. Place the mixture in a mixing bowl, add three of the egg whites and the salt, and stir with a rubber spatula until the mixture is almost a paste. Set the mixture aside.

2. Place the sugar and water in a small saucepan. Place a candy thermometer in the saucepan and cook the mixture over high heat.

3. While the syrup is coming to a boil, wipe out the work bowl of the stand mixer, place the remaining egg whites in it, and whip on medium until they hold firm peaks.

4. Cook the syrup until it is 245°F. Remove the pan from heat and carefully add the syrup to the whipped egg whites, slowly pouring it down the side of the work bowl. When all of the syrup has been added, whip the mixture until it is glossy, holds stiff peaks, and has cooled slightly. If desired, stir in the food coloring.

5. Add half of the meringue to the almond flour mixture and fold to incorporate. Fold in the remaining meringue. When incorporated, the batter should be smooth, very glossy, and not too runny.

6. Fit a piping bag with a plain tip and fill it with the batter. Pipe evenly sized rounds onto baking sheets lined with silicone baking mats, leaving an inch of space between each one. You want the rounds to be about the size of a silver dollar (approximately 2 inches wide) when you pipe them onto the sheet; they will spread slightly as they sit.

7. Gently tap each baking sheet to smooth the tops of the macarons.

8. Let the macarons sit at room temperature, uncovered, for 1 hour. This allows a skin to form on them.

9. Preheat the oven to 325°F.

10. Place the macarons in the oven and bake for 10 minutes. Rotate the baking sheet and let them bake for another 5 minutes. Turn off the oven, crack the oven door, and let the macarons sit in the oven for 5 minutes.

11. Remove the cookies from the oven and let them sit on a cooling rack for 2 hours. When the macarons are completely cool, fill as desired.

INGREDIENTS:

11 OZ. FINE ALMOND FLOUR

11 OZ. CONFECTIONERS' SUGAR

8 EGG WHITES

PINCH OF FINE SEA SALT

11 OZ. SUGAR

½ CUP WATER

2-3 DROPS OF GEL FOOD COLORING (OPTIONAL)

MADELEINES

YIELD: 30 MADELEINES / **ACTIVE TIME:** 40 MINUTES / **TOTAL TIME:** 3 HOURS AND 30 MINUTES

Thanks to the unmatched brilliance of Marcel Proust, this just may be the world's most famous cookie.

1. In the work bowl of a stand mixer fitted with the paddle attachment, beat the sugar, egg whites, and lemon zest on medium until the mixture is light and fluffy. Add the flours and beat until incorporated. Set the mixture aside.

2. Place the butter in a small saucepan and melt it over low heat.

3. Set the mixer to low speed and slowly pour the melted butter into the mixer. When the butter has been incorporated, add the vanilla and beat until incorporated.

4. Place the madeleine batter into two piping bags. Place the bags in the refrigerator to set the batter, about 2 hours.

5. Coat your madeleine pans with nonstick cooking spray. Pipe about 1 tablespoon of batter in the center of each seashell mold.

6. Place the pans in the oven and bake until the edges of the madeleines turn golden brown, about 10 minutes. Remove from the oven, immediately remove the cookies from the pans and onto a cooling rack, and let them cool completely.

7. Once cool, lightly dust the tops of the madeleines with confectioners' sugar.

INGREDIENTS:

8	OZ. SUGAR
8	OZ. EGG WHITES
	ZEST OF 1 LEMON
3.2	OZ. FINE ALMOND FLOUR
3.2	OZ. ALL-PURPOSE FLOUR
7	OZ. UNSALTED BUTTER, MELTED
1	TEASPOON PURE VANILLA EXTRACT
	CONFECTIONERS' SUGAR, FOR DUSTING

BROWNIES FROM SCRATCH

YIELD: 12 BROWNIES / **ACTIVE TIME:** 30 MINUTES / **TOTAL TIME:** 3 HOURS

Toss aside those store-bought mixes for good, as this recipe for homemade brownies has it all.

1. Preheat the oven to 350°F. Line a 9 x 13–inch baking pan with parchment paper and coat it with nonstick cooking spray.

2. Fill a small saucepan halfway with water and bring it to a simmer. Place the dark chocolate and butter in a heatproof bowl, place it over the simmering water, and stir until they have melted and been combined. Remove from heat and set aside.

3. In a separate mixing bowl, whisk the sugar, brown sugar, cocoa powder, and salt, making sure to break up any clumps. Whisk in the eggs, vanilla, and melted chocolate mixture and then gradually add the flour, whisking to thoroughly incorporate before adding the next bit.

4. Pour the batter into the baking pan and use a rubber spatula to even out the top. Lightly tap the baking pan on the counter to remove any air bubbles.

5. Place the brownies in the oven and bake until a cake tester comes out clean, 30 to 40 minutes.

6. Remove from the oven, transfer the brownies to a cooling rack, and let them cool completely. Once they are cool, transfer to the refrigerator and chill for 1 hour.

7. Run a paring knife along the sides of the pan, cut the brownies into squares, and enjoy.

INGREDIENTS:

7.5	OZ. DARK CHOCOLATE (55 TO 65 PERCENT)
12	OZ. UNSALTED BUTTER
12	OZ. SUGAR
12	OZ. LIGHT BROWN SUGAR
¼	CUP COCOA POWDER, PLUS 1 TABLESPOON
1	TEASPOON KOSHER SALT
5	EGGS
1½	TABLESPOONS PURE VANILLA EXTRACT
9.5	OZ. ALL-PURPOSE FLOUR

APRICOT KOLACHES

YIELD: 32 COOKIES / ACTIVE TIME: 30 MINUTES / TOTAL TIME: 2 HOURS AND 30 MINUTES

Y̶ou can nestle any fruit in this dough, but none will be lovelier than the sweet and tart apricot.

1. Place the dried apricots in a saucepan and cover with water. Bring the water to a boil over medium-high heat and cook until the apricots are soft, adding more water if too much evaporates. Add the sugar and reduce the heat so that the mixture simmers. Cook, stirring to dissolve the sugar, until the liquid thickens into a syrup. Transfer the mixture to a blender or a food processor and puree until smooth. Let stand until cool.

2. Sift the flour and salt into a mixing bowl. In the work bowl of a stand mixer fitted with the paddle attachment, beat the cream cheese and butter on high until the mixture is fluffy. Gradually add the dry mixture to the wet mixture and beat to incorporate. Divide the dough into two balls and cover loosely with plastic wrap. Flatten each ball to about ¾-inch thick and refrigerate until the dough is firm, about 2 hours.

3. Preheat the oven to 375°F and line a large baking sheet with parchment paper. Place one of the balls of dough on a flour-dusted work surface and roll it out into a ⅛-inch-thick square. Cut the dough into as many 1½-inch squares as possible.

4. Place approximately 1 teaspoon of the apricot mixture in the center of each square. Gently lift two opposite corners of each square and fold one over the other. Gently press down to seal and transfer to the baking sheet. Repeat until all of the squares have been used.

5. Place in the oven and bake for 12 to 14 minutes, until the cookies are golden brown. Remove, briefly let them cool on the baking sheets, and transfer to a wire rack to cool completely. Repeat with the remaining ball of dough. When all of the kolaches have been baked and cooled, dust with the confectioners' sugar.

INGREDIENTS:

8	OZ. DRIED APRICOTS
3.5	OZ. SUGAR
2.8	OZ. ALL-PURPOSE FLOUR, PLUS MORE AS NEEDED
¼	TEASPOON FINE SEA SALT
2	OZ. CREAM CHEESE, SOFTENED
4	OZ. UNSALTED BUTTER, SOFTENED
¼	CUP CONFECTIONERS' SUGAR, FOR DUSTING

COCONUT MACAROONS

YIELD: 12 MACAROONS / **ACTIVE TIME:** 45 MINUTES / **TOTAL TIME:** 3 HOURS

Coconut can be divisive, but for coconut lovers, these sweet, pillowy, and slightly crispy treats are the jewel of their obsession.

1. Line a baking sheet with parchment paper. In a mixing bowl, mix the sweetened condensed milk, shredded coconut, salt, and vanilla with a rubber spatula until combined. Set the mixture aside.

2. In the work bowl of a stand mixer fitted with the whisk attachment, whip the egg whites until they hold stiff peaks. Add the whipped egg whites to the coconut mixture and fold to incorporate.

3. Scoop 2-oz. portions of the mixture onto the lined baking sheet, making sure to leave enough space between them. Place the baking sheet in the refrigerator and let the dough firm up for 1 hour.

4. Preheat the oven to 350°F.

5. Place the cookies in the oven and bake until they are lightly golden brown, 20 to 25 minutes.

6. Remove the cookies from the oven, transfer them to a cooling rack, and let them cool for 1 hour.

7. Dip the bottoms of the macaroons into the ganache and then place them back on the baking sheet. If desired, drizzle some of the ganache over the tops of the cookies. Refrigerate until the chocolate is set, about 5 minutes, before serving.

INGREDIENTS:

1	(14 OZ.) CAN OF SWEETENED CONDENSED MILK
7	OZ. SWEETENED SHREDDED COCONUT
7	OZ. UNSWEETENED SHREDDED COCONUT
¼	TEASPOON KOSHER SALT
½	TEASPOON PURE VANILLA EXTRACT
2	EGG WHITES
	CHOCOLATE GANACHE (SEE PAGE 99), WARM

ALMOND COOKIES

YIELD: 18 COOKIES / **ACTIVE TIME:** 15 MINUTES / **TOTAL TIME:** 1 HOUR

Toasting the almonds before adding them to the cookies is an alternative well worth experimenting with.

1. Preheat the oven to 350°F and line two baking sheets with parchment paper. Place the flour, confectioners' sugar, sugar, egg whites, and almond paste in a large mixing bowl and work the mixture with your hands until an extremely sticky dough forms.

2. Place the almonds in a bowl. Place teaspoons of the dough in the bowl of almonds and roll the pieces of dough until completely coated. Place on the baking sheets.

3. Place in the oven and bake for about 15 minutes, until golden brown. Remove and let cool on the baking sheets for a few minutes before transferring to a wire rack to cool completely.

INGREDIENTS:

1.25 OZ. ALL-PURPOSE FLOUR

2 OZ. CONFECTIONERS' SUGAR

3.5 OZ. SUGAR

2 EGG WHITES

8 OZ. UNSWEETENED ALMOND PASTE

½ CUP SLIVERED ALMONDS

CORNMEAL COOKIES

YIELD: 24 COOKIES / ACTIVE TIME: 20 MINUTES / TOTAL TIME: 3 HOURS

A brilliantly colored cookie that is lovely with a dollop of raspberry jam.

1. In the work bowl of a stand mixer fitted with the paddle attachment, cream butter and sugar at medium speed until pale and fluffy, scraping down the sides of the bowl as needed. Add the egg and vanilla, reduce speed to low, and beat to incorporate. Gradually incorporate the flour, cornmeal, cornstarch, and salt and beat until the mixture is a stiff dough.

2. Place the dough on a sheet of parchment paper and roll it into a log that is 2½ inches in diameter. Cover in plastic wrap and refrigerate for 2 hours.

3. Preheat the oven to 350°F and line two baking sheets with parchment paper. Cut the chilled dough into ⅓-inch-thick rounds and arrange the cookies on the baking sheets. Place the cookies in the oven and bake until the edges start to brown, about 10 minutes. Remove from the oven, let cool on the sheets for a few minutes, and then transfer the cookies to wire racks to cool completely.

INGREDIENTS:

4	OZ. UNSALTED BUTTER
3	OZ. CONFECTIONERS' SUGAR
1	LARGE EGG, AT ROOM TEMPERATURE
½	TEASPOON PURE VANILLA EXTRACT
3.2	OZ. ALL-PURPOSE FLOUR
¼	CUP FINE CORNMEAL
2	TABLESPOONS CORNSTARCH
¼	TEASPOON FINE SEA SALT

CHOCOLATE-COVERED MARSHMALLOW COOKIES

YIELD: 24 COOKIES / **ACTIVE TIME:** 30 MINUTES / **TOTAL TIME:** 3 HOURS AND 30 MINUTES

Adding a bit of coconut oil to the melted chocolate really helps the coating of these decadent cookies set up.

1. Place the flour, sugar, salt, baking powder, baking soda, and cinnamon in a mixing bowl and whisk to combine. Add the butter and work the mixture with a pastry blender until it is coarse crumbs. Add the eggs and stir until a stiff dough forms. Shape the dough into a ball, cover completely with plastic wrap, and refrigerate for 1 hour.

2. Preheat the oven to 375°F and line two baking sheets with parchment paper. Place the dough on a flour-dusted work surface and roll out to ¼ inch thick. Cut the dough into 24 rounds and place them on the baking sheets.

3. Place in the oven and bake for about 10 minutes, until the edges have browned. Remove from the oven and transfer the cookies to wire racks to cool completely. Leave the oven on.

4. When the cookies are cool, place a marshmallow half on each cookie. Place them back in the oven and, while keeping a close eye on the cookies, bake until marshmallows start to slump. Remove from oven and let cool completely on the baking sheets.

5. Place the chocolate chips in a microwave-safe bowl and microwave on medium until melted and smooth, removing to stir every 15 seconds. Add the coconut oil to the melted chocolate and stir until incorporated. Drop the cookies into the chocolate, turning to coat all sides. Carefully remove the coated cookies with a fork, hold them over the bowl to let any excess chocolate drip off, and place on pieces of parchment paper. Let the chocolate set before serving.

INGREDIENTS:

13.2 OZ. ALL-PURPOSE FLOUR, PLUS MORE FOR DUSTING

⅔ CUP SUGAR

½ TEASPOON FINE SEA SALT

¾ TEASPOON BAKING POWDER

½ TEASPOON BAKING SODA

1 TEASPOON CINNAMON

6 OZ. UNSALTED BUTTER, DIVIDED INTO TABLESPOONS

3 LARGE EGGS, LIGHTLY BEATEN

12 LARGE MARSHMALLOWS, HALVED

2 CUPS DARK CHOCOLATE CHIPS

1 TABLESPOON COCONUT OIL

CHOCOLATE CRINKLE COOKIES

YIELD: 20 COOKIES / **ACTIVE TIME:** 45 MINUTES / **TOTAL TIME:** 2 HOURS AND 30 MINUTES

Somewhere between a brownie and a cookie, these are an ideal blend of chocolatey and chewy.

1. Line two baking sheets with parchment paper. Bring water to a simmer in a small saucepan over low heat. Place the chocolate in a heatproof bowl and place the bowl over the simmering water. Occasionally stir the chocolate until it is melted. Remove the bowl from heat and set aside.

2. In the work bowl of a stand mixer fitted with the paddle attachment, cream the butter, dark brown sugar, and vanilla on medium speed until the mixture is very light and fluffy, about 5 minutes. Scrape down the work bowl and then beat the mixture for another 5 minutes.

3. Reduce the speed to low, add the melted chocolate, and beat until incorporated, scraping down the work bowl as needed.

4. Add the eggs one at a time and beat until incorporated, again scraping the work bowl as needed. When both eggs have been incorporated, beat for another minute.

5. Add the flour, cocoa powder, baking powder, and salt and beat until the mixture comes together as a smooth dough.

6. Drop 2-oz. portions of the dough on the baking sheets, making sure to leave enough space between them. Place the baking sheets in the refrigerator and let the dough firm up for 1 hour.

7. Preheat the oven to 350°F. Place the confectioners' sugar in a mixing bowl, toss the dough balls in the sugar until completely coated, and then place them back on the baking sheet.

8. Place the cookies in the oven and bake until a cake tester comes out clean after being inserted, 12 to 14 minutes.

9. Remove the cookies from the oven, transfer them to a cooling rack, and let them cool for 20 to 30 minutes before enjoying.

INGREDIENTS:

9   OZ. DARK CHOCOLATE (55 TO 65 PERCENT), MELTED

4.5   OZ. UNSALTED BUTTER, SOFTENED

7   OZ. DARK BROWN SUGAR

¾   TEASPOON PURE VANILLA EXTRACT

2   EGGS

7   OZ. ALL-PURPOSE FLOUR

2.5   OZ. COCOA POWDER

2   TEASPOONS BAKING POWDER

1   TEASPOON KOSHER SALT

2   CUPS CONFECTIONERS' SUGAR, FOR COATING

FIORI DI MANDORLE

YIELD: 24 COOKIES / **ACTIVE TIME:** 20 MINUTES / **TOTAL TIME:** 1 HOUR

Also known as almond blossom cookies, these are quick, easy, and good with or without the candied cherries.

1. Preheat the oven to 350°F and line two baking sheets with parchment paper. Place the almond flour, confectioners' sugar, and lemon zest in a large mixing bowl and stir to combine. Add the eggs and milk and work the mixture with your hands until a soft, slightly sticky dough forms.

2. Dust your hands with confectioners' sugar and then roll tablespoons of the dough into balls. Place them on the baking sheets and dust them with additional confectioners' sugar. Make an indent with your thumb in each piece of dough and fill with a candied cherry.

3. Place in the oven and bake for about 18 minutes, until golden brown and dry to the touch. Remove from the oven and transfer to wire racks to cool completely.

INGREDIENTS:

10.2 OZ. FINE ALMOND FLOUR

8 OZ. CONFECTIONERS' SUGAR, PLUS MORE FOR DUSTING

ZEST OF 1 LEMON

2 LARGE EGGS, LIGHTLY BEATEN

1 TABLESPOON MILK

24 CANDIED CHERRIES

ORANGE SPICE COOKIES

YIELD: 24 COOKIES / **ACTIVE TIME:** 20 MINUTES / **TOTAL TIME:** 50 MINUTES

The combination of citrus and a collection of wintry spices makes these perfect for the holiday season.

1. Preheat the oven to 375°F and line two baking sheets with parchment paper. Place one-quarter of the sugar and 2 teaspoons of orange zest in a food processor and pulse until combined. Place the sugar mixture in a square baking dish and set aside. Place the flour, baking soda, spices, and salt in mixing bowl, whisk to combine, and set aside.

2. In the work bowl of a stand mixer fitted with the paddle attachment, beat the butter, remaining orange zest, brown sugar, and remaining sugar at medium speed until pale and fluffy, scraping down the sides of the bowl as needed. Add the egg yolk and vanilla, reduce speed to low, and beat to incorporate. Add the molasses and beat to incorporate. Add the dry mixture and beat until the dough just holds together.

3. Form tablespoons of the dough into balls, roll them in the orange sugar, and place them on the baking sheets. Working with one sheet of cookies at a time, place them in the oven and bake for about 10 minutes, until they are set at their edges but the centers are still soft. Remove from the oven and let cool on the baking sheets for 5 minutes before transferring them to wire racks to cool completely.

INGREDIENTS:

7	OZ. SUGAR
	ZEST OF 1 ORANGE
11.2	OZ. ALL-PURPOSE FLOUR
1	TEASPOON BAKING SODA
1½	TEASPOONS CINNAMON
1½	TEASPOONS GROUND GINGER
½	TEASPOON GROUND CLOVES
¼	TEASPOON ALLSPICE
¼	TEASPOON BLACK PEPPER
¼	TEASPOON FINE SEA SALT
6	OZ. UNSALTED BUTTER, SOFTENED
2.7	OZ. DARK BROWN SUGAR
1	LARGE EGG YOLK
1	TEASPOON PURE VANILLA EXTRACT
½	CUP MOLASSES

ORANGE SPRITZ

YIELD: 48 COOKIES / **ACTIVE TIME:** 15 MINUTES / **TOTAL TIME:** 45 MINUTES

If you're one of those who doesn't want the hint of citrus in their press cookies, feel free to go forward without the orange zest.

1. Preheat the oven to 350°F and line two baking sheets with parchment paper. Place the butter, sugars, and orange zest in a mixing bowl and beat at medium speed with a handheld mixer until pale and fluffy, scraping down the sides of the bowl as needed. Add the egg yolks and beat to combine. Sift the flour, salt, and baking soda into a separate mixing bowl. Gradually add the dry mixture to the butter mixture and work the mixture with your hands until a smooth dough forms.

2. Shape the dough into small logs, place them in cookie press, and press desired shapes onto the baking sheets.

3. Place in the oven and bake for 10 to 12 minutes, until the edges start to brown. Remove from the oven and transfer the cookies to wire racks to cool. Dust with confectioners' sugar before serving.

INGREDIENTS:

8   OZ. UNSALTED BUTTER, SOFTENED

7   OZ. SUGAR

1   TABLESPOON LIGHT BROWN SUGAR

ZEST OF 1 ORANGE

2   EGG YOLKS

11.2 OZ. ALL-PURPOSE FLOUR

¼   TEASPOON FINE SEA SALT

¼   TEASPOON BAKING SODA

CONFECTIONERS' SUGAR, FOR DUSTING

WHITE CHOCOLATE & CRANBERRY COOKIES

YIELD: 48 COOKIES / *ACTIVE TIME*: 15 MINUTES / *TOTAL TIME*: 3 HOURS

An improbably good cookie, with the dried cranberries adding an extra bit of chewiness that proves irresistible.

1. Place the flour, baking soda, and salt in a large mixing bowl and whisk to combine. Place the butter, brown sugar, and sugar in the work bowl of a stand mixer fitted with the paddle attachment and beat at medium speed until pale and fluffy, scraping down the sides of the bowl as needed. Reduce the speed to low and incorporate the eggs one at a time. Add the vanilla and beat to incorporate.

2. With the mixer running on low speed, gradually add the dry mixture to the wet mixture and beat until a smooth dough forms. Add the white chocolate chips and dried cranberries and fold until evenly distributed. Cover the dough with plastic wrap and refrigerate for 2 hours.

3. Preheat the oven to 350°F and line two large baking sheets with parchment paper. Drop tablespoons of the dough onto the baking sheets and, working with one baking sheet at a time, place the cookies in the oven and bake for about 10 minutes, until lightly browned. Remove from the oven and let cool on the baking sheets for 5 minutes before transferring to wire racks to cool completely.

INGREDIENTS:

13.2	OZ. ALL-PURPOSE FLOUR
1	TEASPOON BAKING SODA
1	TEASPOON FINE SEA SALT
8	OZ. UNSALTED BUTTER, SOFTENED
7	OZ. LIGHT BROWN SUGAR
3.5	OZ. SUGAR
2	LARGE EGGS, AT ROOM TEMPERATURE
2	TEASPOONS PURE VANILLA EXTRACT
1½	CUPS WHITE CHOCOLATE CHIPS
1	CUP SWEETENED DRIED CRANBERRIES

FLORENTINES

YIELD: 30 COOKIES / **ACTIVE TIME:** 10 MINUTES / **TOTAL TIME:** 45 MINUTES

Hazelnuts can easily be substituted for the almonds in these thin, crispy marvels.

1. Place the sugar, vanilla, and cream in a saucepan and bring to a boil. Remove from heat, add the butter, and let it melt. Stir in the almonds, candied citrus peels, dried cherries or plums, and the raisins.

2. Preheat the oven to 400°F and line two baking sheets with parchment paper. Place teaspoons of the mixture on the baking sheets, place the cookies in the oven, and bake for 5 to 10 minutes, until golden brown. Remove from the oven and let the cookies cool on the baking sheets for 5 minutes before transferring to wire racks to cool completely.

3. Fill a saucepan halfway with water and bring to a gentle simmer. Place the chocolate chips in a heatproof bowl, place it over the simmering water, and stir until melted. Spread the melted chocolate on the undersides of the florentines and leave to set before serving.

INGREDIENTS:

¾	CUP SUGAR
1	TEASPOON PURE VANILLA EXTRACT
7	TABLESPOONS HEAVY CREAM
1½	OZ. UNSALTED BUTTER
1½	CUPS SLIVERED ALMONDS
⅓	CUP CANDIED CITRUS PEELS
⅓	CUP DRIED CHERRIES OR PLUMS, CHOPPED
⅓	CUP RAISINS
1¼	CUPS DARK CHOCOLATE CHIPS

PFEFFERNÜSSE

YIELD: 24 COOKIES / **ACTIVE TIME:** 30 MINUTES / **TOTAL TIME:** 2 HOURS

If you find yourself falling under the spell of this bewitching, spicy cookie, look into some of the variants local to Germany, where it is a holiday tradition.

1. Place the flour, salt, pepper, and ground spices in a large mixing bowl and whisk to combine. Place the butter, brown sugar, and molasses in the work bowl of a stand mixer fitted with the paddle attachment and beat at medium speed until pale and fluffy, scraping down the sides of the bowl as needed. Add the egg and beat to incorporate. With the mixer running on low speed, gradually add the dry mixture to the wet mixture and beat until the mixture comes together as a dough. Cover the dough completely in plastic wrap and refrigerate for 1 hour.

2. Preheat the oven to 350°F and line two baking sheets with parchment paper. Form tablespoons of the dough into rounded rectangles and place them on the baking sheets. Place the cookies in the oven and bake for 12 to 14 minutes, until the cookies are firm. Remove from the oven and transfer to wire racks to cool briefly.

3. Place the confectioners' sugar in a bowl and toss the warm cookies in it until completely coated. Place the cookies back on the wire racks to cool completely.

INGREDIENTS:

- 11.2 OZ. ALL-PURPOSE FLOUR, SIFTED
- ½ TEASPOON FINE SEA SALT
- ½ TEASPOON BLACK PEPPER
- ½ TEASPOON CINNAMON
- ¼ TEASPOON BAKING SODA
- ¼ TEASPOON ALLSPICE
- ¼ TEASPOON FRESHLY GRATED NUTMEG
- PINCH OF GROUND CLOVES
- 4 OZ. UNSALTED BUTTER, SOFTENED
- 7 OZ. LIGHT BROWN SUGAR
- 3 TABLESPOONS MOLASSES, WARMED
- 1 LARGE EGG
- 2¼ CUPS CONFECTIONERS' SUGAR

KIPFERL BISCUITS

YIELD: 12 COOKIES / **ACTIVE TIME:** 40 MINUTES / **TOTAL TIME:** 2 HOURS

Aheavy dusting of confectioners' sugar is the traditional topping for these beautiful, crescent-shaped cookies. Some Caramelized White Chocolate (see page 85) would be another good option.

1. Place all of the ingredients, except for the white chocolate chips, in the work bowl of a stand mixer fitted with the paddle attachment and beat at medium speed until the mixture comes together as a soft dough. Flatten the dough into a disc, cover it completely with plastic wrap, and refrigerate for 1 hour.

2. Preheat the oven to 350°F and line two large baking sheets with parchment paper. Remove the dough from the fridge and let it stand at room temperature for 5 minutes. Roll the dough into a ¾-inch-thick log, cut them into 2-inch-long pieces, and roll them into cylinders with your hands, while tapering and curling the ends to create crescent shapes. Place them on the baking sheets.

3. Place in the oven and bake for about 15 minutes, until set and firm. Remove from the oven and transfer the cookies to wire racks to cool.

4. Fill a small saucepan halfway with water and bring it to a gentle simmer. Place the white chocolate chips in a heatproof bowl, place it over the simmering water, and stir until melted. Drizzle the melted white chocolate over the cooled biscuits and let it set before serving.

INGREDIENTS:

6.7 OZ. ALL-PURPOSE FLOUR, PLUS MORE FOR DUSTING

1½ OZ. UNSWEETENED COCOA POWDER

½ TEASPOON INSTANT ESPRESSO POWDER

¼ TEASPOON FINE SEA SALT

8 OZ. UNSALTED BUTTER, SOFTENED AND DIVIDED INTO TABLESPOONS

3 OZ. CONFECTIONERS' SUGAR, SIFTED

2.5 OZ. FINE ALMOND FLOUR

1 TEASPOON PURE VANILLA EXTRACT

½ CUP WHITE CHOCOLATE CHIPS

SNOWBALLS

YIELD: 36 COOKIES / **ACTIVE TIME:** 20 MINUTES / **TOTAL TIME:** 1 HOUR

The lime juice and coconut provide this wintry-looking treat a taste of the tropics.

1. Preheat the oven to 350°F and line two baking sheets with parchment paper. Place 1 tablespoon of the cream cheese and the lime juice in a mixing bowl and stir until the mixture is smooth. Add the confectioners' sugar and whisk until the mixture is smooth and thin, adding lime juice as needed until the glaze reaches the desired consistency. Set aside.

2. Place the flour, caster sugar, salt, and lime zest in a separate mixing bowl and whisk to combine. Add the butter one piece at a time and use a pastry blender to work the mixture until it is a coarse meal. Add the vanilla and remaining cream cheese and work the mixture until it is a smooth dough.

3. Form the mixture into balls and place them on the baking sheets. Place in the oven and bake until the cookies are a light brown, about 15 minutes. Remove from the oven and let cool to room temperature. Brush the glaze over the cookies and sprinkle the coconut on top. Let the glaze set before serving.

INGREDIENTS:

1.5 OZ. CREAM CHEESE, SOFTENED

ZEST AND JUICE OF 1 LIME

6 OZ. CONFECTIONERS' SUGAR

12.5 OZ. ALL-PURPOSE FLOUR

6 OZ. CASTER SUGAR

¼ TEASPOON FINE SEA SALT

8 OZ. UNSALTED BUTTER, SOFTENED AND DIVIDED INTO TABLESPOONS

2 TEASPOONS PURE VANILLA EXTRACT

1½ CUPS SWEETENED SHREDDED COCONUT, FINELY CHOPPED

BOURBON BALLS

YIELD: 24 COOKIES / **ACTIVE TIME:** 15 MINUTES / **TOTAL TIME:** 3 HOURS

The inherent sweetness of bourbon makes it a natural to use in desserts.

1. Combine the butter and half of the confectioners' sugar in a mixing bowl and beat at low speed with a handheld mixer to combine. Increase the speed to high and beat until light and fluffy. Add the remaining sugar, bourbon, and salt and beat for 2 minutes. Transfer the mixture to the refrigerator and chill until firm, about 2 hours.

2. Line baking sheets with parchment paper and form tablespoons of the butter-and-bourbon mixture into balls. Coat the balls in melted chocolate, cocoa powder, confectioners' sugar, and/or shredded coconut and then refrigerate for 45 minutes before serving.

INGREDIENTS:

8   OZ. UNSALTED BUTTER, SOFTENED

2   LBS. CONFECTIONERS' SUGAR

½   CUP BOURBON

½   TEASPOON FINE SEA SALT

MELTED CHOCOLATE, COCOA POWDER, CONFECTIONERS' SUGAR, OR SHREDDED COCONUT, FOR TOPPING

OATMEAL RAISIN COOKIES

YIELD: 16 COOKIES / **ACTIVE TIME:** 20 MINUTES / **TOTAL TIME:** 1 HOUR

A classic that has reached its vaunted status by being far more than just the sum of its parts.

1. Preheat the oven to 350°F.

2. Place the butter in a skillet and warm over medium-high heat until it is a dark golden brown and has a nutty aroma. Transfer to a mixing bowl and whisk in the cinnamon, brown sugar, sugar, and canola oil. When the mixture is combined, add the egg, egg yolk, and vanilla and whisk until incorporated.

3. Place the flour, baking soda, and salt in a separate mixing bowl and whisk to combine. Add this mixture to the wet mixture and stir until well combined. Add the oats and raisins and fold the mixture until they are evenly distributed throughout.

4. Form the dough into 16 balls and divide them between two parchment-lined baking sheets. Press down on the balls of dough to flatten them slightly. Place the sheets in the oven and bake the cookies until the edges start to brown, about 10 minutes. Remove from the oven and let cool on the sheets for 5 minutes. Transfer to a wire rack and let cool completely.

INGREDIENTS:

2	OZ. UNSALTED BUTTER
¼	TEASPOON CINNAMON
5.3	OZ. DARK BROWN SUGAR
3.5	OZ. SUGAR
½	CUP CANOLA OIL
1	LARGE EGG
1	LARGE EGG YOLK
1	TEASPOON PURE VANILLA EXTRACT
5	OZ. ALL-PURPOSE FLOUR
½	TEASPOON BAKING SODA
¾	TEASPOON FINE SEA SALT
3	CUPS ROLLED OATS
½	CUP RAISINS

ORANGE & ROSEMARY SHORTBREAD

YIELD: 24 COOKIES / **ACTIVE TIME:** 20 MINUTES / **TOTAL TIME:** 2 HOURS

Rosemary and shortbread were made for each other, and the bit of citrus cuts through just enough of the herb's woodiness.

1. Preheat the oven to 350°F and line two baking sheets with parchment paper.

2. Place all of the ingredients, except the flour and confectioners' sugar, in the work bowl of a stand mixer fitted with the paddle attachment and beat at low speed until the mixture is smooth and creamy.

3. Slowly add the flour and beat until a crumbly dough forms. Press the dough into a rectangle that is approximately ½ inch thick. Cover completely with plastic wrap and place the dough in the refrigerator for 1 hour.

4. Cut rounds out of the dough and place them on the baking sheets. Dust the cookies with confectioners' sugar, place in the oven, and bake until the edges start to brown, about 15 minutes. Remove and let cool before serving.

INGREDIENTS:

1   LB. UNSALTED BUTTER, SOFTENED

1.75 OZ. SUGAR

¼   CUP FRESH ORANGE JUICE

1   TABLESPOON ORANGE ZEST

2   TEASPOONS FINELY CHOPPED FRESH ROSEMARY

22.5 OZ. ALL-PURPOSE FLOUR

      CONFECTIONERS' SUGAR, FOR DUSTING

GINGERBREAD MADELEINES

YIELD: 16 MADELEINES / ACTIVE TIME: 25 MINUTES / TOTAL TIME: 3 HOURS

A holiday spin on the classic French cookie. These are wonderful alongside a cup of coffee or cocoa.

1. Place the butter in a small saucepan and cook over medium heat until lightly brown. Remove from heat and let cool to room temperature.

2. Place the butter and the brown sugar in the work bowl of a stand mixer fitted with the whisk attachment. Beat on high until light and frothy. Reduce the speed to low, add the eggs one at a time, and beat until incorporated. Add the ginger, vanilla, molasses, and milk and beat until incorporated.

3. Sift the flours and baking powder into a bowl. Add the salt, cloves, nutmeg, and cinnamon and stir to combine.

4. Gradually add the dry mixture to the wet mixture and beat until the dry mixture has been thoroughly incorporated. Refrigerate for 2 hours.

5. Preheat the oven to 375°F and brush each shell-shaped depression in the madeleine pan with butter. Place the pan in the freezer for at least 10 minutes.

6. Remove the pan from the freezer and the batter from the refrigerator. Fill each "shell" two-thirds of the way with batter, place the pan in the oven, and bake until a toothpick inserted into the center of a cookie comes out clean, about 12 minutes. Remove from the oven and place the cookies on a wire rack to cool slightly. Serve warm or at room temperature.

INGREDIENTS:

2.5	OZ. UNSALTED BUTTER, PLUS MORE FOR THE PAN
3.5	OZ. BROWN SUGAR
2	EGGS
	1-INCH PIECE OF FRESH GINGER, PEELED AND GRATED
1¼	TEASPOONS PURE VANILLA EXTRACT
1½	TABLESPOONS MOLASSES
⅓	CUP WHOLE MILK
2.5	OZ. ALL-PURPOSE FLOUR
2	OZ. CAKE FLOUR
¼	TEASPOON BAKING POWDER
1½	TEASPOONS FINE SEA SALT
¼	TEASPOON GROUND CLOVES
¼	TEASPOON FRESHLY GRATED NUTMEG
1	TEASPOON CINNAMON

CLASSIC GINGERBREAD COOKIES

YIELD: 24 COOKIES / **ACTIVE TIME:** 20 MINUTES / **ACTIVE TIME:** 2 HOURS

The very idea of these cookies will fill your kitchen with a pleasant warmth.

1. Place the butter and brown sugar in the work bowl of a stand mixer fitted with the paddle attachment and beat at low speed until combined. Increase the speed to high and beat until the mixture is light and fluffy. Add the molasses, egg, baking soda, ginger, apple pie spice, salt, vanilla, and pepper and beat for 1 minute. Slowly add the flour to the mixture and beat until it is a stiff dough.

2. Divide the dough in half and cover each half completely with plastic wrap. Flatten each piece into a disc and refrigerate for 1 hour. The dough will keep in the refrigerator for up to 2 days.

3. Preheat the oven to 350°F and line two baking sheets with parchment paper. Place the dough on a flour-dusted work surface and roll to a thickness of ¼ inch. Dip cookie cutters in flour and cut the dough into desired shapes. Transfer the cookies to the baking sheets and bake until firm, about 10 minutes.

4. Remove cookies from oven, let rest for 2 minutes, and then set on wire racks to cool completely. If desired, decorate with the Royal Icing and candies.

INGREDIENTS:

6   OZ. UNSALTED BUTTER,
       SOFTENED

3.5   OZ. LIGHT BROWN SUGAR

⅔   CUP MOLASSES

1   LARGE EGG, AT ROOM
       TEMPERATURE

1   TEASPOON BAKING SODA

1   TEASPOON GROUND
       GINGER

1   TEASPOON APPLE PIE
       SPICE

½   TEASPOON FINE SEA SALT

½   TEASPOON PURE VANILLA
       EXTRACT

¼   TEASPOON FRESHLY
       GROUND BLACK PEPPER

3   CUPS ALL-PURPOSE FLOUR,
       PLUS MORE FOR DUSTING

       ROYAL ICING (SEE PAGE 65)

       CANDIES, FOR
       DECORATION (OPTIONAL)

POLVORONES

YIELD: 36 COOKIES / **ACTIVE TIME:** 20 MINUTES / **TOTAL TIME:** 1 HOUR

Taking its name from the Spanish word polvo, meaning "powder," these confections are also popularly known as Mexican wedding cookies. But they originated in medieval Arabia, and were brought to Spain by the Moors when they took over Andalusia during the 8th century.

1. Preheat the oven to 350°F and line two baking sheets with parchment paper. Place the butter and 5 oz. of the confectioners' sugar in the work bowl of a stand mixer fitted with the paddle attachment and beat at medium speed until light and fluffy. Add the flours, almonds, and vanilla and beat until the dough is just combined and very stiff. Add a few drops of water, if necessary, to make it pliable.

2. Remove tablespoons of the dough and roll them into balls. Place the balls on the baking sheets and flatten them slightly with the bottom of a glass that has been dipped in flour. Place in oven and bake until lightly browned, about 10 minutes. Remove from oven.

3. Sift the remaining sugar into a shallow bowl and use a spatula to transfer the cookies to the bowl. Roll the cookies in the sugar until they are evenly coated and then transfer them to wire racks to cool completely.

INGREDIENTS:

8	OZ. UNSALTED BUTTER, SOFTENED
7	OZ. CONFECTIONERS' SUGAR
4	OZ. CAKE FLOUR, PLUS MORE FOR DUSTING
5	OZ. SELF-RISING FLOUR
1	CUP ALMONDS, BLANCHED AND MINCED
½	TEASPOON PURE VANILLA EXTRACT
	WARM WATER (110°F), AS NEEDED

CHRUSCIKI

YIELD: 20 COOKIES / **ACTIVE TIME:** 25 MINUTES / **TOTAL TIME:** 1 HOUR AND 30 MINUTES

These delicate cookies, which are also known as "angel wings," are a holiday tradition in Poland.

1. Place the eggs, milk, sugar, and butter in a mixing bowl and whisk until well combined. Whisk in the baking soda, vanilla, salt, and nutmeg, and then add the flour. Mix until a soft dough forms, cover the bowl tightly with plastic wrap, and refrigerate for 1 hour. The dough will keep in the refrigerator for up to 3 days.

2. Dust a work surface with flour and roll out the dough to ¼ inch thick. Cut into 1-inch-wide strips and then cut the strips on a diagonal every 3 inches to form diamond-shaped cookies.

3. Add vegetable oil to a Dutch oven until it is 1½ inches deep. Heat to 375°F and add the cookies a few at a time, using a slotted spoon to turn them as they brown. When cookies are browned all over, remove, set to drain on paper towels, and sprinkle with confectioners' sugar. Serve immediately.

INGREDIENTS:

3   LARGE EGGS, AT ROOM
     TEMPERATURE

¼   CUP WHOLE MILK

5.2 OZ. SUGAR

4   OZ. UNSALTED BUTTER

1   TEASPOON BAKING SODA

1   TEASPOON PURE VANILLA
     EXTRACT

½   TEASPOON FINE SEA SALT

½   TEASPOON FRESHLY
     GRATED NUTMEG

17.5 OZ. ALL-PURPOSE FLOUR,
     PLUS MORE FOR DUSTING

     CANOLA OIL, AS NEEDED

1   CUP CONFECTIONERS'
     SUGAR, FOR DUSTING

SALTED CARAMEL MACAROONS

YIELD: 16 MACAROONS / **ACTIVE TIME:** 20 MINUTES / **TOTAL TIME:** 2 HOURS

A bit of salt elevates the sweet, creamy taste of the coconut in these easy-to-make treats.

1. Place the butter, milk, caramels, and salt in a small saucepan and cook over medium heat. Once the caramels and butter have melted, add the coconut and stir until it is coated.

2. Line a baking sheet with parchment paper and scoop table-spoons of the caramel-and-coconut mixture onto the sheet. Let stand for 1 hour.

3. Fill a small saucepan halfway with water and bring it to a gentle simmer. Place the chocolate chips in a heatproof bowl, place it over the simmering water, and stir until melted.

4. Dip the bottom of each of the cooled macaroons into the melted chocolate and place them back on the baking sheet. Once all the macaroons have been dipped, drizzle the remaining chocolate over the top. Place in the refrigerator and chill until the chocolate has hardened, about 30 minutes.

INGREDIENTS:

3   OZ. UNSALTED BUTTER, MELTED

3   TABLESPOONS WHOLE MILK

¾   LB. SOFT CARAMELS

1   TEASPOON FINE SEA SALT

4   CUPS SWEETENED SHREDDED COCONUT

4   OZ. DARK CHOCOLATE CHIPS

SCOTTISH SHORTBREAD

YIELD: 24 COOKIES / **ACTIVE TIME:** 20 MINUTES / **TOTAL TIME:** 2 HOURS AND 30 MINUTES

The only shortbread recipe you'll ever need.

1. Preheat the oven to 325°F. Grate the butter into a bowl and place it in the freezer for 30 minutes.

2. Place the 3.5 oz. of sugar, flour, salt, and frozen butter in the work bowl of a stand mixer fitted with the paddle attachment and beat slowly until it is fine like sand. Be careful not to overwork the mixture.

3. Press the mixture into a square, 8-inch baking pan and bake for 1 hour and 15 minutes.

4. Remove from oven and sprinkle the remaining sugar over the top. Let cool and then cut the shortbread into bars or circles.

INGREDIENTS:

10   OZ. UNSALTED BUTTER

3.5   OZ. SUGAR, PLUS 2
        TABLESPOONS

12.5   OZ. ALL-PURPOSE FLOUR

1   TEASPOON FINE SEA SALT

MEYER LEMON CRINKLE COOKIES

YIELD: 24 COOKIES / **ACTIVE TIME:** 45 MINUTES / **TOTAL TIME:** 2 HOURS AND 30 MINUTES

The perfect cookie for the spring. The Meyer lemons bring a floral touch to an already light and sweet treat.

1. Line two baking sheets with parchment paper. In the work bowl of a stand mixer fitted with the paddle attachment, cream the butter, sugar, and lemon zest on medium speed until the mixture is very light and fluffy, about 5 minutes. Scrape down the work bowl and then beat the mixture for another 5 minutes.

2. Add the eggs one at a time and beat until incorporated, again scraping the work bowl as needed. When both eggs have been incorporated, scrape down the work bowl, add the lemon juice and food coloring, and beat for another minute. Add the flour, baking powder, baking soda, and salt and beat until the mixture comes together as a smooth dough.

3. Drop 2-oz. portions of the dough on the baking sheets, making sure to leave enough space between them. Place the baking sheets in the refrigerator and let the dough firm up for 1 hour.

4. Preheat the oven to 350°F. Place the confectioners' sugar in a mixing bowl, toss the dough balls in the sugar until completely coated, and then place them back on the baking sheet.

5. Place the cookies in the oven and bake until a cake tester comes out clean after being inserted, 12 to 14 minutes.

6. Remove the cookies from the oven, transfer them to a cooling rack, and let them cool for 20 to 30 minutes before enjoying.

INGREDIENTS:

8   OZ. UNSALTED BUTTER, SOFTENED

1   LB. SUGAR

     ZEST AND JUICE OF 2 MEYER LEMONS

2   EGGS

2-3 DROPS OF LEMON YELLOW GEL FOOD COLORING

15   OZ. ALL-PURPOSE FLOUR

½   TEASPOON BAKING POWDER

¼   TEASPOON BAKING SODA

½   TEASPOON FINE SEA SALT

2   CUPS CONFECTIONERS' SUGAR, FOR COATING

RASPBERRY BARS

YIELD: 12 TO 24 BARS / **ACTIVE TIME:** 15 MINUTES / **TOTAL TIME:** 1 HOUR

The best way to take advantage of raspberry season when it is at its peak.

1. Preheat the oven to 350°F and coat a rimmed 15 x 10–inch baking sheet with nonstick cooking spray. Roll out one of the balls of dough on a lightly floured work surface so that it fits the baking sheet. Place it in the pan, press down to ensure that it is even, and prick it with a fork. Roll out the other crust so that it is slightly larger than the sheet.

2. Place the raspberries, sugar, flour, lemon juice, and salt in a mixing bowl and stir until well combined. Spread this mixture evenly across the dough in the baking sheet.

3. Place the other dough over the filling and trim any excess. Brush the top with the egg and sprinkle additional sugar on top.

4. Place the bars in the oven and bake until golden brown, about 40 minutes. Remove from the oven and let cool before slicing.

INGREDIENTS:

2   BALLS OF PERFECT PIECRUST DOUGH (SEE PAGE 46)

3.2   OZ. ALL-PURPOSE FLOUR, PLUS MORE FOR DUSTING

7   CUPS FRESH RASPBERRIES

14   OZ. SUGAR, PLUS MORE AS NEEDED

2   TABLESPOONS FRESH LEMON JUICE

PINCH OF FINE SEA SALT

1   EGG, BEATEN

MOCHA BALLS

Those who find it difficult to decide between chocolate and coffee get their moment in the sun.

1. Preheat the oven to 350°F.

2. Place the espresso powder and the water in a small bowl and stir until the powder has dissolved. Set aside and let cool.

3. Place the butter and sugar in the work bowl of a stand mixer fitted with the paddle attachment and beat at medium speed until light and fluffy. Add the egg and vanilla, beat until well combined, and then add ¼ cup of the cocoa powder and the espresso mixture. Beat until combined, scraping down the bowl as necessary. Reduce the speed to low, add the flour and salt, and beat until the mixture comes together as a dough.

4. Form tablespoons of the dough into balls and place them on parchment-lined baking sheets. Place in the oven and bake until firm, about 15 minutes.

5. Sift the remaining cocoa powder into a shallow bowl and use a spatula to transfer a few cookies at a time into the bowl. Roll the cookies around until well coated and then transfer them to wire racks to cool completely.

INGREDIENTS:

2	TABLESPOONS ESPRESSO POWDER
2	TABLESPOONS BOILING WATER
4	OZ. UNSALTED BUTTER, SOFTENED AND CUT INTO SMALL PIECES
2.3	OZ. SUGAR
1	LARGE EGG, AT ROOM TEMPERATURE
½	TEASPOON PURE VANILLA EXTRACT
3.75	OZ. UNSWEETENED COCOA POWDER
6.7	OZ. ALL-PURPOSE FLOUR
	PINCH OF FINE SEA SALT

CHEWY PEANUT BUTTER & OAT BARS

YIELD: 12 BARS / **ACTIVE TIME:** 15 MINUTES / **TOTAL TIME:** 45 MINUTES

Use crunchy peanut butter if you find yourself looking for a little bit more texture in these bars.

1. Place the milk, sugar, and salt in a small saucepan and whisk to combine. Cook over medium heat until mixture comes to a boil and thickens, approximately 10 minutes. Remove the pan from heat.

2. Fill a small saucepan halfway with water and bring it to a gentle simmer. Place the chocolate in a heatproof bowl, place it over the simmering water, and stir until melted.

3. Add the vanilla, one-quarter of the melted chocolate, and the peanut butter to the pan and mix until well combined. Fold in the oats and stir until they are completely coated.

4. Line a square, 8-inch cake pan with parchment paper and pour the contents of the saucepan into it. Press into an even layer, spread the remaining melted chocolate over the top, and let sit for 30 minutes. Cut into small bars and serve immediately, or store in the refrigerator until ready to serve.

INGREDIENTS:

¾ CUP WHOLE MILK

7 OZ. SUGAR

¼ TEASPOON FINE SEA SALT

4 OZ. DARK CHOCOLATE, CHOPPED

1 TEASPOON PURE VANILLA EXTRACT

½ CUP CREAMY PEANUT BUTTER

1 CUP ROLLED OATS

BAKLAVA

YIELD: 48 PIECES / **ACTIVE TIME:** 30 MINUTES / **TOTAL TIME:** 1 HOUR

As with pizza, fried chicken, and ice cream, there is no such thing as bad baklava.

1. Place the walnuts, ½ cup of the sugar, cinnamon, and cloves in a food processor. Pulse until very fine and set aside.

2. Preheat the oven temperature to 375°F and coat a 18 x 13–inch baking sheet with nonstick cooking spray. Place the phyllo sheets on a plate and cover with plastic wrap or a damp paper towel to keep them from drying out. Place 1 sheet of phyllo on the baking sheet and brush with some of the melted butter. Repeat with 7 more sheets and spread one-third of the walnut mixture on top. Place 4 more sheets of phyllo dough on top, brushing each with butter. Spread half of the remaining walnut mixture on top, and then repeat. Top the last of the walnut mixture with the remaining sheets of phyllo dough, brushing each one with butter. Trim the edges to make a neat rectangle.

3. Cut pastry into squares or triangles, taking care not to cut through the bottom crust. Place in the oven and bake for 25 to 30 minutes, until the top layer of phyllo is brown.

4. While the pastry is cooking, combine the remaining sugar, water, honey, lemon, and cinnamon stick in a saucepan. Bring to a boil over medium heat while stirring occasionally. Reduce heat to low and simmer for 5 minutes. Strain syrup and keep it hot while the pastry finishes baking.

5. Remove the baklava from the oven and pour the hot syrup over the pastry. Place the pan on a wire rack, allow to cool to room temperature, and then cut through the bottom crust. If desired, garnish with pistachios before serving.

INGREDIENTS:

3½	CUPS WALNUTS, TOASTED
17.5	OZ. SUGAR
1	TEASPOON CINNAMON
¼	TEASPOON GROUND CLOVES
1	LB. FROZEN PHYLLO SHEETS, THAWED
12	OZ. UNSALTED BUTTER, MELTED
1½	CUPS WATER
½	CUP HONEY
½	LEMON, SLICED THIN
1	CINNAMON STICK
	PISTACHIOS, CHOPPED, FOR GARNISH (OPTIONAL)

PEANUT BUTTER & JAM THUMBPRINTS

YIELD: 24 COOKIES / **ACTIVE TIME:** 20 MINUTES / **TOTAL TIME:** 1 HOUR

Anytime this combination shows up, you know you've got a winner on your hands.

1. Preheat the oven to 375°F and line two baking sheets with parchment paper. Combine the brown sugar, butter, and peanut butter in the work bowl of a stand mixer fitted with the paddle attachment and beat at low speed until combined. Increase the speed to high and beat until the mixture is light and fluffy.

2. Add the egg, vanilla, baking soda, and salt and beat for 1 minute. Slowly add the flour and beat until the mixture comes together as a soft dough.

3. Remove tablespoons of the dough and roll them into balls. Place the balls on the baking sheets, 1½ inches apart. Use your index finger to make a depression in the center of each ball. Place the cookies into the oven and bake for 10 to 12 minutes, until the edges are brown. Remove, let cool for 2 minutes, and then transfer to wire racks to cool completely.

4. While the cookies are cooling, place the raspberry jam in a saucepan and cook over medium heat. Bring to a boil, while stirring frequently, and cook until the jam has been reduced by one-quarter. Spoon a teaspoon of the jam into each cookie and allow it to set.

INGREDIENTS:

5.3   OZ. LIGHT BROWN SUGAR

4   OZ. UNSALTED BUTTER, SOFTENED

1   CUP CREAMY PEANUT BUTTER

1   LARGE EGG, AT ROOM TEMPERATURE

½   TEASPOON PURE VANILLA EXTRACT

1   TEASPOON BAKING SODA

⅛   TEASPOON FINE SEA SALT

1   CUP ALL-PURPOSE FLOUR

1½   CUPS SEEDLESS RASPBERRY JAM

MARBLE BROWNIES

YIELD: 16 BROWNIES / **ACTIVE TIME:** 15 MINUTES / **TOTAL TIME:** 1 HOUR AND 15 MINUTES

Cream cheese lifts the already decadent brownie to a whole new realm of richness.

1. Preheat the oven to 350°F. Coat a square, 8-inch cake pan with nonstick cooking spray and dust it with flour, knocking out any excess.

2. Fill a small saucepan halfway with water and bring it to a gentle simmer. Place the butter and chocolate chips in a heatproof bowl, place it over the simmering water, and stir until the mixture is melted and smooth. Remove the mixture from heat and let it cool for 5 minutes.

3. Place 2 of the eggs and three-quarters of the sugar in in the work bowl of a stand mixer fitted with the paddle attachment and beat on medium speed for 1 minute. Add the chocolate-and-butter mixture, beat for 1 minute, and then add the flour and salt. Beat until just combined and then pour into the prepared pan.

4. In a separate bowl, combine the cream cheese, remaining sugar, remaining egg, and vanilla. Beat with a handheld mixer on medium speed until light and fluffy. Spread on top of the batter and use a fork to stir the layers together. Place in the oven and bake for 35 minutes, until the top is springy to the touch. Remove, allow the brownies to cool in the pan, and then cut into bars.

INGREDIENTS:

- 2.5 OZ. ALL-PURPOSE FLOUR, PLUS MORE FOR DUSTING
- 4 OZ. UNSALTED BUTTER
- 4 OZ. MILK CHOCOLATE CHIPS
- 3 LARGE EGGS, AT ROOM TEMPERATURE
- 7 OZ. SUGAR

  PINCH OF FINE SEA SALT
- 8 OZ. CREAM CHEESE, SOFTENED
- ½ TEASPOON PURE VANILLA EXTRACT

LEMON & ALMOND BISCOTTI

YIELD: 24 BISCOTTI / **ACTIVE TIME:** 1 HOUR / **TOTAL TIME:** 4 HOURS AND 30 MINUTES

A light biscotti that is as beautiful as it is delicious. Unless you have considerable willpower, make sure you only whip these up when company is coming over.

1. Line a baking sheet with parchment paper. In the work bowl of a stand mixer fitted with the paddle attachment, cream the butter, lemon zest, sugar, and vanilla extract on medium until the mixture is very light and fluffy, about 5 minutes. Scrape down the work bowl and then beat the mixture for another 5 minutes.

2. Add the eggs one at a time and beat on low until incorporated, again scraping the work bowl as needed. When both eggs have been incorporated, scrape down the work bowl and beat on medium for 1 minute.

3. Add the remaining ingredients, reduce the speed to low, and beat until the mixture comes together as a dough.

4. Place the dough on the baking sheet and form it into a log that is the length of the pan and anywhere from 3 to 4 inches wide. Refrigerate the dough for 1 hour.

5. Preheat the oven to 350°F.

6. Place the dough in the oven and bake until golden brown and a cake tester comes out clean when inserted into the center, 25 to 30 minutes. Remove the biscotti from the oven, transfer it to a cooling rack, and let it cool completely before refrigerating for 2 hours.

7. Preheat the oven to 250°F. Cut the biscotti to the desired size, place them on their sides, and bake for 10 minutes. Remove from the oven, turn them over, and bake for another 6 minutes. Remove from the oven and let them cool completely before enjoying.

INGREDIENTS:

- 8   OZ. UNSALTED BUTTER, SOFTENED
-      ZEST OF 1 LEMON
- 7   OZ. SUGAR
- ¾   TEASPOON PURE VANILLA EXTRACT
- 2   EGGS
- 10   OZ. ALL-PURPOSE FLOUR
- ½   TEASPOON BAKING SODA
- ½   TEASPOON BAKING POWDER
- ½   TEASPOON FINE SEA SALT
- 8   OZ. SLIVERED ALMOND, TOASTED

RED VELVET CRINKLE COOKIES

YIELD: 24 COOKIES / **ACTIVE TIME:** 45 MINUTES / **TOTAL TIME:** 2 HOURS AND 30 MINUTES

This crinkle cookie goes out to all those red velvet cake lovers out there.

1. Line two baking sheets with parchment paper. In a mixing bowl, whisk together the flour, cocoa powder, baking soda, baking powder, and salt and set aside.

2. In the work bowl of a stand mixer fitted with the paddle attachment, cream the butter, sugar, and dark brown sugar on medium speed until the mixture is very light and fluffy, about 5 minutes. Scrape down the work bowl and then beat the mixture for another 5 minutes.

3. Add the eggs one at a time and beat until incorporated, again scraping the work bowl as needed. When both eggs have been incorporated, scrape down the work bowl, add the vanilla and food coloring, and beat for another minute. Add the dry mixture and beat until the mixture comes together as a smooth dough.

4. Drop 2-oz. portions of the dough on the baking sheets, making sure to leave enough space between them. Place the baking sheets in the refrigerator and let the dough firm up for 1 hour.

5. Preheat the oven to 350°F. Place the confectioners' sugar in a mixing bowl, toss the dough balls in the sugar until completely coated, and then place them back on the baking sheet.

6. Place the cookies in the oven and bake until a cake tester comes out clean after being inserted, 12 to 14 minutes.

7. Remove the cookies from the oven, transfer them to a cooling rack, and let them cool for 20 to 30 minutes before enjoying.

INGREDIENTS:

9	OZ. ALL-PURPOSE FLOUR
2	TABLESPOONS COCOA POWDER
1½	TEASPOONS BAKING POWDER
½	TEASPOON KOSHER SALT
4	OZ. UNSALTED BUTTER, SOFTENED
4	OZ. SUGAR
5	OZ. LIGHT BROWN SUGAR
2	EGGS
2	TEASPOONS PURE VANILLA EXTRACT
2-3	RED GEL FOOD COLORING, PLUS MORE AS NEEDED
2	CUPS CONFECTIONERS' SUGAR, FOR COATING

DARK CHOCOLATE & STOUT BROWNIES

YIELD: 16 BROWNIES / **ACTIVE TIME:** 15 MINUTES / **TOTAL TIME:** 1 HOUR AND 15 MINUTES

With its notes of coffee and chocolate, Guinness is a reliably great option here. But as more and more microbreweries are pushing the parameters of stout, it may be worth experimenting with a few of those available in your area.

1. Preheat your oven to 350°F and coat a square, 8-inch cake pan with nonstick cooking spray. Place the stout in a medium saucepan and bring to a boil. Cook until it has reduced by half. Remove pan from the heat and let cool.

2. Fill a small saucepan halfway with water and bring it to a gentle simmer. Place the butter and chocolate chips in a heatproof bowl, place it over the simmering water, and stir until the mixture is melted and smooth. Remove the mixture from heat and let it cool for 5 minutes.

3. Place the sugar, eggs, and vanilla in a large bowl and stir until combined. Slowly whisk in the chocolate-and-butter mixture and then whisk in the stout.

4. Fold in the flour and salt. Pour the batter into a greased pan, and bake for 35 to 40 minutes, until the surface begins to crack and a cake tester inserted in the center comes out with a few moist crumbs attached. Remove the pan from the oven, place on a wire rack, and let cool for at least 20 minutes. When cool, sprinkle the cocoa powder over the top and cut the brownies into squares.

INGREDIENTS:

12 OZ. GUINNESS OR OTHER STOUT

12 OZ. DARK CHOCOLATE CHIPS

8 OZ. UNSALTED BUTTER

10.5 OZ. SUGAR

3 LARGE EGGS

1 TEASPOON PURE VANILLA EXTRACT

3.75 OZ. ALL-PURPOSE FLOUR

1¼ TEASPOONS FINE SEA SALT

COCOA POWDER, FOR DUSTING

ORANGE & PISTACHIO BISCOTTI

YIELD: 24 BISCOTTI / **ACTIVE TIME:** 1 HOUR / **TOTAL TIME:** 4 HOURS AND 30 MINUTES

Feel free to swap in your favorite fruits and nuts for the pistachios and cranberries here.

1. Line a baking sheet with parchment paper. In the work bowl of a stand mixer fitted with the paddle attachment, cream the butter, orange zest, sugar, and vanilla extract on medium until the mixture is very light and fluffy, about 5 minutes. Scrape down the work bowl and then beat the mixture for another 5 minutes.

2. Add the eggs one at a time and beat on low until incorporated, again scraping the work bowl as needed. When both eggs have been incorporated, scrape down the work bowl and beat on medium for 1 minute.

3. Add the remaining ingredients, reduce the speed to low, and beat until the mixture comes together as a dough.

4. Place the dough on the baking sheet and form it into a log that is the length of the pan and anywhere from 3 to 4 inches wide. Place the dough in the refrigerator for 1 hour.

5. Preheat the oven to 350°F.

6. Place the biscotti dough in the oven and bake until golden brown and a cake tester comes out clean when inserted into the center, 25 to 30 minutes. Remove the biscotti from the oven, transfer it to a cooling rack, and let it cool completely before refrigerating for 2 hours.

7. Preheat the oven to 250°F. Cut the biscotti to the desired size, place them on their sides, and bake for 10 minutes. Remove from the oven, turn them over, and bake for another 6 minutes. Remove from the oven and let them cool completely before enjoying.

INGREDIENTS:

4	OZ. UNSALTED BUTTER, SOFTENED
	ZEST OF 1 ORANGE
7	OZ. SUGAR
¾	TEASPOON PURE VANILLA EXTRACT
2	EGGS
10	OZ. ALL-PURPOSE FLOUR
½	TEASPOON BAKING SODA
½	TEASPOON BAKING POWDER
½	TEASPOON FINE SEA SALT
4	OZ. SHELLED PISTACHIOS, TOASTED
1	CUP DRIED CRANBERRIES

PEANUT BUTTER & CHOCOLATE CHIP COOKIES

YIELD: 24 COOKIES / **ACTIVE TIME:** 30 MINUTES / **TOTAL TIME:** 2 HOURS

As we know, no combo can compete with peanut butter and chocolate. These cookies are as buttery as they are sweet, and certain to satisfy.

1. Line two baking sheets with parchment paper. In the work bowl of a stand mixer fitted with the paddle attachment, cream the butter, peanut butter, sugar, dark brown sugar, salt, and baking soda on medium speed until the mixture is very light and fluffy, about 5 minutes. Scrape down the work bowl and then beat the mixture for another 5 minutes.

2. Add the eggs one at a time and beat until incorporated, again scraping the work bowl as needed. When both eggs have been incorporated, scrape down the work bowl, add the vanilla, and beat for another minute. Add the flour and chocolate chips and beat until the mixture comes together as a dough.

3. Drop 2-oz. portions of the dough on the baking sheets, making sure to leave enough space between them. Place the baking sheets in the refrigerator and let the dough firm up for 1 hour.

4. Preheat the oven to 350°F.

5. Place the cookies in the oven and bake until they are lightly golden brown around their edges, 10 to 12 minutes. Do not let the cookies become fully brown or they will end up being too crispy.

6. Remove the cookies from the oven, transfer them to a cooling rack, and let them cool for 20 to 30 minutes before enjoying.

INGREDIENTS:

4   OZ. UNSALTED BUTTER, SOFTENED

4   OZ. SMOOTH PEANUT BUTTER

8   OZ. SUGAR

8   OZ. DARK BROWN SUGAR

1½ TEASPOONS KOSHER SALT

1   TEASPOON BAKING SODA

2   EGGS

1½ TEASPOONS PURE VANILLA EXTRACT

14.5 OZ. ALL-PURPOSE FLOUR

14 OZ. SEMISWEET CHOCOLATE CHIPS

OREO COOKIES

YIELD: 20 COOKIES / **ACTIVE TIME:** 30 MINUTES / **TOTAL TIME:** 2 HOURS AND 15 MINUTES

Finally, a way to make everyone's favorite sandwich cookie at home.

1. Line two baking sheets with parchment paper. In the work bowl of a stand mixer fitted with the paddle attachment, cream the butter and sugar on medium until the mixture is light and fluffy, about 5 minutes. Scrape down the work bowl with a rubber spatula and beat the mixture for another 5 minutes.

2. Reduce the speed to low, add the eggs one at a time, and beat until incorporated, again scraping the work bowl as needed. When both eggs have been incorporated, scrape down the work bowl, add the vanilla, and beat for another minute.

3. Add the flour, cocoa powder, baking soda, baking powder, and salt and beat on low until the dough comes together.

4. Drop 1-oz. portions of the dough on the baking sheets, making sure to leave enough space between them. Place the baking sheets in the refrigerator and let the dough firm up for 1 hour.

5. Preheat the oven to 350°F.

6. Place the cookies in the oven and bake until they are starting to firm up, about 8 minutes.

7. Remove the cookies from the oven, transfer them to a cooling rack, and let them cool for 20 to 30 minutes

8. Place the filling in a piping bag and pipe about 1 tablespoon of filling on half of the cookies. Use the other halves to assemble the sandwich.

INGREDIENTS:

8	OZ. UNSALTED BUTTER, SOFTENED
1	LB. SUGAR
2	EGGS
¾	TEASPOON PURE VANILLA EXTRACT
9.5	OZ. ALL-PURPOSE FLOUR
4.5	OZ. COCOA POWDER
1½	TEASPOONS BAKING SODA
½	TEASPOON BAKING POWDER
¾	TEASPOON KOSHER SALT
1	CUP BUTTERFLUFF FILLING (SEE PAGE 86)

FLOURLESS FUDGE BROWNIES

YIELD: 12 BROWNIES / **ACTIVE TIME:** 30 MINUTES / **TOTAL TIME:** 2 HOURS AND 45 MINUTES

Flourless fudge brownies are the ultimate gluten-free guilty pleasure.

1. Preheat the oven to 350°F. Line a 9 x 13–inch baking pan with parchment paper and coat it with nonstick cooking spray.

2. Fill a small saucepan halfway with water and bring it to a simmer. Place the dark chocolate and butter in a heatproof bowl, place it over the simmering water, and stir until they have melted and been combined. Remove from heat and set aside.

3. In a separate mixing bowl, whisk the sugar, brown sugar, cocoa powder, and salt, making sure to break up any clumps. Whisk in the eggs, vanilla, and melted chocolate mixture. Pour the batter into the baking pan and use a rubber spatula to even out the top. Lightly tap the baking pan on the counter to remove any air bubbles.

4. Place the brownies in the oven and bake until a cake tester comes out clean, 30 to 40 minutes.

5. Remove from the oven, transfer the brownies to a cooling rack, and let them cool completely. Once they are cool, refrigerate for 1 hour.

6. Run a paring knife along the sides of the pan and cut the brownies into squares.

INGREDIENTS:

1	LB. DARK CHOCOLATE (55 TO 65 PERCENT)
8	OZ. UNSALTED BUTTER
12	OZ. SUGAR
4	OZ. LIGHT BROWN SUGAR
¼	CUP COCOA POWDER
¾	TEASPOON KOSHER SALT
6	EGGS
1½	TEASPOONS PURE VANILLA EXTRACT

PRALINE BARS

YIELD: 12 BARS / **ACTIVE TIME:** 30 MINUTES / **TOTAL TIME:** 1 HOUR

A wonderful translation of the beloved Southern confection.

1. Preheat the oven to 350°F. Line a 9 x 13–inch baking pan with parchment paper and coat it with nonstick cooking spray. .

2. To begin preparations for the crust, melt in the butter in a small saucepan over medium-low heat and set aside.

3. In a mixing bowl, combine the graham cracker crumbs, sugar, and flour. Add the melted butter and fold to incorporate. Place the mixture in the baking pan and press down on it so that it is flat and even. Set aside.

4. To prepare the filling, whisk the dark brown sugar and eggs in a mixing bowl until there are no clumps left, about 2 minutes. Add the graham cracker crumbs, salt, baking powder, and vanilla and whisk until thoroughly incorporated. Pour the filling over the crust and evenly distribute the pecans on top, pressing down so they adhere.

5. Place in the oven and bake until the top is golden brown, 25 to 30 minutes. Remove from the oven, transfer to a cooling rack, and let them cool. When cool, cut them into bars.

INGREDIENTS:

FOR THE CRUST

9	OZ. UNSALTED BUTTER
4	CUPS GRAHAM CRACKER CRUMBS
3	TABLESPOONS SUGAR
¼	CUP ALL-PURPOSE FLOUR, PLUS 1 TABLESPOON

FOR THE FILLING

4½	CUPS DARK BROWN SUGAR
6	EGGS
1	CUP GRAHAM CRACKER CRUMBS
1½	TEASPOONS KOSHER SALT
¾	TEASPOON BAKING POWDER
1	TABLESPOON PURE VANILLA EXTRACT
1½	CUPS PECANS, CHOPPED

RICE KRISPIES TREATS

YIELD: 12 BARS / **ACTIVE TIME:** 30 MINUTES / **TOTAL TIME:** 1 HOUR AND 30 MINUTES

Some sweets connoisseurs may view these as a retro dessert, but their appeal is eternal.

1. Line a 9 x 13–baking pan with parchment paper and coat with nonstick cooking spray.

2. Fill a small saucepan halfway with water and bring it to a simmer. Place the marshmallow creme, butter, and salt in a heatproof mixing bowl over the simmering water and stir the mixture with a rubber spatula until the butter has melted and the mixture is thoroughly combined. Remove the bowl from heat, add the cereal and vanilla, and fold until combined. If desired, add the chocolate chips or M&M's and fold until evenly distributed.

3. Transfer the mixture to the baking pan and spread it with a rubber spatula. Place another piece of parchment over the mixture and pack it down with your hands until it is flat and even. Remove the top piece of parchment and refrigerate for 1 hour.

4. Run a knife along the edge of the pan, turn the mixture out onto a cutting board, and into squares.

INGREDIENTS:

12	OZ. MARSHMALLOW CREME
4.5	OZ. UNSALTED BUTTER
¾	TEASPOON FINE SEA SALT
9	CUPS CRISPY RICE CEREAL
¾	TEASPOON PURE VANILLA EXTRACT
2½	CUPS CHOCOLATE CHIPS OR M&M'S (OPTIONAL)

WHITE CHOCOLATE CHIP &
MACADAMIA COOKIES

YIELD: 24 COOKIES / **ACTIVE TIME:** 20 MINUTES / **TOTAL TIME:** 2 HOURS

As far as nuts go, macadamia are the most buttery, making them an ideal pairing with creamy white chocolate.

1. Line two baking sheets with parchment paper. In the work bowl of a stand mixer fitted with the paddle attachment, cream the butter, sugar, dark brown sugar, salt, and baking soda on medium speed until the mixture is very light and fluffy, about 5 minutes. Scrape down the work bowl and then beat the mixture for another 5 minutes.

2. Reduce the speed to low, add the eggs one at a time and beat until incorporated, again scraping the work bowl as needed. When both eggs have been incorporated, scrape down the work bowl, add the vanilla, raise the speed to medium, and beat for 1 minute.

3. Add the flour, macadamia nuts, and white chocolate chips, reduce the speed to low, and beat until the dough comes together.

4. Drop 2-oz. portions of the dough on the baking sheets, making sure to leave enough space between them. Place the baking sheets in the refrigerator and let the dough firm up for 1 hour.

5. Preheat the oven to 350°F.

6. Place the cookies in the oven and bake until lightly golden brown around their edges, 10 to 12 minutes. Remove the cookies from the oven, transfer them to a cooling rack, and let them cool for 20 to 30 minutes before enjoying.

INGREDIENTS:

8	OZ. BUTTER, SOFTENED
8	OZ. SUGAR
8	OZ. DARK BROWN SUGAR
1½	TEASPOONS KOSHER SALT
1	TEASPOON BAKING SODA
2	EGGS
1½	TEASPOON PURE VANILLA EXTRACT
14.5	OZ. ALL-PURPOSE FLOUR
7	OZ. MACADAMIA NUTS, TOASTED
7	OZ. WHITE CHOCOLATE CHIPS

CHEWY GINGER COOKIES

YIELD: 24 COOKIES / **ACTIVE TIME:** 30 MINUTES / **TOTAL TIME:** 2 HOURS

These rich and chewy cookies are a great, grown-up spin on the gingerbread men we know and love.

1. Line two baking sheets with parchment paper. In the work bowl of a stand mixer fitted with the paddle attachment, cream the butter and sugar on medium speed until the mixture is very light and fluffy, about 5 minutes. Scrape down the work bowl and then beat the mixture for another 5 minutes.

2. Reduce the speed to low, add the molasses, and beat to incorporate. Add the eggs one at a time and beat until incorporated, again scraping the work bowl as needed. When both eggs have been incorporated, scrape down the work bowl, add the vinegar, raise the speed to medium, and beat for 1 minute.

3. Add the flour, baking soda, ginger, cinnamon, nutmeg, and salt, reduce the speed to low, and beat until the dough comes together.

4. Drop 2-oz. portions of the dough on the baking sheets, making sure to leave enough space between them. Place the baking sheets in the refrigerator and let the dough firm up for 1 hour.

5. Preheat the oven to 350°F.

6. Place the cookies in the oven and bake until lightly golden brown around their edges, 10 to 12 minutes. Do not allow the cookies to fully brown or they will come out too crispy.

7. Remove the cookies from the oven, transfer them to a cooling rack, and let them cool for 20 to 30 minutes before enjoying.

INGREDIENTS:

- 6.5   OZ. UNSALTED BUTTER, SOFTENED
- 18   OZ. SUGAR
- 6.5   OZ. MOLASSES
- 2   EGGS
- 1½   TABLESPOONS WHITE VINEGAR
- 23   OZ. ALL-PURPOSE FLOUR
- 2   TEASPOONS BAKING SODA
- 2   TEASPOONS GROUND GINGER
- 1   TEASPOON CINNAMON
- ½   TEASPOON FRESHLY GRATED NUTMEG
- ½   TEASPOON KOSHER SALT

ALFAJORES

YIELD: 36 COOKIES / **ACTIVE TIME:** 1 HOUR / **TOTAL TIME:** 3 HOURS

These melt-in-your-mouth cookies are traditional to Spain. If you're a fan of dulce de leche and you get a moment, take a look at some of the delicious iterations that have sprung up around the globe.

1. In the work bowl of a stand mixer fitted with the paddle attachment, cream the butter, sugar, salt, vanilla, and lemon zest on medium speed until the mixture is very light and fluffy, about 5 minutes. Scrape down the work bowl and then beat the mixture for another 5 minutes.

2. Reduce the speed to low, add the egg yolks, and beat until incorporated. Scrape down the work bowl and beat the mixture for 1 minute on medium.

3. Add the cornstarch, flour, and baking soda, reduce the speed to low, and beat until the dough comes together. Form the dough into a ball and then flatten it into a disc. Cover the dough completely with plastic wrap and refrigerate for 2 hours.

4. Preheat the oven to 350°F and line two baking sheets with parchment paper.

5. Remove the dough from the refrigerator and let it sit on the counter for 5 minutes.

6. Place the dough on a flour-dusted work surface and roll it out until it is approximately ¼ inch thick. Use a 2-inch ring cutter to cut cookies out of the dough and place them on the baking sheets. Form any scraps into a ball, roll it out, and cut into cookies. If the dough becomes too sticky or warm, place it back in the refrigerator for 15 minutes to firm up.

7. Place the cookies in the oven and bake until lightly golden brown at their edges, about 8 minutes. Remove from the oven, transfer to a wire rack, and let cool for 10 minutes.

8. Place about a teaspoon of dulce de leche on half of the cookies and use the other cookies to assemble the sandwiches. Dust with confectioners' sugar.

INGREDIENTS:

- 8.9 OZ. UNSALTED BUTTER, SOFTENED
- 5.4 OZ. SUGAR
- ½ TEASPOON KOSHER SALT
- 1 TABLESPOON PURE VANILLA EXTRACT
- ZEST OF 1 LEMON
- 4 EGG YOLKS
- 10.7 OZ. CORNSTARCH
- 7.1 OZ. ALL-PURPOSE FLOUR, PLUS MORE AS NEEDED
- 1 TEASPOON BAKING SODA
- 12 OZ. DULCE DE LECHE
- 1 CUP CONFECTIONERS' SUGAR, FOR DUSTING

VANILLA TUILE

YIELD: 24 COOKIES / **ACTIVE TIME:** 45 MINUTES / **TOTAL TIME:** 3 HOURS

These thin, delicate cookies can be molded into tubes, cups, and small bowls while still warm, and filled with whipped cream, berries, puddings, or a custard.

1. Sift the flour into a small bowl and set aside.

2. In a medium bowl, whisk the egg whites, confectioners' sugar, and vanilla and set aside.

3. In a small saucepan, melt the butter over low heat. Stir it into the egg white mixture, add the sifted flour, and whisk until the mixture is a smooth batter. Cover the bowl with plastic wrap and refrigerate for 2 hours.

4. Preheat the oven to 400°F.

5. Line a 13 x 18–inch baking sheet with a silicone baking mat. Place 2-teaspoon portions of the batter about 5 inches apart from one another. Use a small, offset spatula to spread the batter into 4-inch circles. Tap the pan lightly on the counter to remove any air bubbles and level the circles.

6. Place the tuiles in the oven and bake until the edges begin to color, 4 to 5 minutes. Remove from the oven. Working quickly, carefully remove the tuiles with the offset spatula and transfer them immediately to a cooling rack.

7. Repeat until all of the batter has been used.

INGREDIENTS:

- 3.5 OZ. ALL-PURPOSE FLOUR
- 5 EGG WHITES
- 4.5 OZ. CONFECTIONERS' SUGAR
- ½ TEASPOON PURE VANILLA EXTRACT
- 5.3 OZ. UNSALTED BUTTER

CHOCOLATE TUILE

YIELD: 24 COOKIES / **ACTIVE TIME:** 45 MINUTES / **TOTAL TIME:** 3 MINUTES

For an extra-special treat in the summer, place thin, 5-inch circles of batter on a baking sheet, bake them at 475°F for 2 minutes, and roll them around a wooden citrus reamer to form them into ice cream cones.

1. Sift the flour and cocoa powder into a small bowl and set aside.

2. In a medium bowl, whisk the egg whites, confectioners' sugar, and vanilla and set aside.

3. In a small saucepan, melt the butter over low heat. Stir it into the egg white mixture, add the flour mixture, and whisk until the mixture is a smooth batter. Cover the bowl with plastic wrap and refrigerate for 2 hours.

4. Preheat the oven to 400°F.

5. Line a 13 x 18–inch baking sheet with a silicone baking mat. Place 2-teaspoon portions of the batter about 5 inches apart from one another. Use a small, offset spatula to spread the batter into 4-inch circles. Tap the pan lightly on the counter to remove any air bubbles and level the circles.

6. Place the tuiles in the oven and bake until the edges begin to curl up, 4 to 5 minutes. Remove from the oven. Working quickly, carefully remove the tuiles with the offset spatula and transfer them immediately to a cooling rack.

7. Repeat until all of the batter has been used.

INGREDIENTS:

5   EGG WHITES

4.5   OZ. CONFECTIONERS'
     SUGAR

½   TEASPOON PURE VANILLA
     EXTRACT

5.3   OZ. UNSALTED BUTTER

2.5   OZ. ALL-PURPOSE FLOUR

2   TABLESPOONS COCOA
     POWDER

DOUBLE SHOT COOKIES

YIELD: 18 COOKIES / **ACTIVE TIME:** 30 MINUTES / **TOTAL TIME:** 2 HOURS

Illy's espresso powder, available at stores around the country, is the best choice for these cookies, and all your baking needs.

1. Line two baking sheets with parchment paper. Fill a small saucepan halfway with water and bring it to a simmer. Place the dark chocolate and butter in a heatproof bowl, place it over the simmering water, and stir until they have melted and been combined. Remove from heat and whisk in the eggs, sugar, and vanilla.

2. Add the flour, baking powder, salt, and espresso powder and whisk until the dough comes together. Add the chocolate chips and fold until evenly distributed.

3. Drop 2-oz. portions of the dough on the baking sheets, making sure to leave enough space between them. Place the baking sheets in the refrigerator and let the dough firm up for 1 hour.

4. Preheat the oven to 350°F.

5. Place the cookies in the oven and bake until a cake tester comes out clean after being inserted, 12 to 14 minutes.

6. Remove the cookies from the oven, transfer them to a cooling rack, and let them cool for 20 to 30 minutes before enjoying.

INGREDIENTS:

7.7 OZ. DARK CHOCOLATE (55 TO 65 PERCENT)

1.1 OZ. UNSALTED BUTTER, SOFTENED

2 EGGS

3.6 OZ. SUGAR

¾ TEASPOON PURE VANILLA EXTRACT

1.25 OZ. ALL-PURPOSE FLOUR

¼ TEASPOON BAKING POWDER

¼ TEASPOON KOSHER SALT

¼ CUP ESPRESSO POWDER

6 OZ. CHOCOLATE CHIPS

FIG NEWTONS

YIELD: 60 COOKIES / **ACTIVE TIME:** 1 HOUR / **TOTAL TIME:** 2 HOURS AND 30 MINUTES

If you get nostalgic thinking about eating store-bought versions of these, get ready to create a whole new set of sweet memories with these scrumptious homemade ones.

1. In the work bowl of a stand mixer fitted with the paddle attachment, cream the butter, brown sugar, honey, and orange zest on medium speed until the mixture is very light and fluffy, about 5 minutes. Scrape down the work bowl and then add the egg yolks and orange juice. Beat until combined, add the flour, baking soda, cinnamon, and salt, and beat until the dough comes together.

2. Place the dough on a flour-dusted work surface and divide it into two 6-inch squares. Cover each piece completely with plastic wrap and refrigerate for 1 hour.

3. Preheat the oven to 350°F and line two baking sheets with parchment paper. Place one piece of dough on a flour-dusted work surface and roll out until it is a 15-inch square. Cut the dough into 3-inch-wide strips.

4. Place the preserves or jam in a piping bag and pipe a strip of filling down the center of each strip, leaving 1 inch on either side.

5. Gently fold the dough over the filling so that it is sealed. Flip the strip over so that the seam is facing down. Transfer to the baking sheets, place back in the refrigerator, and let them chill for 10 minutes.

6. Cut the strips into 2-inch squares and place them back on the baking sheets, leaving 1 inch between.

7. Place the cookies in the oven and bake until golden brown, 10 to 12 minutes. Remove from the oven, transfer them to a wire rack to cool, and repeat with the other piece of dough.

INGREDIENTS:

10	OZ. UNSALTED BUTTER, SOFTENED
8	OZ. LIGHT BROWN SUGAR
2	OZ. HONEY
	ZEST OF 1 ORANGE
6	EGG YOLKS
1	OZ. ORANGE JUICE
21	OZ. ALL-PURPOSE FLOUR, PLUS MORE AS NEEDED
1¼	TEASPOONS BAKING SODA
½	TEASPOON CINNAMON
½	TEASPOON KOSHER SALT
6	CUPS FIG PRESERVES OR JAM

MEXICAN CHOCOLATE CRINKLE COOKIES

YIELD: 20 COOKIES / **ACTIVE TIME:** 30 MINUTES / **TOTAL TIME:** 2 HOURS

Spicy, sweet, chocolatey, crunchy, and moist. In other words, a cookie for those who won't rest until they have it all.

1. Line two baking sheets with parchment paper. Fill a small saucepan halfway with water and bring it to a simmer. Place the chocolate in a heatproof bowl, place it over the simmering water, and stir until melted. Remove from heat and set aside.

2. In the work bowl of a stand mixer fitted with the paddle attachment, cream the butter, brown sugar, and vanilla on medium speed until the mixture is very light and fluffy, about 5 minutes. Scrape down the work bowl and then beat the mixture for another 5 minutes.

3. Reduce the speed to low, add the melted chocolate, and beat until incorporated.

4. Add the eggs one at a time and beat until incorporated, again scraping the work bowl as needed. When both eggs have been incorporated, scrape down the work bowl. Set the speed to medium and beat for 1 minute.

5. Add the flour, cocoa powder, baking powder, cinnamon, ancho chile powder, and salt, reduce the speed to low, and beat until the mixture comes together as a dough.

6. Drop 2-oz. portions of the dough on the baking sheets, making sure to leave enough space between them. Place the baking sheets in the refrigerator and let the dough firm up for 1 hour.

7. Preheat the oven to 350°F. Place the confectioners' sugar in a mixing bowl, toss the dough balls in the sugar until completely coated, and then place them back on the baking sheet.

8. Place the cookies in the oven and bake until a cake tester comes out clean after being inserted, 12 to 14 minutes.

9. Remove the cookies from the oven, transfer them to a cooling rack, and let them cool for 20 to 30 minutes before enjoying.

INGREDIENTS:

9	OZ. MEXICAN CHOCOLATE
4.5	OZ. UNSALTED BUTTER, SOFTENED
7	OZ. DARK BROWN SUGAR
¾	TEASPOON PURE VANILLA EXTRACT
2	EGGS
7	OZ. ALL-PURPOSE FLOUR
2.5	OZ. COCOA POWDER
2	TEASPOONS BAKING POWDER
½	TEASPOON CINNAMON
¼	TEASPOON ANCHO CHILE POWDER
1	TEASPOON KOSHER SALT
2	CUPS CONFECTIONERS' SUGAR, FOR COATING

KUDOS BARS

YIELD: 12 KUDOS BARS / **ACTIVE TIME:** 30 MINUTES / **TOTAL TIME:** 2 HOURS AND 30 MINUTES

Consider dipping these bars into the Coating Chocolate on page 107, instead of just drizzling the ganache over the top.

1. Line a 9 x 13–inch baking pan with parchment paper and coat it with nonstick cooking spray. Place the cereal, oats, and 2 cups of the chocolate chips in a mixing bowl and stir to combine. Set the mixture aside.

2. In a medium saucepan, combine the brown sugar, butter, honey, corn syrup, and salt. Bring to a boil over medium heat and cook for another 2 minutes. Remove the pan from heat, whisk in the vanilla, and then pour it over the cereal mixture. Stir with a rubber spatula until combined.

3. Transfer the mixture to the baking pan and press down on it until it is flat and even. Sprinkle the remaining chocolate chips over the mixture and gently press them down into it. Refrigerate for 2 hours.

4. Remove from the refrigerator and cut the mixture into bars.

5. Drizzle the ganache over the bars and enjoy.

INGREDIENTS:

6	CUPS CRISPY RICE CEREAL
3	CUPS ROLLED OATS
4	CUPS CHOCOLATE CHIPS
1	CUP DARK BROWN SUGAR
¾	CUP UNSALTED BUTTER
¾	CUP HONEY
¼	CUP LIGHT CORN SYRUP
4	TEASPOONS KOSHER SALT
2	TABLESPOONS PURE VANILLA EXTRACT
2	CUPS CHOCOLATE GANACHE (SEE PAGE 99), WARM

LEMON BARS

YIELD: 12 BARS / **ACTIVE TIME:** 40 MINUTES / **TOTAL TIME:** 5 HOURS

A confection for those who prefer a fruit-based dessert, and those who aren't afraid of a little tartness at the end of the day.

1. Preheat the oven to 325°F. Line a 9 x 13–inch baking pan with parchment paper and coat it with nonstick cooking spray. To prepare the crust, place all of the ingredients in a mixing bowl and work the mixture with your hands until combined, soft, and crumbly.

2. Firmly press the crust into the baking pan, making sure it is flat and even. Place in the oven and bake until the crust begins to brown at the edges, about 20 minutes. Remove from the oven and place it on a cooling rack.

3. To prepare the filling, place the sugar, flour, lemon zest, and salt in a mixing bowl and whisk until combined. Add the eggs and lemon juice, whisk until incorporated, and spread the mixture over the baked crust.

4. Place in the oven and bake until the center is set, 20 to 25 minutes.

5. Remove from the oven, transfer to a cooling rack, let cool for 2 hours, and then refrigerate for an additional 2 hours.

6. Cut the bars, dust them with confectioners' sugar, and store in the refrigerator until ready to serve.

INGREDIENTS:

FOR THE CRUST

10   OZ. ALL-PURPOSE FLOUR

4   OZ. SUGAR

¼   TEASPOON KOSHER SALT

8   OZ. UNSALTED BUTTER, SOFTENED

FOR THE FILLING

1   LB. SUGAR

¾   CUP ALL-PURPOSE FLOUR

ZEST OF 2 LEMONS

¼   TEASPOON KOSHER SALT

5   EGGS

1   CUP FRESH LEMON JUICE

1   CUP CONFECTIONERS' SUGAR, FOR DUSTING

BUTTERSCOTCH TOFFEE PECAN COOKIES

YIELD: 20 COOKIES / **ACTIVE TIME:** 40 MINUTES / **TOTAL TIME:** 2 HOURS

Toasting the pecans draws their oils to the surface, leading to a richer flavor that stands toe-to-toe with the toffee.

1. Preheat the oven to 350°F and line two baking sheets with parchment paper.

2. Place the pecans on a separate baking sheet, place them in the oven, and bake until toasted and fragrant, about 10 minutes. Remove from the oven and let cool for 15 minutes. Chop the toasted pecans and let them cool. Turn the oven off.

3. In the work bowl of a stand mixer fitted with the paddle attachment, cream the butter, sugar, and brown sugar on medium speed until the mixture is very light and fluffy, about 5 minutes. Scrape down the work bowl and then beat the mixture for another 5 minutes.

4. Reduce the speed to low, add the eggs one at a time, and beat until incorporated, again scraping the work bowl as needed. When both eggs have been incorporated, scrape down the work bowl and then beat for another minute on medium. Add the flour, baking soda, salt, toffee bits, butterscotch chips, and pecans and beat until the mixture comes together as a dough.

5. Drop 2-oz. portions of the dough on the baking sheets, making sure to leave enough space between them. Place the baking sheets in the refrigerator and let the dough firm up for 1 hour.

6. Preheat the oven to 350°F.

7. Place the cookies in the oven and bake until their edges are a light golden brown, 10 to 12 minutes.

8. Remove the cookies from the oven, transfer them to a cooling rack, and let them cool for 20 to 30 minutes before enjoying.

INGREDIENTS:

8	OZ. PECANS
8	OZ. UNSALTED BUTTER, SOFTENED
3.5	OZ. SUGAR
6.5	OZ. LIGHT BROWN SUGAR
2	EGGS
12	OZ. ALL-PURPOSE FLOUR
½	TEASPOON BAKING SODA
½	TEASPOON KOSHER SALT
4	OZ. TOFFEE BITS
10	OZ. BUTTERSCOTCH CHIPS

PEPPERMINT BARS

YIELD: 12 BARS / **ACTIVE TIME:** 1 HOUR / **TOTAL TIME:** 3 HOURS AND 30 MINUTES

In the universe of sweets, the combination of chocolate and mint stands right behind that of chocolate and peanut butter.

1. Preheat the oven to 350°F. Line a 9 x 13–inch baking pan with parchment paper and coat it with nonstick cooking spray. To begin preparations for the crust, fill a small saucepan halfway with water and bring it to a simmer. Place the chocolate and butter in a heatproof bowl, place it over the simmering water, and stir until they are melted and combined. Remove from heat and set aside.

2. In a mixing bowl, whisk the sugar, brown sugar, cocoa powder, and salt, making sure to break up any clumps. Add the eggs and vanilla, whisk to incorporate, and then add the melted chocolate mixture. Whisk to incorporate, pour the batter into the baking pan, and even the surface with a rubber spatula. Lightly tap the baking pan on the counter to settle the batter and remove any air bubbles.

3. Place in the oven and bake until a cake tester comes out clean, 20 to 30 minutes. Remove from the oven and transfer the pan to a cooling rack.

4. To prepare the topping, place the confectioners' sugar, butter, and heavy cream in the work bowl of a stand mixer fitted with the paddle attachment and cream on low until the mixture comes together. Raise the speed to medium and beat until light and fluffy. Add the peppermint candies and beat until just incorporated.

5. Spread the mixture over the baked crust, using an offset spatula to even it out. Transfer the pan to the refrigerator and chill until the topping is set, about 2 hours.

6. Run a sharp knife along the edge of the pan and carefully remove the bars. Place them on a cutting board and cut. Drizzle the ganache over the bars, sprinkle the additional peppermint candies on top, and store in the refrigerator until ready to serve.

INGREDIENTS:

FOR THE CRUST

8	OZ. DARK CHOCOLATE (55 TO 65 PERCENT)
4	OZ. UNSALTED BUTTER
6	OZ. SUGAR
2	OZ. LIGHT BROWN SUGAR
2	TABLESPOONS COCOA POWDER
¼	TEASPOON KOSHER SALT
3	EGGS
¾	TEASPOON PURE VANILLA EXTRACT

FOR THE TOPPING

28.5	OZ. CONFECTIONERS' SUGAR
3	OZ. UNSALTED BUTTER, SOFTENED
4	OZ. HEAVY CREAM
2	CUPS PEPPERMINT CANDY PIECES, PLUS 1 CUP FOR GARNISH
2	CUPS CHOCOLATE GANACHE (SEE PAGE 99), WARM

CAKES

They are universal symbols of celebration. Their presence forces one to acknowledge that something grand is underway, that a transformation has taken place. Birthdays, weddings, graduations, farewells—all of the momentous days of our lives seem to incline toward a gleaming, ornately appointed cake.

This ability to signal distinctiveness is what allowed the elaborate cakes accessible to all today to spread from their exclusive origins in the kitchens of royalty. At present, anyone with a bit of attention and determination can turn out a cake worthy of rejoicing over, whether it be a humble but satisfying pound cake, a beguiling souffle, or the eye-catching complexity of the Opera Torte.

TRIPLE CHOCOLATE CAKE

YIELD: 1 CAKE / **ACTIVE TIME:** 1 HOUR / **TOTAL TIME:** 3 HOURS AND 30 MINUTES

The only chocolate cake recipe you will ever need, moist and fudgy, but also, somehow, light and airy.

1. Preheat the oven to 350°F. Line three round 8-inch cake pans with parchment paper and coat them with nonstick cooking spray.

2. To begin preparations for the cakes, sift the sugar, flour, cocoa powder, baking soda, baking powder, and salt into a medium bowl. Set aside.

3. In the work bowl of a stand mixer fitted with the whisk attachment, combine the sour cream, canola oil, and eggs on medium speed.

4. Reduce the speed to low, add the dry mixture, and whisk until combined. Scrape the sides of the bowl with a rubber spatula as needed. Add the hot coffee and whisk until thoroughly incorporated.

5. Pour 1½ cups of batter into each cake pan. Bang the pans on the countertop to spread the batter and to remove any air bubbles.

6. Place the cakes in the oven and bake until lightly golden brown and baked through, 25 to 30 minutes. Insert a cake tester in the center of each cake to check for doneness.

7. Remove from the oven and place the cakes on a cooling rack. Let them cool completely.

8. To prepare the filling, place 2 cups of the butterfluff and the cocoa powder in a small bowl and whisk to combine.

9. To prepare the frosting, place the buttercream and cocoa powder in another mixing bowl and whisk until combined. Set aside.

10. Trim a thin layer off the tops of each cake to create a flat surface. Transfer 2 cups of the frosting to a piping bag

11. Place one cake on a cake stand and pipe one ring of frosting around the edge. Place 1 cup of the filling in the center and level it with an offset spatula. Place the second cake on top and repeat the process with the frosting and filling. Place the last cake on top, place 1½ cups of the frosting on the cake and frost the top and sides of the cake using an offset spatula. Refrigerate the cake for at least 1 hour.

12. Carefully spoon some the ganache over the edge of the cake so that it drips down. Spread any remaining ganache over the center of the cake.

13. Place the cake in the refrigerator for 30 minutes so that the ganache hardens. To serve, sprinkle the curls of chocolate over the top and slice.

INGREDIENTS:

FOR THE CAKES

20	OZ. SUGAR
13	OZ. ALL-PURPOSE FLOUR
4	OZ. COCOA POWDER
1	TABLESPOON BAKING SODA
1½	TEASPOON BAKING POWDER
1½	TEASPOON KOSHER SALT
1½	CUPS SOUR CREAM
¾	CUP CANOLA OIL
3	EGGS
1½	CUPS BREWED COFFEE, HOT

FOR THE FILLING

	BUTTERFLUFF FILLING (SEE PAGE 86)
¼	CUP COCOA POWDER

FOR THE FROSTING

	ITALIAN BUTTERCREAM (SEE PAGE 75)
1	CUP COCOA POWDER

FOR TOPPING

	CHOCOLATE GANACHE (SEE PAGE 99), WARM
	CHOCOLATE, SHAVED

NEW YORK CHEESECAKE

YIELD: 1 CAKE / **ACTIVE TIME:** 1 HOUR / **TOTAL TIME:** 12 HOURS AND 30 MINUTES

Many who would not tolerate another form of this rich, cheesy treat would be nonplussed if asked to identify what produces the famed dense and satiny texture. That beloved attribute is the result of cream cheese, heavy cream and/or sour cream, eggs, and, occasionally, egg yolks being baked at a low temperature for a long period of time, and very briefly at a high temperature.

1. Preheat the oven to 200°F. Place the cream cheese, half of the sugar, and the salt in the work bowl of a stand mixer fitted with the paddle attachment. Beat at medium-low speed until combined. Add the remaining sugar, beat until combined, and then add the sour cream, lemon juice, and vanilla. Beat at low speed until combined, add the egg yolks, and beat at medium-low speed until incorporated. Scrape down the bowl as needed.

2. Add the eggs two at a time and beat at low speed to incorporate, scraping down the work bowl as needed. When all of the eggs have been incorporated, pour the mixture through a fine sieve, pressing down with a rubber spatula to help push the mixture through.

3. Pour the mixture into the crust and let it rest for 10 minutes. Use a fork to pop any air bubbles that surface. Place the cheesecake in the oven and bake for 45 minutes. Remove from the oven and pop any bubbles that have risen to the surface. Return to the oven and bake until the center of the cake is 165°F, about 2 hours. Remove the cake from the oven and raise the oven temperature to 500°F.

4. Place the cheesecake in the oven and bake until the top is golden brown, 5 to 10 minutes. Remove from the oven and let cool until barely warm, about 2½ hours. Cover in plastic wrap and place in the refrigerator until set, about 6 hours.

5. To serve, remove the sides of the pan and allow the cake to sit at room temperature for 30 minutes before slicing.

INGREDIENTS:

2.5	LBS. CREAM CHEESE, SOFTENED
10.5	OZ. SUGAR
	PINCH OF FINE SEA SALT
⅓	CUP SOUR CREAM
2	TEASPOONS FRESH LEMON JUICE
1	TABLESPOON PURE VANILLA EXTRACT
2	LARGE EGG YOLKS
6	LARGE EGGS
1	GRAHAM CRACKER CRUST (SEE PAGE 50), IN A SPRINGFORM PAN

COCONUT CAKE

YIELD: 1 CAKE / **ACTIVE TIME:** 35 MINUTES / **TOTAL TIME:** 1 HOUR AND 30 MINUTES

The coconut cream filling is perfect for this cake, but don't hesitate to try it out with some of the other cakes in this chapter.

1. Preheat the oven to 350°F and coat two round 9-inch cake pans with nonstick cooking spray.

2. To prepare the coconut cream, place 2 inches of water in a saucepan and bring to a gentle simmer. Place the egg whites, sugar, and salt in a metal mixing bowl and place the bowl over the saucepan. Cook, while whisking constantly, for about 2 minutes. Remove the bowl from heat and beat the mixture until it is shiny. Add the butter one piece at a time and beat until incorporated. Add the cream of coconut and vanilla extract and beat until well combined. Scrape down the bowl as needed while mixing. Set aside.

3. To prepare the cake, place the flour, sugar, baking powder, and salt in a mixing bowl and whisk to combine. Add the butter one piece at a time and work the mixture with a pastry blender until the mixture resembles a coarse meal.

4. Place the egg whites and the egg in a separate bowl and beat until combined. Add the vanilla, cream of coconut, and water and beat until well combined.

5. Add half of the wet mixture to the dry mixture and beat until light and fluffy. Slowly add the remaining half of the wet mixture and beat until incorporated. Scrape down the bowl as needed.

6. Divide the batter between the prepared pans, place in the oven, and bake until they are golden brown and a toothpick inserted into the center of each comes out clean, about 25 minutes. Remove from the oven and let the cakes cool in the pan for 10 minutes.

7. Place the cakes on wire racks and let cool to room temperature.

8. When the cakes are cool, spread some of the coconut cream over the top of one of the cakes. Place the other cake on top, flat-side up, and spread the remaining coconut cream over the entire cake. Sprinkle with the shredded coconut and serve.

INGREDIENTS:

FOR THE COCONUT CREAM

4	LARGE EGG WHITES
1	CUP SUGAR
	PINCH OF FINE SEA SALT
1	LB. UNSALTED BUTTER, SOFTENED AND CUT INTO SMALL PIECES
¼	CUP CREAM OF COCONUT
1	TEASPOON PURE VANILLA EXTRACT

FOR THE CAKE

2¼	CUPS SIFTED CAKE FLOUR, PLUS MORE FOR DUSTING
1	CUP SUGAR
1	TABLESPOON BAKING POWDER
¾	TEASPOON FINE SEA SALT
6	OZ. UNSALTED BUTTER, SOFTENED AND DIVIDED INTO TABLESPOONS
5	LARGE EGG WHITES
1	LARGE EGG
1	TEASPOON PURE VANILLA EXTRACT
¾	CUP CREAM OF COCONUT
¼	CUP WATER
2	CUPS SWEETENED SHREDDED COCONUT

CHOCOLATE SOUFFLES

YIELD: 6 SOUFFLES / **ACTIVE TIME:** 30 MINUTES / **TOTAL TIME:** 1 HOUR

A rich cake with multiple textures—the first layer is crispy, the center is thick, molten chocolate, and the bottom layer is akin to chocolate mousse.

1. Preheat the oven to 375°F. Coat the insides of six 8 oz. ramekins with nonstick cooking spray. Place 2 tablespoons of sugar in each ramekin and spread it to evenly coat the insides of the dishes. Knock out any excess sugar and set the ramekins aside.

2. Place the dark chocolate and butter in a large, heatproof bowl. Add 2 inches of water to a small saucepan and bring it to a simmer. Place the bowl on top and melt the butter and chocolate together.

3. In a medium saucepan, bring the water and heavy cream to a simmer and then whisk in the water-and-cream mixture. Remove the saucepan from heat.

4. Place the egg yolks and the sour cream in a mixing bowl and whisk until combined. Gradually incorporate the cream-and-chocolate mixture, while whisking constantly. Set aside.

5. In the work bowl of a stand mixer fitted with the whisk attachment, whip the egg whites and cream of tartar on high until the mixture holds stiff peaks. Reduce the speed to medium and gradually incorporate the 9 oz. of sugar. Once all of the sugar has been incorporated, raise the speed back to high and whip until it is a glossy, stiff meringue.

6. Working in three increments, add the meringue to the chocolate base, folding gently with a rubber spatula.

7. Spoon the souffle base to the rims of the ramekins. Gently tap the bottoms of the ramekins with the palm of your hand to remove any air, but not so hard as to deflate the meringue.

8. Place in the oven and bake until the souffles have risen significantly and set on the outside, but are still jiggly at the center, 25 to 27 minutes. Remove from the oven and serve immediately.

INGREDIENTS:

9	OZ. SUGAR, PLUS MORE FOR COATING RAMEKINS
20	OZ. DARK CHOCOLATE (55 TO 65 PERCENT)
4	OZ. UNSALTED BUTTER
19	OZ. WATER, PLUS MORE AS NEEDED
2	OZ. HEAVY CREAM
11	EGGS, SEPARATED
1.5	OZ. SOUR CREAM
½	TEASPOON CREAM OF TARTAR

STRAWBERRY RHUBARB RICOTTA CAKES

YIELD: 4 SMALL CAKES / **ACTIVE TIME:** 30 MINUTES / **TOTAL TIME:** 1 HOUR AND 15 MINUTES

An exciting twist on the classic combination of strawberry and rhubarb.

1. Preheat the oven to 350°F and coat a 9 x 5–inch loaf pan with nonstick cooking spray. Place the butter and sugar in the work bowl of a stand mixer fitted with the paddle attachment and beat on high until the mixture is smooth and a pale yellow. Reduce the speed to medium, add the eggs one at a time, and beat until incorporated. Add the vanilla, lemon zest, and ricotta cheese and beat until the mixture is smooth.

2. Place the flour, baking powder, and salt in a mixing bowl and whisk to combine. Reduce the speed of the mixer to low, add the dry mixture to the wet mixture, and beat until incorporated. Scrape the mixing bowl as needed while mixing the batter.

3. Add the strawberries and fold to incorporate. Place the batter in the loaf pan, place it in the oven, and bake until a cake tester inserted into the center comes out clean, about 35 minutes. Remove from the oven and let the cake cool to room temperature in the pan.

4. Remove the cooled cake from the pan and cut it into 8 equal pieces. Spread some of the jam over four of the pieces. Cover the jam with some of the meringue and then place the unadorned pieces of cake on top. Spread more meringue on top, garnish with additional strawberries, and serve.

RHUBARB JAM

1. Place the rhubarb, water, sugar, and salt in a saucepan and cook over high heat, stirring occasionally to prevent sticking, until nearly all of the liquid has evaporated.

2. Add the pectin and stir the mixture for 1 minute. Transfer to a sterilized mason jar and allow to cool completely before applying the lid and placing it in the refrigerator, where the jam will keep for up to 1 week.

INGREDIENTS:

4	OZ. UNSALTED BUTTER, SOFTENED
3.5	OZ. SUGAR
2	EGGS
¼	TEASPOON PURE VANILLA EXTRACT
	ZEST OF 1 LEMON
¾	CUP RICOTTA CHEESE
3.75	OZ. ALL-PURPOSE FLOUR
1	TEASPOON BAKING POWDER
½	TEASPOON KOSHER SALT
½	CUP MINCED STRAWBERRIES, PLUS MORE FOR GARNISH
½	CUP RHUBARB JAM (SEE RECIPE)
	ITALIAN MERINGUE (SEE PAGE 71)

RHUBARB JAM

4	CUPS CHOPPED RHUBARB
1	CUP WATER
¾	CUP SUGAR
½	TEASPOON FINE SEA SALT
1	TEASPOON PECTIN

MOLTEN LAVA CAKES

YIELD: 6 SMALL CAKES / **ACTIVE TIME:** 20 MINUTES / **TOTAL TIME:** 40 MINUTES

Yes, originally this was probably the result of a miscue in the kitchen. But it is also proof that mistakes can be a portal to genius.

1. Preheat the oven to 425°F. Spray six 6 oz. ramekins with nonstick cooking spray and coat each one with cocoa powder. Tap out any excess cocoa powder and set the ramekins aside.

2. Sift the flour and salt into a small bowl and set set aside.

3. Fill a small saucepan halfway with water and bring it to a gentle simmer. Place the chocolate and butter in a heatproof mixing bowl and place it over the simmering water. Stir occasionally until the mixture is melted and completely smooth. Remove from heat and set aside.

4. In another mixing bowl, whisk together the eggs, egg yolks, and sugar. Add the chocolate mixture and whisk until combined. Add the dry mixture and whisk until a smooth batter forms.

5. Pour approximately ½ cup of batter into each of the ramekins. Place them in the oven and bake until the cakes look firm and are crested slightly at the top, 12 to 15 minutes. Remove from the oven and let them cool for 1 minute.

6. Invert each cake onto a plate (be careful, as the ramekins will be very hot). Dust the cakes with confectioners' sugar and serve.

INGREDIENTS:

1 CUP COCOA POWDER, PLUS MORE FOR RAMEKINS

3 OZ. ALL-PURPOSE FLOUR

¼ TEASPOON KOSHER SALT

8 OZ. DARK CHOCOLATE (55 TO 65 PERCENT)

4 OZ. UNSALTED BUTTER

3 EGGS

3 EGG YOLKS

4 OZ. SUGAR

CONFECTIONERS' SUGAR, FOR DUSTING

KING CAKE

YIELD: 1 CAKE / **ACTIVE TIME:** 40 MINUTES / **TOTAL TIME:** 3 HOURS AND 30 MINUTES

Resting somewhere in the space between a coffee cake and cinnamon roll, this is a revered part of New Orleans' Mardi Gras tradition.

1. Place the milk in a saucepan and heat to 100°F. Add the yeast, gently stir, and let the mixture rest for 5 minutes.

2. Place the mixture in a large mixing bowl. Add the flour, the confectioners' sugar, nutmeg, lemon zest, one of the eggs, the egg yolk, and the orange blossom water and beat until combined.

3. Transfer the dough to the work bowl of a stand mixer fitted with the dough hook attachment. Work the dough and gradually incorporate the butter. When all of the butter has been incorporated, add the salt and work the mixture until it is very smooth. This should take about 20 minutes. Place the dough in a naturally warm spot and let it rise until it has doubled in size, about 1 to 1½ hours.

4. Transfer the dough to flour-dusted work surface and shape it into a ball. Place the ball in a 9 x 13–inch baking pan lined with parchment paper and flatten it slightly. Make a small hole in the center of the dough and use your hands to gradually enlarge the hole and create a crown. Cover and let stand for 1 hour.

5. Preheat the oven to 320°F. Place the remaining egg and 1 tablespoon of the warm water in a measuring cup and beat to combine. Brush the crown with the egg wash. Place in the oven and bake until the crown is golden brown and a cake tester comes out clean, about 30 minutes.

6. Place the sugar and the remaining warm water in a mixing bowl and stir until the sugar has dissolved. Add the food coloring, if desired, and stir to combine. Brush the hot crown with the glaze and decorate with the chopped candied fruit.

INGREDIENTS:

⅓ CUP WHOLE MILK

1¾ TEASPOONS ACTIVE DRY YEAST

15 OZ. ALL-PURPOSE FLOUR, PLUS MORE AS NEEDED

⅓ CUP CONFECTIONERS' SUGAR

¼ TEASPOON FRESHLY GRATED NUTMEG

1 TEASPOON LEMON ZEST

2 EGGS

1 EGG YOLK

1 TEASPOON ORANGE BLOSSOM WATER

3 OZ. UNSALTED BUTTER, CUT INTO SMALL PIECES

1 TEASPOON FINE SEA SALT

5 TABLESPOONS WARM WATER (110°F)

3 TABLESPOONS SUGAR

YELLOW, PURPLE, AND GREEN FOOD COLORING (OPTIONAL)

CANDIED FRUIT, ROUGHLY CHOPPED

CARROT CAKE

YIELD: 1 CAKE / **ACTIVE TIME:** 30 MINUTES / **TOTAL TIME:** 2 HOURS AND 30 MINUTES

This cake is a great spot for your carrot trimmings—so make sure you save yours in the freezer. Once you have enough, reward yourself with this cake.

1. Preheat the oven to 350°F and coat a round, 9-inch cake pan with nonstick cooking spray. Place the carrots and sugar in a mixing bowl, stir to combine, and let the mixture sit for 10 minutes.

2. Place the flour, baking soda, salt, and cinnamon in a mixing bowl and stir to combine. Place the eggs, canola oil, and vanilla extract in a separate mixing bowl and stir to combine. Add the wet mixture to the dry mixture and stir until the mixture is a smooth batter. Stir in the carrots and, if desired, the walnuts.

3. Transfer the batter to the cake pan and place the cake in the oven. Bake until the top is browned and a cake tester comes out clean, about 40 to 50 minutes.

4. Remove the cake from the oven, transfer to a wire rack, and let cool for 1 hour before applying the frosting. Top each slice with additional grated carrot before serving.

INGREDIENTS:

2 CUPS GRATED CARROTS, PLUS MORE FOR TOPPING

14 OZ. SUGAR

7.5 OZ. ALL-PURPOSE FLOUR

1½ TABLESPOONS BAKING SODA

1 TEASPOON FINE SEA SALT

1 TABLESPOON CINNAMON

3 EGGS

1¾ CUPS CANOLA OIL

2 TEASPOONS PURE VANILLA EXTRACT

½ CUP CHOPPED WALNUTS (OPTIONAL)

CREAM CHEESE FROSTING (SEE PAGE 76)

DATE & TOFFEE PUDDING CAKES

YIELD: 8 SMALL CAKES / **ACTIVE TIME:** 45 MINUTES / **TOTAL TIME:** 1 HOUR AND 30 MINUTES

Aclassic English dessert that powerfully cuts against the notions that traditional British food is bland and stodgy.

1. Place the ¾ cup of warm water, baking soda, and half of the dates in a large mason jar and soak for 5 minutes. The liquid should cover the dates.

2. Preheat the oven to 350°F and coat eight 4 oz. ramekins with nonstick cooking spray. Bring water to boil in a small saucepan.

3. Place the flour, baking powder, and ½ teaspoon of the salt in a large bowl and whisk to combine.

4. Place ¾ cup of the brown sugar and the remaining dates in a blender or food processor and blitz until the mixture is fine. Drain the soaked dates, reserve the liquid, and set them aside. Add the reserved liquid to the blender with the eggs, melted butter, and vanilla and puree until smooth. Add the puree and soaked dates to the flour mixture and fold to combine.

5. Fill each ramekin two-thirds of the way with the batter, place the filled ramekins in a large roasting pan, and pour the boiling water in the roasting pan so that it goes halfway up each ramekin.

6. Cover tightly with aluminum foil and place the pan in the oven. Bake until each cake is puffy and the surfaces are spongy but firm, about 40 minutes. Remove the ramekins from the roasting pan and let them cool on a wire rack for 10 minutes.

7. Place the remaining butter in a saucepan and warm over medium-high heat. When the butter is melted, add the remaining brown sugar and salt and whisk until smooth. Cook, while stirring occasionally, until the brown sugar has dissolved. Slowly add the cream, while stirring constantly, until it has all been incorporated and the mixture is smooth. Reduce heat to low and simmer until the mixture starts to bubble. Remove from heat and stir in the lemon juice.

8. To serve, invert each cake into a bowl or onto a dish and spoon a generous amount of the sauce over each.

INGREDIENTS:

¾   CUP WARM WATER (110°F), PLUS 1 TABLESPOON

½   TEASPOON BAKING SODA

8   OZ. PITTED DATES, CHOPPED

6.25   OZ. ALL-PURPOSE FLOUR

½   TEASPOON BAKING POWDER

¾   TEASPOON FINE SEA SALT

12.3   OZ. DARK BROWN SUGAR

2   LARGE EGGS

4   OZ. UNSALTED BUTTER, HALF MELTED, HALF SOFTENED

1½   TABLESPOONS PURE VANILLA EXTRACT

1   CUP HEAVY CREAM

1   DASH FRESH LEMON JUICE

BLACK FOREST CAKE

YIELD: 1 CAKE / **ACTIVE TIME:** 1 HOUR / **TOTAL TIME:** 3 HOURS AND 30 MINUTES

Don't be afraid—this improbably moist layered cake is certain to reward the time and energy expended on preparing it.

1. Preheat the oven to 350°F. Line three round 8-inch cake pans with parchment paper and coat them with nonstick cooking spray.

2. In a medium bowl, sift the sugar, flour, cocoa powder, baking soda, baking powder, and salt into a mixing bowl and set aside.

3. In the work bowl of a stand mixer fitted with the whisk attachment, combine the sour cream, canola oil, and eggs on medium speed. Reduce the speed to low, add the dry mixture and beat until combined. Scrape the sides of the work bowl with a rubber spatula as needed.

4. With the mixer running on low, gradually add the hot coffee and beat until fully incorporated. Pour 1½ cups of batter into each cake pan. Bang the pans on the counter to distribute the batter evenly and remove any air bubbles.

5. Place the cakes in the oven and bake until browned and a cake tester comes out clean, 25 to 30 minutes. Remove the cakes from the oven, transfer them to a cooling rack, and let them cool completely.

6. Trim a thin layer off the top of each cake to create a flat surface. Transfer 2 cups of the Chantilly Cream into a piping bag.

7. Place one cake on a cake stand and pipe one ring of cream around the edge. Place 1 cup of the cherry jam in the center and level it with an offset spatula. Place the second cake on top and repeat the process with the Chantilly Cream and cherry jam. Place the last cake on top and spread 1½ cups of the Chantilly Cream over the entire cake using an offset spatula. Refrigerate the cake for at least 1 hour.

8. Carefully spoon some the ganache over the edge of the cake so that it drips down. Spread any remaining ganache over the center of the cake.

9. Place the cake in the refrigerator for 30 minutes so that the ganache hardens.

10. Garnish the cake with the shaved chocolate and fresh cherries before slicing and serving.

INGREDIENTS:

20	OZ. SUGAR
13	OZ. ALL-PURPOSE FLOUR
4	OZ. COCOA POWDER
1	TABLESPOON BAKING SODA
1½	TEASPOONS BAKING POWDER
1½	TEASPOONS KOSHER SALT
1½	CUPS SOUR CREAM
¾	CUP CANOLA OIL
3	EGGS
1½	CUPS BREWED COFFEE, HOT
2	BATCHES OF CHANTILLY CREAM (SEE PAGE 89)
2	CUPS CHERRY JAM
	CHOCOLATE GANACHE (SEE PAGE 99), MADE WITH DARK CHOCOLATE, WARM
	DARK CHOCOLATE, SHAVED, FOR GARNISH
2	CUPS FRESH RED CHERRIES, FOR GARNISH

RED VELVET CAKE

YIELD: 1 CAKE / **ACTIVE TIME:** 1 HOUR / **TOTAL TIME:** 3 HOURS

I t's gorgeous, yes. But the piquant flavor provided by the buttermilk is what has really ushered this cake into the pantheon of great desserts.

1. Preheat the oven to 350°F. Line three round 8-inch cake pans with parchment paper and spray with nonstick cooking spray.

2. In a medium bowl, whisk together the cake flour, cocoa powder, salt, and baking soda. Set aside.

3. In the work bowl of a stand mixer fitted with the paddle attachment, cream the butter and sugar on high speed until the mixture is creamy and fluffy, about 5 minutes. Reduce the speed to low, add the eggs two at a time and beat until incorporated, scraping down the sides of the bowl with a rubber spatula between additions. Add the vinegar, beat until incorporated, and then add the dry mixture. Beat until thoroughly incorporated, add the buttermilk, vanilla extract, and food coloring, and beat until they have been combined.

4. Pour 1½ cups of batter into each cake pan, bang the pans on the counter to distribute the batter evenly and remove any air bubbles.

5. Place the cakes in the oven and bake until set and cooked through and a cake tester comes out clean, 26 to 28 minutes. Remove the cakes from the oven, transfer to a cooling rack, and let them cool completely.

6. Trim a thin layer off the top of each cake to create a flat surface. Transfer 2 cups of the Chantilly Cream into a piping bag.

7. Place one cake on a cake stand and pipe one ring of cream around the edge. Place 1 cup of the buttercream in the center and level it with an offset spatula. Place the second cake on top and repeat the process with the buttercream. Place the last cake on top and spread 2 cups of the buttercream over the entire cake using an offset spatula. Refrigerate the cake for at least 1 hour before slicing and serving.

INGREDIENTS:

12.7 OZ. CAKE FLOUR

1 OZ. COCOA POWDER

½ TEASPOON KOSHER SALT

1 TEASPOON BAKING SODA

13.4 OZ. UNSALTED BUTTER, SOFTENED

14.5 OZ. SUGAR

6 EGGS

1 TEASPOON WHITE VINEGAR

2.5 OZ. BUTTERMILK

1 TEASPOON PURE VANILLA EXTRACT

2 TEASPOONS RED FOOD COLORING

CREAM CHEESE FROSTING (SEE PAGE 76)

PINEAPPLE UPSIDE DOWN CAKE

YIELD: 1 CAKE / **ACTIVE TIME:** 1 HOUR / **TOTAL TIME:** 2 HOURS

If a series of arid upside down cakes have kept you from returning to this American classic for a while, this version will restore your faith.

1. Preheat the oven to 350°F. To prepare the topping, place a cast-iron skillet over medium-high heat. Add the butter, the juice from the can of pineapples, and the brown sugar and stir until the liquid comes to a boil and starts to thicken. Continue cooking until the sauce darkens and gains the consistency of caramel. Remove from heat and place the pineapple rings in the liquid, working from the outside in. Put the skillet in the oven while preparing the batter.

2. To prepare the cake, place the butter and sugar in a mixing bowl and beat until light and creamy. Add the eggs one at a time and incorporate thoroughly before adding the next. Add the sour cream and vanilla extract, stir to incorporate, and set aside.

3. Sift the flour, baking powder, and salt into a separate bowl. Add the dry mixture to the wet mixture and stir to combine.

4. Remove the skillet from the oven and pour the batter over the topping. Return to the oven and bake until the cake is golden and a cake tester inserted into the middle comes out clean, 35 to 40 minutes. Remove from the oven and let the cake rest for 10 minutes.

5. While using oven mitts to hold the skillet, invert the cake onto a plate. If some of the topping is stuck to the skillet, gently remove it and place it back on the cake. Let cool for a few more minutes before slicing.

INGREDIENTS:

FOR THE TOPPING

2	OZ. UNSALTED BUTTER
1	(20 OZ.) CAN OF PINEAPPLE RINGS, WITH THE JUICE
3.5	OZ. DARK BROWN SUGAR

FOR THE CAKE

4	OZ. UNSALTED BUTTER, CHILLED
7	OZ. SUGAR, PLUS 2 TABLESPOONS
4	EGGS
⅔	CUP SOUR CREAM
1½	TEASPOONS PURE VANILLA EXTRACT
7.5	OZ. ALL-PURPOSE FLOUR
1½	TEASPOONS BAKING POWDER
½	TEASPOON FINE SEA SALT

ELDERFLOWER SOUFFLES

YIELD: 4 SOUFFLES / **ACTIVE TIME:** 30 MINUTES / **TOTAL TIME:** 2 HOURS

St.-Germain liqueur, which brings notes of lychee, sweet blossoms, and peach nectar, is the overwhelming preference for the elderflower liqueur used here.

1. Coat four 8 oz. ramekins with nonstick cooking spray. Place 2 tablespoons of sugar in each ramekin and spread it to evenly coat the insides of the dishes. Knock out any excess sugar and set the ramekins aside.

2. In a small bowl, whisk together the cornstarch and cold water. Set aside.

3. Bring the milk and lemon zest to a boil over medium heat in a medium saucepan. Gradually pour in the cornstarch mixture while continually whisking. Continue to whisk until the mixture has thickened and has boiled for 30 seconds. Immediately remove the pan from heat and whisk in the elderflower liqueur.

4. Transfer the souffle base to a medium bowl. Take plastic wrap and place it directly on the mixture so that no air can get to it. This will prevent a skin from forming. Place the bowl in the refrigerator until it reaches room temperature, about 1 hour.

5. Preheat the oven to 375°F. In the work bowl of a stand mixer fitted with the whisk attachment, whip the egg whites and cream of tartar on high until the mixture holds stiff peaks. Reduce the speed to medium and gradually incorporate the sugar. Once all of the sugar has been incorporated, raise the speed back to high and whip until it is a glossy, stiff meringue.

6. Working in three increments, add the meringue to the souffle base, folding gently with a rubber spatula.

7. Spoon the souffle base to the rims of the ramekins. Gently tap the bottoms of the ramekins with the palm of your hand to remove any air, but not so hard as to deflate the meringue.

8. Place in the oven and bake until the souffles have risen significantly and set on the outside, but are still jiggly at the center, 22 to 25 minutes. Remove from the oven and serve immediately.

INGREDIENTS:

- 3.5 OZ. SUGAR, PLUS MORE FOR COATING RAMEKINS
- 2 TABLESPOONS CORNSTARCH
- ¼ CUP COLD WATER
- 10.5 OZ. MILK
   ZEST OF ½ LEMON
- 2 OZ. ELDERFLOWER LIQUEUR
- 4 EGG WHITES
- ¼ TEASPOON CREAM OF TARTAR

LEMON TEA CAKE

YIELD: 1 CAKE / **ACTIVE TIME:** 30 MINUTES / **TOTAL TIME:** 1 HOUR AND 30 MINUTES

A simple cake that will brighten the day of anyone who takes a step back from the world and spends some time with it.

1. Preheat the oven to 350°F and coat a round, 9-inch cake pan with nonstick cooking spray. In a large bowl, combine the sugar and lemon zest. Add the butter and beat until the mixture is light and fluffy. Add the eggs one at a time, stirring to incorporate thoroughly before adding the next one.

2. Place the flour and baking powder in a measuring cup and stir to combine. Alternate adding the flour mixture and the milk to the butter-and-sugar mixture, stirring after each addition until incorporated.

3. Transfer the batter to the cake pan, place it in the oven, and bake until the top is golden brown and a cake tester inserted in the middle comes out clean, 30 to 35 minutes. Remove and let cool before dusting with confectioners' sugar and cutting into wedges.

INGREDIENTS:

5.3	OZ. SUGAR
	ZEST OF 2 LEMONS
3	OZ. UNSALTED BUTTER, CUT INTO SMALL PIECES
2	EGGS
5	OZ. ALL-PURPOSE FLOUR
1	TEASPOON BAKING POWDER
½	CUP WHOLE MILK
	CONFECTIONERS' SUGAR, FOR DUSTING

SUNSET CAKE

YIELD: 1 CAKE / **ACTIVE TIME:** 30 MINUTES / **TOTAL TIME:** 24 HOURS

Reducing the strawberry juice to a syrup is the key to this striking and delicious cake.

1. Place the strawberries in a large mixing bowl and let them thaw overnight.

2. Preheat the oven to 350°F and coat two round, 9-inch cake pans with nonstick cooking spray.

3. Place the juice from the thawed strawberries in a small saucepan and bring to a boil over medium-high heat. Cook, while stirring occasionally, until the mixture is syrupy and has reduced by two-thirds, about 6 minutes. Remove from the heat and briefly let cool. Add the milk and stir to combine.

4. Place the strawberry juice-and-milk mixture, egg whites, and vanilla in a mixing bowl and whisk to combine. Set aside. Place the flour, sugar, baking powder, and salt in a mixing bowl and whisk to combine. Add the butter 1 tablespoon at a time and work the mixture with a pastry blender until it is a coarse meal consisting of pea-sized pieces. Add half of the egg white mixture and beat until the batter is light and fluffy. Add the remaining egg white mixture and beat until incorporated.

5. Divide the batter between the cake pans, place in the oven, and bake until a cake tester inserted in the center of each comes out clean, about 20 minutes. Remove from the oven and let the cakes cool in the pans for 10 minutes. Remove the cakes from the pans and place on wire racks to cool completely.

6. Pat the thawed strawberries dry. Spread some of the frosting on top of one of the cakes. Place the other cake on top, flat-side up, and cover the entire cake with the rest of the frosting. Arrange the whole strawberries on top and serve.

INGREDIENTS:

2 CUPS FROZEN WHOLE STRAWBERRIES

¾ CUP WHOLE MILK, AT ROOM TEMPERATURE

6 LARGE EGG WHITES, AT ROOM TEMPERATURE

2 TEASPOONS PURE VANILLA EXTRACT

9 OZ. CAKE FLOUR, PLUS MORE AS NEEDED

12.3 OZ. SUGAR

4 TEASPOONS BAKING POWDER

1 TEASPOON FINE SEA SALT

6 OZ. UNSALTED BUTTER, SOFTENED AND DIVIDED INTO TABLESPOONS

AMERICAN BUTTERCREAM (SEE PAGE 72)

LAVENDER & LEMON CUPCAKES

YIELD: 24 CUPCAKES / **ACTIVE TIME:** 30 MINUTES / **TOTAL TIME:** 1 HOUR AND 30 MINUTES

Lavender has a lovely, but very powerful, flavor. Pairing it with another strong flavor, such as lemon, is the key to getting the most out of it when using it in a dessert.

1. Preheat the oven to 350°F and line a 24-well cupcake pan with liners.

2. In a medium bowl, whisk together the flour, baking powder, salt, and lavender. Set aside.

3. In the work bowl of a stand mixer fitted with the paddle attachment, cream the butter, sugar, and lemon zest on high until the mixture is light and fluffy, about 5 minutes. Reduce the speed to low and gradually incorporate the egg whites, scraping the sides of the bowl with a rubber spatula as needed. Add the dry mixture and beat until incorporated.

4. Add the milk and beat until the mixture is a smooth batter. Pour approximately ¼ cup of batter into each cupcake liner, place them in the oven, and bake until they are lightly golden brown, 15 to 18 minutes.

5. Remove the cupcakes from the oven and transfer them to a cooling rack. Let them cool completely.

6. Place the buttercream and violet gel coloring in the work bowl of a stand mixer fitted with the paddle attachment and beat until combined. Place the frosting in a piping bag and frost the cupcakes. Place the cupcakes in the refrigerator and let the frosting set before garnishing with the dried lavender buds.

INGREDIENTS:

14	OZ. ALL-PURPOSE FLOUR
1	TABLESPOON BAKING POWDER, PLUS 2 TEASPOONS
½	TEASPOON KOSHER SALT
1	TABLESPOON GROUND DRIED LAVENDER
8	OZ. UNSALTED BUTTER, SOFTENED
15	OZ. SUGAR
	ZEST OF 2 LEMONS
7	EGG WHITES
¾	CUP MILK
	AMERICAN BUTTERCREAM (SEE PAGE 72)
1-2	DROPS OF VIOLET GEL FOOD COLORING
	DRIED LAVENDER BUDS, FOR GARNISH

STRAWBERRY SHORTCAKE

YIELD: 6 SERVINGS / **ACTIVE TIME:** 30 MINUTES / **TOTAL TIME:** 1 HOUR AND 15 MINUTES

If you find these cakes to be a little too dry for your liking, add an egg to the batter when you add the heavy cream to the batter.

1. Preheat the oven to 400°F and line a baking sheet with parchment paper. Place the strawberries and 1.75 oz. of sugar in a large bowl and cover it with plastic wrap. Let the mixture sit until the strawberries start to release their juice, about 45 minutes.

2. Place the flour, baking powder, remaining sugar, lemon zest, and cinnamon in a mixing bowl and whisk to combine. Add the heavy cream very slowly and beat with a handheld mixer until a smooth dough comes together.

3. Transfer the dough to a flour-dusted work surface and roll it out into a 9 x 6-inch rectangle that is approximately ¾ inch thick. Use a floured biscuit cutter or mason jar to cut six rounds from the dough. Place the rounds on the baking sheet, place the sheet in the oven, and bake the cakes until golden brown, about 12 minutes. Remove from the oven and let them cool for 10 minutes.

4. Starting at the equator, cut each of the cakes in half. Place a dollop of the Chantilly Cream on top of one of the halves, followed by a few scoops of the strawberries and their juices. Top with the other half and serve.

INGREDIENTS:

2   LBS. STRAWBERRIES, HULLED AND HALVED

1.75   OZ. SUGAR, PLUS 2 TABLESPOONS

10   OZ. ALL-PURPOSE FLOUR, PLUS MORE AS NEEDED

2   TEASPOONS BAKING POWDER

½   TEASPOON LEMON ZEST

¼   TEASPOON CINNAMON

1½   CUPS HEAVY CREAM

CHANTILLY CREAM (SEE PAGE 89)

GLUTEN-FREE VANILLA CAKE

YIELD: 1 CAKE / **ACTIVE TIME:** 15 MINUTES / **TOTAL TIME:** 1 HOUR AND 30 MINUTES

At last, gluten-free fans can have their cake and eat it, too.

1. Preheat the oven to 350°F. Liberally coat a Bundt pan with non-stick cooking spray and then lightly dust it with flour, making sure to knock out the excess.

2. Place the butter and sugar in the mixing bowl of a stand mixer fitted with the paddle attachment and beat on medium until the mixture is light and fluffy. Add the eggs one at a time, beating until each one is incorporated before adding the next. Scrape down the bowl after incorporating each egg. Add the vanilla and beat to incorporate.

3. Place the flour, xanthan gum, baking soda, and salt in a separate mixing bowl and whisk to combine.

4. Divide the flour mixture and the buttermilk into three portions and alternate adding them to the butter-and-sugar mixture. Incorporate each portion completely before adding the next.

5. Transfer the batter to the prepared Bundt pan and ensure that it is spread evenly. Place in the oven and bake until a toothpick inserted into the center comes out with just a few crumbs, about 45 minutes.

6. Remove from the oven and let cool in the pan for 30 minutes. Invert the cake onto a wire rack and let cool completely before dusting with the confectioners' sugar.

INGREDIENTS:

8.5 OZ. GLUTEN-FREE FLOUR, PLUS MORE AS NEEDED

6 OZ. UNSALTED BUTTER, SOFTENED

9.6 OZ. SUGAR

2 EGGS, AT ROOM TEMPERATURE

1 TEASPOON PURE VANILLA EXTRACT

1 TEASPOON XANTHAN GUM

2 TEASPOONS BAKING SODA

½ TEASPOON FINE SEA SALT

1 CUP BUTTERMILK

CONFECTIONERS' SUGAR, FOR DUSTING

BUTTERSCOTCH SOUFFLES

YIELD: 4 SOUFFLES / **ACTIVE TIME:** 30 MINUTES / **TOTAL TIME:** 2 HOURS

Butterscotch is created by boiling butter and brown sugar together, a process that manages to approximate the flavor of a rich caramel astonishingly well.

1. Preheat the oven to 375°F. Coat four 8 oz. ramekins with non-stick cooking spray. Place 2 tablespoons of sugar in each ramekin and spread it to evenly coat the insides of the dishes. Knock out any excess sugar and set the ramekins aside.

2. In a medium bowl, whisk together the cornstarch and the egg. Set aside.

3. Bring the milk, dark brown sugar, and butter to a boil over medium heat in a medium saucepan.

4. Gradually add the heated milk mixture into the egg-and-corn-starch mixture while whisking constantly. When fully incorporated, transfer the tempered mixture back into the saucepan.

5. Cook the mixture over medium heat, whisking until the mixture has thickened. Immediately remove the saucepan from heat and whisk in the vanilla.

6. Take plastic wrap and place it directly on the mixture so that no air can get to it. This will prevent a skin from forming. Place the bowl in the refrigerator until it reaches room temperature, about 1 hour.

7. In the work bowl of a stand mixer fitted with the whisk attachment, whip the egg whites and cream of tartar on high until the mixture holds stiff peaks. Reduce the speed to medium and gradually incorporate the sugar. Once all of the sugar has been incorporated, raise the speed back to high and whip until it is a glossy, stiff meringue.

8. Working in three increments, add the meringue to the souffle base, folding gently with a rubber spatula.

9. Spoon the souffle base to the rims of the ramekins. Gently tap the bottoms of the ramekins with the palm of your hand to remove any air, but not so hard as to deflate the meringue.

10. Place in the oven and bake until the souffles have risen significantly and set on the outside, but are still jiggly at the center, 22 to 25 minutes. Remove from the oven and serve immediately.

INGREDIENTS:

3	OZ. SUGAR, PLUS MORE FOR COATING RAMEKINS
2	TABLESPOONS CORNSTARCH
1	EGG
10.5	OZ. MILK
3	OZ. DARK BROWN SUGAR
1	OZ. UNSALTED BUTTER
½	TEASPOON PURE VANILLA EXTRACT
4	EGG WHITES
¼	TEASPOON CREAM OF TARTAR

CHOCOLATE BEET CAKE

YIELD: 1 CAKE / **ACTIVE TIME:** 45 MINUTES / **TOTAL TIME:** 3 HOURS AND 15 MINUTES

Their detractors will say their taste is too earthy to even be considered using in a dessert, but devotees understand that beets' sweetness makes them a natural.

1. Preheat the oven to 350°F. Coat a round 9-inch cake pan with nonstick cooking spray.

2. Place the beets in a large saucepan, cover them with water, and bring to a boil. Cook the beets until they are very tender when poked with a knife, about 1 hour. Drain and let the beets cool. When cool enough to handle, place the beets under cold, running water and rub off their skins. Cut the beets into 1-inch chunks, place them in a food processor, and puree. Set aside.

3. Whisk the flour, cocoa powder, baking powder, and salt together in a small bowl. Set aside.

4. Bring a small saucepan filled halfway with water to a gentle simmer. Add the chocolate and butter to a heatproof mixing bowl and set it over the simmering water until it melts, stirring occasionally. Remove from heat and set aside.

5. Heat the milk in a clean saucepan, warm it over medium-low heat until it starts to steam, and pour it into the chocolate mixture. Stir to combine, add the eggs and sugar, and whisk until incorporated. Add the beet puree, stir to incorporate, and add the dry mixture. Whisk until the mixture comes together as a smooth batter.

6. Pour the batter into the prepared cake pan, place it in the oven, and bake until baked through and a cake tester comes out clean, 40 to 45 minutes. Remove from the oven, transfer the cake to a cooling rack, and let it cool completely.

7. Carefully remove the cake from the pan and transfer to a serving plate.

8. Spread the warm ganache over the top of the cake, garnish with blackberries, and serve.

INGREDIENTS:

2	MEDIUM RED BEETS, RINSED
4.5	OZ. ALL-PURPOSE FLOUR
3	TABLESPOONS COCOA POWDER
1¼	TEASPOONS BAKING POWDER
¼	TEASPOON KOSHER SALT
7	OZ. DARK CHOCOLATE (55 TO 65 PERCENT)
7	OZ. UNSALTED BUTTER
¼	CUP MILK
5	EGGS
7	OZ. SUGAR
1	CUP CHOCOLATE GANACHE (SEE PAGE 99), WARM
	FRESH BLACKBERRIES, FOR GARNISH

BLUEBERRY BUCKLE

YIELD: 1 CAKE / **ACTIVE TIME:** 20 MINUTES / **TOTAL TIME:** 2 HOURS

A classic country-style cake that can soothe a sweet tooth any time of day.

1. Preheat the oven to 350°F and coat a 9 x 13–inch baking pan with nonstick cooking spray.

2. Place one-quarter of the flour, 2 tablespoons of the sugar, the brown sugar, cinnamon, and a pinch of the salt in a mixing bowl and mix until combined. Add 2 ounces of the butter and work the mixture with a pastry blender until it resembles wet sand. Set the crumble aside.

3. Place the remaining flour and the baking powder in a small bowl and whisk to combine. Set the mixture aside.

4. In the work bowl of a stand mixer fitted with the paddle attachment, combine the remaining butter, sugar, salt, and the lemon zest and beat on medium speed until the mixture is light and fluffy, about 5 minutes.

5. Add the vanilla, beat until incorporated, and then incorporate the eggs one at a time, scraping down the work bowl as needed. Gradually add the flour-and-baking soda mixture and beat until the mixture is a smooth batter.

6. Add the blueberries and fold until they have been evenly distributed.

7. Transfer the batter to the baking pan and smooth the surface with a rubber spatula. Sprinkle the crumble over the batter, place the cake in the oven, and bake until it is golden brown and a cake tester inserted into the center comes out clean, about 50 minutes. Remove from the oven and let the cake cool in the pan for 15 minutes.

8. Remove the cake from the pan, transfer to a wire rack, and let cool to room temperature before serving.

INGREDIENTS:

10	OZ. ALL-PURPOSE FLOUR
5.25	OZ. SUGAR
3.5	OZ. LIGHT BROWN SUGAR
¼	TEASPOON CINNAMON
¾	TEASPOON FINE SEA SALT
7	OZ. UNSALTED BUTTER, CUT INTO SMALL PIECES AND SOFTENED
1½	TEASPOONS BAKING POWDER
½	TEASPOON LEMON ZEST
1½	TEASPOONS PURE VANILLA EXTRACT
2	LARGE EGGS, AT ROOM TEMPERATURE
1	QUART OF FRESH BLUEBERRIES

ANGEL FOOD CAKE

YIELD: 1 CAKE / **ACTIVE TIME:** 30 MINUTES / **TOTAL TIME:** 2 HOURS

It's not just a clever nickname: this light and airy cake is heavenly with some Chantilly Cream (see page 89) or preserves.

1. Preheat the oven to 325°F. Coat a 10-inch Bundt pan with nonstick cooking spray.

2. Sift the cake flour and ½ cup of the sugar into a medium bowl.

3. In the work bowl of a stand mixer fitted with the whisk attachment, whip the egg whites and salt on high until soft peaks begin to form. Reduce the speed to low and add the remaining sugar a few tablespoons at a time until all of it has been incorporated. Add the vanilla, raise the speed back to high, and whisk the mixture until it holds stiff peaks.

4. Remove the work bowl from the mixer and gently fold in the dry mixture. Pour the batter into the prepared Bundt pan.

5. Place in the oven and bake until the cakes are lightly golden brown and a cake tester comes out clean, 45 to 55 minutes.

6. Remove the cake from the oven and transfer it to a cooling rack. Let it cool for 30 minutes.

7. Invert the cake onto a cake stand or serving tray, dust the top with confectioners' sugar, and serve with the preserves.

INGREDIENTS:

1	CUP CAKE FLOUR
1½	CUPS SUGAR
12	EGG WHITES, AT ROOM TEMPERATURE
¼	TEASPOON KOSHER SALT
1	TEASPOON PURE VANILLA EXTRACT
	CONFECTIONERS' SUGAR, FOR DUSTING
	STRAWBERRY PRESERVES (SEE PAGE 622), FOR SERVING

HOSTESS CUPCAKES

YIELD: 24 CUPCAKES / **ACTIVE TIME:** 40 MINUTES / **TOTAL TIME:** 2 HOURS

An American classic that almost every child continually pined for.

1. Preheat the oven to 350°F. Line a 24-well cupcake pan with liners.

2. In a medium bowl, whisk together the sugar, flour, cocoa powder, baking soda, baking powder, and salt. Sift the mixture into a separate bowl and set aside.

3. In the work bowl of a stand mixer fitted with the whisk attachment, combine the sour cream, canola oil, and eggs on medium speed.

4. Reduce the speed to low, add the dry mixture, and beat until incorporated, scraping the sides of the bowl with a rubber spatula as needed. Gradually add the hot coffee and beat until thoroughly incorporated. Pour about ¼ cup of batter into each cupcake liner.

5. Place the cupcakes in the oven and bake until browned and a cake tester comes out clean, 18 to 22 minutes. Remove from the oven and place the cupcakes on a cooling rack until completely cool.

6. Using an apple corer or a sharp paring knife, carefully remove the centers of each cupcake. Place 2 cups of the Butterfluff Filling in a piping bag and fill the centers of the cupcakes with it.

7. While the ganache is warm, dip the tops of the cupcakes in the ganache and place them on a flat baking sheet. Refrigerate the cupcakes for 20 minutes so that the chocolate will set.

8. Place 1 cup of the Butterfluff Filling in a piping bag fit with a thin, plain tip and pipe decorative curls on top of each cupcake. Allow the curls to set for 10 minutes before serving.

INGREDIENTS:

20	OZ. SUGAR
13	OZ. ALL-PURPOSE FLOUR
4	OZ. COCOA POWDER
1	TABLESPOON BAKING SODA
1½	TEASPOONS BAKING POWDER
1½	TEASPOONS KOSHER SALT
1½	CUPS SOUR CREAM
¾	CUP CANOLA OIL
3	EGGS
1½	CUPS BREWED COFFEE, HOT
	BUTTERFLUFF FILLING (SEE PAGE 86)
	CHOCOLATE GANACHE (SEE PAGE 99), WARM

BLUEBERRY & LEMON CHEESECAKE

YIELD: 1 CHEESECAKE / **ACTIVE TIME:** 1 HOUR / **TOTAL TIME:** 8 HOURS

Swirling the blueberry and lemon mixtures as recommended produces a stunning cake, but will have no impact on the final flavor if your style is more staid.

1. Preheat the oven to 350°F. Bring 8 cups of water to a boil in a medium saucepan.

2. In a small saucepan, cook the blueberries, water, and sugar over medium heat until the blueberries burst and start to become fragrant, about 5 minutes. Remove the pan from heat.

3. In the work bowl of a stand mixer fitted with the paddle attachment, cream the cream cheese, sugar, and salt on high until the mixture is soft and airy, about 10 minutes. Scrape down the sides of the bowl with a rubber spatula as needed.

4. Reduce the speed of the mixer to medium and incorporate the eggs one at a time, scraping the bowl as needed. Add the vanilla extract and mix until incorporated.

5. Divide the mixture between two mixing bowls. Add the blueberry mixture to one bowl and whisk to combine. Whisk the lemon juice into the mixture in the other bowl.

6. Starting with the lemon mixture, add 1 cup to the crust. Add 1 cup of the blueberry mixture, and then alternate between the mixtures until all of them have been used.

7. If desired, use a paring knife to gently swirl the blueberry and lemon mixtures together, making sure not to overmix.

8. Place the cheesecake in a large baking pan with high sides. Gently pour the boiling water into the pan until it reaches halfway up the sides of the cheesecake pan. Cover the baking pan with aluminum foil and place it in the oven. Bake until the cheesecake is set and only slightly jiggly in the center, 50 minutes to 1 hour.

9. Turn off the oven and leave the oven door cracked. Allow the cheesecake to rest in the cooling oven for 45 minutes.

10. Remove the cheesecake from the oven and transfer the springform pan to a cooling rack. Let it sit at room temperature for 1 hour.

11. Transfer the cheesecake to the refrigerator and let it cool for at least 4 hours before slicing and serving.

INGREDIENTS:

2	PINTS OF BLUEBERRIES
1	TABLESPOON WATER
2	TABLESPOONS SUGAR
2	LBS. CREAM CHEESE, SOFTENED
⅔	CUP SUGAR
¼	TEASPOON KOSHER SALT
4	EGGS
1	TEASPOON PURE VANILLA EXTRACT
2	TABLESPOONS FRESH LEMON JUICE
1	GRAHAM CRACKER CRUST (SEE PAGE 50), IN A SPRINGFORM PAN

CHERRY AMARETTO SOUFFLES

YIELD: 6 SOUFFLES / **ACTIVE TIME:** 30 MINUTES / **TOTAL TIME:** 2 HOURS

The richness and acidity provided by the cherries are balanced by the sweetness and nuttiness of the amaretto.

INGREDIENTS:

8	OZ. SUGAR, PLUS MORE FOR COATING RAMEKINS
5	TABLESPOONS CORNSTARCH
½	CUP COLD WATER
10	OZ. MORELLO CHERRIES, PUREED
10	OZ. MILK
2	OZ. AMARETTO
8	EGG WHITES
½	TEASPOON CREAM OF TARTAR

1. Preheat the oven to 375°F. Coat six 8 oz. ramekins with nonstick cooking spray. Place 2 tablespoons of sugar in each ramekin and spread it to evenly coat the insides of the dishes. Knock out any excess sugar and set the ramekins aside.

2. In a small bowl, whisk together the cornstarch and cold water. Set aside.

3. Bring the cherry puree and milk to a boil over medium heat in a medium saucepan. Gradually pour in the cornstarch slurry while continually whisking. Continue to whisk until the mixture has thickened and has boiled for 30 seconds. Immediately remove the pan from heat and whisk in the amaretto liqueur.

4. Transfer the cherry mixture to a medium bowl. Cover with plastic wrap, placing it directly on the mixture so that no air can get to it. This will prevent a skin from forming. Place the bowl in the refrigerator until it reaches room temperature, about 1 hour.

5. In the work bowl of a stand mixer fitted with a whisk attachment, whip the egg whites and cream of tartar on high until the mixture holds stiff peaks. Reduce the speed to medium and gradually incorporate the sugar. Once all of the sugar has been added, raise the speed back to high and whip until it is a glossy, stiff meringue.

6. Working in three increments, add the meringue to the cherry base, folding gently with a rubber spatula.

7. Spoon the souffle base to the rims of the ramekins. Gently tap the bottoms of the ramekins with the palm of your hand to remove any air, but not so hard as to deflate the meringue.

8. Place in the oven and bake until the souffles have risen significantly and set on the outside, but are still jiggly at the center, 25 to 27 minutes. Remove from the oven and serve immediately.

LEMON RICOTTA CHEESECAKE

YIELD: 1 CHEESECAKE / **ACTIVE TIME:** 1 HOUR / **TOTAL TIME:** 8 HOURS

Whole milk ricotta is a must for this (and, really, any dessert that calls for ricotta cheese). When shopping, keep an eye out for BelGioioso's offering, as it provides the best results.

1. Preheat the oven to 350°F. Bring 8 cups of water to a boil in a medium saucepan.

2. In the work bowl of a stand mixer fitted with the paddle attachment, cream the ricotta, cream cheese, sugar, and lemon zest on high until the mixture is soft and airy, about 10 minutes. Scrape down the work bowl with a rubber spatula as needed. Reduce the speed of the mixer to medium and incorporate the egg, scraping the bowl as needed. Add the lemon juice and mix until incorporated. Add the cornstarch and flour and beat until incorporated. Reduce the speed to low, add the butter and sour cream, and beat until the mixture is very smooth.

3. Pour the mixture into the crust, place the cheesecake in a large baking pan with high sides, and gently pour the boiling water into the baking pan until it reaches halfway up the sides of the spring-form pan.

4. Cover the baking pan with aluminum foil, place it in the oven, and bake until the cheesecake is set and only slightly jiggly in the center, 50 minutes to 1 hour.

5. Turn off the oven and leave the oven door cracked. Allow the cheesecake to rest in the cooling oven for 45 minutes.

6. Remove the cheesecake from the oven and transfer to a cooling rack. Let it sit at room temperature for 1 hour.

7. Transfer the cheesecake to the refrigerator and let it cool for at least 4 hours before serving and slicing. To serve, top each slice with a dollop of the Chantilly Cream.

INGREDIENTS:

8 OZ. WHOLE MILK RICOTTA CHEESE

8 OZ. CREAM CHEESE, SOFTENED

6 OZ. SUGAR

1 EGG

ZEST AND JUICE OF 1 LEMON

¼ TEASPOON PURE VANILLA EXTRACT

1 TABLESPOON CORNSTARCH, PLUS 1½ TEASPOONS

1½ TABLESPOONS ALL-PURPOSE FLOUR

1 OZ. UNSALTED BUTTER, MELTED

1 CUP SOUR CREAM

1 GRAHAM CRACKER CRUST (SEE PAGE 50), IN A SPRINGFORM PAN

CHANTILLY CREAM (SEE PAGE 89)

VANILLA CAKE

YIELD: 1 CAKE / **ACTIVE TIME:** 1 HOUR / **TOTAL TIME:** 3 HOURS AND 30 MINUTES

An updated classic, with the buttermilk providing a lovely, unexpected tanginess.

1. Preheat the oven to 350°F. Line three round 8-inch cake pans with parchment paper and coat them with nonstick cooking spray.

2. In a medium bowl, whisk together the cake flour, baking powder, and salt. Sift this mixture into another mixing bowl and set aside.

3. In the work bowl of a stand mixer fitted with the paddle attachment, cream the butter, canola oil, and sugar until the mixture is smooth and creamy, about 5 minutes.

4. Incorporate the eggs one at a time, scraping down the sides of the work bowl with a rubber spatula as needed.

5. Reduce the speed to low, add the dry mixture and beat until combined.

6. Gradually add the milk, buttermilk, and vanilla extract. When they have been thoroughly incorporated, pour 1½ cups of batter into each cake pan. Bang the pans on the countertop to spread the batter evenly and to dissolve any air bubbles.

7. Place the cakes in the oven and bake until lightly golden brown and baked through, 25 to 30 minutes. Insert a cake tester in the center of each cake to check for doneness.

8. Remove from the oven and place the cakes on a cooling rack. Let them cool completely.

9. Trim a thin layer off the tops of each cake to create a flat surface. Transfer 2 cups of the buttercream to a piping bag and cut a ½-inch slit in it.

10. Place one cake on a cake stand and pipe one ring of buttercream around the edge. Place 1 cup of the Butterfluff Filling in the center and level it with an offset spatula. Place the second cake on top and repeat the process with the buttercream and filling. Place the last cake on top Place 1½ cups of the buttercream on the cake and frost the top and sides of the cake using an offset spatula. Refrigerate the cake for at least 1 hour before slicing and serving.

INGREDIENTS:

13	OZ. CAKE FLOUR
2	TEASPOONS BAKING POWDER
¼	TEASPOON KOSHER SALT
8	OZ. UNSALTED BUTTER, SOFTENED
½	CUP CANOLA OIL
3	CUPS SUGAR
5	EGGS
½	CUP MILK
½	CUP BUTTERMILK
1	TABLESPOON PURE VANILLA EXTRACT
	ITALIAN BUTTERCREAM (SEE PAGE 75)
	BUTTERFLUFF FILLING (SEE PAGE 86)

MANGO SHORTCAKE

YIELD: 1 CAKE / **ACTIVE TIME:** 1 HOUR AND 30 MINUTES / **TOTAL TIME:** 8 HOURS

Don't hesitate to serve the mango mousse on its own, or as the filling for a pie.

1. Preheat the oven to 325°F. Coat a 9 x 13–inch baking pan with nonstick cooking spray.

2. To begin preparations for the cake, sift the flour and ¼ cup of the sugar into a mixing bowl. Set aside.

3. In the work bowl of a stand mixer fitted with the whisk attachment, whip the egg whites and salt on high until soft peaks begin to form. Reduce the speed to low and add the remaining sugar a few tablespoons at a time. When all of the sugar has been incorporated, add the vanilla, raise the speed back to high, and whip until the mixture holds stiff peaks.

4. Remove the work bowl from the mixer and gently fold in the dry mixture. Pour the batter into the prepared pan, place it in the oven, and bake until the cake is lightly golden brown and a cake tester comes out clean, 20 to 25 minutes. Remove the cake from the oven, transfer it to a cooling rack, and let it cool completely.

5. Place the gelatin sheets for the mousse in a small bowl, add 1 cup of ice, and enough cold water to cover the sheets. In a small saucepan, bring the mango puree, confectioners' sugar, and lime zest to a simmer over medium heat. Immediately remove the pan from heat. Remove the gelatin from the ice bath and squeeze out as much water as possible. Whisk the gelatin into the mango mixture until fully dissolved. Let the mixture cool to room temperature.

6. Place the heavy cream in the work bowl of a stand mixer fitted with the paddle attachment and whip on high until soft peaks form. Fold the whipped cream into the mousse base.

7. Pour the mousse over the angel cake and use a rubber spatula to spread it evenly. Refrigerate for 4 hours.

8. To prepare the mango gelee, place the gelatin sheets in a small bowl, add 1 cup of ice, and enough cold water to cover the sheets. Place the water, mango puree, and sugar in a small saucepan and bring to a simmer over medium heat.

9. Remove the pan from heat. Remove the gelatin from the ice bath and squeeze out as much water as possible. Whisk the gelatin into the mango mixture until fully dissolved. Let the gelee cool to room temperature.

10. Pour the gelee over the mousse layer and refrigerate the cake for 2 hours.

11. To serve, cut the shortcake into bars.

INGREDIENTS:

FOR THE CAKE

½	CUP CAKE FLOUR
¾	CUP SUGAR
6	EGG WHITES, ROOM TEMPERATURE
⅛	TEASPOON KOSHER SALT
½	TEASPOON PURE VANILLA EXTRACT

FOR THE MANGO MOUSSE

4	SILVER GELATIN SHEETS
1¼	CUPS MANGO PUREE
2.6	OZ. CONFECTIONERS' SUGAR
	ZEST OF 1 LIME
1¼	CUPS HEAVY CREAM

FOR THE MANGO GELEE

4	SHEETS OF SILVER GELATIN
½	CUP WATER
1¼	CUPS MANGO PUREE
2	TABLESPOONS SUGAR

CHEESECAKE WITH CITRUS & BRIE

YIELD: 1 CHEESECAKE / **ACTIVE TIME:** 1 HOUR / **TOTAL TIME:** 8 HOURS

A light and tangy cheesecake that benefits greatly from the Grand Marnier and a triple-cream Brie.

1. Preheat the oven to 350°F. Bring 8 cups of water to a boil in a small saucepan.

2. In the work bowl of a stand mixer fitted with the paddle attachment, cream the cream cheese, Brie, sugar, salt, and orange zest on high until the mixture is fluffy, about 10 minutes. Scrape down the sides of the work bowl as needed.

3. Reduce the speed of the mixer to medium and incorporate one egg at a time, scraping the bowl as needed. Add the vanilla extract and Grand Marnier and mix until incorporated.

4. Pour the mixture into the crust, place the cheesecake in a large baking pan with high sides, and gently pour the boiling water into the baking pan until it reaches halfway up the sides of the spring-form pan.

5. Cover the baking pan with aluminum foil, place it in the oven, and bake until the cheesecake is set and only slightly jiggly in the center, 50 minutes to 1 hour.

6. Turn off the oven and leave the oven door cracked. Allow the cheesecake to rest in the cooling oven for 45 minutes.

7. Remove the cheesecake from the oven and transfer to a cooling rack. Let it sit at room temperature for 1 hour.

8. Transfer the cheesecake to the refrigerator and let it cool for at least 4 hours before serving and slicing. To serve, top each slice with a heaping spoonful of the Strawberry Preserves.

INGREDIENTS:

- 1.5 LBS. CREAM CHEESE, SOFTENED
- 8 OZ. TRIPLE-CREAM BRIE CHEESE, RIND REMOVED
- ⅔ CUP SUGAR
- ¼ TEASPOON KOSHER SALT
- ZEST OF 1 ORANGE
- 4 EGGS
- 1 TABLESPOON PURE VANILLA EXTRACT
- 2 TABLESPOONS GRAND MARNIER
- 1 GRAHAM CRACKER CRUST (SEE PAGE 50), IN A SPRINGFORM PAN
- STRAWBERRY PRESERVES (SEE PAGE 622)

GLUTEN-FREE ALMOND TORTE

YIELD: 1 CAKE / **ACTIVE TIME:** 40 MINUTES / **TOTAL TIME:** 2 HOURS

With the crispy outside, moist and chewy interior, and the homemade almond syrup, even gluten evangelists would be wise to give this one a try.

1. Preheat the oven to 375°F. Line a round 9-inch cake pan with parchment paper and coat it with nonstick cooking spray.

2. In a medium bowl, whisk together the flour, xanthan gum, baking powder, and salt. Set aside.

3. In the work bowl of a stand mixer fitted with the paddle attachment, cream the almond paste, butter, sugar, vanilla, and almond extract on high until the mixture is smooth and fluffy, about 10 minutes. Reduce the speed to low and incorporate the eggs one at a time. Scrape down the sides of the bowl with a rubber spatula between each addition. Add the dry mixture, beat until combined, and raise the speed to high. Beat the mixture for 2 minutes to thicken it.

4. Pour the batter into the prepared cake pan. Bang the pan on the countertop to evenly distribute the batter and remove any air bubbles. Sprinkle the slivered almonds over the batter and place it in the oven.

5. Bake the cake until lightly golden brown and a cake tester comes out clean, 20 to 25 minutes. Remove from the oven, transfer the cake to a cooling rack, and let it cool completely.

6. Gently brush the syrup over the torte and dust with confectioners' sugar before slicing and serving.

ALMOND SYRUP

1. Place the water and sugar in a small saucepan and bring to a boil over medium heat, stirring to dissolve the sugar.

2. Remove the saucepan from heat, stir in the almond extract, and let the syrup cool completely before using.

INGREDIENTS:

2.5	OZ. GLUTEN-FREE FLOUR
¼	TEASPOON XANTHAN GUM
¾	TEASPOON BAKING POWDER
¼	TEASPOON KOSHER SALT
4	OZ. ALMOND PASTE
4	OZ. UNSALTED BUTTER, SOFTENED
4.7	OZ. SUGAR
¼	TEASPOON PURE VANILLA EXTRACT
¼	TEASPOON ALMOND EXTRACT
3	EGGS
½	CUP SLIVERED ALMONDS
	ALMOND SYRUP (SEE RECIPE)
	CONFECTIONERS' SUGAR, FOR DUSTING

ALMOND SYRUP

½	CUP WATER
½	CUP SUGAR
¼	TEASPOON ALMOND EXTRACT

FLOURLESS CHOCOLATE TORTE

YIELD: 1 CAKE / *ACTIVE TIME*: 30 MINUTES / *TOTAL TIME*: 3 HOURS AND 30 MINUTES

This flourless torte is rich and decadent, sure to assuage any chocolate lover's yearning.

1. Preheat the oven to 375°F. Line a round 9-inch cake pan with parchment paper and coat it with nonstick cooking spray.

2. Fill a small saucepan halfway with water and bring it to a gentle simmer. In a heatproof medium bowl, combine the chocolate and butter. Place the bowl over the simmering water and stir the mixture with a rubber spatula until it has melted. Remove the mixture from heat and set aside.

3. In another small saucepan, bring the water, salt, and sugar to a boil over medium heat. Pour the mixture into the melted chocolate and whisk to combine. Incorporate the eggs and vanilla and then pour the batter into the prepared cake pan.

4. Place the cake in the oven and bake until set and the internal temperature reaches 200°F, 25 to 30 minutes. Remove the cake from the oven and let it cool on a wire rack for 30 minutes.

5. Place the torte in the refrigerator for 2 hours.

6. Run a paring knife along the edge of the pan and invert the torte onto a serving plate. Dust the top of the torte with confectioners' sugar and garnish with fresh raspberries.

INGREDIENTS:

- 9 OZ. DARK CHOCOLATE (55 TO 65 PERCENT)
- 4 OZ. UNSALTED BUTTER
- ¼ CUP WATER, PLUS MORE AS NEEDED
- PINCH OF KOSHER SALT
- 3 OZ. SUGAR
- 3 EGGS
- ½ TEASPOON PURE VANILLA EXTRACT
- CONFECTIONERS' SUGAR, FOR DUSTING
- FRESH RASPBERRIES, FOR GARNISH

TRES LECHES CAKE

YIELD: 1 CAKE / **ACTIVE TIME:** 45 MINUTES / **TOTAL TIME:** 2 HOURS AND 30 MINUTES

A recipe that appeared on cans of Nestlé condensed milk during the 1940s is believed to be responsible for the proliferation of this simple, delicious cake.

1. Preheat the oven to 350°F. Line a 9 x 13–inch baking pan with parchment paper and coat it with nonstick cooking spray.

2. Sift the flour, baking powder, and salt into a medium bowl and set aside.

3. In the work bowl of a stand mixer fitted with the paddle attachment, cream the butter, sugar, and orange zest on medium speed until the mixture is smooth and creamy, about 5 minutes.

4. Incorporate the eggs two at a time, scraping down the sides of the work bowl with a rubber spatula between each addition.

5. Reduce the speed of the mixer to low, add the dry mixture, and beat until combined. Incorporate the vanilla and then pour the batter into the prepared pan. Gently tap the pan on the countertop to evenly distribute the batter and remove any air bubbles.

6. Place the cake in the oven and bake until golden brown and a cake tester comes out clean, 30 to 35 minutes. Remove the cake from the oven and transfer to a cooling rack. Let cool for 1 hour.

7. While the cake is cooling, combine the evaporated milk, sweetened condensed milk, milk, and heavy cream in a small bowl.

8. Once the cake has cooled for 1 hour, poke holes in it using a fork. Slowly pour the milk mixture over the entire top of the cake. Refrigerate the cake for at least 1 hour, allowing the cake to soak up the milk.

9. Spread the Chantilly Cream over the top of the cake, slice it into squares, and serve with the sliced strawberries.

INGREDIENTS:

14 OZ. ALL-PURPOSE FLOUR

1 TEASPOON BAKING POWDER

½ TEASPOON KOSHER SALT

8 OZ. UNSALTED BUTTER, SOFTENED

1 LB. SUGAR

ZEST OF 1 ORANGE

10 EGGS

1½ TEASPOONS PURE VANILLA EXTRACT

1 (12 OZ.) CAN OF EVAPORATED MILK

1 (14 OZ.) CAN OF SWEETENED CONDENSED MILK

½ CUP MILK

½ CUP HEAVY CREAM

CHANTILLY CREAM (SEE PAGE 89)

FRESH STRAWBERRIES, SLICED, FOR SERVING

OPERA TORTE

YIELD: 1 CAKE / **ACTIVE TIME:** 3 HOURS / **TOTAL TIME:** 3 HOURS AND 45 MINUTES

A classic French dessert that beautifully marries chocolate, coffee, and almond. This cake is a bit of a process to put together, but a wonderful project for some winter weekend.

1. Preheat the oven to 400°F. Coat two 9 x 13–inch baking pans with nonstick cooking spray.

2. To begin preparations for the joconde, sift the almond flour, confectioners' sugar, and all- purpose flour into a large bowl. Add the eggs and whisk until combined. Set aside.

3. In the work bowl of a stand mixer, fitted with the whisk attachment, whip the egg whites and salt on high until soft peaks begin to form. Reduce the speed to low and gradually incorporate the sugar. Raise the speed back to high and continue to whip until stiff peaks form. Add the meringue to the dry mixture and fold until thoroughly incorporated. Divide batter between the two prepared pans, place them in the oven, and bake until they are set and lightly browned, 8 to 10 minutes. Remove from the oven, transfer to a cooling rack, and let them cool completely.

4. To prepare the coffee syrup, place the water, sugar and espresso in a small saucepan and bring to a simmer over medium heat while stirring frequently to dissolve the sugar and espresso. Remove from heat and let the syrup cool completely.

5. To prepare the hazelnut and praline crunch, bring a small saucepan filled halfway with water to a gentle simmer. Place the chocolate in a small heatproof bowl, place it over the simmering water, and stir until the chocolate is melted. Remove from heat, stir in the praline paste and the feuilletine flakes, and spread the mixture over the two joconde. Place the cakes in the refrigerator.

6. To begin preparations for the mocha cream, place the sugar and water in a small saucepan over high heat. Cook until the mixture reaches 245°F on a candy thermometer.

7. While the sugar and water are heating up, place the egg yolks and espresso powder in the work bowl of a stand mixer fitted with the whisk attachment and whip the mixture on high.

INGREDIENTS:

FOR THE JOCONDE

5	OZ. FINE ALMOND FLOUR
5	OZ. CONFECTIONERS' SUGAR
1	OZ. ALL-PURPOSE FLOUR
5	EGGS
5	EGG WHITES
¼	TEASPOON KOSHER SALT
2	TABLESPOONS SUGAR

FOR THE COFFEE SYRUP

½	CUP WATER
½	CUP SUGAR
1	TABLESPOON GROUND ESPRESSO

FOR THE HAZELNUT & PRALINE CRUNCH

4	OZ. DARK CHOCOLATE (55 TO 65 PERCENT)
4	OZ. PRALINE PASTE
3	OZ. FEUILLETINE FLAKES

FOR THE MOCHA CREAM

1	CUP SUGAR
¼	CUP WATER
6	EGG YOLKS
3	TABLESPOONS ESPRESSO POWDER
8	OZ. UNSALTED BUTTER, SOFTENED

FOR TOPPING

	CHOCOLATE GANACHE (SEE PAGE 99), AT ROOM TEMPERATURE

8. When the syrup reaches the correct temperature, gradually add it to egg yolk mixture. Continue to whip on high until the mixture cools slightly. Reduce the speed to low and gradually add the softened butter. When all of the butter has been incorporated, raise the speed back to high and whip the mixture until smooth and fluffy. Set aside.

9. Remove both cakes from the refrigerator and carefully remove them from the pans. Place one cake on a serving tray with the coated layer facing down. Brush the cake with some of the coffee syrup and spread half of the mocha cream over the top. Lay the second cake on top so that the mocha and hazelnut layers are touching. Brush the top of this cake with the remaining coffee syrup and then spread the remaining mocha cream over the cake.

10. Place the cake in the refrigerator for 30 minutes. Spread the Chocolate Ganache over the cake and let it sit for 10 minutes. To serve, use a hot knife to cut the cake into rectangles.

NOTE: Feuilletine flakes are a crispy confection made from thin, sweetened crepes. They can be found at many baking shops, and are also available online.

EGGNOG CUPCAKES

YIELD: 24 CUPCAKES / **ACTIVE TIME:** 30 MINUTES / **TOTAL TIME:** 1 HOUR AND 30 MINUTES

These deliciously light cupcakes are perfect for the holidays.

1. Preheat the oven to 350°F. Line a 24-well cupcake pan with liners.

2. To begin preparations for the cupcakes, whisk the flour, sugar, baking powder, and kosher salt in a medium bowl. Set aside.

3. In the work bowl of a stand mixer fitted with the paddle attachment, combine the butter, egg whites, vanilla, and nutmeg on medium speed. The batter will look separated and broken. Reduce the speed to low, add the dry mixture, and beat until incorporated, scraping the sides of the bowl with a rubber spatula as needed.

4. Gradually add the heavy cream and milk until the mixture comes together as a smooth cake batter. Pour approximately ¼ cup of the batter into each cupcake liner.

5. Place in the oven and bake until the cupcakes are lightly golden brown and a cake tester comes out clean, 16 to 20 minutes.

6. Remove from the oven and place the cupcakes on a cooling rack.

7. To prepare the frosting, place the buttercream in the work bowl of a stand mixer fitted with a paddle attachment and add the nutmeg. Beat on medium speed until combined. Spoon the frosting into a piping bag, frost the cupcakes, and top each one with a little more nutmeg.

INGREDIENTS:

FOR THE CUPCAKES

11.4	OZ. ALL-PURPOSE FLOUR
9.5	OZ. SUGAR
1¾	TEASPOONS BAKING POWDER
½	TEASPOON KOSHER SALT
8	OZ. UNSALTED BUTTER, SOFTENED
4	EGG WHITES
½	TEASPOON PURE VANILLA EXTRACT
2¾	TEASPOONS FRESHLY GRATED NUTMEG
1	CUP HEAVY CREAM
⅓	CUP MILK

FOR THE FROSTING

AMERICAN BUTTERCREAM (SEE PAGE 72)

| 1 | TABLESPOON FRESHLY GRATED NUTMEG, PLUS MORE FOR GARNISH |

RASPBERRY CHIFFON CAKE

YIELD: 1 CAKE / **ACTIVE TIME:** 30 MINUTES / **TOTAL TIME:** 2 HOURS AND 30 MINUTES

A light and rich cake that is a cross between a moist, buttery treat and an airy, fluffy sponge cake.

1. Preheat the oven to 325°F. Place a 10-inch tube pan with a removable bottom near your workspace. Do not grease the pan.

2. Sift the cake flour, 6 oz. of the sugar, salt, and baking powder into a small bowl. Set aside.

3. In a medium bowl, whisk together the canola oil, eggs, pureed raspberries, and vanilla. Add the dry mixture and whisk until thoroughly incorporated.

4. In the work bowl of a stand mixer fitted with the whisk attachment, whip the egg whites and cream of tartar on high until soft peaks begin to form. Decrease the speed to low and add the remaining sugar a few tablespoons at a time. When all of the sugar has been incorporated, raise the speed back to high and whip until the mixture holds stiff peaks.

5. Remove the work bowl from the mixer and gently fold half of the meringue into the cake batter base. Add the remaining meringue and fold the mixture until no white streaks remain. Pour the batter into the tube pan, place it in the oven, and bake until the cake is lightly golden brown and a cake tester comes out clean, about 1 hour.

6. Remove the cake from the oven and let it cool completely.

7. Run a long metal spatula around the inside of the tube pan and center. Turn the cake out onto a serving platter, dust the top with confectioners' sugar, and serve with the Chantilly Cream and fresh raspberries.

INGREDIENTS:

6	OZ. CAKE FLOUR
10	OZ. SUGAR
½	TEASPOON KOSHER SALT
1½	TEASPOONS BAKING POWDER
¼	CUP CANOLA OIL
2	EGGS
¾	CUP PUREED RASPBERRIES
1½	TEASPOONS PURE VANILLA EXTRACT
6	EGG WHITES
¼	TEASPOON CREAM OF TARTAR
	CONFECTIONERS' SUGAR, FOR DUSTING
	CHANTILLY CREAM (SEE PAGE 89), FOR SERVING
	FRESH RASPBERRIES, FOR SERVING

OLIVE OIL CAKE

YIELD: 1 CAKE / ACTIVE TIME: 30 MINUTES / TOTAL TIME: 1 HOUR

The olive oil will keep this cake moist for an alarming amount of time, making this a good option for the summer, when people are less likely to keep to a set schedule.

1. Preheat the oven to 325°F. Coat a round 9-inch cake pan with nonstick cooking spray.

2. Place the lemon juice and ½ cup sugar in a small saucepan and bring the mixture to a boil, stirring to dissolve the sugar. Remove from heat and let cool.

3. Sift the flour, baking soda, and baking powder into a small bowl and set the mixture aside.

4. In a medium bowl, whisk the lemon zest, remaining sugar, salt, yogurt, olive oil, and eggs until the mixture smooth and combined. Add the dry mixture and whisk until a smooth batter forms.

5. Pour the batter into the prepared cake pan, place it in the oven, and bake until the cake is lightly golden brown and a cake tester comes out clean, 45 minutes to 1 hour.

6. Remove the cake from the oven, transfer to a cooling rack, and gently pour the lemon syrup over the hot cake. Let the cake cool completely.

7. Carefully remove the cake from the pan, transfer to a serving plate, dust with confectioners' sugar, and serve.

INGREDIENTS:

ZEST AND JUICE OF 3 LEMONS

½ CUP SUGAR, PLUS 7 OZ.

7 OZ. ALL-PURPOSE FLOUR

1 TEASPOON BAKING SODA

1 TEASPOON BAKING POWDER

½ TEASPOON KOSHER SALT

¾ CUP FULL-FAT PLAIN YOGURT

¾ CUP EXTRA-VIRGIN OLIVE OIL

3 EGGS

CONFECTIONERS' SUGAR, FOR DUSTING

AUTUMN SPICE CAKE

YIELD: 1 CAKE / **ACTIVE TIME:** 1 HOUR / **TOTAL TIME:** 3 HOURS AND 30 MINUTES

F all spices have started to be categorized as "basic." But when done right, they produce results as magical as the season.

1. Preheat the oven to 350°F. Line three round, 8-inch cake pans with parchment paper and coat them with nonstick cooking spray.

2. To begin preparations for the cakes, sift the flour, baking soda, baking powder, cinnamon, cloves, nutmeg, ginger, and salt into a mixing bowl. Set aside.

3. In the work bowl of a stand mixer fitted with the whisk attachment, beat the eggs, sugar, brown sugar, pumpkin puree, canola oil, and vanilla on medium until combined. Add the buttermilk and melted butter and beat until incorporated.

4. Reduce the speed to low, add the dry mixture, and whisk until a smooth batter forms. Pour 1½ cups of batter into each cake pan. Bang the pans on the counter to evenly distribute the batter and to remove any air bubbles.

5. Place the cakes in the oven and bake until lightly golden brown and a cake tester comes out clean, 35 to 45 minutes. Remove from the oven, transfer the cakes to a cooling rack, and let them cool completely.

6. To prepare the frosting, combine the butterfluff and maple extract in a mixing bowl. In a separate bowl, whisk the cinnamon and the buttercream together. Set both aside.

7. Trim a thin layer off the top of each cake to create a flat surface. Place 2 cups of the cinnamon buttercream in a piping bag and cut a ½-inch slit in it. Place one cake on a cake stand and pipe one ring of cream around the edge. Place 1 cup of the maple butterfluff in the center and level it with an offset spatula. Place the second cake on top and repeat the process with the cinnamon buttercream and maple butterfluff. Place the last cake on top and spread 1½ cups of the cinnamon buttercream over the entire cake. Dust the top of the cake with additional cinnamon and refrigerate for 1 hour before slicing and serving.

INGREDIENTS:

FOR THE CAKE

14	OZ. ALL-PURPOSE FLOUR
2	TEASPOONS BAKING SODA
1	TABLESPOON BAKING POWDER
2	TEASPOONS CINNAMON
2	TEASPOONS GROUND CLOVES
2	TEASPOONS FRESHLY GRATED NUTMEG
1	TEASPOON GROUND GINGER
1	TEASPOON KOSHER SALT
8	EGGS
12	OZ. SUGAR
3	OZ. LIGHT BROWN SUGAR
12	OZ. PUMPKIN PUREE
1	CUP CANOLA OIL
2	TEASPOONS PURE VANILLA EXTRACT
4	OZ. BUTTERMILK
12	OZ. UNSALTED BUTTER, MELTED

FOR THE FROSTING

	BUTTERFLUFF FILLING (SEE PAGE 86)
1	TABLESPOON MAPLE EXTRACT
2	TABLESPOONS CINNAMON, PLUS MORE FOR DUSTING
	ITALIAN BUTTERCREAM (SEE PAGE 75)

CHOCOLATE CAKE ROLL

YIELD: 10 TO 12 SERVINGS / **ACTIVE TIME:** 45 MINUTES / **TOTAL TIME:** 3 HOURS

Rolling up a light chocolate sponge cake with a sweet, airy filling and drizzling ganache over the top ushers this childhood favorite into maturity.

1. Preheat the oven to 350°F. Line an 18 x 13–inch baking sheet with parchment paper and coat it with nonstick cooking spray.

2. Sift the flour, cocoa powder, 7 oz. of the sugar, salt, and the baking powder into a small bowl. Set aside.

3. In a medium bowl, whisk the canola oil, eggs, and water until combined. Add the dry mixture and whisk until combined.

4. In the work bowl of a stand mixer fitted with the whisk attachment, whip the egg whites and cream of tartar on high until soft peaks begin to form. Reduce the speed to low and add the remaining sugar a few tablespoons at a time. When all of the sugar has been incorporated, raise the speed back to high and whip until the mixture holds stiff peaks.

5. Remove the work bowl from the mixer. Gently fold half of the meringue into the cake batter. Add the remaining meringue and fold until no white streaks remain. Spread the cake batter over the baking sheet, place it in the oven, and bake until the center of the cake springs back when poked with a finger and a cake tester comes out clean, 10 to 12 minutes. Remove the cake from the oven and immediately dust the top with cocoa powder. Turn the sponge cake onto a fresh piece of parchment paper. Peel the parchment away from the bottom side of the cake. Place a fresh piece of parchment on the bottom of the cake and turn it over so that the dusted side of the cake is facing up.

6. Using a rolling pin, gently roll the cake up into a tight roll, starting with the narrow end. Let the cake cool to room temperature while coiled around the rolling pin.

7. Gently unroll the cake and spread the filling evenly over the top, leaving an approximately ½-inch border around the edges. Carefully roll the cake back up with your hands (do not use the rolling pin). Place the cake roll on a cooling rack that has parchment paper beneath it.

8. Pour the ganache over the cake roll. Refrigerate for at least 1 hour to let the chocolate set before slicing and serving.

INGREDIENTS:

7.5	OZ. ALL-PURPOSE FLOUR
1.8	OZ. COCOA POWDER, PLUS MORE AS NEEDED
12	OZ. SUGAR
1½	TEASPOONS KOSHER SALT
¾	TEASPOON BAKING POWDER
5	OZ. CANOLA OIL
5	EGGS
5	OZ. WATER
7	EGG WHITES
½	TEASPOON CREAM OF TARTAR
	BUTTERFLUFF FILLING (SEE PAGE 86)
	CHOCOLATE GANACHE (SEE PAGE 99), WARM

BROWN BUTTER CAKE

YIELD: 1 CAKE / **ACTIVE TIME:** 1 HOUR / **TOTAL TIME:** 3 HOURS AND 30 MINUTES

Browning butter caramelizes the milk solids in butterfat, giving it a unique, nutty taste that is wonderful in a number of desserts. If you like this cake, don't hesitate to experiment with brown butter in your favorite confections.

1. Preheat the oven to 350°F. Line three, round 8-inch cake pans with parchment paper and coat them with nonstick cooking spray.

2. Sift the flour, baking powder, and salt into a medium bowl and set aside.

3. In the work bowl of a stand mixer fitted with the paddle attachment, cream the brown butter and sugar on high until the mixture is smooth and creamy, about 5 minutes.

4. Incorporate the eggs two at a time, scraping down the sides of the work bowl with a rubber spatula in between each addition. Reduce the speed to low, add the dry mixture, and beat until combined.

5. Pour 1½ cups of batter into each cake pan. Bang the pans on the countertop to evenly distribute the batter and remove any air bubbles.

6. Place the cakes in the oven and bake until they are lightly golden brown, 35 to 40 minutes. Remove from the oven, transfer to a cooling rack, and let the cakes cool completely.

7. While the cakes cool, place the buttercream and 1 cup of the caramel in the work bowl of a stand mixer fitted with the paddle attachment and beat on medium speed until combined. Set aside.

8. Trim a thin layer off the top of each cake to create a flat surface. Place one cake on a cake stand and pipe one ring of cream around the edge. Place 1 cup of the frosting in the center and level it with an offset spatula. Place the second cake on top and repeat the process with the frosting. Place the last cake on top and spread 1½ cups of the frosting over the entire cake using an offset spatula.

9. Gently spoon some of the remaining caramel over the edge of the cake and let it drip down the side. Spread ½ cup of the caramel over the top of the cake.

10. Place the cake in the refrigerator for 1 hour before slicing and serving.

INGREDIENTS:

18	OZ. ALL-PURPOSE FLOUR
1	TABLESPOON BAKING POWDER
2	TEASPOONS KOSHER SALT
1	LB. BROWN BUTTER (SEE RECIPE)
1	LB. SUGAR
8	EGGS
	AMERICAN BUTTERCREAM (SEE PAGE 72)
	CARAMEL SAUCE (SEE PAGE 103)

BROWN BUTTER

1. Place the butter in a large saucepan and melt it over medium heat, stirring frequently, until the butter gives off a nutty smell and turns golden brown (let your nose lead the way here, frequently wafting the steam toward you).

2. Remove the pan from heat and strain the butter through a fine sieve. Let the butter cool and solidify before using it in this preparation.

INGREDIENTS:

1.5   LBS. UNSALTED BUTTER

PIES, TARTS & GALETTES

"Anytime is a good time for pie."

When Maria de Medeiros's Fabienne offered this response after Bruce Willis's Butch questioned her choice of blueberry pie for breakfast in the 1994 film *Pulp Fiction*, it was easy to imagine millions nodding along.

Simply put, pie, though frequently grouped behind other beloved treats like cake, cookies, and ice cream, has the most fervent devotees in the dessert game. As far as these folks are concerned, nothing else will do when the time comes for a treat. Dubious? Consider, for a minute, the apple pie's place as a stand-in for what is good about the American way of life—clearly, pie has transcended to a level few foods ever reach.

Cherry, blueberry, and strawberry rhubarb in the summer. Pumpkin during the holidays. Chocolate or banana cream at the diner after a late-night meal with a loved one. The presence of pie signals that something special is happening, and the warm memories we hold of our encounters with our favorites indicate that this communication comes through loud and clear.

Pie's humbler, but no less delicious, cousins, tarts and galettes, can also be found in this chapter.

APPLE PIE

YIELD: 1 PIE / **ACTIVE TIME:** 30 MINUTES / **TOTAL TIME:** 1 HOUR AND 45 MINUTES

The combination of Granny Smith and Honeycrisp provides the most balanced flavor. However, those who have access to the Northern Spy, which prefers cooler climes, should give it a try, as a strong contingent identifies it as the very best option.

1. Preheat the oven to 375°F. Coat a 9-inch pie pan with nonstick cooking spray and place one of the crusts in it.

2. Place the apples, sugar, brown sugar, cornstarch, cinnamon, nutmeg, cardamom, lemon juice, lemon zest, and salt in a mixing bowl and toss until the apples are evenly coated.

3. Fill the crust with the apple filling, lay the other crust over the top, and crimp the edge to seal. Brush the top crust with the egg and sprinkle the coarse sugar over it. Cut several slits in the top crust.

4. Place the pie in the oven and bake until the filling is bubbly and has thickened, about 50 minutes. Remove from the oven and let the pie cool completely before serving.

INGREDIENTS:

2	PERFECT PIECRUSTS (SEE PAGE 46), ROLLED OUT
3	HONEYCRISP APPLES, PEELED, CORED, AND SLICED
3	GRANNY SMITH APPLES, PEELED, CORED, AND SLICED
½	CUP SUGAR
¼	CUP LIGHT BROWN SUGAR
1½	TABLESPOONS CORNSTARCH
1	TEASPOON CINNAMON
½	TEASPOON FRESHLY GRATED NUTMEG
¼	TEASPOON CARDAMOM
	ZEST AND JUICE OF 1 LEMON
¼	TEASPOON KOSHER SALT
1	EGG, BEATEN
	COARSE SUGAR, FOR TOPPING

BLUEBERRY PIE

YIELD: 1 PIE / **ACTIVE TIME:** 30 MINUTES / **TOTAL TIME:** 1 HOUR AND 30 MINUTES

The rare dessert that has been honored with its own day, as April 28 is National Blueberry Pie Day in the United States of America. Interestingly, this is far too early for those who live in Maine—where blueberry pie is the official state dessert—to enjoy a slice made with fresh berries, as blueberry season in the New England state typically runs from July to September.

1. Preheat the oven to 350°F. Place the blueberries, sugar, cornstarch, nutmeg, lemon juice, lemon zest, and salt in a large mixing bowl and stir to combine.

2. Place one of the crusts in a greased 9-inch pie plate and fill it with the blueberry mixture. Place the other crust over the mixture and crimp the edge to seal.

3. Brush the top crust with the egg white and then sprinkle sugar over it. Cut 4 or 5 slits in the middle, place the pie in the oven, and bake until the top crust is golden brown and the filling is bubbling, about 40 minutes.

4. Remove the pie from the oven and let it cool before serving.

INGREDIENTS:

6 CUPS FRESH BLUEBERRIES

1 CUP SUGAR, PLUS MORE TO TASTE

2 TABLESPOONS CORNSTARCH

½ TEASPOON FRESHLY GRATED NUTMEG

1 TABLESPOON FRESH LEMON JUICE

1 TEASPOON LEMON ZEST

¼ TEASPOON FINE SEA SALT

2 PERFECT PIECRUSTS (SEE PAGE 46), ROLLED OUT

1 EGG WHITE

LEMON MERINGUE PIE

YIELD: 1 PIE / **ACTIVE TIME:** 30 MINUTES / **TOTAL TIME:** 1 HOUR AND 30 MINUTES

In the early days of the American experiment, Elizabeth Goodfellow opened a pastry shop and a cooking school in Philadelphia, the latter of which was one of the country's first. While Elizabeth never published her own recipes, her students (Eliza Leslie, a popular cookbook author of the early 19th century, was counted among Goodfellow's flock) served as the Plato to Goodfellow's Socrates. While handing down her recipes and knowledge to the public, they couldn't help but convey her propensity for covering lemon custard pie with meringue. Unknown before the 19th century, in part because lemons were rare outside of the large cities, Goodfellow's pie took the burgeoning nation by storm and quickly became one of its classic desserts.

1. Place the cornstarch, flour, sugar, and salt in a saucepan and stir until well combined. Add the water in a slow stream and stir until incorporated. Cook the mixture over medium heat, stirring occasionally, until it is thick, about 20 minutes. Remove from heat.

2. While whisking constantly, add ¼ cup of the mixture in the saucepan into the beaten egg yolks. Stir the tempered eggs into the saucepan and place it over medium-low heat.

3. Add the lemon juice, lemon zest, and butter and stir constantly until the mixture is thick enough to coat the back of a wooden spoon. Remove the mixture from heat and let it cool completely. Preheat the oven to 400°F.

4. Add the cooled filling to the baked piecrust and use a rubber spatula to smooth the top.

5. Spread the meringue over the filling and use a large spoon or a spatula to create swirled peaks. Place in the oven and bake until peaks of meringue are light brown, about 6 minutes. Remove from the oven and let the pie cool completely before serving.

INGREDIENTS:

¼   CUP CORNSTARCH

¼   CUP ALL-PURPOSE FLOUR

1¾   CUPS SUGAR

¼   TEASPOON FINE SEA SALT

2   CUPS WATER

4   EGG YOLKS, LIGHTLY BEATEN

½   CUP FRESH LEMON JUICE

1½   TABLESPOONS LEMON ZEST

1   OZ. UNSALTED BUTTER

1   PERFECT PIECRUST (SEE PAGE 46), BLIND BAKED

    SWISS MERINGUE (SEE PAGE 70)

BANANA CREAM PIE

YIELD: 1 PIE / **ACTIVE TIME:** 30 MINUTES / **TOTAL TIME:** 2 HOURS AND 30 MINUTES

Rich and silky, decadent and irresistibly beautiful, this may be the optimal use of the banana.

1. Place the bananas, milk, heavy cream, and vanilla in a blender and puree until smooth.

2. Place the puree in a medium saucepan and bring to a boil over medium heat. Remove the pan from heat once it comes to a boil.

3. While the puree is coming to a boil, place the sugar, salt, cornstarch, and egg whites in a small bowl and whisk for 2 minutes.

4. While whisking constantly, incorporate small amounts of the puree into the egg white mixture. When half of the puree has been incorporated, add the tempered mixture to the saucepan and place it over medium heat. While whisking continually, cook until the mixture thickens and begins to bubble. Remove the pan from heat, add the butter, and whisk until incorporated.

5. Strain the custard through a fine mesh strainer and into a small bowl. Pour the strained custard into the crust and place plastic wrap directly onto the custard to prevent a skin from forming. Place the pie in the refrigerator for 2 hours.

6. Spread the Chantilly Cream over the filling, slice the pie, and enjoy.

INGREDIENTS:

2	BANANAS, PEELED AND SLICED
1½	CUPS MILK
1	CUP HEAVY CREAM
¾	TEASPOON PURE VANILLA EXTRACT
4	OZ. SUGAR
½	TEASPOON KOSHER SALT
¼	CUP CORNSTARCH
4	EGG WHITES
1	OZ. UNSALTED BUTTER, SOFTENED
1	GRAHAM CRACKER CRUST (SEE PAGE 50)
	CHANTILLY CREAM (SEE PAGE 89)
	DARK CHOCOLATE (55 TO 65 PERCENT), SHAVED, FOR TOPPING

CHERRY PIE

YIELD: 1 PIE / **ACTIVE TIME:** 30 MINUTES / **TOTAL TIME:** 1 HOUR AND 45 MINUTES

This pie is all about the Stradivarius of the cherry clan, the Rainier, which occasionally goes for $1 a piece in the fresh markets in Japan.

1. Preheat oven to 350°F. Place the cherries, sugar, and lemon juice in a saucepan and cook, stirring occasionally, over medium heat until the mixture is syrupy.

2. Combine the cornstarch and water in a small bowl and then stir this mixture into the saucepan. Reduce the heat to low and cook, while stirring, until the mixture is thick and syrupy. Remove from heat, stir in the almond extract, and let the filling cool.

3. When the cherry mixture has cooled, place the bottom crust in a greased 9-inch pie plate and pour the filling into the crust. Top with the other crust, make a few slits in the top, and brush the top crust with the beaten egg.

4. Place the pie in the oven and bake until the top crust is golden brown and the filling is bubbly, about 45 minutes. Remove and let cool before serving.

INGREDIENTS:

4	CUPS RAINIER CHERRIES, PITTED
2	CUPS SUGAR
2	TABLESPOONS FRESH LEMON JUICE
3	TABLESPOONS CORNSTARCH
1	TABLESPOON WATER
¼	TEASPOON ALMOND EXTRACT
2	PERFECT PIECRUSTS (SEE PAGE 46), ROLLED OUT
1	EGG, BEATEN

WHOOPIE PIES

YIELD: 6 WHOOPIE PIES / **ACTIVE TIME:** 15 MINUTES / **TOTAL TIME:** 1 HOUR

This has been categorized as a cookie, cake, sandwich, and pie. Pennsylvania, Maine, Massachusetts, Virginia, and New Hampshire have proclaimed themselves the birthplace of this treat. In the interest of avoiding controversy, we'll simply say this: it is uniquely delicious, and deserving of its growing following.

1. Preheat the oven to 350°F and line two baking sheets with parchment paper.

2. Place the flour, cocoa powder, baking soda, and salt in a bowl and whisk to combine.

3. In the work bowl of a stand mixer fitted with the paddle attachment, cream the butter and brown sugar on medium speed until the mixture is light and fluffy, about 10 minutes. Add the egg, beat until incorporated, and then add the remaining vanilla. Gradually add the dry mixture and the buttermilk, alternating between them. Beat until incorporated and then scoop the batter onto parchment-lined baking sheets, making sure to leave plenty of room between the scoops.

4. Place the baking sheets in the oven and bake, while rotating and switching their positions halfway through, for 15 minutes. The cakes should feel springy to the touch when done. Remove from the oven and let them cool on the baking sheets.

5. Place the filling in the center of one cake, top with another cake, and press down to spread the filling to the edges. Repeat with the remaining filling and cakes and then serve.

INGREDIENTS:

10 OZ. ALL-PURPOSE FLOUR

1.5 OZ. COCOA POWDER

1 TEASPOON BAKING SODA

PINCH OF FINE SEA SALT

4 OZ. UNSALTED BUTTER

7 OZ. LIGHT BROWN SUGAR

1 LARGE EGG, AT ROOM TEMPERATURE

1 TEASPOON PURE VANILLA EXTRACT

1 CUP BUTTERMILK

BUTTERFLUFF FILLING (SEE PAGE 86)

LEMONY RICE PUDDING PIE

YIELD: 1 PIE / **ACTIVE TIME:** 20 MINUTES / **TOTAL TIME:** 2 HOURS AND 30 MINUTES

Leftover rice? Lemons that are overripe? Both are tremendous invitations for you to go ahead and make this pie.

1. Place the Lemon Curd and milk in a large mixing bowl and whisk to combine. Add the vanilla and cooked rice and fold to combine.

2. Evenly distribute the filling in the piecrust, smoothing the top with a rubber spatula. Cover the pie with plastic wrap and place in the refrigerator for 2 hours.

3. Preheat the oven's broiler to high. Remove the pie from the refrigerator and place it underneath the broiler. Broil until the top starts to brown, about 5 minutes. Remove and top each slice with Chantilly Cream and, if desired, cinnamon.

INGREDIENTS:

3   CUPS LEMON CURD (SEE PAGE 476)

2   CUPS WHOLE MILK

1   TEASPOON PURE VANILLA EXTRACT

1½ CUPS COOKED, LEFTOVER RICE

1   GRAHAM CRACKER CRUST (SEE PAGE 50)

CHANTILLY CREAM (SEE PAGE 89), FOR SERVING

CINNAMON, FOR DUSTING (OPTIONAL)

BLUE CHEESE & WALNUT TART
WITH PEARS AND HONEY

YIELD: 1 TART / **ACTIVE TIME:** 15 MINUTES / **TOTAL TIME:** 45 MINUTES

Gorgonzola is a lovely option for the blue cheese here, as it partners well with the walnuts, honey, and creamy pears.

1. Preheat the oven to 450°F. Roll the dough out to approximately ¼ inch thick and form it into the desired shape. Place it on a parchment-lined baking sheet and place it in the oven until it starts to turn golden brown, 10 to 15 minutes. Remove from the oven and let cool.

2. Sprinkle the thyme, blue cheese, and walnuts evenly over the dough. Distribute the pear slices over the tart, place it in the oven, and cook until the crust is crispy and the cheese is melted, about 10 to 15 minutes.

3. Remove from the oven, let cool for 5 minutes, and drizzle the honey over the tart. Slice and serve immediately.

INGREDIENTS:

1 BALL OF PÂTE SUCRÉE DOUGH (SEE PAGE 49)

1 TABLESPOON FRESH THYME, CHOPPED

1 CUP CRUMBLED BLUE CHEESE

1 HANDFUL OF WALNUTS

1 PEAR, CORED AND SLICED THIN

   HONEY, TO TASTE

NUTTY CARAMEL & CRANBERRY PIE

YIELD: 1 PIE / **ACTIVE TIME:** 45 MINUTES / **TOTAL TIME:** 3 HOURS

With a bedeviling texture, considerable lusciousness, and a complex play of flavors, this simple pie is far more than the sum of its parts.

1. Preheat the oven to 375°F. Coat a 9-inch pie pan with nonstick cooking spray and place the piecrust in it.

2. Place the almonds and cashews on a parchment-lined baking sheet, place them in the oven, and toast until they are fragrant and starting to brown, 8 to 10 minutes. Remove from the oven and let them cool. Leave the oven on.

3. In a medium saucepan, bring the sugar and water to a boil over high heat. Cook, swirling the pan occasionally, until the mixture is a deep amber color. Remove the pan from heat.

4. While continually whisking, gradually add the cream to the caramel, taking care as the mixture may splatter. Whisk in the butter, vanilla, and salt and let the caramel cool.

5. Place the toasted nuts and cranberries in a mixing bowl and toss to combine. Place the mixture in the piecrust and pour the caramel over it until the crust is filled. Save any remaining caramel for another preparation.

6. Place the pie in the oven and bake until the filling is set at the edge and the center barely jiggles when you shake the pie plate, about 1 hour. Remove from the oven and let the pie cool completely before slicing and serving.

INGREDIENTS:

1	PERFECT PIECRUST (SEE PAGE 46), ROLLED OUT
1⅓	CUPS SUGAR
½	CUP WATER
6	TABLESPOONS BUTTER
1	TEASPOON PURE VANILLA EXTRACT
¼	TEASPOON KOSHER SALT
1	CUP SLIVERED ALMONDS
1	CUP CASHEWS, CHOPPED
1½	CUPS FRESH CRANBERRIES

RASPBERRY CREAM PIE

YIELD: 1 PIE / **ACTIVE TIME:** 15 MINUTES / **TOTAL TIME:** 4 HOURS AND 30 MINUTES

The contrast of sweet and tart that makes raspberries beloved has never been presented in a more luscious package.

1. Place the cream cheese in the work bowl of a stand mixer fitted with the paddle attachment and beat until smooth and creamy.

2. Add the condensed milk and beat the mixture until it is smooth and thick, about 5 minutes. Remove the bowl from the stand mixer, add the Chantilly Cream, vanilla, and raspberries and fold to incorporate.

3. Spoon the filling into the crust and use a rubber spatula to even out the top. Cover with plastic wrap and freeze until set, about 4 hours.

4. To serve, remove the pie from the freezer and let it sit at room temperature for 10 minutes before slicing.

INGREDIENTS:

8   OZ. CREAM CHEESE, SOFTENED

1⅔   CUPS SWEETENED CONDENSED MILK

1½   CUPS CHANTILLY CREAM (SEE PAGE 89)

1   TEASPOON PURE VANILLA EXTRACT

1⅓   CUPS RASPBERRIES

1   COOKIE CRUST (SEE PAGE 53)

GRASSHOPPER PIE

YIELD: 1 PIE / **ACTIVE TIME:** 20 MINUTES / **TOTAL TIME:** 4 HOURS AND 45 MINUTES

The great New Orleans cocktail lends its lovely flavor and eye-catching color to this confection.

1. Place the milk and the marshmallows in a large saucepan and cook over low heat, stirring frequently, until the marshmallows have melted. Place the pan in the refrigerator and chill for 20 minutes, stirring occasionally.

2. Stir the crème de menthe and the crème de cacao into the mixture. Fold the marshmallow mixture into the Chantilly Cream and then stir in the green food coloring.

3. Place the filling in the crust and smooth the top with a rubber spatula. Refrigerate for 4 hours before serving.

INGREDIENTS:

½ CUP WHOLE MILK

32 LARGE MARSHMALLOWS

¼ CUP GREEN CRÈME DE MENTHE

¼ CUP WHITE CRÈME DE CACAO

1½ CUPS CHANTILLY CREAM (SEE PAGE 89)

1-2 DROPS OF GREEN GEL FOOD COLORING

1 COOKIE CRUST (SEE PAGE 53)

VANILLA & COCONUT CREAM PIE

YIELD: 1 PIE / **ACTIVE TIME:** 30 MINUTES / **TOTAL TIME:** 24 HOURS

I f you don't have any piecrusts in the freezer and are also without the patience to whip a couple up, simply turn this filling into a pudding.

1. Preheat the oven to 350°F. Place the coconut in a dry skillet and toast it, stirring frequently, over medium heat until fragrant and golden brown, about 2 to 3 minutes. Transfer to a bowl and set aside.

2. Place the sugar, cornstarch, and salt in a saucepan and stir to combine. Whisk in the milk and cream and cook the mixture over medium heat until it has thickened and started to bubble, about 2 to 3 minutes. Remove from heat and set aside.

3. Place the eggs in a heatproof bowl and whisk until scrambled. Gradually whisk in about 1 cup of the hot milk mixture and then pour the tempered eggs into the pan. Cook, stirring constantly, over medium heat until the mixture is just about to come to a boil. Reduce the heat to low and continue stirring the mixture as it cooks for another 2 minutes.

4. Remove the pan from heat and whisk in the butter, vanilla, and toasted coconut.

5. Pour the mixture into the piecrust, place it in the oven, and bake until it is set and golden brown on top, 25 to 30 minutes. Remove from the oven and transfer to a wire rack to cool completely. Cover with plastic wrap and refrigerate overnight before topping with the Chantilly Cream and serving.

INGREDIENTS:

1	CUP SWEETENED SHREDDED COCONUT
¾	CUP SUGAR
3	TABLESPOONS CORNSTARCH
¼	TEASPOON KOSHER SALT
2½	CUPS WHOLE MILK
½	CUP HEAVY CREAM
3	LARGE EGGS
1	TABLESPOON UNSALTED BUTTER
1	TABLESPOON PURE VANILLA EXTRACT
1	PERFECT PIECRUST (SEE PAGE 46), BLIND BAKED
	CHANTILLY CREAM (SEE PAGE 89)

CARAMELIZED PEACH CUSTARD PIE

YIELD: 1 PIE / **ACTIVE TIME:** 25 MINUTES / **TOTAL TIME:** 2 HOURS

The texture and sweetness of peaches make them a natural to be flambéed.

1. Place the butter in a skillet and melt it over medium heat. Add the peaches to the melted butter and cook, turning the slices occasionally, until they are brown all over.

2. Sprinkle 3 tablespoons of the sugar and all of the cinnamon over the peaches and shake the pan until they are evenly coated. Cook until the peaches start to caramelize, about 8 minutes.

3. Remove the pan from heat, tilt it away from you, add the brandy, and use a long match or wand lighter to ignite it. Place the pan back on the burner and shake it until the flames are extinguished and the alcohol cooks off. Pour the mixture into a heatproof mixing bowl and let cool.

4. Preheat the oven to 300°F. When the flambéed peaches are close to cool, place the milk, heavy cream, eggs, egg yolk, remaining sugar, vanilla, and salt in a mixing bowl and whisk to combine.

5. Evenly distribute the flambéed peaches in the piecrust and then strain the egg mixture over the top. Place the pie in the oven and bake until the filling is just set, 20 to 25 minutes. Remove from the oven and let cool before serving.

INGREDIENTS:

1	OZ. UNSALTED BUTTER
2	LARGE PEACHES, PITTED AND SLICED
7	TABLESPOONS SUGAR
¼	TEASPOON CINNAMON
2	TABLESPOONS BRANDY
½	CUP WHOLE MILK
½	CUP HEAVY CREAM
2	EGGS
1	EGG YOLK
½	TEASPOON PURE VANILLA EXTRACT
¼	TEASPOON KOSHER SALT
1	PERFECT PIECRUST (SEE PAGE 46), BLIND BAKED

PEAR & FRANGIPANE TART

YIELD: 1 TART / **ACTIVE TIME:** 30 MINUTES / **TOTAL TIME:** 2 HOURS AND 15 MINUTES

A classic French pastry that features ingenuously spiced poached pears and a lush almond cream.

1. Preheat the oven to 375°F. In a medium saucepan, combine the water, sugar, cinnamon sticks, star anise, vanilla, lemon juice, and lemon zest and bring the mixture to a simmer over medium heat.

2. Peel the pears and slice them in half lengthwise. Core the pears and gently lay them in the simmering poaching liquid. Let them simmer until tender, about 15 minutes. Transfer the poached pears to a paper towel–lined plate and let them cool to room temperature. When the pears are cool enough to handle, slice them into ⅛-inch-wide strips. Set the pears aside.

3. Spread the Frangipane evenly over the bottom of the tart shell and arrange the pears over it, making sure the thinnest parts are pointing toward the center. Place the tart in the oven and bake until the Frangipane has risen up around the pears and is golden brown. Remove from the oven and let the tart cool for 1 hour before dusting with confectioners' sugar and slicing.

INGREDIENTS:

6 CUPS WATER

2 CUPS SUGAR

2 CINNAMON STICKS

1 STAR ANISE POD

1 TABLESPOON PURE VANILLA EXTRACT

ZEST AND JUICE OF 1 LEMON

3 ANJOU PEARS

2 CUPS FRANGIPANE (SEE PAGE 66)

1 PÂTÉ SUCRÉE (SEE PAGE 49), BLIND BAKED IN A TART PAN

CONFECTIONERS' SUGAR, FOR DUSTING

WHITE CHOCOLATE PIE

YIELD: 1 PIE / **ACTIVE TIME:** 15 MINUTES / **TOTAL TIME:** 1 HOUR AND 30 MINUTES

For decades the debate has raged: Is white chocolate actually chocolate? Who cares. This pie is too delicious to bother with such nitpicking.

1. Preheat the oven to 350°F. Fill a small saucepan halfway with water and bring it to a simmer. Place the white chocolate chips and butter in a large heatproof bowl, place it over the simmering water, and stir occasionally until the mixture is melted and combined. Remove from heat and aside.

2. In a mixing bowl, whisk together the eggs, cream, sugar, vanilla, and salt. While whisking constantly, gradually add white chocolate mixture. Pour the filling into the crust and gently tap the pie plate on the counter to evenly distribute.

3. Place the pie in the oven and bake until the filling is set around the edges but still soft in the center, 15 to 20 minutes. Remove from the oven and let cool completely before topping with the white chocolate shavings and strawberries.

INGREDIENTS:

12   OZ. WHITE CHOCOLATE CHIPS

4   OZ. UNSALTED BUTTER, CUT INTO SMALL PIECES

2   EGGS

1   CUP HEAVY CREAM

½   CUP SUGAR

1   TEASPOON PURE VANILLA EXTRACT

     PINCH OF FINE SEA SALT

1   PÂTE SUCRÉE (SEE PAGE 49), BLIND BAKED

     WHITE CHOCOLATE, SHAVED, FOR GARNISH

¼   CUP HULLED AND SLICED STRAWBERRIES, FOR GARNISH

SWEET POTATO PIE

YIELD: 1 PIE / **ACTIVE TIME:** 25 MINUTES / **TOTAL TIME:** 2 HOURS

When this pie is tended by a true master, there may not be a more delicious dessert. This recipe won't automatically make you an old hand, but it's going to deliver a result good enough that you just may decide to devote yourself to becoming one.

1. Preheat the oven to 400°F. Place the mashed sweet potato, evaporated milk, eggs, sugar, salt, cinnamon, ginger, and nutmeg in a bowl and stir until combined.

2. Place a 10-inch cast-iron skillet over medium heat and melt the butter in it. Add the brown sugar and cook, stirring constantly, until the sugar has melted. Remove the pan from heat.

3. Place the piecrust over the butter-and-brown sugar mixture in the skillet. Line the crust with aluminum foil and fill it with uncooked rice, dried beans, or pie weights. Place the skillet in the oven and bake for 15 minutes.

4. Remove the skillet from the oven, remove the weight and foil, and briefly let the crust cool.

5. Evenly distribute the sweet potato mixture in the crust. Place the pie in the oven and bake for 15 minutes.

6. Reduce the oven temperature to 325°F and bake until the filling is set and a cake tester inserted in its center comes out clean, about 30 minutes. Remove the skillet from the oven and let cool completely before serving.

INGREDIENTS:

- 2 CUPS MASHED ROASTED SWEET POTATO
- 1½ CUPS EVAPORATED MILK
- 2 EGGS, LIGHTLY BEATEN
- ½ CUP SUGAR
- ½ TEASPOON FINE SEA SALT
- 1 TEASPOON CINNAMON
- ¼ TEASPOON GROUND GINGER
- ¼ TEASPOON FRESHLY GRATED NUTMEG
- 4 OZ. UNSALTED BUTTER
- 1 CUP PACKED LIGHT BROWN SUGAR
- 1 PERFECT PIECRUST (SEE PAGE 46), ROLLED OUT

CRANBERRY CURD PIE

YIELD: 1 PIE / **ACTIVE TIME:** 35 MINUTES / **TOTAL TIME:** 24 HOURS

Astunning and inventive dessert that is worthy of a place on the dessert table around the holidays, right alongside the classics.

1. Place the cranberries and orange juice in a large saucepan and cook, stirring occasionally over medium heat until the cranberries soften and split, about 10 to 15 minutes.

2. Strain the mixture through a fine sieve into a clean saucepan. Add the sugar, eggs, egg yolks, butter, vanilla, and salt and stir to combine. Cook over low heat, stirring frequently, until the curd thickens, about 10 minutes. Strain the curd into a mixing bowl and let it cool slightly. Preheat the oven to 350°F.

3. Pour the curd into the crust, place the pie in the oven, and bake for 10 to 12 minutes, until the curd is just set. Remove from the oven, let cool completely on a wire rack, and refrigerate overnight before topping with the Chantilly Cream and serving.

INGREDIENTS:

3	CUPS CRANBERRIES
	JUICE OF 1 ORANGE
1¼	CUPS SUGAR
2	LARGE EGGS
2	LARGE EGG YOLKS
4	OZ. UNSALTED BUTTER, SOFTENED
1	TEASPOON PURE VANILLA EXTRACT
1	PERFECT PIECRUST (SEE PAGE 46), BLIND BAKED
	CHANTILLY CREAM (SEE PAGE 89)

BUTTERMILK PIE

YIELD: 1 PIE / **ACTIVE TIME:** 10 MINUTES / **TOTAL TIME:** 1 HOUR AND 30 MINUTES

Sometimes, buttermilk's creaminess and slightly tart taste are all one needs to ensure the day comes to a satisfying close.

1. Preheat the oven to 350°F. Place all of the ingredients, except for the piecrust, in the work bowl of a stand mixer fitted with the paddle attachment and beat on medium until the mixture is fluffy and thoroughly combined, about 3 to 4 minutes.

2. Pour the mixture into the piecrust, place the pie in the oven, and bake for about 45 minutes, until the filling is set and starting to brown. Remove from the oven and let cool slightly before serving.

INGREDIENTS:

3 LARGE EGGS

1 CUP WHITE SUGAR

¼ CUP HONEY

3 TABLESPOONS ALL-PURPOSE FLOUR

4 OZ. UNSALTED BUTTER, MELTED AND SLIGHTLY COOLED

1¼ CUPS BUTTERMILK

1 TEASPOON PURE VANILLA EXTRACT

1 TABLESPOON FRESH LEMON JUICE

1 TEASPOON LEMON ZEST

¼ TEASPOON KOSHER SALT

1 PERFECT PIECRUST (SEE PAGE 46), BLIND BAKED

APPLE PIE WITH QUARK

YIELD: 1 PIE / **ACTIVE TIME:** 20 MINUTES / **TOTAL TIME:** 1 HOUR AND 30 MINUTES

A soft, creamy cheese that is beloved in Eastern Europe, quark's unique flavor transforms an American classic.

1. Preheat the oven to 350°F, coat a 9-inch pie plate with nonstick cooking spray, and place the piecrust in it. Place the sugar, butter, eggs, quark, vanilla, lemon zest, and lemon juice in a food processor and puree until smooth, scraping the work bowl as needed.

2. Sift the flour, baking powder, and salt into a mixing bowl. Add the mixture to the food processor and pulse until incorporated. Evenly distribute the mixture in the crust and arrange the apples in the mixture.

3. Place the pie in the oven and bake until the filling is set and golden brown, about 40 minutes. Remove from the oven and let cool before serving. To serve, sprinkle the almonds and confectioners' sugar on top.

INGREDIENTS:

1	PERFECT PIECRUST (SEE PAGE 46), ROLLED OUT
½	CUP SUGAR
4	OZ. UNSALTED BUTTER, SOFTENED
3	LARGE EGGS, LIGHTLY BEATEN
2	CUPS QUARK CHEESE
1	TEASPOON PURE VANILLA EXTRACT
1	TEASPOON LEMON ZEST
1	TEASPOON FRESH LEMON JUICE
½	CUP ALL-PURPOSE FLOUR
1	TEASPOON BAKING POWDER
¼	TEASPOON KOSHER SALT
3	LARGE BRAEBURN APPLES, PEELED, CORED, AND SLICED
⅓	CUP SLIVERED ALMONDS
2	TABLESPOONS CONFECTIONERS' SUGAR

RASPBERRY PIE

YIELD: 1 PIE / **ACTIVE TIME:** 15 MINUTES / **TOTAL TIME:** 1 HOUR AND 30 MINUTES

A good opportunity to fashion a lattice crust, as the sight of deep red filling will entice everyone to finish what's on their plate and get to the good stuff.

1. Preheat the oven to 350°F. Coat a 9-inch pie plate with nonstick cooking spray and place one of the crusts in it.

2. Place the raspberries, sugar, flour, lemon juice, and salt in a mixing bowl and stir until well combined. Evenly distribute this mixture in the crust in the pie plate.

3. Place the top crust over the filling, trim any excess, and crimp the edge to seal. Brush the top crust with the egg, make four to five slits in it, and sprinkle additional sugar on top.

4. Place the pie in the oven and bake until golden brown, about 45 minutes. Remove from the oven and let cool before serving.

INGREDIENTS:

2   PERFECT PIECRUSTS (SEE PAGE 46), ROLLED OUT

7   CUPS FRESH RASPBERRIES

2   CUPS SUGAR, PLUS MORE TO TASTE

⅔   CUP ALL-PURPOSE FLOUR

2   TABLESPOONS FRESH LEMON JUICE

    PINCH OF KOSHER SALT

1   EGG, BEATEN

GRAPE PIE

YIELD: 1 PIE / **ACTIVE TIME:** 20 MINUTES / **TOTAL TIME:** 2 HOURS

The legend, Larry David, once asked on *Curb Your Enthusiasm*, "Grape works as a soda. . . . I wonder why it doesn't work as a pie. Grape pie? There's no grape pie." Well, Larry, there is. And it's spectacular.

1. Preheat the oven to 350°F. Coat a 9-inch pie plate with nonstick cooking spray and place one of the crusts in it. Place the grapes and sugar in a saucepan and let the mixture stand for 15 minutes.

2. Place the cornstarch and lemon juice in a small bowl and whisk to combine. Pour the mixture into the saucepan, add the butter, and stir to combine. Cook over medium heat, stirring frequently, until the grapes start to collapse, about 5 minutes. Remove the pan from heat and let the mixture cool slightly.

3. Evenly distribute the grape mixture in the crust in the pie plate. Place the remaining crust on top, crimp the edge to seal, and make a hole in the center of the pie. Brush the top crust with the milk.

4. Place the pie in the oven and bake for about 45 minutes, until the crust is golden brown and the filling is bubbling. Remove from the oven and let cool before serving.

INGREDIENTS:

2	PERFECT PIECRUSTS (SEE PAGE 46), ROLLED OUT
4	CUPS SEEDLESS PURPLE GRAPES, HALVED
⅔	CUP SUGAR
3	TABLESPOONS CORNSTARCH
2	TABLESPOONS FRESH LEMON JUICE
1	OZ. UNSALTED BUTTER
2	TABLESPOONS MILK

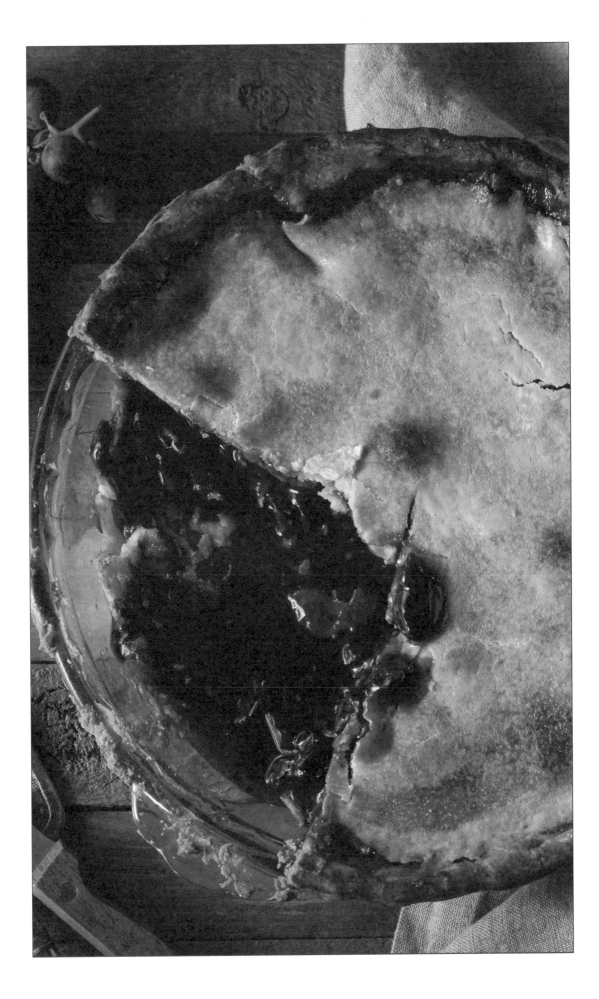

CHOCOLATE & BOURBON PECAN PIE

YIELD: 1 PIE / **ACTIVE TIME:** 25 MINUTES / **TOTAL TIME:** 1 HOUR AND 30 MINUTES

Don't be afraid to experiment with different bourbons until you find one that's just to your taste. We've found that those with a higher rye content, which will add spice, tend to work best.

1. Preheat the oven to 325°F. Evenly distribute the pecans and chocolate chips in the piecrust.

2. Place the corn syrup, sugar, light brown sugar, and bourbon in a saucepan and cook, stirring constantly, over medium heat until the mixture comes to a boil. Remove the saucepan from heat. While whisking constantly, gradually add the mixture into the eggs. When all of the mixture has been incorporated, stir in the butter, vanilla, and sea salt and pour the tempered mixture into the piecrust. Tap the pie plate so that it gets distributed evenly.

3. Place the pie in the oven and bake for about 1 hour, until a knife inserted into the center of the filling comes out clean. Remove from the oven and let cool completely before serving.

INGREDIENTS:

- 1½ CUPS CHOPPED PECANS, TOASTED
- 1 CUP SEMISWEET CHOCOLATE CHIPS
- 1 COCOA CRUST (SEE PAGE 54)
- 1 CUP DARK CORN SYRUP
- ⅓ CUP SUGAR
- ½ CUP FIRMLY PACKED LIGHT BROWN SUGAR
- ¼ CUP BOURBON
- 4 LARGE EGGS, BEATEN
- 2 OZ. UNSALTED BUTTER, MELTED
- 2 TEASPOONS PURE VANILLA EXTRACT
- ½ TEASPOON FINE SEA SALT

WALNUT PIE

YIELD: 1 PIE / **ACTIVE TIME:** 20 MINUTES / **TOTAL TIME:** 1 HOUR AND 30 MINUTES

For fans of baklava, pie doesn't get any better than this.

1. Preheat the oven to 325°F. Coat a 9-inch pie plate with nonstick cooking spray and place the piecrust in it.

2. Place the walnuts, brown sugar, sugar, and cinnamon in a mixing bowl and stir to combine.

3. Pour half of the melted butter over the crust and then spread the walnut mixture evenly on top. Pour the remaining butter over the walnut mixture, place the pie in the oven, and bake for about 50 minutes, until the crust is golden brown. Remove from the oven and let the pie cool slightly.

4. Place the honey and lemon juice in a small saucepan and warm over medium heat, stirring constantly, until the mixture acquires a watery consistency. Drizzle the mixture over the pie and let the pie cool completely before serving.

INGREDIENTS:

1	PERFECT PIECRUST (SEE PAGE 46), ROLLED OUT
2½	CUPS WALNUTS, FINELY CHOPPED
¼	CUP PACKED DARK BROWN SUGAR
2	TABLESPOONS SUGAR
1½	TEASPOONS CINNAMON
4	OZ. UNSALTED BUTTER, MELTED
¾	CUP HONEY
1	TABLESPOON FRESH LEMON JUICE

CRACK PIE

YIELD: 1 PIE / **ACTIVE TIME:** 45 MINUTES / **TOTAL TIME:** 24 HOURS

One of the inventive and uncommonly delicious recipes that powered Christina Tosi's rise to the top of the culinary world.

1. Preheat the oven to 350°F and line a 9 x 13–inch baking inch baking sheet with parchment paper. To begin preparations for the crust, place 5 tablespoons of the butter, ¼ cup of the brown sugar, and the sugar in the work bowl of a stand mixer fitted with the paddle attachment and beat on medium speed until pale and fluffy.

2. Add the egg, beat to incorporate, and then stir in the ¾ cup of oats, the flour, baking powder, baking soda, and salt. Press the mixture into the baking sheet, place it in the oven, and bake for 16 to 18 minutes, until it is dry to the touch. Remove and let cool completely.

3. When the crust has cooled, break it up into pieces, place them in a food processor and pulse until they are fine crumbs. Add the remaining butter, brown sugar, and oats and pulse until incorporated. Coat a 9-inch pie plate with nonstick cooking spray and press the mixture into it. Place the crust in the refrigerator.

4. To begin preparations for the filling, place the sugars, milk powder, and salt in the work bowl of a stand mixer fitted with the paddle attachment and stir to combine. Add the melted butter and beat on medium speed until pale and fluffy. Add the cream, egg yolks, and vanilla and beat until the mixture is thoroughly combined.

5. Pour the filling into the piecrust and tap the pie plate to distribute evenly. Place the pie in the oven and bake for 30 minutes. Reduce the oven temperature to 325°F and bake for another 20 minutes, until the filling is set and the center wobbles slightly when poked. Remove from the oven, let cool completely, cover with plastic wrap, and chill overnight. When ready to serve, sprinkle the confectioners' sugar over the top.

INGREDIENTS:

FOR THE CRUST

4	OZ. UNSALTED BUTTER, AT ROOM TEMPERATURE
2.7	OZ. LIGHT BROWN SUGAR
2	TABLESPOONS SUGAR
1	LARGE EGG, AT ROOM TEMPERATURE
¾	CUP OATS, PLUS 2 TABLESPOONS
2.5	OZ. ALL-PURPOSE FLOUR
⅛	TEASPOON BAKING POWDER
⅛	TEASPOON BAKING SODA
¼	TEASPOON FINE SEA SALT

FOR THE FILLING

¾	CUP SUGAR
½	CUP PACKED LIGHT BROWN SUGAR
1	TABLESPOON NONFAT MILK POWDER
¼	TEASPOON KOSHER SALT
4	OZ. UNSALTED BUTTER, MELTED AND SLIGHTLY COOLED
½	CUP HEAVY CREAM
4	LARGE EGG YOLKS
1	TEASPOON PURE VANILLA EXTRACT
¼	CUP CONFECTIONERS' SUGAR

SHOO-FLY PIE

YIELD: 1 PIE / **ACTIVE TIME:** 15 MINUTES / **TOTAL TIME:** 1 HOUR AND 15 MINUTES

This pie originated in Pennsylvania Dutch country during the late 19th century, when it was seen as the ideal accompaniment to a powerful cup of coffee first thing in the morning.

1. Preheat the oven to 350°F. Place the molasses, baking soda, and boiling water in a large mixing bowl and stir to combine. Evenly distribute the mixture in the piecrust.

2. Place flour, brown sugar, cinnamon, nutmeg, and salt in a large mixing bowl and stir to combine. Add the butter and work the mixture with your hands until it is sticking together in clumps. Distribute the mixture over the pie.

3. Place the pie in the oven and bake until the crust is golden brown and the topping is dry to the touch, about 45 minutes. Remove from the oven and let cool before serving.

INGREDIENTS:

- 1 CUP MOLASSES
- 1 TEASPOON BAKING SODA
- ¾ CUP BOILING WATER
- 1 PÂTE SUCRÉE (SEE PAGE 49), ROLLED OUT
- 1½ CUPS ALL-PURPOSE FLOUR
- ½ CUP PACKED DARK BROWN SUGAR
- ½ TEASPOON CINNAMON
-    PINCH OF FRESHLY GRATED NUTMEG
-    PINCH OF FINE SEA SALT
- 4 OZ. UNSALTED BUTTER, CHILLED AND DIVIDED INTO TABLESPOONS

MISSISSIPPI MUD PIE

YIELD: 1 PIE / ACTIVE TIME: 15 MINUTES / TOTAL TIME: 1 HOUR AND 45 MINUTES

The name comes from its resemblance to the dark, dank soil that make up the banks of the Mississippi River. To counter that density, don't hesitate to scoop a bit of vanilla ice cream beside each slice.

1. Preheat the oven to 350°F. Place the butter and sugar in the work bowl of a stand mixer fitted with the paddle attachment and beat on medium until pale and fluffy, about 5 minutes. Add the eggs and cocoa powder, beat to incorporate, and then fold in the chocolate chips and espresso powder. Add the cream and beat until incorporated.

2. Evenly distribute the mixture in the piecrust, place the pie in the oven, and bake until the filling is set, about 35 minutes. Remove from the oven and let the pie cool completely. Top with the Chantilly Cream and shaved chocolate before serving.

INGREDIENTS:

6 OZ. UNSALTED BUTTER

4 LARGE EGGS, LIGHTLY BEATEN

¼ CUP COCOA POWDER

1 CUP PACKED DARK BROWN SUGAR

1¼ CUPS BITTERSWEET CHOCOLATE CHIPS, MELTED AND SLIGHTLY COOLED

2 TEASPOONS ESPRESSO POWDER

1¼ CUPS HEAVY CREAM

1 COCOA CRUST (SEE PAGE 54)

CHANTILLY CREAM (SEE PAGE 89), FOR TOPPING

DARK CHOCOLATE, SHAVED, FOR TOPPING

PLUM TART WITH HAZELNUT CRUMBLE

YIELD: 1 TART / **ACTIVE TIME:** 20 MINUTES / **TOTAL TIME:** 1 HOUR AND 30 MINUTES

The simple addition of hazelnuts' sweet and buttery flavor will leave people gobsmacked by your abilities in the kitchen.

1. Preheat the oven to 350°F. To begin preparations for the tart, place the butter in a saucepan and melt over medium heat. Add the plums, sugar, and water and cook, stirring occasionally, until the plums start to break down, 7 to 10 minutes.

2. Remove from heat and stir in the cornstarch and lemon juice. Evenly distribute the mixture in the tart shell, making sure the plums are cut side up.

3. To prepare the crumble, place all of the ingredients, except for the hazelnuts, in a food processor and pulse until the mixture is a coarse meal. Spread the mixture over the tart and sprinkle the hazelnuts on top.

4. Place in the oven and bake until the crumble is golden brown, about 40 minutes. Remove from the oven and let cool before serving.

INGREDIENTS:

FOR THE TART

1	OZ. UNSALTED BUTTER
10	RIPE PLUMS, PITTED AND HALVED
½	CUP SUGAR
¼	CUP WATER
2	TABLESPOONS CORNSTARCH
1	TABLESPOON FRESH LEMON JUICE
1	PÂTÉ SUCRÉE (SEE PAGE 49), BLIND BAKED IN A TART PAN

FOR THE CRUMBLE

¼	CUP LIGHT BROWN SUGAR
¼	CUP SUGAR
½	CUP ALL-PURPOSE FLOUR
⅓	CUP ALMOND MEAL
1.5	OZ. UNSALTED BUTTER
¼	TEASPOON GROUND CINNAMON
¼	TEASPOON KOSHER SALT
⅓	CUP BLANCHED HAZELNUTS, CHOPPED

FUNFETTI WHOOPIE PIES

YIELD: 20 WHOOPIE PIES / **ACTIVE TIME:** 30 MINUTES / **TOTAL TIME:** 1 HOUR AND 45 MINUTES

Too much fun, and too delicious, for you to bother trying to act like you're above it.

1. Preheat the oven to 350°F and line two baking sheets with parchment paper. Sift the flour, baking soda, baking powder, and salt into a mixing bowl and set the mixture aside.

2. In the work bowl of a stand mixer fitted with the paddle attachment, cream the butter and sugar on medium speed until the mixture is very light and fluffy, about 5 minutes. Scrape down the work bowl and then beat the mixture for another 5 minutes.

3. Add the egg and vanilla, reduce the speed to low, and beat until incorporated, again scraping the work bowl as needed.

4. Add the dry mixture and beat on low until the batter comes together. Gradually add in the buttermilk and beat until incorporated. When all of the buttermilk has been combined, add the sprinkles and fold the mixture until they are evenly distributed.

5. Drop 2-oz. portions of the dough on the baking sheets, making sure to leave 2 inches of space between them.

6. Place in the oven and bake until a cake tester inserted into the centers of the cakes comes out clean, about 12 minutes. Remove from the oven and let the cakes cool completely.

7. Spread the filling on half of the cakes and use the other cakes to assemble the whoopie pies.

INGREDIENTS:

12	OZ. ALL-PURPOSE FLOUR
1	TEASPOON BAKING SODA
¾	TEASPOON BAKING POWDER
¾	TEASPOON KOSHER SALT
4	OZ. UNSALTED BUTTER, SOFTENED
9	OZ. SUGAR
1	EGG
1½	TEASPOONS PURE VANILLA EXTRACT
⅔	CUP BUTTERMILK
½	CUP RAINBOW SPRINKLES
2	CUPS BUTTERFLUFF FILLING (SEE PAGE 86)

LINZER TART

YIELD: 1 TART / **ACTIVE TIME:** 30 MINUTES / **TOTAL TIME:** 2 HOURS AND 45 MINUTES

Toasting the almond flour is key to getting the crust to where its crumbly, subtly flavored loveliness allows the preserves to shine.

1. Preheat the oven to 250°F. Place the almond flour on a baking sheet, place it in the oven, and toast for 5 minutes. Remove from the oven and set it aside.

2. In the work bowl of a stand mixer fitted with the paddle attachment, combine the sugar, butter, and lemon zest and beat on medium speed until the mixture is pale and fluffy.

3. Incorporate two of the eggs one at a time, scraping down the mixing bowl as needed.

4. Place the flour, almond flour, cinnamon, ground cloves, cocoa powder, and salt in a separate bowl and whisk to combine. Gradually add this mixture to the wet mixture and beat until the mixture comes together as a dough. Divide the dough in half, envelop each piece in plastic wrap, and refrigerate for 1 hour.

5. Preheat the oven to 350°F and coat a 9-inch tart pan with non-stick cooking spray. Place the pieces of dough on a flour-dusted work surface and roll them out to fit the tart pan. Place one piece of dough in the pan and then cut the other piece of dough into ¾-inch-wide strips.

6. Fill the crust in the pan with the raspberry jam. Lay some of the strips over the tart and trim any excess. To make a lattice crust, lift every other strip and fold back so you can place another strip across those strips that remain flat. Lay the folded strips back down over the cross-strip. Fold back the strips that you laid the cross-strip on top of and repeat until the lattice covers the surface of the tart. Beat the remaining egg until scrambled and brush the strips with it, taking care not to get any egg on the filling.

7. Place the tart in the oven and bake for about 45 minutes, until the lattice crust is golden brown. Remove from the oven and let cool before serving.

INGREDIENTS:

3.3	OZ. FINE ALMOND FLOUR
7	OZ. SUGAR
6	OZ. UNSALTED BUTTER, SOFTENED
1	TEASPOON LEMON ZEST
3	EGGS
6.25	OZ. ALL-PURPOSE FLOUR, PLUS MORE AS NEEDED
½	TEASPOON CINNAMON
¼	TEASPOON GROUND CLOVES
1	TABLESPOON UNSWEETENED COCOA POWDER
¼	TEASPOON KOSHER SALT
1½	CUPS RASPBERRY JAM

NECTARINE PIE

YIELD: 1 PIE / **ACTIVE TIME:** 30 MINUTES / **TOTAL TIME:** 1 HOUR AND 45 MINUTES

Whenever you come across ripe nectarines, the temptation is to buy as many as you can. This pie turns that impulse into a prudent play.

1. Preheat the oven to 375°F. Coat a 9-inch pie pan with nonstick cooking spray and place one of the crusts in it.

2. Place the nectarines, sugar, brown sugar, cornstarch, cinnamon, nutmeg, lemon juice, lemon zest, and salt in a mixing bowl and toss until the nectarines are evenly coated.

3. Fill the crust with the nectarine mixture, lay the other crust over the top, and crimp the edge to seal. Brush the top crust with the egg and sprinkle the sanding sugar over it. Cut several slits in the top crust.

4. Place the pie in the oven and bake until the filling is bubbly and has thickened, about 50 minutes. Remove from the oven and let the pie cool completely before serving.

INGREDIENTS:

2	PERFECT PIECRUSTS (SEE PAGE 46), ROLLED OUT
7	NECTARINES, PITTED AND SLICED
½	CUP SUGAR
½	CUP LIGHT BROWN SUGAR
3	TABLESPOONS CORNSTARCH
¼	TEASPOON CINNAMON
¼	TEASPOON FRESHLY GRATED NUTMEG
	ZEST AND JUICE OF 1 LEMON
¼	TEASPOON KOSHER SALT
1	EGG, BEATEN
	SANDING SUGAR, FOR TOPPING

STRAWBERRY RHUBARB PIE

YIELD: 1 PIE / **ACTIVE TIME:** 30 MINUTES / **TOTAL TIME:** 1 HOUR AND 45 MINUTES

The floral aspect of the cardamom and the brightness added by the orange zest lift this classic combination to all-new heights.

1. Preheat the oven to 375°F. Coat a 9-inch pie pan with nonstick cooking spray and place one of the crusts in it.

2. Place the strawberries, rhubarb, sugar, cornstarch, cardamom, orange zest, and salt in a mixing bowl and toss until the strawberries and rhubarb are evenly coated.

3. Fill the crust with the strawberry mixture, lay the other crust over the top, and crimp the edge to seal. Brush the top crust with the egg and sprinkle the sanding sugar over it. Cut several slits in the top crust.

4. Place the pie in the oven and bake until the filling is bubbly and has thickened, about 50 minutes. Remove from the oven and let the pie cool completely before serving.

INGREDIENTS:

2   PERFECT PIECRUSTS (SEE PAGE 46), ROLLED OUT

3   CUPS STRAWBERRIES, HULLED AND QUARTERED

3   CUPS CHOPPED RHUBARB

1   CUP SUGAR

2   TABLESPOONS CORNSTARCH

¼   TEASPOON CARDAMOM

    ZEST OF 2 ORANGES

¼   TEASPOON KOSHER SALT

1   EGG, BEATEN

    SANDING SUGAR, FOR TOPPING

FIG & PECAN TART

YIELD: 1 TART / **ACTIVE TIME:** 25 MINUTES / **TOTAL TIME:** 1 HOUR AND 15 MINUTES

A sweet and earthy tart that provides a perfect introduction to baking with the underutilized and underrated fig.

1. Preheat the oven to 350°F. Place the pecans, brown sugar, vanilla, and egg whites in a food processor and pulse until the pecans are finely ground.

2. Pour the mixture into the tart shell and lay the sliced figs over the top. Place the tart in the oven and bake until the filling has set and the figs have caramelized, about 30 minutes. Remove from the oven and let the tart cool completely before slicing and serving.

INGREDIENTS:

1½   CUPS PECANS

⅔   CUP DARK BROWN SUGAR

1   TEASPOON PURE VANILLA EXTRACT

2   EGG WHITES

1   PÂTÉ SUCRÉE (SEE PAGE 49), BLIND BAKED IN A TART PAN

6   FIGS, SLICED

SOUR CHERRY CRUMBLE PIE

YIELD: 1 PIE / **ACTIVE TIME:** 30 MINUTES / **TOTAL TIME:** 1 HOUR AND 45 MINUTES

The Morello cherry is more acidic than its family members, lending it a vibrant sour taste that will linger in the mind long after you've left the table.

1. Preheat the oven to 375°F. Coat a 9-inch pie pan with nonstick cooking spray and place the crust in it.

2. Place the cherries, sugar, cornstarch, ginger, lemon juice, lemon zest, and salt in a mixing bowl and toss until the cherries are evenly coated.

3. Fill the crust with the cherry mixture and sprinkle the topping over it.

4. Place the pie in the oven and bake until the filling is bubbly and has thickened, about 50 minutes. Remove from the oven and let the pie cool completely before serving.

INGREDIENTS:

1   PERFECT PIECRUST (SEE PAGE 46), ROLLED OUT

6   CUPS MORELLO CHERRIES, PITTED AND HALVED

½   CUP SUGAR

3   TABLESPOONS CORNSTARCH

¼   TEASPOON GROUND GINGER

    ZEST AND JUICE OF 1 LEMON

¼   TEASPOON KOSHER SALT

    STREUSEL TOPPING (SEE PAGE 110)

KEY LIME PIE

YIELD: 1 PIE / **ACTIVE TIME:** 40 MINUTES / **TOTAL TIME:** 4 HOURS AND 30 MINUTES

When selecting key limes, keep in mind that the green ones are actually unripe. They will have higher levels of acidity and tartness, which can be fine in some preparations, but for desserts you'll want to seek out yellow key limes, as they are sweeter.

1. Preheat the oven to 350°F. In a mixing bowl, whisk together the condensed milk, egg yolks, key lime juice, salt, and vanilla extract. When the mixture is smooth, pour it into the crust.

2. Place the pie in the oven and bake until the filling is just set, about 16 minutes. Remove from the oven and let the pie cool at room temperature for 30 minutes before transferring it to the refrigerator. Chill the pie for 3 hours.

3. Place the meringue in a piping bag fit with a star tip. Pipe the meringue around the border of the pie and lightly brown it with a kitchen torch. Slice and serve.

INGREDIENTS:

1 (14 OZ.) CAN OF SWEETENED CONDENSED MILK

4 EGG YOLKS

½ CUP FRESH KEY LIME JUICE

¼ TEASPOON KOSHER SALT

½ TEASPOON PURE VANILLA EXTRACT

1 GRAHAM CRACKER CRUST (SEE PAGE 50)

SWISS MERINGUE (SEE PAGE 70)

PUMPKIN PIE

YIELD: 1 PIE / **ACTIVE TIME:** 3 MINUTES / **TOTAL TIME:** 5 HOURS

Don't believe the hype: while using anything other than fresh pumpkin is verboten in contemporary cooking cliques, the actual difference appears to exist only in the mind. For almost every preparation, fresh is better than canned. Not so for this one, yet another way that pumpkin pie defies convention.

1. Preheat the oven to 350°F. In a mixing bowl, whisk together the pumpkin puree, evaporated milk, eggs, light brown sugar, cinnamon, ginger, nutmeg, cloves, and salt. When the mixture is smooth, pour it into the crust.

2. Place the pie in the oven and bake until the filling is just set, about 40 minutes. Remove from the oven and let the pie cool at room temperature for 30 minutes before transferring it to the refrigerator. Chill the pie for 3 hours.

3. Slice the pie, top each piece with a dollop of the Chantilly Cream, and serve.

INGREDIENTS:

1   (15 OZ.) CAN OF PUMPKIN PUREE

1   (12 OZ.) CAN OF EVAPORATED MILK

2   EGGS

6   OZ. LIGHT BROWN SUGAR

1   TEASPOON CINNAMON

1   TEASPOON GROUND GINGER

½   TEASPOON FRESHLY GRATED NUTMEG

¼   TEASPOON GROUND CLOVES

½   TEASPOON KOSHER SALT

1   PERFECT PIECRUST (SEE PAGE 46), BLIND BAKED

CHANTILLY CREAM (SEE PAGE 89)

SQUASH WHOOPIE PIES WITH GINGER CREAM

YIELD: 12 WHOOPIE PIES / **ACTIVE TIME:** 20 MINUTES / **TOTAL TIME:** 1 HOUR

Using a microplane to grate the ginger is essential here, as it is the only way to get the right texture for the filling.

1. Preheat the oven to 350°F and line two baking sheets with parchment paper. Sift the flour, cinnamon, ground ginger, cloves, nutmeg, baking soda, baking powder, and salt into a mixing bowl.

2. Place the brown sugar, maple syrup, pureed squash, egg, and olive oil in a separate mixing bowl and stir until combined. Sift the dry mixture into the squash mixture and stir until it has been incorporated.

3. Use an ice cream scoop to place dollops of the batter onto the baking sheets. Make sure to leave plenty of space between each scoop. Place the sheets in the oven and bake until golden brown, about 10 to 15 minutes. Remove and let the cakes cool.

4. While the squash cakes are cooling, place the remaining ingredients in a bowl and beat with a handheld mixer until the mixture thoroughly combined and fluffy.

5. When the cakes have cooled completely, spread the filling on half of the cakes. Use the other cakes to assemble the whoopie pies and enjoy.

INGREDIENTS:

- 6.3 OZ. ALL-PURPOSE FLOUR
- 1 TEASPOON CINNAMON
- 1 TEASPOON GROUND GINGER
- ¼ TEASPOON GROUND CLOVES
- ½ TEASPOON FRESHLY GRATED NUTMEG
- ½ TEASPOON BAKING SODA
- ½ TEASPOON BAKING POWDER
- 1 TEASPOON FINE SEA SALT
- 7 OZ. LIGHT BROWN SUGAR
- 2 TABLESPOONS MAPLE SYRUP
- 1 CUP PUREED BUTTERNUT OR ACORN SQUASH
- 1 EGG
- 1 CUP EXTRA-VIRGIN OLIVE OIL
- 5.3 OZ. CONFECTIONERS' SUGAR
- 2 OZ. UNSALTED BUTTER
- 8 OZ. CREAM CHEESE, AT ROOM TEMPERATURE
- 1-INCH PIECE OF FRESH GINGER, PEELED AND GRATED
- ½ TEASPOON PURE VANILLA EXTRACT

PEAR GALETTE WITH MAPLE CARAMEL

YIELD: 1 GALETTE / **ACTIVE TIME:** 30 MINUTES / **TOTAL TIME:** 1 HOUR AND 45 MINUTES

A spicy dough and the subtle notes of vanilla in the pears make this easy-to-prepare dessert seem anything but.

1. To begin preparations for the dough, place the flour, cinnamon, nutmeg, cloves, salt, and brown sugar in a bowl and whisk to combine. Divide the butter into tablespoons and place them in the freezer for 15 minutes.

2. Place the flour mixture and the frozen pieces of butter in a food processor and blitz until combined. Gradually add the water and blitz until the dough just holds together. Remove from the food processor, place on a lightly floured work surface, and knead until all of the ingredients are thoroughly incorporated. Place in the refrigerator for 20 minutes before rolling out.

3. Preheat the oven to 400°F and prepare the filling. Place the sugar and cinnamon in a bowl, stir to combine, and set aside. Place the pears, lemon zest, ginger, and butter in a separate bowl and gently toss, being careful not to break the slices of pear.

4. Place the dough on a lightly floured work surface and roll out into a 12-inch circle that is approximately ¼ inch thick. Place it on a parchment-lined baking sheet and then place the pear slices on the dough in layers, making sure to leave a 1½-inch border. Sprinkle each layer with the sugar-and-cinnamon mixture before adding the next layer.

5. Fold the edge of the dough over the filling and crimp. Brush the crust with the egg yolk and sprinkle with the sugar-and-cinnamon mixture. Place the galette in the oven and bake until the crust is golden brown and the pears are tender, about 25 minutes.

6. While the galette is baking, prepare the maple caramel. Place the butter in a saucepan and melt over medium heat. Add the sugar and salt and cook, stirring constantly, until the sugar is dissolved, about 5 minutes. Add the maple syrup and cook until the mixture is smooth and thick. Remove from heat.

7. Remove the galette from the oven, drizzle the maple caramel over the top, and let cool for 5 to 10 minutes before serving.

INGREDIENTS:

FOR THE DOUGH

7.5	OZ. ALL-PURPOSE FLOUR, PLUS MORE AS NEEDED
1	TEASPOON CINNAMON
¼	TEASPOON FRESHLY GRATED NUTMEG
¼	TEASPOON GROUND CLOVES
1½	TEASPOONS FINE SEA SALT
2	TEASPOONS BROWN SUGAR
8	OZ. UNSALTED BUTTER
½	CUP ICE WATER
1	EGG YOLK, BEATEN

FOR THE FILLING

¼	CUP SUGAR
2	TEASPOONS CINNAMON
3	ANJOU PEARS, CORED AND CUT INTO ¼-INCH SLICES
1½	TABLESPOONS LEMON ZEST
	½-INCH PIECE OF FRESH GINGER, PEELED AND GRATED
1	OZ. UNSALTED BUTTER, CUT INTO SMALL PIECES

FOR THE MAPLE CARAMEL

4	OZ. UNSALTED BUTTER
1	CUP DARK BROWN SUGAR
½	TEASPOON FINE SEA SALT
½	CUP MAPLE SYRUP

GRACELAND PIE

YIELD: 1 PIE / **ACTIVE TIME:** 30 MINUTES / **TOTAL TIME:** 1 HOUR

The trio of bacon, peanut butter, and banana is a strange one, but as any fan of Elvis will tell you, it's fit for a King.

1. Place the sugar, flour, and salt in a saucepan and whisk to combine. Whisk the milk into the mixture and bring to a simmer, while stirring constantly, over medium heat. Simmer, while stirring, for 2 minutes and then remove the pan from heat.

2. While whisking constantly, stir a small amount of the warmed mixture into the beaten egg yolks. Add the tempered egg yolks to the saucepan, place the pan back over medium heat, and cook until the mixture thickens and starts bubbling, while whisking constantly. Remove from heat, add the butter and vanilla, and stir until combined. Add half of the sliced bananas, stir to coat, and let the mixture cool.

3. While the mixture is cooling, place the peanut butter in a saucepan and warm over medium heat until it starts to melt.

4. Place the remaining bananas in the piecrust and then pour the cooled banana cream over the bananas. Cover with the Chantilly Cream, drizzle the peanut butter over it, and arrange the dehydrated banana chips and bacon pieces (if desired) on top.

INGREDIENTS:

¾ CUP SUGAR

⅓ CUP ALL-PURPOSE FLOUR

¼ TEASPOON FINE SEA SALT

2 CUPS WHOLE MILK

3 EGG YOLKS, BEATEN

1 OZ. UNSALTED BUTTER

1¼ TEASPOONS PURE VANILLA EXTRACT

4 BANANAS, SLICED

½ CUP CREAMY NATURAL PEANUT BUTTER

1 GRAHAM CRACKER CRUST (SEE PAGE 50), MADE WITH CHOCOLATE GRAHAM CRACKERS

CHANTILLY CREAM (SEE PAGE 89)

DEHYDRATED BANANA CHIPS, FOR GARNISH

¼ CUP CRISPY, CHOPPED BACON, FOR GARNISH (OPTIONAL)

TARTE TATIN

YIELD: 1 TART / **ACTIVE TIME:** 30 MINUTES / **TOTAL TIME:** 1 TO 2 DAYS

In the late 19th century, the Tatin sisters, Caroline and Stephanie, ran the Hotel Tatin in Lamotte-Beuvron, a small town in France's Loire Valley. Stephanie, who was in charge of the kitchen, was renowned for her apple tart. But during one lunch rush she accidently placed it in the oven upside down. She shrugged off the mistake and served it anyway, and word of her wonderful misstep soon reached Paris. There, it quickly ascended onto the menu at the famed restaurant Maxim's, assuring the Tarte Tatin's place in history.

1. Place the apples in a mixing bowl and let them sit in the refrigerator for 24 to 48 hours. This will allow them to dry out.

2. Whisk together the flour, confectioners' sugar, and salt in a large bowl. Add half of the butter and use your fingers or a pastry blender to work the mixture until it is a collection of coarse clumps. Add the egg and work the mixture until the dough just holds together. Shape it into a ball, cover it with plastic wrap, flatten into a 4-inch disc, and refrigerate for 1 hour. If preparing ahead of time, the dough will keep in the refrigerator overnight.

3. Preheat the oven to 375°F. Coat a 10-inch cast-iron skillet with the butter. When the butter is melted, remove the skillet from heat and sprinkle the sugar evenly over the butter. Place the apple slices in a circular pattern, starting at the center of the pan and working out to the edge. The pieces should overlap and face the same direction.

4. Place the dough on a flour-dusted work surface and roll it out to ⅛ inch thick. Use the roller to carefully roll up the dough. Place it over the apples and tuck it in around the edges.

5. Place the skillet over low heat and gradually raise it until the juices in the pan are a deep amber color, about 7 minutes.

6. Place the skillet in the oven and bake until the crust is golden brown and firm, 35 to 40 minutes.

7. Remove the tart from the oven, allow to cool for about 5 minutes, and then run a knife around the edges to loosen the tart. Using oven mitts, carefully invert the tart onto a large plate. Place any apples that are stuck to the skillet back on the tart and enjoy.

INGREDIENTS:

- 6-8 BRAEBURN OR HONEYCRISP APPLES, PEELED, CORED, AND QUARTERED
- 6.3 OZ. ALL-PURPOSE FLOUR, PLUS MORE AS NEEDED
- 1 OZ. CONFECTIONERS' SUGAR
- ½ TEASPOON FINE SEA SALT
- 4 OZ. UNSALTED BUTTER, CHILLED
- 1 EGG, BEATEN
- 3 OZ. SALTED BUTTER, SOFTENED
- ⅔ CUP SUGAR

MIXED BERRY PIE

YIELD: 1 PIE / **ACTIVE TIME:** 30 MINUTES / **TOTAL TIME:** 1 HOUR AND 30 MINUTES

A pie made to celebrate the glory of berry season.

1. Preheat the oven to 375°F and grease a 9-inch pie plate.

2. Place all of the berries, lemon juice, brown sugar, and cornstarch in a large bowl and toss to combine. Transfer the fruit to a large saucepan and cook over medium heat until the berries start to collapse, 7 to 10 minutes. Stir in the preserves, remove the pan from heat, and set the mixture aside.

3. Place the balls of piecrust dough on a flour-dusted work surface and roll them out to fit the pie plate. Transfer one of the crusts to the pie plate and fill it with the berry mixture.

4. Cut the other crust into 1-inch-wide strips. Lay some of the strips over the pie and trim the strips so that they fit. To make a lattice crust, lift every other strip and fold them back so you can place another strip across those strips that remain flat. Lay the folded strips back down over the cross-strip. Fold back the strips that you laid the cross-strip on top of and repeat until the lattice covers the surface of the pie. Brush the strips with the beaten egg, taking care not to get any egg on the filling.

5. Place the pie in the oven and bake for 45 minutes, until the crust is golden brown and the filling is bubbling. Remove from the oven and let cool before serving.

INGREDIENTS:

1½ CUPS FRESH BLUEBERRIES

1 CUP FRESH BLACKBERRIES

1 CUP FRESH RASPBERRIES

1½ CUPS FRESH STRAWBERRIES, HULLED AND HALVED

1 TABLESPOON FRESH LEMON JUICE

½ CUP LIGHT BROWN SUGAR

2 TABLESPOONS CORNSTARCH

½ CUP UNSWEETENED RASPBERRY PRESERVES

2 PERFECT PIECRUSTS (SEE PAGE 46)

ALL-PURPOSE FLOUR, AS NEEDED

1 EGG, BEATEN

BLACK & BLUE GALETTE

YIELD: 1 GALETTE / **ACTIVE TIME:** 20 MINUTES / **TOTAL TIME:** 1 HOUR AND 30 MINUTES

Far less painless than the name implies, and far more enjoyable.

1. Preheat the oven to 400°F. Place the ball of dough on a flour-dusted work surface, roll it out to 9 inches, and then place it on a parchment-lined baking sheet.

2. Place the berries, brown sugar, lemon juice, cornstarch, and salt in a large mixing bowl and stir until the berries are evenly coated.

3. Spread the berry mixture over the dough, making sure to leave a 1½-inch border. Fold the crust over the filling, brush the folded-over crust with the beaten egg, and sprinkle the sugar over it.

4. Place the galette in the oven and bake until the crust is golden brown and the filling is bubbly, about 35 to 40 minutes. Remove from the oven and let cool before serving.

INGREDIENTS:

1	BALL OF PERFECT PIECRUST DOUGH (SEE PAGE 46)
	ALL-PURPOSE FLOUR, AS NEEDED
1½	CUPS FRESH BLUEBERRIES
1½	CUPS FRESH BLACKBERRIES
½	CUP LIGHT BROWN SUGAR
	JUICE OF ½ LEMON
3	TABLESPOONS CORNSTARCH
	PINCH OF FINE SEA SALT
1	EGG, BEATEN
1	TABLESPOON SUGAR

ROASTED STRAWBERRY HANDPIES

YIELD: 8 HANDPIES / **ACTIVE TIME:** 40 MINUTES / **TOTAL TIME:** 2 HOURS

Roasting the strawberries caramelizes the sugars and concentrates the flavor, guaranteeing that these seemingly small pockets are extremely deep.

1. Preheat the oven to 400°F. Place the strawberries on a baking sheet, place it in the oven, and roast until they start to darken and release their juice, about 20 to 30 minutes. If you prefer, you can roast them for up to an hour. Cooking the strawberries for longer will caramelize the sugars and lend them an even richer flavor.

2. Remove the strawberries from the oven and place them in a saucepan with the sugar and lemon juice. Bring to a simmer over medium heat and cook for 20 minutes, until the mixture has thickened slightly.

3. Place the cornstarch and water in a small cup and stir until there are no lumps in the mixture. Add to the saucepan and stir until the mixture is syrupy. Remove the pan from heat.

4. Divide the ball of piecrust dough into two pieces, place on a flour-dusted work surface, roll them out into squares that are about ⅛ inch thick, and then cut each square into quarters. Spoon some of the strawberry mixture into the center of each quarter.

5. Take a bottom corner of each pie and fold to the opposite top corner. Press down to ensure that none of the mixture leaks out and then use a fork to seal the edge. Place the pies on a baking sheet and brush them with the beaten egg. Place in the oven and bake until golden brown, about 20 to 30 minutes.

6. While the pies are cooking, place the confectioners' sugar, milk, and cinnamon in a bowl and stir until well combined.

7. Remove the pies from the oven, brush them with the sugar-and-cinnamon glaze, and allow to cool before serving.

INGREDIENTS:

3   QUARTS OF FRESH STRAWBERRIES, HULLED AND SLICED

1   CUP SUGAR

2   TEASPOONS FRESH LEMON JUICE

1   TABLESPOON CORNSTARCH

½   TABLESPOON WATER

1   BALL OF PERFECT PIECRUST DOUGH (SEE PAGE 46)

   ALL-PURPOSE FLOUR, AS NEEDED

2   EGGS, BEATEN

1½   CUPS SIFTED CONFECTIONERS' SUGAR

3   TABLESPOONS WHOLE MILK

1   TEASPOON CINNAMON

PLUM GALETTE

YIELD: 1 GALETTE / **ACTIVE TIME:** 20 MINUTES / **TOTAL TIME:** 1 HOUR

It should be illegal for something this beautiful to be so simple.

1. Preheat the oven to 400°F. Place the ball of dough on a flour-dusted work surface, roll it out to 9 inches, and place it on a parchment-lined baking sheet.

2. Place the plums, the ½ cup of sugar, lemon juice, cornstarch, and salt in a mixing bowl and stir until the plums are evenly coated.

3. Spread the jam over the crust, making sure to leave a 1½-inch border. Distribute the plum mixture on top of the jam and fold the crust over it. Brush the folded-over crust with the beaten egg and sprinkle it with the remaining sugar.

4. Put the galette in the oven and bake until the crust is golden brown and the filling is bubbly, about 35 to 40 minutes. Remove from the oven and allow to cool before serving.

INGREDIENTS:

1	BALL OF PERFECT PIECRUST DOUGH (SEE PAGE 46)
	ALL-PURPOSE FLOUR, AS NEEDED
5	PLUMS, PITTED AND SLICED
½	CUP SUGAR, PLUS 1 TABLESPOON
	JUICE OF ½ LEMON
3	TABLESPOONS CORNSTARCH
	PINCH OF FINE SEA SALT
2	TABLESPOONS BLACKBERRY JAM
1	EGG, BEATEN

PECAN PIE

YIELD: 1 PIE / **ACTIVE TIME:** 20 MINUTES / **TOTAL TIME:** 1 HOUR AND 30 MINUTES

It is not a pie that one can have every day. But, much like Christmas, its approach creates feverish anticipation among its devotees.

1. Preheat the oven to 350°F. Place all of the ingredients, except for the piecrust and flour, in a large mixing bowl and stir to combine. Set the filling aside.

2. Roll out the piecrust on a flour-dusted work surface. Place the dough in a greased 9-inch pie plate, trim the edges, and then crimp the crust. Place the crust in the refrigerator for 15 minutes.

3. Pour the filling into the crust. Place the pie in the oven and bake until the crust is golden brown and the filling is set, 45 to 50 minutes. Remove from the oven and let cool completely before serving.

INGREDIENTS:

1   CUP LIGHT CORN SYRUP

1   CUP PACKED DARK BROWN SUGAR

3   EGGS, LIGHTLY BEATEN

3   OZ. UNSALTED BUTTER, MELTED

½   TEASPOON FINE SEA SALT

1   CUP PECAN HALVES

1   PERFECT PIECRUST (SEE PAGE 46)

     ALL-PURPOSE FLOUR, AS NEEDED

BOSTON CREAM PIE

YIELD: 1 PIE / **ACTIVE TIME:** 1 HOUR / **TOTAL TIME:** 6 HOURS AND 30 MINUTES

Yes, it's functionally a cake. But the misnomer may be the ultimate testament to the Boston cream pie's greatness—the combination of flavors and textures is so remarkable that no one who has encountered it can bear to be bothered with such trivialities as nomenclature.

1. To begin preparations for the filling, place the sugar, salt, and egg yolks in a mixing bowl and whisk until smooth. Add the flour and whisk to incorporate.

2. Place the half-and-half in a saucepan and bring to a simmer over medium heat. Remove the pan from heat and slowly pour ½ cup into the flour-and-egg yolk mixture while whisking constantly. Whisk the tempered mixture into the half-and-half that remains in the saucepan. Place the saucepan over medium heat and cook, whisking constantly, until the mixture thickens, about 1 minute. Reduce heat to medium-low and simmer, while whisking constantly, for 8 minutes.

3. Raise the heat to medium and cook, while whisking vigorously, until the mixture starts to bubble, 1 to 2 minutes. Remove saucepan from heat, add the butter and vanilla seeds, and whisk until the butter is melted and incorporated. Strain the filling through a fine sieve and let cool. When cool, press plastic wrap directly onto the surface and place in the refrigerator for 2 hours.

4. To begin preparations for the cakes, preheat the oven to 325°F. Line two round, 9-inch cake pans with parchment paper and coat with nonstick cooking spray. Place the flour, baking powder, and salt in mixing bowl and whisk to combine. Place the milk and butter in a small saucepan and warm over low heat until the butter has melted. Remove the pan from heat, stir in the vanilla, and cover it.

5. Place the eggs and sugar in the work bowl of a stand mixer fitted with the paddle attachment and beat on high until the mixture is light and fluffy, about 5 minutes. Add the warm milk mixture and beat on medium until it has all been incorporated. Add the flour mixture and beat until incorporated.

6. Divide the batter between the prepared pans and place them in the oven. Bake until the tops are light brown and a cake tester inserted into the center of each cake comes out clean, about 20 minutes. Remove pans from the oven and let cool completely, about 2 hours.

INGREDIENTS:

FOR THE FILLING

½	CUP SUGAR
	PINCH OF FINE SEA SALT
6	LARGE EGG YOLKS
¼	CUP ALL-PURPOSE FLOUR
2	CUPS HALF-AND-HALF
2	OZ. UNSALTED BUTTER, CHILLED AND DIVIDED INTO TABLESPOONS
	SEEDS OF 1 VANILLA BEAN

FOR THE CAKES

7.5	OZ. ALL-PURPOSE FLOUR
1½	TEASPOONS BAKING POWDER
¾	TEASPOON FINE SEA SALT
¾	CUP WHOLE MILK
3	OZ. UNSALTED BUTTER
1½	TEASPOONS PURE VANILLA EXTRACT
3	LARGE EGGS
10.5	OZ. SUGAR
	CLASSIC CHOCOLATE FROSTING (SEE PAGE 79)

7. After 2 hours, invert the cakes onto wire racks and remove the parchment paper. Remove the filling from the refrigerator and whisk to loosen it slightly. Spoon the filling onto the top of one of the cakes and spread it evenly over the surface. Place the second cake, flat-side up, on top of the filling.

8. Spread the frosting over the top of the cake. Place the cake in the refrigerator for at least 3 hours before serving.

CHOCOLATE CREAM PIE

YIELD: 1 PIE / **ACTIVE TIME:** 10 MINUTES / **TOTAL TIME:** 1 HOUR AND 10 MINUTES

You've no doubt been tempted by this siren's song while she sat calmly behind the glass at an all-night diner. Armed with this simple recipe, you don't even have to venture beyond the comfort of your own home.

1. Place the pudding in the piecrust, smooth the top with a rubber spatula, and cover with plastic wrap. Refrigerate for 1 hour.

2. When ready to serve, spread the Chantilly Cream on top of the filling in a thick layer. Garnish with the chocolate shavings, raspberries, or strawberries, if desired.

INGREDIENTS:

6   CUPS CHOCOLATE PUDDING (SEE PAGE 493)

1   PERFECT PIECRUST (SEE PAGE 46), BLIND BAKED

2   CUPS CHANTILLY CREAM (SEE PAGE 89)

CHOCOLATE SHAVINGS, RASPBERRIES, OR SLICED STRAWBERRIES, FOR GARNISH

PASTRIES

*M*any a foodie will tell you that a pastry was their first love. One day, while accompanying a parent to the store in order to pick up things for dinner, they caught an unimaginably beautiful and promising sight out of the corner of their eye. A delicate, golden beauty, sequestered behind glass. They held their breath, feeling wonder but also pain, sure that this wonder could never be theirs. Try as they may to forget, it remained front of mind, growing in force until, eventually, they could no longer remain apart from it. And, somehow, the actual experience managed to match the ideal that had been fashioned.

This section offers considerable opportunities to create similarly lovely collisions for those you love. These recipes also offer a chance to stretch yourself in the kitchen once you've cut your teeth on some of the more rudimentary preparations in this book. So when it is time to really dazzle someone, or you've got one of those precious weekends with no plans and snow coming in, pass your time composing one of the confections in this chapter. You won't regret it.

CANELÉS

YIELD: 18 CANELÉS / ACITVE TIME: 1 HOUR / **TOTAL TIME:** 2 DAYS

A bit of infrastructure is needed here if you want your canelés to achieve their highest form—expensive (though beautiful) copper molds to conduct the heat well enough to get the proper level of caramelization, as well as beeswax to coat them.

1. To begin preparations for the pastries, place the milk and butter in a saucepan. If using the vanilla bean, halve it, scrape the seeds into the saucepan, and add the pod as well. Place the pan over medium heat and bring the mixture to a simmer. Immediately remove the pan from heat and let it sit for 10 minutes.

2. In a large mixing bowl, whisk the flour, sugar, and salt together. Set the mixture aside. Place the eggs and egg yolks in a heatproof mixing bowl and whisk to combine, making sure not to add any air to the mixture.

3. While whisking the egg mixture, add the milk mixture in small increments. When all of the milk mixture has been thoroughly incorporated, whisk in the rum or Cognac.

4. Remove the vanilla bean pod and reserve. While whisking, add the tempered eggs to the dry mixture and whisk until just combined, taking care not to overwork the mixture. Strain the custard through a fine sieve. If the mixture is still warm, place the bowl in an ice bath until it has cooled.

5. Add the vanilla bean pod to the custard, cover it with plastic wrap, and refrigerate for at least 24 hours; however, 48 hours is strongly recommended.

6. Preheat the oven to 500°F. To prepare the molds, grate the beeswax into a mason jar and add the butter. Place the jar in a saucepan filled with a few inches of water and bring the water to a simmer. When the beeswax mixture is melted and combined, pour it into one mold, immediately pour it back into the jar, and set the mold, right side up, on a wire rack to drain. When all of the molds have been coated, place them in the freezer for 15 minutes. Remove the custard from the refrigerator and let it come to room temperature.

7. Pour the custard into the molds so that they are filled about 85 percent of the way. Place the filled molds, upside down, on a baking sheet, place them in the oven, and bake for 10 minutes. Reduce the oven's temperature to 375°F and bake until they are a deep brown, about 40 minutes. Turn the canelés out onto a wire rack and let them cool completely before enjoying. Reheat the beeswax mixture and let the molds cool before refilling them with the remaining batter.

INGREDIENTS:

FOR THE PASTRIES

17.1 OZ. WHOLE MILK

1.75 OZ. CULTURED BUTTER, SOFTENED

1 VANILLA BEAN OR 1 TABLESPOON PURE VANILLA EXTRACT

3.5 OZ. ALL-PURPOSE FLOUR

7 OZ. SUGAR

PINCH OF FINE SEA SALT

2 EGGS

2 EGG YOLKS

1.75 OZ. DARK RUM OR COGNAC

FOR THE MOLDS

1.75 OZ. BEESWAX

1.75 OZ. UNSALTED BUTTER

BRIOCHE DOUGHNUTS

YIELD: 15 DOUGHNUTS / **ACTIVE TIME:** 1 HOUR / **TOTAL TIME:** 24 HOURS

The preparation here is for the classic, centerless treats coated in a simple sweet glaze, but if you want to fill them with jam, Lemon Curd (see page 476), or Pastry Cream (see page 80), make sure you keep the centers intact.

1. In the work bowl of a stand mixer, combine the milk, water, yeast, sugar, nutmeg, egg, and egg yolk.

2. Add the flour and salt, fit the mixer with the dough hook, and knead on low speed for 5 minutes.

3. Gradually add the butter and knead to incorporate. When all of the butter has been incorporated, knead at low speed for 5 minutes.

4. Raise the speed to medium and knead until the dough starts to pull away from the sides of the bowl, about 6 minutes. Cover the bowl with plastic wrap and place it in the refrigerator overnight.

5. Place the vegetable oil in a Dutch oven fitted with a candy thermometer and warm the oil to 350°F over medium heat. Set a cooling rack in a rimmed baking sheet beside the stove.

6. Remove the dough from the refrigerator and place it on a flour-dusted work surface. Roll the dough out until it is ½ inch thick. Cut out the donuts using a round, 4-inch cookie cutter and then use a round, 1-inch cookie cutter to cut out the centers. If you want to fill the doughnuts, leave the centers in the rounds.

7. Transfer the doughnuts to the cooling rack and let them sit at room temperature for 10 minutes.

8. Working in batches, carefully place the doughnuts in the oil and fry, turning them once, until browned and cooked through, 2 to 4 minutes. Transfer the cooked doughnuts to the wire rack to drain and cool.

9. When the doughnuts have cooled, coat them in the glaze and enjoy.

INGREDIENTS:

1   CUP MILK

1   CUP WATER

2   TABLESPOONS ACTIVE DRY YEAST

4   OZ. SUGAR

¼   TEASPOON FRESHLY GRATED NUTMEG

1   EGG

1   EGG YOLK

28 OZ. BREAD FLOUR, PLUS MORE AS NEEDED

1   TEASPOON KOSHER SALT

3   OZ. UNSALTED BUTTER, SOFTENED

4   CUPS VEGETABLE OIL

HONEY GLAZE (SEE PAGE 92)

MILLE-FEUILLE

YIELD: 6 SERVINGS / **ACTIVE TIME:** 20 MINUTES / **TOTAL TIME:** 45 MINUTES

An impressive, delicious dessert that will have company thinking you're some kind of preter-naturally gifted maker of confections.

1. Preheat the oven to 400°F and line two baking sheets with parchment paper. Roll out the sheets of puff pastry and place each one on a baking sheet. Dust the sheets generously with confectioners' sugar, place them in the oven, and bake for 12 to 15 minutes, until golden brown. Remove from the oven, transfer to a wire rack, and let cool.

2. Place the Pastry Cream in a bowl, add the orange zest and Grand Marnier, and fold to incorporate. Transfer the mixture into a piping bag fitted with a plain tip and place it in the refrigerator to chill while the puff pastry continues to cool.

3. Divide each sheet of the cooled puff pastry into 3 equal portions. Remove the piping bag from the freezer and place a thick layer of cream on one of the pieces of puff pastry. Dot the edges of the cream with raspberries and press down on them gently. Fill the space between the raspberries with more of the cream and place another piece of puff pastry on top. Repeat the process with the cream and raspberries and then place the last piece of puff pastry on top. Carefully cut into the desired number of portions and serve.

INGREDIENTS:

2   **SHEETS OF FROZEN PUFF PASTRY, THAWED**

      CONFECTIONERS' SUGAR, FOR DUSTING

      PASTRY CREAM (SEE PAGE 80)

      ZEST OF 1 ORANGE

1   **TABLESPOON GRAND MARNIER**

1   **PINT OF FRESH RASPBERRIES**

ECLAIRS

YIELD: 12 ECLAIRS / **ACTIVE TIME:** 40 MINUTES / **TOTAL TIME:** 1 HOUR AND 30 MINUTES

A decadent dessert that manages to return everyone to the excitement they felt as a child, when procuring something sweet was the primary focus.

1. Preheat the oven to 425°F and line two baking sheets with parchment paper. In a medium saucepan, combine the water, butter, salt, and sugar and warm the mixture over medium heat until the butter is melted.

2. Add the flour to the pan and use a rubber spatula or a wooden spoon to fold the mixture until it comes together as a thick, shiny dough, taking care not to let the dough burn.

3. Transfer the dough to the work bowl of a stand mixer fitted with the paddle attachment and beat on medium speed until the dough is no longer steaming and the bowl is just warm to the touch, at least 10 minutes.

4. Incorporate the eggs two at a time, scraping down the work bowl between each addition. Transfer the dough to a piping bag fit with a plain tip. Pipe 12 eclairs onto the baking sheets, leaving 1½ inches between them. They should be approximately 5 inches long.

5. Place the eclairs in the oven and bake for 10 minutes. Lower the oven's temperature to 325°F and bake until golden brown and a cake tester inserted in their centers comes out clean, 20 to 25 minutes. Remove from the oven and let them cool on a wire rack.

6. Fill a piping bag fitted with a plain tip with the Pastry Cream.

7. Using a paring knife, cut 3 small slits on the undersides of the eclairs and fill them with the Pastry Cream.

8. Carefully dip the top halves of the eclairs in the ganache, or drizzle the ganache over the pastries. Allow the chocolate to set before serving.

INGREDIENTS:

17	OZ. WATER
8.5	OZ. UNSALTED BUTTER
1	TEASPOON FINE SEA SALT
2.4	OZ. SUGAR
12.5	OZ. ALL-PURPOSE FLOUR
6	EGGS
	PASTRY CREAM (SEE PAGE 80)
	CHOCOLATE GANACHE (SEE PAGE 99), WARM

BEIGNETS

YIELD: 15 BEIGNETS / **ACTIVE TIME:** 1 HOUR / **TOTAL TIME:** 24 HOURS

While these originated in France, beignets are now most commonly associated with New Orleans, where their alchemical interaction with a café au lait lends a considerable amount to that city's mystique.

1. In the work bowl of a stand mixer fitted with the paddle attachment, combine the milk, eggs, egg yolks, sugar, and butter and beat on medium speed for 2 minutes.

2. Add the yeast, flour, and salt and beat until the mixture comes together as a dough, about 5 minutes.

3. Coat a medium heatproof bowl with nonstick cooking spray, transfer the dough to the bowl, and cover with plastic wrap. Refrigerate overnight.

4. Place the vegetable oil in a Dutch oven fitted with a candy thermometer and warm the oil to 350°F over medium heat. Set a paper towel–lined baking sheet beside the stove.

5. Remove the dough from the refrigerator and place it on a flour-dusted work surface. Roll the dough out until it is ½ inch thick. Cut the dough into 2-inch squares.

6. Working in batches, carefully place the beignets in the oil and fry, turning them once, until browned and cooked through, 2 minutes. Transfer the cooked doughnuts to the baking sheet to drain and cool.

7. When the beignets have cooled, dust them generously with confectioners' sugar and enjoy.

INGREDIENTS:

1½ CUPS MILK

2 EGGS

2 EGG YOLKS

½ CUP SUGAR

4 OZ. UNSALTED BUTTER, MELTED

2 TABLESPOONS ACTIVE DRY YEAST

25 OZ. ALL-PURPOSE FLOUR, PLUS MORE AS NEEDED

1¼ TEASPOONS KOSHER SALT

4 CUPS VEGETABLE OIL

1 CUP CONFECTIONERS' SUGAR, FOR DUSTING

APPLE DUTCH BABY

YIELD: 4 SERVINGS / **ACTIVE TIME:** 20 MINUTES / **TOTAL TIME:** 1 HOUR

Part popover, part pancake, part crêpe, this offspring is far more delicious than any one of those.

INGREDIENTS:

2	OZ. UNSALTED BUTTER
2	FIRM AND TART APPLES, CORED, PEELED, AND SLICED
¼	CUP SUGAR, PLUS 3 TABLESPOONS
1	TABLESPOON CINNAMON
¾	CUP ALL-PURPOSE FLOUR
¼	TEASPOON FINE SEA SALT
¾	CUP MILK
4	EGGS
1	TEASPOON PURE VANILLA EXTRACT
	CONFECTIONERS' SUGAR, FOR DUSTING

1. Preheat the oven to 425°F and place a rack in the middle position. Warm a cast-iron skillet over medium-high heat. Add the butter and apples to the pan and cook, stirring frequently, until the apples start to soften, 3 to 4 minutes. Add the ¼ cup of sugar and the cinnamon and cook, stirring occasionally, for another 3 or 4 minutes. Distribute the apple mixture evenly over the bottom of the skillet and remove it from heat.

2. In a large bowl, mix the remaining sugar, flour, and salt together. In a smaller bowl, whisk together the milk, eggs, and vanilla extract. Add the wet mixture to the dry mixture and stir until the mixture comes together as a smooth batter. Pour the batter over the apples.

3. Put the skillet in the oven and bake until the baby is puffy and golden brown, about 20 minutes. Remove the skillet from the oven and let it cool for a few minutes.

4. Run a knife along the edge of the skillet to loosen the baby, dust it with confectioners' sugar, and serve warm.

ALMOND CROISSANTS

YIELD: 16 CROISSANTS / **ACTIVE TIME:** 45 MINUTES / **TOTAL TIME:** 17 HOURS

Cultured butter, where the cream is fermented after being pasteurized, is essential here. American-style butter, which uses a sweet cream, will leave you with lacking returns on the considerable investment of time.

1. To make the dough, combine the flour, sugar, salt, yeast, milk, and butter in the work bowl of a stand mixer fitted with the paddle attachment. Add the Poolish and beat on low speed until the mixture is just combined, about 2 minutes. Let rest for 20 minutes and then mix for 2 minutes on low speed. Transfer the dough to a separate bowl, cover with plastic wrap, and let stand at room temperature for 1 hour.

2. To prepare the lamination layer, place the cultured butter in a mixing bowl and beat until it is smooth and free of lumps. Place the butter on a piece of parchment paper and smash until it is a 6½ x 9–inch rectangle of uniform thickness. Place the butter in the refrigerator when the dough has 20 minutes left to stand.

3. Place the dough on a flour-dusted work surface and roll it out into a 13 x 9–inch rectangle. Remove the butter from the refrigerator and place it on the right half of the dough. Fold the left side of the dough over the butter, making sure that the dough completely covers the butter. Essentially, you want to make a "butter sandwich."

4. Roll the dough out to a 12 x 27–inch rectangle, fold it in half, and then fold it in half again. Wrap the dough in plastic, place in the refrigerator, and chill for 1 hour.

5. Place the dough on a flour-dusted work surface and gently roll it out into a 12 x 30–inch rectangle. Cut the rectangle into 4-inch squares and then cut each square into two triangles. Spread some of the Frangipane in the center of each triangle.

6. Roll up the croissants, starting at the 90° angle and working toward the wide side (aka the hypotenuse). Place the croissants on parchment-lined baking sheets, making sure to leave enough space between them. Cover with a kitchen towel at let them stand at room temperature for 4 hours. The croissants can be refrigerated until the next day after this period of rest.

7. When you are ready to bake the croissants, preheat the oven to 420°F. Place the egg yolk and heavy cream in a mug and stir to combine. Brush the egg wash on the tops of the croissants, place them in the oven, and bake until golden brown, 20 to 25 minutes.

INGREDIENTS:

FOR THE DOUGH

28.4 OZ. ALL-PURPOSE FLOUR, PLUS MORE AS NEEDED

3.5 OZ. SUGAR

1 TABLESPOON FINE SEA SALT

1¼ TEASPOONS INSTANT YEAST

1 CUP WHOLE MILK

1.5 OZ. CULTURED BUTTER

POOLISH (SEE RECIPE)

1 EGG YOLK

1 TEASPOON HEAVY CREAM

FOR THE LAMINATION LAYER

18 OZ. CULTURED BUTTER

FOR THE FILLING

FRANGIPANE (SEE PAGE 66)

POOLISH

1. Place the all-purpose flour, ½ teaspoon of the yeast, and 1 cup of the water in a mixing bowl, stir to combine, and transfer the mixture to the refrigerator for 8 hours. Place the whole wheat flour, remaining yeast, and remaining water in a separate bowl and stir to combine. Let stand at room temperature for 1 hour and then place in the refrigerator for 8 hours.

INGREDIENTS:

POOLISH

1¾	CUPS ALL-PURPOSE FLOUR
1	TEASPOON INSTANT YEAST
1⅓	CUPS LUKEWARM WATER (90°F)
¾	CUP WHOLE WHEAT FLOUR

APPLE CIDER DOUGHNUTS

YIELD: 12 DOUGHNUTS / **ACTIVE TIME:** 1 HOUR / **TOTAL TIME:** 24 HOURS

The only thing that can distract one from the glory of fall in the Northeast is the smell of a fresh batch of these doughnuts carrying on the air.

1. In the work bowl of a stand mixer fitted with the paddle attachment, combine the apple cider, eggs, egg yolk, butter, and brown sugar and beat on medium speed for 2 minutes.

2. Add the baking powder, baking soda, salt, ½ teaspoon cinnamon, nutmeg, cardamom, allspice, and the flours and beat until the mixture comes together as a dough, about 5 minutes.

3. Coat a medium heatproof bowl with nonstick cooking spray, transfer the dough to the bowl, and cover with plastic wrap. Refrigerate overnight.

4. Place the vegetable oil in a Dutch oven fitted with a candy thermometer and warm the oil to 350°F over medium heat. Set a cooling rack in a rimmed baking sheet beside the stove.

5. Remove the dough from the refrigerator and place it on a flour-dusted work surface. Roll the dough out until it is ½ inch thick. Cut out the donuts using a round, 4-inch cookie cutter and then use a round, 1-inch cookie cutter to cut out the centers.

6. Transfer the doughnuts to the wire rack and let them sit at room temperature for 10 minutes.

7. Working in batches, carefully place the doughnuts in the oil and fry, turning them once, until browned and cooked through, 2 to 4 minutes. Transfer the cooked doughnuts to the wire rack to drain and cool.

8. Place the sugar and remaining cinnamon in a small bowl and stir to combine.

9. When the doughnuts have cooled, toss them in the cinnamon sugar and serve.

INGREDIENTS:

1¼	CUPS APPLE CIDER
2	EGGS
1	EGG YOLK
4	OZ. UNSALTED BUTTER, MELTED
6	OZ. LIGHT BROWN SUGAR
2½	TEASPOONS BAKING POWDER
1	TEASPOON BAKING SODA
1	TEASPOON KOSHER SALT
½	TEASPOON CINNAMON, PLUS 1 TABLESPOON
½	TEASPOON FRESHLY GRATED NUTMEG
½	TEASPOON CARDAMOM
½	TEASPOON ALLSPICE
19	OZ. ALL-PURPOSE FLOUR, PLUS MORE AS NEEDED
1.4	OZ. WHOLE WHEAT FLOUR
4	CUPS VEGETABLE OIL
2	CUPS SUGAR

APPLE STRUDEL

YIELD: 6 SERVINGS / **ACTIVE TIME:** 25 MINUTES / **TOTAL TIME:** 1 HOUR AND 30 MINUTES

In a traditional Austrian strudel, the apples will be one of the more tart varieties, and grated. We're not so specific here, but those looking to dig into the origins of their favorite preparations would do well to keep this in mind.

1. Preheat the oven to 350°F and line a baking sheet with parchment paper. Place the apples, lemon zest, lemon juice, sugar, cinnamon, ginger, and a pinch of salt in a large mixing bowl and toss until the apples are evenly coated. Place the mixture in a skillet and cook over medium heat until the apples begin to release their liquid. Remove the pan from heat and let it cool for 10 minutes before draining the mixture.

2. Place the melted butter in a bowl and stir in the remaining salt.

3. Brush a sheet of phyllo dough with some of the salted butter and lightly dust it with some of the confectioners' sugar. Repeat with the remaining sheets of phyllo dough, stacking them on top of one another after they have been dressed.

4. Place the apple mixture in the center of the phyllo sheets, leaving a 2-inch border of dough on the sides. Fold the border over the filling so that they overlap and gently press down to seal.

5. Place the strudel on the baking sheet, place it in the oven, and bake, rotating the sheet halfway through, until the strudel is golden brown, 30 to 40 minutes. Remove from the oven, transfer to a cutting board, and let cool slightly. Slice into desired portions and dust with additional confectioners' sugar before serving.

INGREDIENTS:

12 OZ. APPLES, PEELED, CORED, AND CHOPPED

¼ TEASPOON LEMON ZEST

1 TEASPOON FRESH LEMON JUICE

1½ TABLESPOONS SUGAR

DASH OF CINNAMON

¼ TEASPOON GROUND GINGER

2 PINCHES OF FINE SEA SALT

2 OZ. UNSALTED BUTTER, MELTED

7 SHEETS OF FROZEN PHYLLO DOUGH, THAWED

1 TABLESPOON CONFECTIONERS' SUGAR, PLUS MORE FOR DUSTING

CHOCOLATE CAKE DOUGHNUTS

YIELD: 12 DOUGHNUTS / **ACTIVE TIME:** 1 HOUR / **TOTAL TIME:** 24 HOURS

For those who prize tenderness while tending to their sweet tooth, these doughnuts are a godsend.

1. In the work bowl of a stand mixer fitted with the paddle attachment, cream the sugar and butter on medium speed until light and fluffy, about 5 minutes.

2. Incorporate the egg yolks one at a time, scraping down the work bowl as needed. When all of the egg yolks have been incorporated, add the sour cream and beat until incorporated. Add the flour, cocoa powder, baking powder, and salt and beat until the mixture comes together as a dough.

3. Coat a medium heatproof bowl with nonstick cooking spray, transfer the dough to the bowl, and cover with plastic wrap. Refrigerate overnight.

4. Place the vegetable oil in a Dutch oven fitted with a candy thermometer and warm the oil to 350°F over medium heat. Set a cooling rack in a rimmed baking sheet beside the stove.

5. Remove the dough from the refrigerator and place it on a flour-dusted work surface. Roll the dough out until it is ½ inch thick. Cut out the donuts using a round, 4-inch cookie cutter and then use a round, 1-inch cookie cutter to cut out the centers.

6. Transfer the doughnuts to the wire rack and let them sit at room temperature for 10 minutes.

7. Working in batches, carefully place the doughnuts in the oil and fry, turning them once, until browned and cooked through, about 4 minutes. A cake tester inserted into the center of the doughnuts should come out clean. Transfer the cooked doughnuts to the wire rack to drain and cool.

8. When cool, dip the top half of the doughnuts in the ganache, place them on a piece of parchment paper, and let the chocolate set before enjoying.

INGREDIENTS:

6   OZ. SUGAR

1   OZ. UNSALTED BUTTER, SOFTENED

3   EGG YOLKS

10.8 OZ. SOUR CREAM

11.4 OZ. ALL-PURPOSE FLOUR, PLUS MORE AS NEEDED

2.9 OZ. COCOA POWDER

2   TEASPOONS BAKING POWDER

1   TABLESPOON KOSHER SALT

4   CUPS VEGETABLE OIL

CHOCOLATE GANACHE (SEE PAGE 99), WARM

PARIS-BREST

YIELD: 6 PASTRIES / **ACTIVE TIME:** 50 MINUTES / **TOTAL TIME:** 2 HOURS

A classic French pastry that was created in 1910 to commemorate the Paris-Brest-Paris bicycle race, with its circular shape representing a wheel.

1. Preheat the oven to 425°F and line two baking sheets with parchment paper. In a medium saucepan, combine the water, butter, salt, and sugar and warm the mixture over medium heat until the butter is melted.

2. Add the flour to the pan and use a rubber spatula or a wooden spoon to fold the mixture until it comes together as a thick, shiny dough, taking care not to let the dough burn.

3. Transfer the dough to the work bowl of a stand mixer fitted with the paddle attachment and beat on medium speed until the dough is no longer steaming and the bowl is just warm to the touch, at least 10 minutes.

4. Incorporate six of the eggs two at a time, scraping down the work bowl between each addition. Transfer the dough to a piping bag fitted with a #867 tip (this will be called a "French Star Tip" on occasion).

5. Pipe a 5-inch ring of dough onto a baking sheet and then pipe another ring inside the first ring. Pipe another ring atop the seam between the first two rings. Repeat until all of the dough has been used.

6. In a small bowl, whisk the remaining egg and brush the tops of the dough with it. Arrange the almonds on top and gently press down to ensure they adhere.

7. Place the pastries in the oven and bake for 10 minutes. Lower the oven's temperature to 300°F and bake until golden brown and a cake tester inserted into each one comes out clean, 30 to 35 minutes. Remove from the oven and let them cool on a wire rack.

8. Fill a piping bag fit with a plain tip with the mousseline. Using a serrated knife, slice the pastries in half along their equators. Pipe rosettes of the mousseline around the inside. Place the top half of the pastries on top, dust them with confectioners' sugar, and enjoy.

INGREDIENTS:

17	OZ. WATER
8.5	OZ. UNSALTED BUTTER
1	TEASPOON FINE SEA SALT
2.4	OZ. SUGAR
12.5	OZ. ALL-PURPOSE FLOUR
7	EGGS
1	CUP SLIVERED ALMONDS
	HAZELNUT MOUSSELINE (SEE RECIPE)
	CONFECTIONERS' SUGAR, FOR DUSTING

HAZELNUT MOUSSELINE

1. Place the sugar, egg yolks, and cornstarch in a mixing bowl and whisk for 2 minutes, so that the mixture is thoroughly combined. Set aside.

2. Place the milk in a medium saucepan and bring to a simmer over medium heat. While whisking continually, gradually add the warm milk to the egg yolk mixture until it has all been incorporated.

3. Pour the tempered egg yolks into the saucepan and cook over medium heat, stirring constantly. When the custard has thickened and begins to simmer, cook for another 30 seconds and then remove the pan from heat.

4. Whisk in the remaining ingredients, strain the mousseline into a bowl through a fine-mesh sieve, and place plastic wrap directly on the top to keep a skin from forming. Place the mousseline in the refrigerator and chill for 2 hours before using. The mousseline will keep in the refrigerator for 5 days.

HAZELNUT PRALINE PASTE

1. Place the hazelnuts in a large, dry skillet and toast over medium heat until they just start to brown, about 5 minutes. Transfer the nuts to a clean, dry kitchen towel, fold the towel over the nuts, and rub them together until the skins have loosened. Place the toasted nuts on a parchment-lined baking sheet and discard the skins.

2. Place the sugar and water in a small saucepan and warm over medium heat, swirling the pan occasionally instead of stirring the mixture. Cook until the mixture is a deep golden brown and then pour it over the toasted hazelnuts. Let the mixture sit at room temperature until it has set.

3. Break the hazelnut brittle into pieces, place them in a blender, and add the canola oil and salt. Puree until the mixture is a smooth paste and use as desired. The paste will keep in the refrigerator for up to 1 month.

INGREDIENTS:

HAZELNUT MOUSSELINE

½	CUP SUGAR
6	EGG YOLKS
3	TABLESPOONS CORNSTARCH
2	CUPS WHOLE MILK
¼	TEASPOONS KOSHER SALT
1½	TEASPOONS PURE VANILLA EXTRACT
2	OZ. UNSALTED BUTTER, SOFTENED
¼	CUP HAZELNUT PRALINE PASTE (SEE RECIPE)

HAZELNUT PRALINE PASTE

2	CUPS HAZELNUTS
1	CUP SUGAR
3	TABLESPOONS WATER
2	TEASPOONS CANOLA OIL
¼	TEASPOON FINE SEA SALT

APPLE TURNOVERS

YIELD: 4 SERVINGS / **ACTIVE TIME:** 25 MINUTES / **TOTAL TIME:** 1 HOUR AND 15 MINUTES

Should time allow, prepare the apples two days before you are going to make this pastry and store them in the refrigerator. This will allow them to dry out some, causing the flavor to become more concentrated.

1. Preheat the oven to 375°F and line a baking sheet with parchment paper. Place the apples, 10 tablespoons of the sugar, lemon juice, and salt in a food processor and pulse until the apples are minced. Strain the juice into a bowl through a fine sieve, reserve the juice, and place the solids in another small bowl. Stir in the applesauce and let the mixture sit for 5 minutes.

2. Place the sheet of puff pastry on a flour-dusted work surface and cut it into quarters. Place 2 tablespoons of the apple mixture in the middle of each quarter and brush the edges with some of the reserved liquid. Fold a bottom corner of each quarter to the opposing top corner and crimp to seal. Place the sealed pastries in the refrigerator for 10 minutes.

3. Place the remaining sugar and the cinnamon in a small bowl and stir to combine.

4. Place the turnovers on the baking sheet and brush the tops with some of the reserved liquid. Sprinkle the cinnamon-and-sugar mixture over the turnovers, place the sheet in the oven, and bake, rotating the baking sheet halfway through, until the turnovers are golden brown, about 25 minutes. Remove from the oven, transfer to wire racks, dust with the sanding sugar, and let them cool before enjoying.

INGREDIENTS:

2   APPLES, PEELED, CORED, AND CHOPPED

¾   CUP SUGAR

1   TABLESPOON FRESH LEMON JUICE

     PINCH OF FINE SEA SALT

¼   CUP APPLESAUCE

1   SHEET OF FROZEN PUFF PASTRY, THAWED

     ALL-PURPOSE FLOUR, AS NEEDED

1   TEASPOON CINNAMON

     SANDING SUGAR, FOR TOPPING

CINNAMON TWISTS

YIELD: 24 TWISTS / **ACTIVE TIME:** 15 MINUTES / **TOTAL TIME:** 30 MINUTES

The quality of readily available frozen puff pastry is a godsend for those evenings when you need something inventive and delicious right this minute. Like these cinnamon twists, for instance.

1. Preheat oven to 375°F, line a baking sheet with parchment paper, and roll out the sheets of puff pastry. Combine the sugar, cinnamon, and nutmeg in a mixing bowl. Beat the egg in a separate bowl.

2. Lightly brush the top of each pastry sheet with the egg and then sprinkle the sugar-and-spice mixture evenly across both sheets of puff pastry.

3. Cut the pastries into long strips and twist them. Place strips on the baking sheet and bake until golden brown, 10 to 15 minutes. Remove from the oven, flip each pastry over, and bake for an additional 2 to 3 minutes.

4. Remove twists from oven and let cool until just slightly warm. Serve with the Caramel Sauce on the side.

INGREDIENTS:

2   SHEETS OF FROZEN PUFF PASTRY, THAWED

1   CUP SUGAR

3½   TABLESPOONS CINNAMON

1   TEASPOON FRESHLY GRATED NUTMEG

1   EGG

1   CUP CARAMEL SAUCE (SEE PAGE 103), WARMED, FOR SERVING

RED VELVET DOUGHNUTS

YIELD: 12 DOUGHNUTS / **ACTIVE TIME:** 1 HOUR / **TOTAL TIME:** 24 HOURS

I f you're a red velvet fanatic and find that the flavor of these doughnuts isn't quite hitting the mark, try substituting a little buttermilk for a portion of the sour cream.

1. In the work bowl of a stand mixer fitted with the paddle attachment, cream the sugar and butter on medium speed until light and fluffy, about 5 minutes.

2. Incorporate the egg yolks one at a time, scraping down the work bowl as needed. When all of the egg yolks have been incorporated, add the sour cream and beat until incorporated. Add the flour, cocoa powder, baking powder, salt, and food coloring and beat until the mixture comes together as a dough.

3. Coat a medium heatproof bowl with nonstick cooking spray, transfer the dough to the bowl, and cover with plastic wrap. Refrigerate overnight.

4. Place the vegetable oil in a Dutch oven fitted with a candy thermometer and warm the oil to 350°F over medium heat. Set a cooling rack in a rimmed baking sheet beside the stove.

5. Remove the dough from the refrigerator and place it on a flour-dusted work surface. Roll the dough out until it is ½ inch thick. Cut out the donuts using a round, 4-inch cookie cutter and then use a round, 1-inch cookie cutter to cut out the centers.

6. Transfer the doughnuts to the wire rack and let them sit at room temperature for 10 minutes.

7. Working in batches, carefully place the doughnuts in the oil and fry, turning them once, until browned and cooked through, about 4 minutes. A cake tester inserted into the center of the doughnuts should come out clean. Transfer the cooked doughnuts to the wire rack to drain and cool.

8. When cool, spread the frosting over the doughnuts and enjoy.

9. Once the donuts are cool, dip in the Cream Cheese Frosting and serve immediately.

INGREDIENTS:

6	OZ. SUGAR
1	OZ. UNSALTED BUTTER, SOFTENED
3	EGG YOLKS
10.8	OZ. SOUR CREAM
12.9	OZ. ALL-PURPOSE FLOUR, PLUS MORE AS NEEDED
1.5	OZ. COCOA POWDER
2	TEASPOONS BAKING POWDER
1	TABLESPOON KOSHER SALT
4	DROPS OF RED GEL FOOD COLORING
4	CUPS VEGETABLE OIL
	CREAM CHEESE FROSTING (SEE PAGE 76)

FRENCH CRULLERS

YIELD: 12 CRULLERS / **ACTIVE TIME:** 1 HOUR / **TOTAL TIME:** 1 HOUR AND 30 MINUTES

Made from choux pastry, these doughnuts are dangerously light and airy.

1. In a medium saucepan, combine the water, butter, salt, and sugar and warm the mixture over medium heat until the butter has melted.

2. Add the flour to the pan and use a rubber spatula or a wooden spoon to fold the mixture until it comes together as a thick, shiny dough, taking care not to let the dough burn.

3. Transfer the dough to the work bowl of a stand mixer fitted with the paddle attachment and beat on medium speed until the dough is no longer steaming and the bowl is just warm to the touch, at least 10 minutes.

4. Incorporate the eggs two at a time, scraping down the work bowl between each addition. Transfer the dough to a piping bag fitted with a star tip.

5. Cut parchment paper into a dozen 4-inch squares, place them on a baking sheet, and coat with nonstick cooking spray. Pipe 4-inch circles of dough onto the parchment and place the baking sheet in the refrigerator for 30 minutes.

6. Place the vegetable oil in a Dutch oven fitted with a candy thermometer and warm the oil to 350°F over medium heat. Set a cooling rack in a rimmed baking sheet beside the stove.

7. Working in batches, carefully lower the dough, with the parchment attached, into the hot oil. Cook for 2 minutes, turn them over, and use tongs to remove the parchment paper. Cook until the crullers are a deep golden brown and then transfer them to the wire rack to drain and cool.

8. When the crullers are cool, dip them in the glaze and enjoy.

INGREDIENTS:

17	OZ. WATER
8.5	OZ. UNSALTED BUTTER
1	TEASPOON FINE SEA SALT
2.4	OZ. SUGAR
12.5	OZ. ALL-PURPOSE FLOUR
6	EGGS
4	CUPS VEGETABLE OIL
	HONEY GLAZE (SEE PAGE 92)

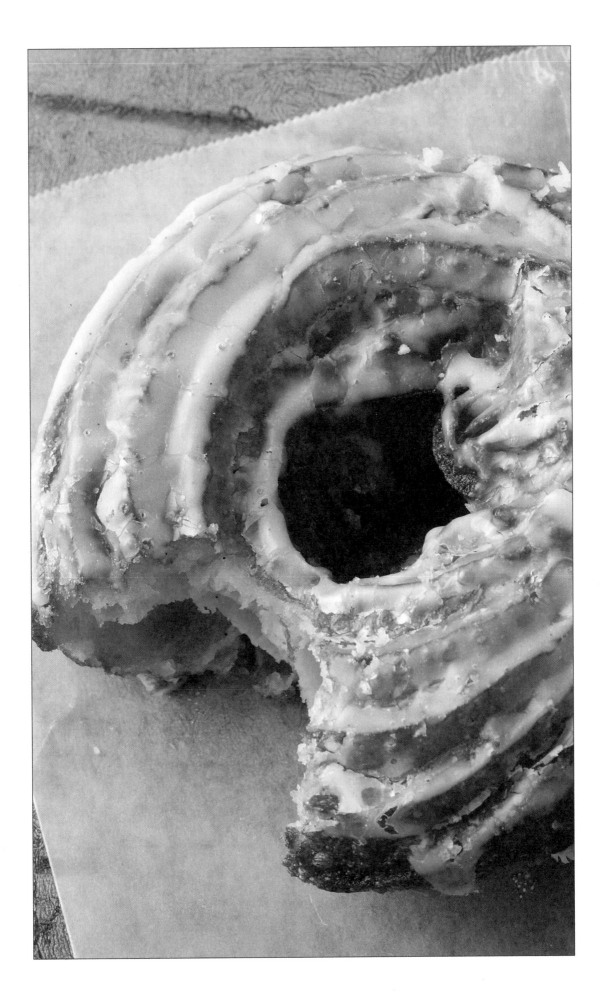

CANNOLI

YIELD: 10 CANNOLI / **ACTIVE TIME:** 45 MINUTES / **TOTAL TIME:** 4 HOURS

At the end of the day, few things in this world deliver on the promise of their appearance as well as the cannoli.

1. Line a colander with three pieces of cheesecloth and place it in sink. Place the ricotta in the colander, form the cheesecloth into a pouch and twist to remove as much liquid as possible from the ricotta. Keep the pouch taut and twisted, place it in a baking dish, and place a cast-iron skillet on top. Weight the skillet down with 2 large, heavy cans and place in the refrigerator for 1 hour.

2. Discard the drained liquid and transfer the ricotta to a mixing bowl. Add the mascarpone, half of the grated chocolate, the confectioners' sugar, vanilla, and salt and stir until well combined. Cover the bowl and refrigerate for at least 1 hour. The mixture will keep in the refrigerator for up to 24 hours.

3. Line an 18 x 13–inch baking sheet with parchment paper. Fill a small saucepan halfway with water and bring it to a gentle simmer. Place the chocolate in a heatproof mixing bowl, place it over the simmering water, and stir until it is melted. Add the remaining grated chocolate and stir until melted.

4. Dip the ends of the cannoli shells in chocolate, let the excess drip off, and transfer them to the baking sheet. Let the shells sit until the chocolate is firm, about 1 hour.

5. Place the cannoli filling in a piping bag and cut a ½-inch slit in it. Pipe the filling into the shells, working from both ends in order to ensure they are filled evenly. When all of the cannoli have been filled, dust them with confectioners' sugar and enjoy.

INGREDIENTS:

- 12 OZ. WHOLE MILK RICOTTA CHEESE
- 12 OZ. MASCARPONE CHEESE
- 4 OZ. CHOCOLATE, GRATED
- ¾ CUP CONFECTIONERS' SUGAR, PLUS MORE FOR DUSTING
- 1½ TEASPOONS PURE VANILLA EXTRACT
-   PINCH OF FINE SEA SALT
- 10 CANNOLI SHELLS

SOPAIPILLAS

YIELD: 24 SOPAIPILLAS / **ACTIVE TIME:** 35 MINUTES / **TOTAL TIME:** 1 HOUR

The "doughnut of the Southwest" isn't going to meet the expectations of New Englanders get when they hear that term, but that doesn't mean it isn't delicious.

1. In the bowl of a stand mixer fitted with the whisk attachment, combine the flour, baking powder, salt, and sugar. Turn the mixer on low speed and slowly drizzle in the warm water. Beat until the mixture comes together as a soft, smooth dough. Cover the bowl with a kitchen towel and let the dough rest for 20 minutes.

2. Place the vegetable oil in a Dutch oven and warm it over medium heat until it is 325°F. Line a baking sheet with paper towels and place it beside stove.

3. Divide the dough in half and pat each piece into a rectangle. Cut each rectangle into 12 squares and roll each square to ⅛ inch thick.

4. Working in batches of three, place the sopaipillas in the oil and use a pair of tongs to gently submerge them until puffy and golden brown, about 1 minute. Transfer the fried pastries to the baking sheet to drain and cool. When all of the sopaipillas have been fried, dust them with confectioners' sugar and cinnamon and serve with honey.

INGREDIENTS:

3 CUPS SELF-RISING FLOUR

1½ TEASPOONS BAKING POWDER

1 TEASPOON FINE SEA SALT

1 TEASPOON SUGAR

1 CUP WARM WATER (105°F)

4 CUPS VEGETABLE OIL

CONFECTIONERS' SUGAR, FOR DUSTING

CINNAMON, FOR DUSTING

HONEY, FOR SERVING

BLUEBERRY VARENYKY

YIELD: 36 VARENYKY / **ACTIVE TIME:** 1 HOUR / **TOTAL TIME:** 1 HOUR AND 30 MINUTES

Blueberries are wonderful in these dumplings, but don't hesitate to fill them with your favorite custard, pudding, or spread. The dough can also accommodate savory fillings.

1. Place two-thirds of the blueberries in a medium saucepan. Add the sugar and lemon zest and cook over medium heat, stirring occasionally, until the blueberries burst and release their juice, about 4 minutes. Reduce the heat to low and simmer until the mixture is very thick, about 18 minutes. Stir in the remaining blueberries, remove the pan from heat, and let the mixture cool completely.

2. Place the flour and salt in the work bowl of a stand mixer fitted with the paddle attachment. Add half of the butter and the sour cream and beat on medium speed until the mixture comes together as a crumbly dough, about 5 minutes.

3. Place the egg in a measuring cup and add enough water for the mixture to measure ¾ cup. Beat until combined and pour into the work bowl. Beat on medium speed until the dough holds together and is no longer sticky. If the dough is sticky, incorporate more flour, 1 teaspoon at a time.

4. Place the dough on a flour-dusted work surface and roll it out to ⅛ inch thick. Use a cookie cutter to cut as many 3-inch rounds from the dough as possible. Place the rounds on a parchment-lined baking sheet and lightly dust them with flour. When you have as many as you can fit in a single layer, cover with another piece of parchment.

5. To fill the varenyky, place a round in a slightly cupped hand and hold it so that it takes the shape of a taco. Place 1 teaspoon of the filling in the center. Using your thumb and index finger, firmly pinch the edges together to form a tight seal. You'll want this seal, or seam, to be approximately ¼ inch wide. Pat the sealed varenyky gently to evenly distribute the filling. Check for holes (patch any with a little bit of dough) and make sure the seal is tight. Reserve any leftover filling.

6. Bring a large pot of salted water to a boil. Once it's boiling, add the oil and stir. Working in batches, add the varenyky to the water and stir for 1 minute to keep them from sticking to the bottom. After the dumplings float to the surface, cook for another 3 minutes.

INGREDIENTS:

3½	CUPS FRESH BLUEBERRIES
1	TABLESPOON SUGAR
	ZEST OF 1 LEMON
3	CUPS ALL-PURPOSE FLOUR, PLUS MORE AS NEEDED
½	TEASPOON FINE SEA SALT, PLUS MORE TO TASTE
4.5	OZ. UNSALTED BUTTER
⅔	CUP SOUR CREAM, AT ROOM TEMPERATURE
1	LARGE EGG, BEATEN
	WATER, AS NEEDED
1	TABLESPOON CANOLA OIL
	CONFECTIONERS' SUGAR, FOR DUSTING

7. While the first batch of varenyky boils, melt the remaining butter in a skillet over low heat. Remove the varenyky from the water using a large slotted spoon and let them drain for a few seconds over the pot. Transfer to a warmed platter, top them with some of the melted butter, and gently toss to coat. Tent the platter loosely with aluminum foil to keep the dumplings warm while you cook the remaining varenyky.

8. To serve, dust the varenyky with the confectioners' sugar and top with any remaining filling.

FRISSANTS

YIELD: 8 FRISSANTS / **ACTIVE TIME:** 2 HOURS / **TOTAL TIME:** 5 HOURS

Feel free to use active dry or instant yeast here, but know that the floral aroma added by the fresh cake yeast is a considerable boon to these light, lovely pastries.

1. In the work bowl of stand mixer fitted with the dough hook, combine the flour, sugar, salt, yeast, egg yolk, 1⅓ tablespoons butter, and water and knead on low speed until the mixture just comes together as a dough, about 5 minutes.

2. Transfer the dough to a parchment-lined baking sheet, flatten the dough, cover it with plastic wrap, and place in the freezer for 1 hour.

3. Place the remaining butter in a large resealable plastic bag and flatten with a rolling pin until it is pliable and fills up as much of the bag as possible. The butter should not be melted.

4. Remove the dough from the freezer and place it onto a flour-dusted work surface. Roll it out so it is twice the size of the butter in the bag. Remove the butter from the bag and place it on one side of the dough. Fold the other side over the butter, making sure that the butter is fully enclosed by dough. Roll out the dough and fold it over itself. Transfer to the refrigerator and let it rest for 30 minutes.

5. Remove the dough from the refrigerator and roll it out. Fold it as you would a letter before placing it in an envelope, return the dough to the refrigerator, and chill for 30 minutes.

6. Remove the dough from the refrigerator and roll it out. Repeat the envelope fold made in Step 5, return the dough to the refrigerator, and chill for 30 minutes.

7. Place the dough on a flour-dusted work surface and roll it out until it is ¼ inch thick. Cut the dough into 8 pieces, place the pieces on a greased piece of parchment paper in a naturally warm area, and let them sit until they have doubled in size, about 2 hours.

8. Add the vegetable oil to a large Dutch oven and warm them to 350°F over medium heat.

9. Working in batches, place the frissants in the oil and fry, turning once, until they are golden brown all over. Transfer the cooked frissants to a paper towel–lined plate to drain.

10. Use a toothpick to poke 4 holes in the undersides of each frissant and, using a piping bag fitted with a plain tip, pipe the Pastry Cream into them. Dust with confectioners' sugar and serve.

INGREDIENTS:

3 CUPS ALL-PURPOSE FLOUR, PLUS MORE AS NEEDED

3¼ TABLESPOONS SUGAR

¾ TEASPOON FINE SEA SALT

2¼ TABLESPOONS CAKE YEAST

⅔ TABLESPOON EGG YOLK

4 OZ. UNSALTED BUTTER, PLUS 1⅓ TABLESPOONS

¾ CUP WATER

4 CUPS VEGETABLE OIL

PASTRY CREAM (SEE PAGE 80)

CONFECTIONERS' SUGAR, FOR DUSTING

PAIN AU CHOCOLAT

YIELD: 16 CROISSANTS / ACTIVE TIME: 45 MINUTES / TOTAL TIME: 17 HOURS

The stories that Marie Antoinette introduced this and the croissant to France are apocryphal, as they followed her famous demise by nearly 50 years.

1. To begin preparations for the croissants, combine the flour, sugar, salt, yeast, milk, and butter in the work bowl of a stand mixer fitted with the paddle attachment. Add the Poolish and beat on low speed until the mixture is just combined, about 2 minutes. Let rest for 20 minutes and then mix for 2 minutes on low speed. Transfer the dough to a separate bowl, cover with plastic wrap, and let stand at room temperature for 1 hour.

2. Place the butter for the lamination layer in a mixing bowl and beat until it is smooth and free of lumps. Place the butter on a piece of parchment paper and smash until it is a 6½ x 9–inch rectangle of uniform thickness. Place the butter in the refrigerator when the dough has 20 minutes left to stand.

3. Place the dough on a flour-dusted work surface and roll it out into a 13 x 9–inch rectangle. Remove the butter from the refrigerator and place it on half of the dough. Fold the other half over the butter, making sure that the dough completely covers the butter.

4. Roll the dough out into a 12 x 27–inch rectangle, fold it in half, and then fold it in half again. Cover the dough completely with plastic wrap, place it in the refrigerator, and chill for 1 hour.

5. Place the dough on a flour-dusted work surface and gently roll it out into a 12 x 30–inch rectangle. Cut the rectangle in half and then cut each half every 3½ inches. Place a piece of chocolate in the center of each piece of dough. Fold the dough over the chocolate and place the croissants, seam side down, on parchment-lined baking sheets, making sure to leave enough space between them. Let them stand at room temperature for 4 hours or refrigerate until the next day.

6. When you are ready to bake the croissants, preheat the oven to 420°F. Place the egg yolk and heavy cream in a mug and stir to combine. Brush the egg wash on the tops of the croissants, place them in the oven, and bake until golden brown, 20 to 25 minutes.

INGREDIENTS:

FOR THE CROISSANTS

28.4 OZ. ALL-PURPOSE FLOUR, PLUS MORE FOR DUSTING

3.5 OZ. SUGAR

1 TABLESPOON FINE SEA SALT

1¼ TEASPOONS INSTANT YEAST

1 CUP WHOLE MILK

1.5 OZ. CULTURED BUTTER POOLISH (SEE PAGE 419)

16 PIECES OF PREFERRED CHOCOLATE

1 EGG YOLK

1 TEASPOON HEAVY CREAM

FOR THE LAMINATION LAYER

18 OZ. CULTURED BUTTER

ZEPPOLE

YIELD: 18 ZEPPOLE / **ACTIVE TIME:** 30 MINUTES / **TOTAL TIME:** 1 HOUR

A treat concocted to celebrate Saint Joseph's Day, a Catholic feast day, you should treat these as you would a doughnut. Either sprinkle with sugar, roll in cinnamon, or inject them with your favorite filling.

1. Combine the flour, sugar, yeast, baking powder, and salt in large bowl and whisk in the water and vanilla. Cover the bowl with plastic wrap and let the batter rest at room temperature until it doubles in size, 15 to 25 minutes.

2. Add oil to a Dutch oven until it is about 1½ inches deep and warm to 350°F over medium heat.

3. Using a greased tablespoon, add six heaping tablespoons of the batter to the oil and fry until golden brown and cooked through, 2 to 3 minutes, turning halfway through. Make sure the oil remains around 350°F while frying the zeppole.

4. Transfer the cooked zeppole to a paper towel–lined plate. When all of the zeppole have been cooked, dust them with confectioners' sugar (if desired) and serve.

INGREDIENTS:

6.7 OZ. ALL-PURPOSE FLOUR

1 TABLESPOON SUGAR

2 TEASPOONS INSTANT YEAST

1 TEASPOON BAKING POWDER

½ TEASPOON FINE SEA SALT

1 CUP WARM WATER (105°F)

½ TEASPOON PURE VANILLA EXTRACT

CANOLA OIL, AS NEEDED

CONFECTIONERS' SUGAR, FOR DUSTING (OPTIONAL)

PUDDINGS & CUSTARDS

*S*imple, yes. But so delicious and affirming that they carry an ability all too rare in this world: making you realize how little one needs to actually be happy.

Many of the classic preparations in this chapter have been pushed aside by the instant varieties that are now widely available. And while those effortless offerings can certainly scratch the itch when you need the luscious comfort that only a pudding or custard can provide, these recipes are here to remind you that convenience always comes at a great cost.

Puddings and custards made from scratch may seem to be something from the past, but a quick scan of the ingredients required will reveal something important—everything you need to prepare them is probably already in the house, and many are a wonderful landing spot for odds and ends left over from other preparations—egg yolks, milk, bread, and fruit.

Cutting down on waste and costs and getting to treat yourself—sounds like something worth investing a bit of time in.

CHOCOLATE MOUSSE

YIELD: 6 SERVINGS / **ACTIVE TIME:** 45 MINUTES / TOTAL TIME 2 HOURS AND 45 MINUTES

With its perfect balance of bitter and sweet and silky texture, this is a dish that will never go out of style.

1. Fill a small saucepan halfway with water and bring it to a simmer. Place the chocolate in a heatproof mixing bowl and place it over the simmering water. Stir until the chocolate is melted and then set aside.

2. In the work bowl of a stand mixer fitted with the whisk attachment, whip 15 oz. of the heavy cream until it holds soft peaks. Transfer the whipped cream to another bowl and place it in the refrigerator.

3. Place the egg yolks and sugar in a mixing bowl, whisk to combine, and set the mixture aside.

4. In a small saucepan, combine the milk, salt, and remaining cream and bring the mixture to a simmer. Remove the pan from heat.

5. Whisking constantly, gradually add the warm mixture to the egg yolk mixture. When all of the warm mixture has been incorporated, add the tempered egg yolks to the saucepan and cook over low heat, stirring constantly, until the mixture thickens enough to coat the back of a wooden spoon.

6. Remove the pan from heat, pour the mixture into the melted chocolate, and whisk until thoroughly combined. Add half of the whipped cream, fold until incorporated, and then fold in the rest of the whipped cream.

7. Divide the mousse between six 8 oz. ramekins and lightly tap the bottom of each one to settle the mousse and to remove any air bubbles. Transfer to the refrigerator and chill for 2 hours.

8. To serve, top each mousse with Chantilly Cream.

INGREDIENTS:

17	OZ. DARK CHOCOLATE (55 TO 65 PERCENT)
19	OZ. HEAVY CREAM
2	EGG YOLKS
1	OZ. SUGAR
½	CUP WHOLE MILK
¼	TEASPOON KOSHER SALT
	CHANTILLY CREAM (SEE PAGE 89)

LEMON POSSET

YIELD: 6 SERVINGS / **ACTIVE TIME:** 30 MINUTES / **TOTAL TIME:** 4 HOURS

An English classic that allows us to appreciate all the good that is available when you keep things simple in the kitchen.

1. Place the heavy cream, sugar, and lemon zest in a saucepan and bring the mixture to a simmer over medium heat, stirring constantly. Cook until the sugar has dissolved and the mixture has reduced slightly, about 10 minutes.

2. Remove the saucepan from heat and stir in the lemon juice. Let the mixture stand until a skin forms on the top, about 20 minutes. Strain the mixture through a fine sieve and transfer it to the refrigerator. Chill until set, about 3 hours.

3. About 10 minutes before you are ready to serve the posset, remove the mixture from the refrigerator and let it come to room temperature. Cover the bottom of the serving dishes with whipped cream and then alternate layers of the posset and whipped cream. Top each serving with a generous amount of blueberries and enjoy.

INGREDIENTS:

2   CUPS HEAVY CREAM

⅔   CUP SUGAR

1   TABLESPOON LEMON ZEST

6   TABLESPOONS FRESH LEMON JUICE

2   CUPS CHANTILLY CREAM (SEE PAGE 89)

FRESH BLUEBERRIES, FOR TOPPING

GRAPE-NUT CUSTARD

YIELD: 12 SERVINGS / **ACTIVE TIME:** 15 MINUTES / **TOTAL TIME:** 1 HOUR AND 15 MINUTES

This is another revered New England oddity, perhaps for its miraculous ability to make Grape-Nuts enjoyable.

1. Preheat the oven to 350°F. Place the milk, cereal, eggs, vanilla, and sugar in a bowl and stir until thoroughly combined.

2. Transfer the mixture to a baking dish and then place the dish in a roasting pan. Fill the roasting pan with hot water until it reaches halfway up the sides of the baking dish. Place the custard in the oven and bake for 15 minutes.

3. Remove the baking dish from the oven and stir the custard. Return to the oven and cook until it is golden brown and a cake tester inserted into the center comes out clean, about 15 minutes.

4. Remove the custard from the oven, sprinkle with cinnamon, and grate nutmeg over the top. Let the custard cool completely.

5. When the custard is cool, top each serving with a drizzle of maple syrup and a dollop of Chantilly Cream.

INGREDIENTS:

4   CUPS WHOLE MILK, WARMED

½   CUP GRAPE-NUTS CEREAL

5   EGGS

1   TEASPOON PURE VANILLA EXTRACT

½   CUP SUGAR

1   TEASPOON CINNAMON

FRESHLY GRATED NUTMEG, TO TASTE

MAPLE SYRUP, FOR GARNISH

CHANTILLY CREAM (SEE PAGE 89), FOR SERVING

CHERRY CLAFOUTIS

YIELD: 6 SERVINGS / **ACTIVE TIME:** 20 MINUTES / **TOTAL TIME:** 45 MINUTES

One of those invaluable whatever's-on-hand recipes, as almost any fruit can be swapped in for the cherries. Also, don't hesitate to experiment with substituting almond extract for some amount of the vanilla.

1. Preheat the oven to 400°F. Place three-quarters of the butter, ½ cup of the sugar, the flour, salt, vanilla, eggs, and milk in a large mixing bowl and stir until the mixture is well combined and smooth. Set the batter aside.

2. Grease a cast-iron skillet with the remaining butter and put the skillet in the oven to warm up.

3. When the skillet is warm, remove from the oven, place ½ cup of the sugar in the skillet, and shake to distribute it evenly. Distribute the cherries in the skillet and then pour in the batter. Sprinkle the remaining granulated sugar on top, place the skillet in the oven, and bake until the custard is golden brown and set in the middle, about 30 minutes.

4. Remove from the oven, sprinkle confectioners' sugar over the clafoutis, and serve immediately.

INGREDIENTS:

4 OZ. UNSALTED BUTTER, MELTED

1 CUP SUGAR, PLUS 2 TEASPOONS

⅔ CUP ALL-PURPOSE FLOUR

½ TEASPOON FINE SEA SALT

1 TEASPOON PURE VANILLA EXTRACT

3 EGGS, BEATEN

1 CUP WHOLE MILK

3 CUPS CHERRIES, PITTED

CONFECTIONERS' SUGAR, FOR TOPPING

VANILLA PANNA COTTA

YIELD: 4 SERVINGS / **ACTIVE TIME**: 30 MINUTES / **TOTAL TIME**: 4 HOURS AND 30 MINUTES

This eggless custard, which translates to "cooked cream" in Italian, is great on its own, or with fresh berries on top.

1. Place the gelatin sheets in a small bowl. Add 1 cup of ice and water until the sheets are submerged. Let the mixture rest.

2. Combine the heavy cream, milk, sugar, and the vanilla seeds and pod in a saucepan and bring to a simmer. Cook for 15 minutes and then remove the pan from heat. Remove the vanilla bean pod and discard.

3. Remove the bloomed gelatin from the ice water. Squeeze to remove as much water from the sheets as possible, add them to the warm mixture, and whisk until they have completely dissolved.

4. Strain the mixture into a bowl through a fine-mesh sieve and divide it between four 8 oz. ramekins, leaving about ½ inch of space at the top. Carefully transfer the ramekins to the refrigerator and chill until the panna cottas are fully set, about 4 hours.

INGREDIENTS:

3½	SHEETS OF SILVER GELATIN
13	OZ. HEAVY CREAM
13	OZ. MILK
3.5	OZ. SUGAR
	SEEDS AND POD OF ½ VANILLA BEAN

CHOCOLATE POTS DE CRÈME

YIELD: 6 SERVINGS / **ACTIVE TIME:** 30 MINUTES / **TOTAL TIME:** 6 HOURS AND 30 MINUTES

A loose, easy-to-prepare custard that occupies the space between a mousse and a pudding.

1. Preheat the oven to 325°F. Bring 8 cups of water to a boil and then set aside.

2. Place the chocolate in a heatproof mixing bowl. Place the heavy cream in a saucepan and bring it to a simmer over medium heat. Pour the cream over the chocolate and whisk until the chocolate has melted and the mixture is combined. Set aside.

3. In the work bowl of a stand mixer fitted with the whisk attachment, combine the sugar, egg yolks, liqueur, and salt and whip on high speed until the mixture is pale yellow and ribbony, about 10 minutes.

4. Pour the mixture into the chocolate mixture and fold to incorporate.

5. Fill six 8 oz. ramekins three-quarters of the way with the custard.

6. Place the ramekins in a 9 x 13–inch baking pan and pour the boiling water into the pan until it reaches halfway up the sides of the ramekins. Place the pan in the oven and bake until the custards are set at their edges and jiggle slightly at their centers, about 50 minutes. Remove from the oven and carefully transfer the ramekins to a wire rack. Let cool for 1 hour

7. Place the ramekins in the refrigerator and chill for 4 hours before enjoying.

INGREDIENTS:

5	OZ. CHOCOLATE
2	CUPS HEAVY CREAM
4	OZ. SUGAR
4	EGG YOLKS
1	TABLESPOON CHOCOLATE LIQUEUR
¼	TEASPOON KOSHER SALT

QUARK PANNA COTTA
WITH ROSÉ RASPBERRY SAUCE

YIELD: 6 SERVINGS / ACTIVE TIME: 40 MINUTES / TOTAL TIME: 24 HOURS

Using quark as the base of the panna cotta lends the custard a tartness that pairs beautifully with the raspberry-forward sauce.

1. To prepare the panna cotta, place the cream, milk, sugar, salt, and vanilla in a saucepan and bring to a simmer over medium heat, taking care that the mixture does not come to a boil. Remove the pan from heat.

2. Place the quark in a small mixing bowl and ladle about 1 cup of the warm milk mixture into the bowl. Whisk to combine and then pour the tempered quark into the saucepan.

3. Bring the mixture back to a boil and then remove the saucepan from heat. Place the gelatin in a large mixing bowl and pour the warmed mixture into it, whisking constantly to prevent lumps from forming. Pour the mixture into six ramekins and place them in the refrigerator to set overnight.

4. Approximately 2 hours before you will serve the panna cotta, prepare the sauce. Place the Rosé in a small saucepan and cook over medium-high heat until it has reduced by half. Add the remaining ingredients for the sauce, bring the mixture to a boil, and then reduce heat so that the mixture simmers. Simmer for 20 minutes.

5. Transfer the mixture to a blender and puree until smooth. Strain through a fine sieve and place the sauce in the refrigerator to cool completely.

6. When the panna cottas are set, pour 1 tablespoon of honey over each serving. Pour the sauce on top of the honey and garnish with raspberries, toasted almonds, and mint.

INGREDIENTS:

FOR THE PANNA COTTA

2½	CUPS HEAVY CREAM
⅔	CUP WHOLE MILK
⅔	CUP SUGAR
½	TEASPOON FINE SEA SALT
1	TEASPOON PURE VANILLA EXTRACT
2	CUPS QUARK CHEESE
½	OZ. GELATIN (2 ENVELOPES)
6	TABLESPOONS HONEY
	RASPBERRIES, FOR GARNISH
	TOASTED ALMONDS, FOR GARNISH
	MINT LEAVES, FOR GARNISH

FOR THE SAUCE

2	CUPS ROSÉ
⅓	CUP SUGAR
¼	TEASPOON FINE SEA SALT
2	CUPS RASPBERRIES

TIRAMISU

YIELD: 8 TO 10 SERVINGS / **ACTIVE TIME:** 20 MINUTES / **TOTAL TIME:** 3 HOURS AND 30 MINUTES

To be blunt: the ladyfingers available at the grocery store are a travesty. If you want this coffee-laced dessert, you'll want to use the homemade version provided here.

1. Place the espresso, 1 tablespoon of sugar, and Kahlúa in a bowl and stir to combine. Set the mixture aside.

2. Place two inches of water in a saucepan and bring to a simmer. Place the remaining sugar and egg yolks in a metal mixing bowl and set the bowl over the simmering water. Whisk the mixture continually until it has nearly tripled in size, approximately 10 minutes. Remove from heat, add the mascarpone, and fold to incorporate.

3. Pour the heavy cream into a separate bowl and whisk until soft peaks start to form. Gently fold the whipped cream into the mascarpone mixture.

4. Place the Ladyfingers in the espresso mixture and briefly submerge them. Place an even layer of the soaked Ladyfingers on the bottom of a 9 x 13–inch baking pan. This will use up approximately half of the Ladyfingers. Spread half of the mascarpone mixture on top of the Ladyfingers and then repeat until the Ladyfingers and mascarpone have been used up.

5. Cover with plastic and place in the refrigerator for 3 hours. Sprinkle the cocoa powder over the top before serving.

INGREDIENTS:

2	CUPS FRESHLY BREWED ESPRESSO
½	CUP GRANULATED SUGAR, PLUS 1 TABLESPOON
3	TABLESPOONS KAHLÚA
4	LARGE EGG YOLKS
2	CUPS MASCARPONE CHEESE
1	CUP HEAVY CREAM
30	LADYFINGERS (SEE RECIPE)
2	TABLESPOONS COCOA POWDER

LADYFINGERS

1. Preheat the oven to 300°F. Line two baking sheets with parchment paper and dust with flour. Shake to remove any excess.

2. Place the egg yolks in a mixing bowl and gradually incorporate the sugar, using a handheld mixer at high speed. When the mixture is thick and a pale yellow, whisk in the vanilla.

3. In the work bowl of a stand mixer fitted with the whisk attachment, beat the egg whites and salt until the mixture holds soft peaks. Scoop one-quarter of the whipped egg whites into the egg yolk mixture and sift one-quarter of the flour on top. Fold to combine and repeat until all of the egg whites and flour have been incorporated and the mixture is light and airy.

4. Spread the batter in 4-inch-long strips on the baking sheets, leaving 1 inch between them. Sprinkle the confectioners' sugar over the top and place them in the oven.

5. Bake until lightly golden brown and just crispy, about 20 minutes. Remove from the oven and transfer the ladyfingers to a wire rack to cool completely before using.

INGREDIENTS:

LADYFINGERS

- 3.3 OZ. ALL-PURPOSE FLOUR, PLUS MORE AS NEEDED
- 3 EGGS, SEPARATED
- 3.5 OZ. SUGAR, PLUS 1 TABLESPOON
- 1 TEASPOON PURE VANILLA EXTRACT
- PINCH OF FINE SEA SALT
- 3 OZ. CONFECTIONERS' SUGAR

INDIAN PUDDING

YIELD: 8 SERVINGS / **ACTIVE TIME:** 30 MINUTES / **TOTAL TIME:** 8 HOURS AND 30 MINUTES

This recipe dates back to 18th-century America, when New Englanders who had a hankering for the hasty pudding they left behind in England had to make the most of what was available, resulting in this dessert that leans heavily upon molasses and cornmeal. This latter ingredient, which the colonists referred to as "Indian flour," is what lends the dish its name.

1. Preheat the oven to 275°F and coat a baking dish with nonstick cooking spray.

2. Place the milk in a large saucepan and cook over medium-high heat until it comes to a simmer. Remove the saucepan from heat and set aside.

3. Place all of the remaining ingredients, except for the eggs, butter, and Chantilly Cream, in a mixing bowl and stir to combine. Whisk this mixture into the warm milk, place the saucepan over medium-low heat, and cook, stirring, until the mixture begins to thicken.

4. Remove the saucepan from heat, crack the eggs into a bowl, and whisk them until combined. While whisking, add the hot molasses-and-cornmeal mixture ½ cup at a time until all of it has been incorporated. Add the butter and whisk until it has been incorporated.

5. Pour the pudding into the prepared baking dish. Place the dish in a roasting pan and fill the roasting pan with warm water until it reaches halfway up the sides of the baking dish. Place the pudding in the oven and bake until it is set, about 2 hours.

6. Remove the pudding from the oven and let it cool to room temperature. When cool, transfer to the refrigerator and chill for at least 6 hours before serving with the Chantilly Cream.

INGREDIENTS:

3	CUPS WHOLE MILK
1	CUP HEAVY CREAM
½	CUP CORNMEAL
½	CUP BLACKSTRAP MOLASSES
½	CUP LIGHT BROWN SUGAR
½	TEASPOON GROUND GINGER
½	TEASPOON FRESHLY GRATED NUTMEG
½	TEASPOON ALLSPICE
2	TEASPOONS CINNAMON
2	TEASPOONS FINE SEA SALT
5	EGGS
2.5	OZ. UNSALTED BUTTER
	CHANTILLY CREAM (SEE PAGE 89), FOR SERVING

COCONUT PUDDING PANCAKES

YIELD: 30 PANCAKES / **ACTIVE TIME**: 20 MINUTES / **TOTAL TIME**: 50 MINUTES

This is a take on a very popular street food in Thailand that is known as khanom krok, or "candy bowl" because of the traditional shape, and the sweetness. To make the perfectly spherical cakes found on the streets of Bangkok, you will need to purchase a khanom krok pan, which is similar to the aebleskiver pan used here.

1. Preheat the oven to 350°F and coat an aebleskiver pan with non-stick cooking spray.

2. Place the coconut milk, 1 cup of the rice flour, the coconut, 1 tablespoon of the sugar, and the salt in a bowl and whisk vigorously until the sugar has dissolved. Set the mixture aside.

3. Place the coconut cream, remaining rice flour, remaining sugar, and tapioca starch or cornstarch in another bowl and whisk until the starch has dissolved. Add this mixture to the coconut milk mixture and stir until combined.

4. Fill the wells of the aebleskiver pan with the batter and top with some of the corn, if using.

5. Place the pan in the oven and bake until they are firm, 15 to 20 minutes. Remove from the oven, transfer the cooked cakes to a platter, and tent it with aluminum foil to keep warm. Repeat Steps 4 and 5 with any remaining batter.

INGREDIENTS:

1½	CUPS COCONUT MILK
1½	CUPS RICE FLOUR
½	CUP SWEETENED SHREDDED COCONUT
5	TABLESPOONS CASTER SUGAR
½	TEASPOON FINE SEA SALT
1	CUP COCONUT CREAM
½	TABLESPOON TAPIOCA STARCH OR CORNSTARCH
¼	CUP CORN KERNELS (OPTIONAL)

LEMON CURD

YIELD: 2 CUPS / **ACTIVE TIME:** 15 MINUTES / **TOTAL TIME:** 2 HOURS

This will most often find its way into a tart or pie, or atop a shortbread or cake. But its combination of buttery, sweet, and tart make it good enough to go it alone.

1. In the work bowl of a stand mixer fitted with the paddle attachment, combine all of the ingredients and beat on medium speed until well combined.

2. Pour the mixture into a saucepan and cook over low heat until it is thick enough to coat the back of a wooden spoon, about 15 minutes.

3. Pour the lemon curd into a serving dish, place in the refrigerator, and chill until it thickens further, about 1½ hours.

INGREDIENTS:

1	CUP FRESH LEMON JUICE
4	TEASPOONS LEMON ZEST
6	LARGE EGGS
1⅓	CUPS SUGAR
8	OZ. UNSALTED BUTTER

STRAWBERRY CONSOMMÉ
WITH CARDAMOM PANNA COTTA

YIELD: 4 SERVINGS / **ACTIVE TIME:** 30 MINUTES / **TOTAL TIME:** 5 HOURS

Adding sugar to the consommé helps extract all the flavor from the strawberries—try one after straining, and you'll be pleased to discover that all of their flavor is in the soup.

1. To begin preparations for the consommé, place all of the ingredients in a heatproof mixing bowl, stir to combine, and cover with plastic wrap.

2. Bring 2 cups of water to boil in a saucepan. Place the bowl over the saucepan and reduce the heat so that the water simmers. Cook the consommé for 1 hour, turn off the burner, and let stand for 1 hour.

3. After 1 hour, strain the mixture through a fine sieve and place it in the refrigerator for 1 hour.

4. While the consommé is chilling in the refrigerator, begin preparations for the panna cotta. Place half of the buttermilk in a bowl and set aside. Place the remaining buttermilk, heavy cream, vanilla seeds and pod, cardamom, and sugar in a small saucepan and bring to a simmer over medium-low heat. Remove the pan from heat and let the mixture steep for 10 minutes.

5. Place the gelatin in the bowl of cold buttermilk and stir briskly to combine. Bring the contents of the saucepan to a boil over medium heat and add the buttermilk-and-gelatin mixture. Remove the pan from heat and stir gently for 2 minutes. Strain through a fine sieve and chill in the refrigerator for 15 minutes, removing to stir every 5 minutes. Pour the panna cotta into ramekins and refrigerate for 3 hours.

6. To serve, ladle the consommé over the panna cotta and serve with Scottish Shortbread.

INGREDIENTS:

FOR THE CONSOMMÉ

2	QUARTS OF STRAWBERRIES, HULLED AND CHOPPED
½	CUP SUGAR
	SEEDS OF 1 VANILLA BEAN
1	CINNAMON STICK
1	STAR ANISE POD
	JUICE AND ZEST OF 2 LEMONS
1	SPRIG OF FRESH MINT
2	TABLESPOONS GRAND MARNIER

FOR THE PANNA COTTA

¾	CUP BUTTERMILK
¾	CUP HEAVY CREAM
	SEEDS AND POD OF ½ VANILLA BEAN
	SEEDS OF 2 CARDAMOM PODS, CHOPPED
2	TABLESPOONS SUGAR
1¼	TEASPOONS GELATIN
	SCOTTISH SHORTBREAD (SEE PAGE 174), FOR SERVING

KATAIFI PUDDING

YIELD: 8 SERVINGS / ACTIVE TIME: 15 MINUTES / TOTAL TIME: 1 HOUR AND 30 MINUTES

A wonderful twist on the beloved Greek dessert.

1. Preheat the oven to 300°F and coat a square, 8-inch cake pan with nonstick cooking spray.

2. Bring a large saucepan of water to a boil. When the water is boiling, add salt and the pasta and cook for 3 minutes less than the directed time. Reserve ¼ cup of the pasta water, drain the pasta, and set aside.

3. Return the empty pan to the stove. Immediately turn the heat to high and add half of the butter and all of the reserved pasta water. Add the drained pasta and cook. Add the cinnamon and cook, while tossing to coat, for 1 to 2 minutes. Remove from heat.

4. Transfer one-third of the cooked pasta to the prepared pan. Sprinkle half of the almonds, raisins, pistachios, and ¼ cup of the sugar on top. Add half of the remaining pasta and sprinkle with the remaining almonds, raisins, pistachios, and another ¼ cup of the sugar. Top with the remaining pasta. Cut the remaining butter into small pieces and dot the mixture with them.

5. Place the pan in the oven and bake for 25 minutes.

6. While it bakes, put the remaining sugar in a small saucepan over low heat and stir until it melts and turns golden brown. Remove from heat and very slowly and carefully (the mixture will splatter a bit) add the ice water. Return the pan to the heat and stir until the mixture thickens, about 4 minutes.

7. After 25 minutes, remove the dish from the oven and pour the sauce evenly over the top. Return to the oven to bake until the top is golden brown, about 5 minutes. Let cool briefly before serving with Chantilly Cream.

INGREDIENTS:

	SALT, TO TASTE
8	OZ. ANGEL HAIR PASTA
3.5	OZ. UNSALTED BUTTER
1	TEASPOON CINNAMON
¾	CUP SLIVERED ALMONDS
¾	CUP RAISINS
¾	CUP CHOPPED PISTACHIOS
¾	CUP CASTER SUGAR
¼	CUP ICE WATER
	CHANTILLY CREAM (SEE PAGE 89), FOR SERVING

THE PERFECT FLAN

YIELD: 6 SERVINGS / **ACTIVE TIME:** 30 MINUTES / **TOTAL TIME:** 6 HOURS AND 30 MINUTES

Listen Mamet, you're a great writer, but you're wrong about this: there most definitely *is* a difference between good and bad flan.

1. Preheat the oven to 350°F. Bring 2 quarts of water to a boil and set aside.

2. Place the 1 cup of the sugar and the water in a small saucepan and bring to a boil over high heat, swirling the pan instead of stirring. Cook until the caramel is a deep golden brown, taking care not to burn it. Remove the pan from heat and pour the caramel into a round, 8-inch cake pan. Place the cake pan on a cooling rack and let it sit until it has set.

3. Place the egg yolks, eggs, cream cheese, remaining sugar, condensed milk, evaporated milk, heavy cream, almond extract, and vanilla in a blender and puree until emulsified.

4. Pour the mixture over the caramel and place the cake pan in a roasting pan. Pour the boiling water into the roasting pan until it reaches halfway up the side of the cake pan.

5. Place the flan in the oven and bake until is just set, 60 to 70 minutes. The flan should still be jiggly without being runny. Remove from the oven, place the cake pan on a cooling rack, and let it cool for 1 hour.

6. Place the flan in the refrigerator and chill for 4 hours.

7. Run a knife along the edge of the pan and invert the flan onto a plate so that the caramel layer is on top. Slice the flan and serve.

INGREDIENTS:

2	CUPS SUGAR
¼	CUP WATER
5	EGG YOLKS
5	EGGS
5	OZ. CREAM CHEESE, SOFTENED
1	(14 OZ.) CAN OF SWEETENED CONDENSED MILK
1	(12 OZ.) CAN OF EVAPORATED MILK
1½	CUPS HEAVY CREAM
½	TEASPOON ALMOND EXTRACT
½	TEASPOON PURE VANILLA EXTRACT

BEET PANNA COTTA

YIELD: 4 SERVINGS / **ACTIVE TIME:** 30 MINUTES / **TOTAL TIME:** 4 HOURS AND 30 MINUTES

A gorgeous variation on the traditional Italian panna cotta, with the goat cheese cutting beautifully against the sweetness of the beets.

1. Place the gelatin sheets in a small bowl. Add 1 cup of ice and water until the sheets are submerged. Let the mixture rest.

2. Combine the heavy cream, milk, sugar, honey, and beets in a saucepan and bring to a simmer. Cook for 15 minutes and then remove the pan from heat.

3. Remove the bloomed gelatin from the ice water. Squeeze to remove as much water from the sheets as possible, add them to the warm mixture, and whisk until they have completely dissolved.

4. Transfer the mixture to a blender, add the goat cheese, and puree until emulsified, about 45 seconds.

5. Strain the mixture into a bowl through a fine-mesh sieve and divide it between four 8 oz. ramekins, leaving about ½ inch of space at the top. Carefully transfer the ramekins to the refrigerator and chill until the panna cottas are fully set, about 4 hours.

INGREDIENTS:

4	SHEETS OF SILVER GELATIN
13	OZ. HEAVY CREAM
9	OZ. MILK
4	OZ. SUGAR
1.8	OZ. HONEY
12	OZ. RED BEETS, PEELED AND FINELY DICED
4	OZ. GOAT CHEESE, CRUMBLED

TAPIOCA PUDDING

YIELD: 6 SERVINGS / **ACTIVE TIME:** 15 MINUTES / **TOTAL TIME:** 4 HOURS AND 15 MINUTES

So delicious and comforting that not even a discomforting nickname like "Eyeball Pudding" could keep it from becoming a classic.

1. Place the eggs, sugar, tapioca, and vanilla seeds and pod in a saucepan and whisk until the mixture is frothy.

2. Stir in the half-and-half and bring the mixture to a simmer over medium-low heat while stirring constantly. Cook until the mixture has thickened considerably, about 10 minutes, taking care not to let it come to a boil.

3. Remove the pan from heat, remove the vanilla pod, and discard it. Transfer the mixture to a bowl and stir in the salt and nutmeg. Place the pudding in the refrigerator and chill for 4 hours before serving.

INGREDIENTS:

2	LARGE EGGS
1	CUP SUGAR
½	CUP INSTANT TAPIOCA
	SEEDS AND POD OF 1 VANILLA BEAN
4	CUPS HALF-AND-HALF
½	TEASPOON FINE SEA SALT
¼	TEASPOON FRESHLY GRATED NUTMEG

CRÈME BRÛLÉE

YIELD: 6 SERVINGS / **ACTIVE TIME:** 1 HOUR / **TOTAL TIME:** 3 HOURS AND 30 MINUTES

Originating in France in 1691, this luscious dessert disappeared shortly after and lay dormant until the 1980s, when it was resurrected as a symbol of that decade's emphasis on lavish living.

1. Preheat the oven to 325°F. Place the cream and vanilla seeds and pod in a saucepan and bring to a simmer over medium-high heat. Remove from heat, cover the pan, and let sit for 15 minutes.

2. Remove the vanilla bean pod and discard it. Place ½ cup of the sugar and the egg yolks in a bowl and whisk until combined. While whisking constantly, add the cream mixture in ¼-cup increments. When all of the cream mixture has been incorporated, divide the mixture between six 8 oz. ramekins.

3. Transfer the ramekins to a 9 x 13–inch baking pan. Add hot water (about 125°F) until it reaches halfway up the sides of the ramekins, place the dish in the oven, and bake until the custard is just set, about 40 minutes. Remove from the oven, transfer the ramekins to the refrigerator, and chill for 2 hours.

4. Remove the ramekins 30 minutes before you are ready to serve them and let them to come to room temperature.

5. Divide the remaining sugar between the ramekins and spread evenly on top. Use a kitchen torch to caramelize the sugar, let the crème brûlées sit for 5 minutes, and then serve.

INGREDIENTS:

4   CUPS HEAVY CREAM

     SEEDS AND POD OF 1
     VANILLA BEAN

1   CUP SUGAR

6   LARGE EGG YOLKS

VANILLA PUDDING

YIELD: 8 SERVINGS / **ACTIVE TIME:** 20 MINUTES / **TOTAL TIME:** 2 HOURS AND 20 MINUTES

Switching out some of the cornstarch for egg yolks grants this pudding an irresistible creaminess, and keeps the flavor from being negatively impacted.

1. Place the egg yolks in a bowl and beat until combined.

2. Place the sugar, cornstarch, and salt in a saucepan, stir to combine, and warm over medium heat. Slowly add the milk and whisk constantly as the mixture comes to a simmer.

3. Remove the saucepan from heat and, whisking continually, add approximately one-third of the warm mixture into the beaten egg yolks. Pour the tempered egg yolks into the saucepan, place it back over medium heat, and cook for 1 minute while stirring constantly. Remove from heat.

4. Stir in the butter and vanilla. Transfer the pudding into serving dishes and place plastic wrap directly on the surface of each one to prevent a skin from forming. Place the pudding in the refrigerator and chill for 2 hours before serving.

INGREDIENTS:

3	LARGE EGG YOLKS
⅓	CUP SUGAR
2	TABLESPOONS CORNSTARCH
¼	TEASPOON FINE SEA SALT
2	CUPS WHOLE MILK
1	OZ. UNSALTED BUTTER, AT ROOM TEMPERATURE
2	TABLESPOONS PURE VANILLA EXTRACT

ZABAGLIONE

YIELD: 6 SERVINGS / **ACTIVE TIME:** 20 MINUTES / **TOTAL TIME:** 20 MINUTES

Any sweet wine can be substituted for the Marsala in this classic Italian dessert, which is thought to date back to the 15th century.

1. Fill a small saucepan halfway with water and bring it to a gentle simmer. Combine the egg yolks and sugar in a heatproof bowl and place it over the simmering water. Whisk the mixture until it is pale yellow and creamy.

2. While whisking continually, slowly add the Marsala. The mixture will begin to foam and then it will swell considerably. Whisk until it is very soft with a number of gentle peaks and valleys. Ladle into the serving dishes and garnish with fresh raspberries.

INGREDIENTS:

4   EGG YOLKS

¼   CUP SUGAR

½   CUP DRY MARSALA WINE

       FRESH RASPBERRIES, FOR
       GARNISH

MAPLE POTS DE CRÈME

YIELD: 4 SERVINGS / **ACTIVE TIME:** 30 MINUTES / **TOTAL TIME:** 6 HOURS AND 30 MINUTES

Using maple sugar instead of maple syrup allows this custard to retain the lightness you want in a pot de crème.

1. Preheat the oven to 325°F. Bring 8 cups of water to a boil and then set aside.

2. Place the heavy cream, two-thirds of the maple sugar, and the salt in a saucepan and bring it to a simmer over medium heat.

3. Place the egg yolks and remaining maple sugar in a mixing bowl and whisk until the sugar has dissolved.

4. Whisking constantly, gradually add the warm mixture to the egg yolk mixture. When all of the warm mixture has been incorporated, pour the custard into four 8 oz. ramekins until they are three-quarters full.

5. Place the ramekins in a 9 x 13–inch baking pan and pour the boiling water into the pan until it reaches halfway up the sides of the ramekins. Place the pan in the oven and bake until the custards are set at their edges and jiggle slightly at their centers, about 50 minutes. Remove from the oven and carefully transfer the ramekins to a wire rack. Let cool for 1 hour

6. Place the ramekins in the refrigerator and chill for 4 hours before enjoying.

INGREDIENTS:

18	OZ. HEAVY CREAM
6	OZ. MAPLE SUGAR
¼	TEASPOON KOSHER SALT
5	EGG YOLKS

CHOCOLATE PUDDING

YIELD: 8 SERVINGS / **ACTIVE TIME:** 15 MINUTES / **TOTAL TIME:** 2 HOURS AND 15 MINUTES

To replicate the famed snack packs of your youth, simply swirl this pudding with some of the Chantilly Cream on page 89.

1. Place the egg yolks in a heatproof bowl and whisk to combine.

2. Place the sugar, cocoa powder, cornstarch, and salt in a saucepan and whisk to combine. Cook over medium heat and, whisking continually, gradually add the milk. Cook until the mixture thickens and comes to a simmer, approximately 8 to 10 minutes.

3. Reduce the heat to low and simmer for 1 to 2 minutes. Remove the saucepan from heat and stir in the butter and vanilla.

4. While whisking continually, gradually add the warm milk mixture to the egg yolks. When all of the milk mixture has been incorporated, transfer the pudding into serving dishes and place plastic wrap directly on the pudding's surface to prevent a skin from forming. Place in the refrigerator and chill for 2 hours before serving.

INGREDIENTS:

3	LARGE EGG YOLKS
¼	CUP SUGAR
½	CUP COCOA POWDER
2	TABLESPOONS CORNSTARCH
¾	TEASPOON FINE SEA SALT
2½	CUPS WHOLE MILK
3	OZ. UNSALTED BUTTER, AT ROOM TEMPERATURE
2	TEASPOONS PURE VANILLA EXTRACT

CARAMEL BREAD PUDDING

YIELD: 16 SERVINGS / **ACTIVE TIME:** 45 MINUTES / **TOTAL TIME:** 24 HOURS

A classic bread pudding that elects to omit the raisins that so often make their way into the preparation. If you find yourself missing their sweetness and chewiness, toss in anywhere from ¼ to ½ cup.

1. Place the bread in a mixing bowl and let it rest overnight at room temperature, uncovered, to dry out.

2. Place the cream, milk, cinnamon, cloves, sugar, and salt in a medium saucepan and bring the mixture to a simmer. Remove the pan from heat.

3. Place the eggs and vanilla in a heatproof mixing bowl and whisk to combine. Whisking constantly, gradually add the warm mixture. When half of the warm mixture has been incorporated, add the tempered eggs to the saucepan and whisk to combine.

4. Coat a 9 x 13–inch baking pan with cooking spray and then distribute the bread pieces in it. Slowly pour the custard over the bread and gently shake the pan to ensure it is evenly distributed. Press down on the bread with a rubber spatula so that they soak up the custard. Cover the baking dish with aluminum foil, place it in the refrigerator, and chill for 2 hours.

5. Preheat the oven to 350°F.

6. Place the baking pan in the oven and bake for 45 minutes. Remove the aluminum foil and bake until the bread pudding is golden brown on top, about 15 minutes. Remove from the oven and let the bread pudding cool slightly before slicing and serving with the toffee sauce.

INGREDIENTS:

8	CUPS TORN CHALLAH OR BRIOCHE
9	OZ. HEAVY CREAM
3	OZ. MILK
1	TEASPOON CINNAMON
¼	TEASPOON GROUND CLOVES
3	OZ. SUGAR
¼	TEASPOON KOSHER SALT
3	EGGS
½	TEASPOON PURE VANILLA EXTRACT
2	CUPS BOURBON TOFFEE SAUCE (SEE PAGE 106)

EGGNOG MOUSSE

YIELD: 6 SERVINGS / **ACTIVE TIME:** 30 MINUTES / **TOTAL TIME:** 2 HOURS AND 30 MINUTES

Heavy desserts tend to reign around the holidays, making this light and fluffy offering a welcome sight on the dessert table.

1. In the work bowl of a stand mixer fitted with the whisk attachment, whip the egg whites on high until they hold stiff peaks. Transfer the egg whites to another bowl and place it in the refrigerator.

2. Wipe out the work bowl of the stand mixer, add the heavy cream, confectioners' sugar, vanilla, nutmeg, cinnamon, and ginger and whip until the mixture holds stiff peaks.

3. Transfer the whipped cream to a mixing bowl. Add the whipped egg whites and fold to incorporate.

4. Divide the mousse between six 8 oz. ramekins and lightly tap the bottom of each one to settle the mousse and to remove any air bubbles. Transfer to the refrigerator and chill for 2 hours.

5. To serve, top each mousse with Chantilly Cream.

INGREDIENTS:

4   EGG WHITES

4   CUPS HEAVY CREAM

1   CUP CONFECTIONERS' SUGAR

2   TEASPOONS PURE VANILLA EXTRACT

2   TABLESPOONS FRESHLY GRATED NUTMEG, OR TO TASTE

2   TABLESPOONS CINNAMON

1   TABLESPOON GROUND GINGER, OR TO TASTE

2   CUPS CHANTILLY CREAM (SEE PAGE 89)

CHOCOLATE & SOURDOUGH BREAD PUDDING

YIELD: 16 SERVINGS / **ACTIVE TIME:** 45 MINUTES / **TOTAL TIME:** 24 HOURS

Using sourdough in bread pudding gives this humble offering a bit more texture and tanginess.

1. Place the bread in a mixing bowl and let it rest overnight at room temperature, uncovered, to dry out.

2. Place the chocolate chips in a heatproof mixing bowl. Place the milk, butter, sugar, cream, cinnamon, nutmeg, and salt in a medium saucepan and bring the mixture to a simmer. Remove the pan from heat, pour it over the chocolate chips, and stir until the chocolate has melted and the mixture is combined.

3. Place the eggs and vanilla in a heatproof mixing bowl and whisk to combine. Whisking constantly, gradually add the melted chocolate mixture until all of it has been incorporated.

4. Coat a 9 x 13–inch baking pan with cooking spray and then distribute the bread pieces in it. Slowly pour the custard over the bread and gently shake the pan to ensure it is evenly distributed. Press down on the bread with a rubber spatula so that they soak up the custard. Cover the baking dish with aluminum foil, place it in the refrigerator, and chill for 2 hours.

5. Preheat the oven to 350°F.

6. Place the baking pan in the oven and bake for 45 minutes. Remove the aluminum foil and bake until the bread pudding is golden brown on top, about 15 minutes. Remove from the oven and let the bread pudding cool slightly before slicing and serving.

INGREDIENTS:

8	CUPS SOURDOUGH BREAD PIECES
2	CUPS CHOCOLATE CHIPS
3	CUPS WHOLE MILK
3	TABLESPOONS UNSALTED BUTTER
2¼	CUPS SUGAR
¾	CUP HEAVY CREAM
1½	TEASPOONS CINNAMON
½	TEASPOON FRESHLY GRATED NUTMEG
¼	TEASPOON KOSHER SALT
3	EGGS
1½	TEASPOONS PURE VANILLA EXTRACT

GINGERBREAD MOUSSE

YIELD: 6 SERVINGS / **ACTIVE TIME:** 30 MINUTES / **TOTAL TIME:** 2 HOURS AND 45 MINUTES

The earthy sweetness of molasses is the perfect companion to all of the baking spice in this mousse.

1. Fill a small saucepan halfway with water and bring it to a simmer. Place the white chocolate in a heatproof mixing bowl and place it over the simmering water. Stir until the white chocolate is melted and then set aside.

2. In the work bowl of a stand mixer fitted with the whisk attachment, whip the heavy cream until it holds soft peaks. Transfer the whipped cream to another bowl and place it in the refrigerator.

3. Wipe out the work bowl of the stand mixer, add the molasses, confectioners' sugar, egg yolks, eggs, vanilla, cinnamon, allspice, cardamom, nutmeg, and ginger and whip until the mixture has doubled in size and is pale, about 15 minutes. Transfer the mixture to a mixing bowl. Add the white chocolate and whisk to incorporate. Add the whipped cream and fold to incorporate.

4. Divide the mousse between six 8 oz. ramekins and lightly tap the bottom of each one to settle the mousse and to remove any air bubbles. Transfer to the refrigerator and chill for 2 hours.

5. To serve, top each mousse with Chantilly Cream.

INGREDIENTS:

10.5	OZ. WHITE CHOCOLATE
14	OZ. HEAVY CREAM
2	OZ. MOLASSES
1	OZ. CONFECTIONERS' SUGAR
2	EGG YOLKS
2	EGGS
1	TEASPOON PURE VANILLA EXTRACT
1	TEASPOON CINNAMON
1	TEASPOON ALLSPICE
1	TEASPOON CARDAMOM
1	TEASPOON FRESHLY GRATED NUTMEG
½	TEASPOON GROUND GINGER
2	CUPS CHANTILLY CREAM (SEE PAGE 89)

CREMA CATALANA

YIELD: 4 SERVINGS / **ACTIVE TIME:** 30 MINUTES / **TOTAL TIME:** 6 HOURS AND 30 MINUTES

This is the Spanish version of Crème Brûlée, made with a touch more milk and the zest of an orange.

1. Place the egg yolks in a mixing bowl, whisk to combine, and set them aside.

2. Combine the heavy cream, milk, vanilla, three-quarters of the sugar, orange zest, and salt in a saucepan and bring the mixture to a simmer. Remove the pan from heat and strain the mixture into a clean bowl through a fine-mesh sieve.

3. Whisking constantly, gradually add the warm mixture to the egg yolk mixture. When all of the warm mixture has been incorporated, place the custard in the refrigerator and chill for 4 hours.

4. Preheat the oven to 325°F. Bring 8 cups of water to a boil and then set aside.

5. Fill four 8 oz. ramekins three-quarters of the way with the custard.

6. Place the ramekins in a 9 x 13–inch baking pan and pour the boiling water into the pan until it reaches halfway up the sides of the ramekins. Place the pan in the oven and bake until the custards are set at their edges and jiggle slightly at their centers, about 50 minutes. Remove from the oven and carefully transfer the ramekins to a wire rack. Let cool for 1 hour.

7. Place the ramekins in the refrigerator and chill for 4 hours.

8. Divide the remaining sugar between the ramekins and spread evenly on top. Use a kitchen torch to caramelize the sugar and serve.

INGREDIENTS:

8	EGG YOLKS
12	OZ. HEAVY CREAM
7	OZ. MILK
	SEEDS OF ½ VANILLA BEAN
1	CUP SUGAR
	ZEST OF ½ ORANGE
¼	TEASPOON KOSHER SALT

PUMPKIN MOUSSE

YIELD: 6 SERVINGS / **ACTIVE TIME:** 30 MINUTES / **TOTAL TIME:** 2 HOURS AND 30 MINUTES

I f someone around your house just can't take the plunge on pumpkin pie, try warming them up a little with this brilliant, in taste and appearance, mousse.

1. Place the pumpkin puree, 1 cup of the heavy cream, and sugar in a saucepan and bring the mixture to a simmer, stirring to combine. Remove the pan from heat, pour the mixture into a heatproof bowl, and set aside.

2. In the work bowl of a stand mixer fitted with the whisk attachment, add the cinnamon, nutmeg, cloves, vanilla, and remaining heavy cream and whip on medium speed until the mixture holds medium peaks.

3. Transfer the whipped cream to the bowl containing the pumpkin mixture and fold to incorporate.

4. Divide the mousse between six 8 oz. ramekins and lightly tap the bottom of each one to settle the mousse and to remove any air bubbles. Transfer to the refrigerator and chill for 2 hours.

5. To serve, top each mousse with Cinnamon Chantilly Cream.

INGREDIENTS:

15	OZ. PUMPKIN PUREE
3	CUPS HEAVY CREAM
¾	CUP SUGAR
1	TABLESPOON CINNAMON
1	TEASPOON FRESHLY GRATED NUTMEG
1	TEASPOON GROUND CLOVES
1	TABLESPOON PURE VANILLA EXTRACT
2	CUPS CINNAMON CHANTILLY CREAM (SEE PAGE 90)

ICE CREAM & OTHER FROZEN DELIGHTS

*W*hen it is OK, it is still enough to make one's day. When it is good, it is worth driving the better part of an afternoon to acquire. And, on those rare occasions when one encounters great ice cream—as one might if they happen to be in Seattle when the Strawberry Balsamic at Molly Moon's is available—it feels as though heaven is half as far.

In a book filled with the very best sweets humanity has devised, ice cream stands alone, above them all. An argument could be made that it is the apex of culinary achievement, and we would enthusiastically nod along.

This chapter will teach you how to bring this wonder closer to home. It will not immediately be that divine offering you occasionally come across, but with a little bit of an investment into an ice cream maker—a solid one runs about $50—you can make very, very good ice cream at home, good enough to entice you along until you become a master capable of producing something transcendent.

CUSTARD ICE CREAM BASE

YIELD: 1 QUART / **ACTIVE TIME:** 30 MINUTES / **TOTAL TIME:** 5 HOURS

This rich custard base is the key to getting the most out of your other ingredients. Don't believe us? It's actually why French vanilla is recognized as its own flavor.

1. In a small saucepan, combine the heavy cream, milk, sugar, and salt and bring to a simmer over medium-low heat, stirring until sugar completely dissolves, about 5 minutes.

2. Remove the saucepan from heat. Place the egg yolks in a heat-proof mixing bowl and whisk them until combined. While whisking constantly, slowly whisk about a third of the hot cream mixture into the yolks. Whisk the tempered egg yolks into the saucepan.

3. Warm the mixture over medium-low heat, stirring constantly, until the mixture is thick enough to coat the back of a wooden spoon (about 170°F on an instant-read thermometer).

4. Strain the custard through a fine-mesh sieve into a bowl and let it cool to room temperature. Cover the bowl, place it in the refrigerator, and let it chill for at least 4 hours.

5. Flavor the custard as desired and churn it in an ice cream maker until it has the desired consistency.

INGREDIENTS:

2	CUPS HEAVY CREAM
1	CUP WHOLE MILK
⅔	CUP SUGAR
⅛	TEASPOON FINE SEA SALT
6	LARGE EGG YOLKS

PHILADELPHIA ICE CREAM BASE

YIELD: 1 QUARTS / **ACTIVE TIME:** 10 MINUTES / **TOTAL TIME:** 5 HOURS

An eggless ice cream base that will be slightly less creamy, but no less delicious.

1. In a saucepan, combine the cream, milk, sugar, corn syrup or honey, and salt and bring the mixture to a simmer, stirring until the sugar has dissolved.

2. Pour the mixture into a heatproof bowl and let it cool to room temperature. Cover it with plastic wrap and store in the refrigerator for at least 4 hours.

3. Flavor the ice cream base as desired and churn it in an ice cream maker until it has the desired consistency.

INGREDIENTS:

3   CUPS HEAVY CREAM

1   CUP WHOLE MILK

½   CUP GRANULATED SUGAR

½   CUP LIGHT CORN SYRUP OR ⅓ CUP HONEY

½   TEASPOON FINE SEA SALT

VEGAN ICE CREAM BASE

YIELD: 1 QUART / **ACTIVE TIME:** 15 MINUTES / **TOTAL TIME:** 4 HOURS AND 15 MINUTES

The natural creaminess of coconut milk allows vegans to not feel left out when it's time for a frozen treat.

1. Place the coconut milk, maple syrup, vanilla seeds, and salt in a blender or food processor and blitz until combined. Transfer the mixture to a bowl, cover it, and refrigerate for 4 hours.

2. Flavor the base as desired and churn in an ice cream maker until it has the desired consistency.

INGREDIENTS:

2 (14 OZ.) CANS OF COCONUT MILK

¾ CUP MAPLE SYRUP

SEEDS OF 2 VANILLA BEANS

1 TEASPOON FINE SEA SALT

CHOCOLATE ICE CREAM

YIELD: 1 QUART / **ACTIVE TIME:** 30 MINUTES / **TOTAL TIME:** 9 HOURS

This may well be the best delivery system for the miraculous flavor of chocolate.

1. While the ice cream base is still warm, combine the cream and cocoa powder in a saucepan and bring to a simmer over medium-low heat.

2. Place the chocolate in a heatproof bowl and pour the warm milk mixture over it. Stir until melted and smooth.

3. Stir the melted chocolate mixture, crème fraîche, and vanilla into the base. Let the mixture cool to room temperature. Strain into a bowl through a fine-mesh sieve, cover the bowl, and store in the refrigerator for 4 hours.

4. Churn the base in an ice cream maker until it reaches the desired texture. Place the ice cream in an airtight container and freeze it for 4 to 6 hours before serving.

INGREDIENTS:

1	QUART ICE CREAM BASE
¾	CUP HEAVY CREAM
3	TABLESPOONS COOCA POWDER
4	OZ. CHOCOLATE, CHOPPED
¾	CUP CRÈME FRAÎCHE
1	TEASPOON PURE VANILLA EXTRACT

VANILLA ICE CREAM

YIELD: 1 QUART / **ACTIVE TIME:** 30 MINUTES / **TOTAL TIME:** 9 HOURS

While it has become synonymous with bland, or plain, using fresh vanilla beans will show you that this ice cream is anything but.

1. While preparing the ice cream base, halve the vanilla beans, scrape the seeds into the saucepan, and add the pods as well. When the base is ready, pour it into the heatproof bowl and let steep for 1 hour.

2. Remove the vanilla bean pods, cover the bowl, and place it in the refrigerator for 4 hours.

3. Churn the mixture in an ice cream maker until it is the desired texture. Place the ice cream in an airtight container and freeze it for 4 to 6 hours before serving.

INGREDIENTS:

1   QUART ICE CREAM BASE

2   VANILLA BEANS

PISTACHIO ICE CREAM

YIELD: 1 QUART / **ACTIVE TIME:** 30 MINUTES / **TOTAL TIME:** 9 HOURS

A silky, flavor-packed paste made from raw pistachios is the key to getting this ice cream's flavor as intense and the color as brilliant as it is when idealized in the mind.

1. Add your preferred ice cream base to the ice cream maker and churn for 5 minutes.

2. Add the Pistachio Paste and almond extract and churn for 5 minutes.

3. Gradually add the chopped pistachios to the mixture and churn until they have been evenly distributed. Transfer the ice cream to an airtight container and freeze for 4 to 6 hours before serving.

PISTACHIO PASTE

1. Place the pistachios in a food processor and blitz until they are a smooth, oily paste.

2. Add the confectioners' sugar, salt, and orange blossom water and blitz until the paste is smooth and thick.

3. With the food processor running, drizzle in the pistachio oil and blitz until the paste is silky. Use immediately or store in the refrigerator, where the paste will keep for up to 1 month.

INGREDIENTS:

1   QUART ICE CREAM BASE

1   CUP PISTACHIO PASTE (SEE RECIPE)

¼   TEASPOON ALMOND EXTRACT

      PISTACHIOS, CHOPPED, TO TASTE

PISTACHIO PASTE

9   OZ. RAW PISTACHIOS, BLANCHED AND PEELED

10   OZ. CONFECTIONERS' SUGAR

½   TEASPOON KOSHER SALT

¼   TEASPOON ORANGE BLOSSOM WATER

2   OZ. ROASTED PISTACHIO OIL

COCONUT ICE CREAM

YIELD: 1 QUART / **ACTIVE TIME:** 30 MINUTES / **TOTAL TIME:** 9 HOURS

Don't hesitate to experiment with the amounts of sweetened and unsweetened coconut here until you find a ratio that produces the flavor you want.

1. While preparing your preferred ice cream base, add the coconut cream and toasted unsweetened coconut to the pot and proceed with the preparation as normal.

2. After removing the pan from heat, let the mixture steep for 1 hour.

3. Strain into a bowl through a fine-mesh sieve, pressing down on the coconut to extract as much liquid from it as possible. Cover the bowl and refrigerate for 4 hours.

4. Place the mixture in an ice cream maker and churn until it almost has the desired texture. Add the toasted sweetened coconut and churn for 2 minutes, or until it is equally distributed. Place the ice cream in an airtight container and freeze for 4 to 6 hours before serving.

INGREDIENTS:

1   QUART ICE CREAM BASE

1   CUP COCONUT CREAM

1   CUP SHREDDED UNSWEETENED COCONUT, TOASTED

½   CUP SHREDDED SWEETENED COCONUT, TOASTED

LEMON GELATO

YIELD: 1 PINT / **ACTIVE TIME:** 30 MINUTES / **TOTAL TIME:** 6 HOURS

The quality of lemons available in Italy means that you still have to travel if you want to experience this frozen treat at its apex. That said, this recipe will tide you over for some time.

1. In a small saucepan, combine the milk and lemon zest and warm over medium-low heat until the mixture starts to steam. Remove the pan from heat, cover it, and let the mixture steep for about 20 minutes.

2. Put a few inches of ice water in a large bowl. In a mixing bowl, whisk together the egg yolks and sugar. Strain the infused milk into a pitcher, then whisk it into the yolk mixture.

3. Pour the mixture into a clean saucepan and place it over medium-low heat. While stirring constantly with a wooden spoon, warm until it is a custard thick enough to coat back of the spoon, about 10 minutes. Take care not to overheat the mixture; it will curdle.

4. Place the pan in the ice water bath and stir until cool. Transfer to a bowl, cover it, and refrigerate for about 1 hour.

5. Pour the mixture into an ice cream maker and churn until it has the desired consistency. Transfer to an airtight container and freeze for 4 to 6 hours before serving.

INGREDIENTS:

2	CUPS WHOLE MILK
	ZEST OF ½ LEMON
5	LARGE EGG YOLKS
½	CUP SUGAR

AFFOGATO

Starbucks has transformed the concept of affogato in the minds of the public. By going back to its roots, you start to see all that has been lost.

1. Scoop ice cream into four small glasses. Pour some of the Sambuca over each scoop and sprinkle a bit of nutmeg on top.

2. Pour the espresso or coffee over the ice cream. Top each portion with whipped cream and serve.

INGREDIENTS:

1   PINT OF VANILLA ICE CREAM (SEE PAGE 516 FOR HOMEMADE)

¼   CUP SAMBUCA

1   TEASPOON FRESHLY GRATED NUTMEG

1¼   CUPS FRESHLY BREWED ESPRESSO OR VERY STRONG COFFEE

CHANTILLY CREAM (SEE PAGE 89), FOR GARNISH

BANANA ICE CREAM

YIELD: 1 QUART / **ACTIVE TIME:** 30 MINUTES / **TOTAL TIME:** 9 HOURS

The pungent sweetness of the banana may be at its best when swaddled in layer upon layer of luscious frozen cream. The riper they are, the better, as they begin to pick up notes of vanilla, honey, and rum as they brown.

1. While the ice cream base is still warm, place all of the remaining ingredients, except for the crème fraîche, in a blender and puree until smooth. Stir the puree and crème fraîche into the base and let the mixture cool to room temperature. Strain into a bowl, cover the bowl, and store in the refrigerator for 4 hours.

2. Churn the base in an ice cream maker until it reaches the desired texture. Place the ice cream in an airtight container and freeze it for 4 to 6 hours before serving.

INGREDIENTS:

1   QUART ICE CREAM BASE

4   VERY RIPE BANANAS

2   TABLESPOONS SUGAR

1   TEASPOON FRESH LEMON
     JUICE

     PINCH OF FINE SEA SALT

½   CUP CRÈME FRAÎCHE

SALTED CARAMEL ICE CREAM

YIELD: 1 QUART / **ACTIVE TIME:** 30 MINUTES / **TOTAL TIME:** 9 HOURS

Just a little salt is all that's required to make the flavor of caramel explode. That said, don't be afraid to add another pinch or two if this recipe doesn't quite get you there.

1. While the ice cream base is still warm, place the sugar and water in a saucepan and warm over medium heat, swirling the pan frequently, until the mixture is a deep golden brown. Add the mixture to the base and let the mixture cool to room temperature. Cover the bowl and store in the refrigerator for 4 hours.

2. Churn the base in an ice cream maker until it is approaching the desired texture. Sprinkle the sea salt into the ice cream and churn for another 2 minutes. Place the ice cream in an airtight container and freeze it for 4 to 6 hours before serving.

INGREDIENTS:

1	QUART ICE CREAM BASE
¾	CUP SUGAR
3	TABLESPOONS WATER
¼	TEASPOON FLAKY SEA SALT

THE ICE STORM

YIELD: 4 TO 6 SERVINGS / **ACTIVE TIME:** 30 MINUTES / **TOTAL TIME:** 2 HOURS

Part souffle, part Italian ice, this citrus-centered dessert is here to provide a cool breeze on those brutal summer days where the air hangs like a damp sheet.

1. Place the milk and ½ cup of the sugar in a saucepan and cook over medium-low heat, stirring occasionally, until the sugar has dissolved, about 5 minutes. Remove the pan from heat and set it aside.

2. Place the lime juice in a small bowl, add the gelatin, and stir to combine. Set the mixture aside and prepare an ice water bath in a large bowl.

3. Place the egg yolks, half of the remaining sugar, and the cornstarch in a bowl and beat until the mixture has thickened. While whisking constantly, gradually add the hot milk mixture to the egg yolk mixture until it has all been incorporated.

4. Place the tempered eggs in the saucepan and cook, while stirring, over medium-low heat until it is thick enough to coat a wooden spoon. Strain the mixture into a mixing bowl, stir in the lime juice-and-gelatin mixture and the lime zest, and place the bowl in the prepared ice water bath. Stir the mixture occasionally as it cools and thickens.

5. Place the egg whites and cream of tartar in a mixing bowl and beat until foamy. Add the remaining sugar and beat until soft peaks form. Remove the bowl containing the custard from the ice water bath and whisk in one-third of the egg white mixture. Add the remaining egg white mixture and fold to incorporate it.

6. Beat the heavy cream until it holds soft peaks. Fold the whipped cream into the custard and transfer that mixture into a bowl or souffle dish. Place in the freezer for approximately 1½ hours, until it is set. Garnish with lime wheels and additional lime zest before serving.

INGREDIENTS:

1   CUP WHOLE MILK

¾   CUP SUGAR

½   CUP FRESH LIME JUICE

1   PACKAGE OF GELATIN

2   LARGE EGG YOLKS, AT ROOM TEMPERATURE

¼   TEASPOON CORNSTARCH

2½   TEASPOONS LIME ZEST, PLUS MORE FOR GARNISH

5   LARGE EGG WHITES, AT ROOM TEMPERATURE

    PINCH OF CREAM OF TARTAR

¾   CUP HEAVY CREAM

    LIME WHEELS, FOR GARNISH

CRANBERRY SORBET

YIELD: 1 QUART / **ACTIVE TIME:** 40 MINUTES / **TOTAL TIME:** 6 HOURS

The straightforward nature of a sorbet makes it the best vehicle to convey the unique flavor of a fruit like the cranberry.

1. Place the cranberries, 9 oz. of the water, and 5 tablespoons of the sugar in a medium saucepan and cook over medium heat until all of the cranberries burst. Transfer the mixture to the blender and puree until smooth, starting at a low speed and increasing to high. Strain into a bowl through a fine-mesh sieve and place in the refrigerator until chilled.

2. Place the remaining water and sugar in a saucepan and bring to a boil, while stirring, until the sugar is dissolved. Remove from heat and let cool completely.

3. Place the cranberry puree, simple syrup, orange juice, and cornstarch in a bowl and stir until combined.

4. Pour the mixture into an ice cream maker and churn until it has the desired texture. Place the sorbet in an airtight container and freeze for 4 to 6 hours.

INGREDIENTS:

8   OZ. FRESH CRANBERRIES

2¾   CUPS WATER

13   TABLESPOONS SUGAR

1   CUP ORANGE JUICE

½   TEASPOON CORNSTARCH

COFFEE ICE CREAM

YIELD: 1 QUART / **ACTIVE TIME:** 30 MINUTES / **TOTAL TIME:** 9 HOURS

It should go without saying, but you need great coffee to make great coffee ice cream. Consider bypassing the grocery store and heading instead to a coffee shop that roasts its own, as they're guaranteed to have better beans on hand.

1. While the base is still warm, stir in the ground coffee and let the mixture steep for 1 hour.

2. Strain into a bowl through a fine-mesh sieve, cover the bowl, and store in the refrigerator for 4 hours.

3. Churn the base in an ice cream maker until it reaches the desired texture. Place the ice cream in an airtight container and freeze it for 4 to 6 hours before serving.

INGREDIENTS:

1   QUART ICE CREAM BASE

½   CUP COFFEE BEANS, COARSELY GROUND

MINT CHOCOLATE CHIP ICE CREAM

YIELD: 1 QUART / **ACTIVE TIME:** 30 MINUTES / **TOTAL TIME:** 9 HOURS

Dark chocolate works best with the bright freshness of mint, but feel free to use whatever chocolate is your favorite.

1. Place the mint leaves and sugar in a food processor and pulse until well combined.

2. Prepare the base, adding the mint-and-sugar mixture in place of the plain sugar in your chosen preparation. When the base is ready, pour the mixture into a heatproof bowl and let it steep for 30 minutes.

3. Strain into a bowl through a fine-mesh sieve, cover the bowl, and refrigerate for 4 hours.

4. Churn the base in an ice cream maker until it is almost the desired texture. Add the chocolate and churn until evenly distributed. Place the ice cream in an airtight container and freeze it for 4 to 6 hours before serving.

INGREDIENTS:

1   CUP FRESH MINT LEAVES

½   CUP SUGAR

1   QUART ICE CREAM BASE (NO SUGAR)

1   CUP CHOPPED DARK CHOCOLATE

PROFITEROLES

YIELD: 36 CREAM PUFFS / **ACTIVE TIME:** 30 MINUTES / **TOTAL TIME:** 1 HOUR

Profiteroles are baby cream puffs filled with ice cream and traditionally topped with a chocolate sauce. You can go that route, but those with *aficion* know that caramel is far and away the best topping.

1. Preheat the oven to 425°F and line two baking sheets with parchment paper. In a medium saucepan, combine the water, butter, salt, and sugar and warm the mixture over medium heat until the butter is melted.

2. Add the flour to the pan and use a rubber spatula or a wooden spoon to fold the mixture until it comes together as a thick, shiny dough, taking care not to let the dough burn.

3. Transfer the dough to the work bowl of a stand mixer fitted with the paddle attachment and beat on medium speed until the dough is no longer steaming and the bowl is just warm to the touch, at least 10 minutes.

4. Incorporate the eggs two at a time, scraping down the work bowl between each addition. Transfer the dough to a piping bag fit with a plain tip. Pipe 1-inch-wide mounds onto the baking sheets, place them in the oven, and bake until golden brown and dry to the touch, about 15 minutes.

5. Remove from the oven and use a paring knife to cut a slit in the side of each pastry to allow the steam to escape. Turn off the oven, place the pastries back in the oven, leave the door ajar, and let the pastries sit for 5 minutes before transferring them to a wire rack to cool completely.

6. To serve, split the puffs in half, fill the bottom half with ice cream, and set the other half atop the ice cream. Drizzle the caramel over the top and serve.

INGREDIENTS:

17	OZ. WATER
8.5	OZ. UNSALTED BUTTER
1	TEASPOON FINE SEA SALT
2.4	OZ. SUGAR
12.5	OZ. ALL-PURPOSE FLOUR
6	EGGS
3	CUPS ICE CREAM
	CARAMEL SAUCE (SEE PAGE 103)

ALMOND GRANITA

YIELD: 4 SERVINGS / **ACTIVE TIME:** 15 MINUTES HOURS / **TOTAL TIME:** 2 HOURS AND 15 MINUTES

Believe it or not, this is a breakfast food in Italy, alongside a piece of brioche.

1. Place all of the ingredients in a blender and puree until smooth.

2. Place a fine-mesh sieve over a square, metal 9-inch baking pan. Strain the puree into the pan, pressing down on the solids to extract as much liquid as possible. Discard the solids.

3. Cover the pan with plastic wrap and freeze until the mixture is firm, about 2 hours.

4. Using a fork, vigorously scrape the mixture until it is a collection of icy flakes. Cover with aluminum foil and store in freezer. Scrape again with a fork before enjoying.

INGREDIENTS:

1¼ CUPS WHOLE MILK

1¼ CUPS WATER

3 OZ. SLIVERED ALMONDS (ABOUT ½ CUP), TOASTED, COOLED, CHOPPED

2.7 OZ. SUGAR (ABOUT ⅓ CUP)

2.5 OZ. ALMOND PASTE (ABOUT ¼ CUP)

1 TEASPOON ALMOND EXTRACT

CINNAMON ICE CREAM

YIELD: 1 QUART / **ACTIVE TIME:** 30 MINUTES / **TOTAL TIME:** 9 HOURS

Y ou want the cinnamon to be as fragrant as possible in this ice cream, so hold out for the Ceylon variety if you can.

1. Place the cinnamon stick and sugar in a food processor and pulse until finely ground.

2. Prepare the base, adding the cinnamon sugar in place of the plain sugar in your chosen preparation. When the base is ready, pour the mixture into a heatproof bowl and let it steep for 30 minutes.

3. Strain into a bowl through a fine-mesh sieve, cover the bowl, and refrigerate for 4 hours.

4. Churn the base in an ice cream maker until it is the desired texture. Place the ice cream in an airtight container and freeze it for 4 to 6 hours before serving.

INGREDIENTS:

1   CINNAMON STICK, CHOPPED

½   CUP SUGAR

1   QUART ICE CREAM BASE (NO SUGAR)

STRAWBERRY & BALSAMIC ICE CREAM

YIELD: 1 QUART / *ACTIVE TIME*: 30 MINUTES / *TOTAL TIME*: 9 HOURS

If you've got a bit of basil kicking around, it's worth adding to the base along with the puree.

1. While the base is warm, place the berries, sugar, vinegar, and salt in a blender and puree until smooth. Taste and adjust the amount of sugar or vinegar as desired.

2. Stir the puree into the base and let the mixture cool to room temperature. Cover the bowl with plastic wrap and refrigerate for 4 hours.

3. Place the base in an ice cream maker and churn until it is the desired texture. Place the ice cream in an airtight container and freeze it for 4 to 6 hours before serving.

INGREDIENTS:

1	QUART ICE CREAM BASE (NO MILK)
1	LB. STRAWBERRIES
3	TABLESPOONS SUGAR
½	TEASPOON BALSAMIC VINEGAR
	PINCH OF FINE SEA SALT

PEACH ICE CREAM

YIELD: 1 QUART / **ACTIVE TIME:** 30 MINUTES / **TOTAL TIME:** 9 HOURS

The only thing better than a ripe peach is putting that peach in ice cream.

1. While the base is warm, place the peaches and sugar in a saucepan and warm over medium heat. Simmer gently for 10 minutes and then stir the mixture into the base along with the crème fraîche and almond extract. Let the mixture cool to room temperature, cover the bowl with plastic wrap, and refrigerate it for 4 hours.

2. Churn the base in an ice cream maker until it is the desired texture. Place the ice cream in an airtight container and freeze it for 4 to 6 hours before using.

INGREDIENTS:

1	QUART ICE CREAM BASE (NO MILK USED)
1.5	LBS. PEACHES, PITTED
¼	CUP SUGAR
½	CUP CRÈME FRAÎCHE
2	DROPS OF ALMOND EXTRACT

ROSÉ SORBET

YIELD: 6 SERVINGS / **ACTIVE TIME:** 30 MINUTES / **TOTAL TIME:** 7 HOURS

A combination of two of the summer's great pleasures: relaxing with a glass of wine, and enjoying a frozen treat.

1. Place all of the ingredients in a saucepan and cook, while stirring, over medium-low heat until the sugar has dissolved. Raise the heat and bring to a boil.

2. Remove the pan from heat and let the mixture cool completely. Cover and place the mixture in the refrigerator for 2 hours.

3. Pour the mixture into an ice cream maker and churn until the desired consistency has been achieved. Transfer to the freezer and freeze for 4 to 6 hours before serving.

INGREDIENTS:

1⅓   CUPS SUGAR

1   (750 ML) BOTTLE OF ROSÉ

1   CUP WATER

LAVENDER ICE CREAM

YIELD: 1 QUART / **ACTIVE TIME:** 30 MINUTES / **TOTAL TIME:** 9 HOURS

Equal parts earthy, floral, and sweet, lavender adds incredible depth and beauty to ice cream. Once you've gotten the hang of making ice cream, this is a great one to break out for company.

1. While the base is still warm, stir in the lavender and let it steep for 30 minutes.

2. Strain into a bowl through a fine-mesh sieve, cover the bowl with plastic wrap, and refrigerate for 4 hours.

3. Churn the base in an ice cream maker until it almost has the desired consistency. Sprinkle in the sea salt and churn for another 2 minutes. Place the ice cream in an airtight container and freeze for 4 to 6 hours before serving.

INGREDIENTS:

1   QUART ICE CREAM BASE

2   TABLESPOONS DRIED
     LAVENDER

     PINCH OF FINE SEA SALT

ROASTED PARSNIP ICE CREAM

YIELD: 6 SERVINGS / **ACTIVE TIME:** 30 MINUTES / **TOTAL TIME:** 24 HOURS

A great way to cut down on food waste, as the recipe intends for you to use the stuff you would normally just throw away, since there's still good flavor in there. Carrot trimmings would also do well here.

1. While the base is still warm, stir in the roasted parsnip trimmings and let the mixture steep for 1 hour.

2. Strain into a bowl through a fine-mesh sieve, pressing down on the pieces of parsnip to extract as much liquid from them as possible. Cover the bowl with plastic wrap and refrigerate for 4 hours.

3. Churn in an ice cream maker until it has the desired consistency. Place the ice cream in an airtight container and freeze for 4 to 6 hours before serving.

INGREDIENTS:

1   QUART ICE CREAM BASE

3-4   CUPS ROASTED PARSNIP TRIMMINGS

GINGERBREAD ICE CREAM

YIELD: 1 QUART / **ACTIVE TIME:** 30 MINUTES / **TOTAL TIME:** 9 HOURS

Infusing the bright flavors of the classic holiday cookie into ice cream is certain to start another holiday tradition.

1. While the base is still warm, stir in the remaining ingredients and let the mixture steep for 1 hour.

2. Strain into a bowl through a fine-mesh sieve, cover the bowl, and refrigerate for 4 hours.

3. Churn the base in an ice cream maker until it has the desired texture. Place in an airtight container and freeze for 4 to 6 hours before serving.

INGREDIENTS:

1 QUART ICE CREAM BASE

2 TEASPOONS GRATED FRESH GINGER

2 TEASPOONS CINNAMON

1 TEASPOON FRESHLY GRATED NUTMEG

¼ TEASPOON GROUND CLOVES

2 TABLESPOONS MOLASSES

PINCH OF FINE SEA SALT

STRAWBERRY SORBET

YIELD: 1 QUART / **ACTIVE TIME:** 30 MINUTES / **TOTAL TIME:** 9 HOURS AND 30 MINUTES

If you'd prefer the creamier texture of ice cream, simply add the strawberries, lemon juice, and lemon zest to your preferred ice cream base and omit the sugar, water, and salt from this preparation.

1. Place the sugar and water in a saucepan and cook over medium heat, while stirring, until the sugar has dissolved. Remove from heat and let cool completely.

2. Place the strawberries, lemon juice, salt, and lemon zest in a food processor and puree until smooth. Add the cooled simple syrup and blitz to incorporate. Place the mixture in a bowl, cover it, and refrigerate for 4 hours.

3. Churn the mixture in an ice cream maker until it has the desired consistency. Place the sorbet in an airtight container and freeze for 4 to 6 hours.

INGREDIENTS:

1	CUP SUGAR
½	CUP WATER
3	PINTS OF FRESH STRAWBERRIES, HULLED
¼	CUP FRESH LEMON JUICE
½	TEASPOON FINE SEA SALT
1	TEASPOON LEMON ZEST

BLACK RASPBERRY ICE CREAM

YIELD: 4 CUPS / **ACTIVE TIME:** 30 MINUTES / **TOTAL TIME:** 9 HOURS

Rarely seen outside of the ice cream stand, most folks assume that the black raspberry is just another name for the blackberries they regularly encounter at the farmers market or grocery store. But the black raspberry is less tart than the blackberry and its red counterpart. It is also fruitier and not as sweet as the blackberry, which has high levels of sugar. This diminished sweetness and tartness lend the black raspberry's flavor a floral quality that shines in an ice cream.

1. While the ice cream base is still warm, stir in the vanilla.

2. Place the raspberries in a blender and puree until smooth. Strain to remove the seeds and stir the puree into the ice cream base. Let the mixture cool completely, cover it, and refrigerate for 4 hours.

3. Churn the base in an ice cream maker until it has the desired consistency. Place in an airtight container and store in the freezer for 4 to 6 hours before serving.

INGREDIENTS:

1   QUART ICE CREAM BASE

1   TEASPOON PURE VANILLA EXTRACT

5   CUPS BLACK RASPBERRIES

HONEY-GINGER FROZEN YOGURT

YIELD: 3 CUPS / **ACTIVE TIME:** 15 MINUTES / **TOTAL TIME:** 4 HOURS AND 30 MINUTES

This is extremely easy to make, and is wonderful with sliced, fresh summer fruit.

1. Place the yogurt, evaporated milk, vanilla, ginger, corn syrup, salt, and honey in a mixing bowl and stir to combine.

2. Pour the mixture into an ice cream maker and churn until it has the desired texture. Transfer to the freezer and freeze for 4 to 6 hours before serving.

INGREDIENTS:

2½ CUPS PLAIN GREEK YOGURT

½ CUP EVAPORATED MILK

¼ TEASPOON PURE VANILLA EXTRACT

1 TEASPOON GRATED FRESH GINGER

⅛ CUP LIGHT CORN SYRUP

½ TEASPOON FINE SEA SALT

⅓ CUP HONEY

CLASSIC ICE CREAM SANDWICHES

YIELD: 4 SERVINGS / **ACTIVE TIME:** 10 MINUTES / **TOTAL TIME:** 1 HOUR AND 45 MINUTES

Feel free to swap in your favorite cookie for these decadent sandwiches.

1. Preheat the oven to 350°F and line two baking sheets with parchment paper.

2. Drop 4-oz. portions of the dough on the baking sheets, making sure to leave enough space between them. Place them in the oven and bake until golden brown and the edges are set, 14 to 18 minutes.

3. Remove the cookies from the oven and transfer them to wire racks to cool completely.

4. When the cookies have cooled completely, scoop ice cream onto half of the cookies. Carefully press down with the other cookies to assemble the sandwiches and store in the freezer until ready to serve.

INGREDIENTS:

DOUGH FROM CHOCOLATE CHIP COOKIES (SEE PAGE 116)

1 PINT OF VANILLA ICE CREAM (SEE PAGE 516 FOR HOMEMADE)

HOT FUDGE SUNDAES

YIELD: 4 SERVINGS / **ACTIVE TIME:** 5 MINUTES / **TOTAL TIME:** 5 MINUTES

The key is getting the hot fudge on the bottom, as it allows you to control the distribution of it.

1. Place the Hot Fudge in the bottom of four tulip sundae dishes or bowls.

2. Scoop the ice cream into the bowls.

3. Top each portion with Chantilly Cream, pecans or walnuts, and a maraschino cherry and serve.

INGREDIENTS:

HOT FUDGE (SEE PAGE 100)

2 PINTS OF VANILLA ICE CREAM (SEE PAGE 516 FOR HOMEMADE)

CHANTILLY CREAM (SEE PAGE 89)

½ CUP CHOPPED PECANS OR WALNUTS

4 LUXARDO MARASCHINO CHERRIES, FOR GARNISH

CANDIES & OTHER DECADENT CONFECTIONS

*N*o, you will not find the secrets needed to produce M & M's, Starburst, Skittles, or Snickers bars. You will find nougat, but not the mysterious and ubiquitous iteration that likely popped into your mind.

This chapter features the more refined offerings from the sweet shop—the truffles, pralines, peppermint bark, meringues, and pâte de fruit that allow us to embrace our inner child while also exhibiting how much our palates have evolved.

There are also decadent dumplings plucked from cuisines across the world, the exhilaration offered by carnival fare such as the caramel apple, and the boozy, showy singularity that is the Bananas Foster.

PEANUT BUTTER CUPS

YIELD: 12 CUPS / **ACTIVE TIME:** 15 MINUTES / **TOTAL TIME:** 1 HOUR AND 15 MINUTES

Sure, it's easier to run down to the store when you need to soothe your craving for this confection, but it's a whole lot less fun.

1. Line a cupcake pan with 12 liners and coat them with nonstick cooking spray. Place the peanut butter, confectioners' sugar, salt, and vanilla in a mixing bowl and stir to combine. Set the mixture aside

2. Fill a small saucepan with water and bring it to a gentle simmer. Place the chocolate in heatproof bowl, place it over the simmering water, and stir until it is melted.

3. Place a spoonful of the melted chocolate in each muffin liner and then use spoon to drag chocolate halfway up the sides. When you have done this for each liner, place in refrigerator and let chill until chocolate has hardened, 15 to 20 minutes.

4. Remove from the refrigerator, scoop the peanut butter mixture into each chocolate shell and smooth it with a rubber spatula. Return to the refrigerator and chill for 10 to 15 minutes.

5. Remove from the refrigerator, top each filled shell with another spoonful of melted chocolate, and smooth the top with a rubber spatula. Return to the refrigerator and chill for 25 to 30 minutes before serving.

INGREDIENTS:

1 CUP CREAMY PEANUT BUTTER

½ CUP CONFECTIONERS' SUGAR

½ TEASPOON FINE SEA SALT

¼ TEASPOON PURE VANILLA EXTRACT

12 OZ. MILK CHOCOLATE

CLASSIC CHOCOLATE TRUFFLES

YIELD: 36 TRUFFLES / **ACTIVE TIME:** 20 MINUTES / **TOTAL TIME:** 24 HOURS

It's important to use the best possible ingredients here, as compromises have nowhere to hide.

1. Break the chocolate into small pieces, place it in a food processor, and blitz until it is finely chopped. Place it in a heatproof bowl and add the salt.

2. Place the cream in a saucepan and bring to a simmer over medium heat, stirring frequently. Pour the warm cream over the chocolate and whisk until it has melted and the mixture is smooth. Transfer the chocolate to a square 9-inch baking pan and let it cool completely. Cover with plastic wrap and refrigerate overnight.

3. Line two baking sheets with parchment paper and place the cocoa powder in a shallow bowl. Form heaping tablespoons of the chocolate mixture into balls and roll them in the cocoa powder. Place them on the baking sheets and refrigerate for 30 minutes before serving.

INGREDIENTS:

1	LB. DARK CHOCOLATE (55 TO 65 PERCENT)
	PINCH OF FINE SEA SALT
1¼	CUPS HEAVY CREAM
½	CUP COCOA POWDER

PEPPERMINT BARK

YIELD: 24 SERVINGS / **ACTIVE TIME:** 15 MINUTES / **TOTAL TIME:** 1 HOUR

A simple bark that will make the considerable labor of preparing for the holidays bearable.

1. Line a rimmed baking sheet with parchment paper and place the crushed peppermint candies in a mixing bowl.

2. Fill a small saucepan halfway with water and bring it to a gently simmer. Place the semisweet chocolate chips in a heatproof bowl, place it over the simmering water, and stir until melted. Keep the water at a simmer.

3. Stir 1 teaspoon of the canola oil into the melted chocolate and then pour the chocolate onto the baking sheet, using a rubber spatula to distribute evenly. Place in the refrigerator until it has set, about 30 minutes.

4. Place the white chocolate chips in a heatproof bowl, place it over the simmering water, and stir until melted. Stir in the remaining oil and pour the melted white chocolate on top of the hardened semisweet chocolate, using a rubber spatula to distribute evenly.

5. Sprinkle the peppermint pieces liberally over the white chocolate and press down on them lightly. Refrigerate until set, about 30 minutes. Break the bark into pieces and refrigerate until ready to serve.

INGREDIENTS:

- ¾ CUP CRUSHED PEPPERMINT CANDIES
- 12 OZ. SEMISWEET CHOCOLATE CHIPS
- 2 TEASPOONS CANOLA OIL
- 12 OZ. WHITE CHOCOLATE CHIPS

TANG YUAN DANGO

YIELD: 4 TO 6 SERVINGS / **ACTIVE TIME:** 30 MINUTES / **TOTAL TIME:** 2 HOURS

A sweet rice dumpling that is both beautiful and bursting with flavor thanks to the freeze-dried berries.

1. Place the strawberries and sugar in a glass mixing bowl and stir to combine. Place 1 inch of water in a small saucepan and bring it to a boil. Cover the bowl with plastic wrap, place it over the saucepan, and let cook for 1 hour. Check the water level every 15 minutes and add more if it has evaporated. After 1 hour, turn off the heat and let the syrup cool. When cool, strain and discard the solids.

2. Bring water to a boil in a large saucepan. Place the flour, water, and ¾ cup of the syrup in a large mixing bowl and use a fork to work the mixture until it is combined and very dry. Remove 2 tablespoons of the mixture and roll each tablespoon into a ball. Place the balls in the boiling water and cook until they float to the surface and double in size, about 5 minutes. Return the balls to the mixture, add the canola oil, and use the fork to incorporate.

3. Bring the water back to a boil and prepare an ice water bath. Place the mixture on a flour-dusted work surface and knead until it is a smooth and slightly tacky dough. If the dough is too dry or too sticky, incorporate water or flour as needed.

4. Divide the dough into 18 pieces, roll them into balls, and use a slotted spoon to gently lower them into the pot. Gently stir to keep them from sticking to the bottom and then cook until they float to the surface and double in size, about 8 minutes. Remove with a slotted spoon, refresh in the ice water bath, drain, and place 3 balls on each of the skewers. Garnish with the freeze-dried strawberries, drizzle some of the remaining syrup over the top, and enjoy..

INGREDIENTS:

4   CUPS FRESH STRAWBERRIES, HULLED AND CHOPPED

8.75   OZ. SUGAR

8.5   OZ. SWEET RICE FLOUR (GLUTINOUS RICE FLOUR), PLUS MORE AS NEEDED

⅓   CUP WATER, PLUS MORE AS NEEDED

2   TABLESPOONS CANOLA OIL

6   WOODEN SKEWERS

FREEZE-DRIED STRAWBERRIES, FOR GARNISH

PRALINES

YIELD: 24 PRALINES / **ACTIVE TIME:** 15 MINUTES / **TOTAL TIME:** 50 MINUTES

Originating in France and initially containing almonds, the praline came into its own in Louisiana, where the plentiful pecan lent its natural sweetness to the treat. The transformation proved to be addictive, becoming so popular that they were being hawked on the streets of New Orleans as far back as the 1860s, a time when markets and vendors were largely concerned with providing the necessities of everyday life.

1. Place the sugars and evaporated milk in a saucepan fitted with a candy thermometer and cook, stirring constantly, until the sugars have dissolved. Continue cooking, stirring frequently, until the mixture reaches 225°F.

2. Add the pecans and butter, stir until the butter melts, and then remove from heat.

3. Stir in the vanilla and let the mixture cool, stirring occasionally. When the mixture starts to thicken, place tablespoons of the mixture on a piece of parchment paper. They will settle into thin patties as they cool. Let stand for 30 minutes before enjoying. To store the pralines, wrap each one in wax paper.

INGREDIENTS:

1	CUP PACKED DARK BROWN SUGAR
1	CUP SUGAR
½	CUP EVAPORATED MILK
1	CUP PECAN HALVES
1	OZ. UNSALTED BUTTER
1½	TEASPOONS PURE VANILLA EXTRACT

HONEY NUT TRUFFLES

YIELD: 16 TRUFFLES / **ACTIVE TIME:** 10 MINUTES / **TOTAL TIME:** 2 HOURS

Honey proves that perfection—the combination of peanut butter and chocolate—is possible to improve upon.

1. Place the peanut butter, honey, and salt in a mixing bowl and stir until well combined. Drop teaspoons of the mixture on a parchment-lined baking sheet and then place it in the refrigerator for 1 hour.

2. Remove the baking sheet from the refrigerator. Fill a small saucepan with water and bring it to a gentle simmer. Place the chocolate in heatproof bowl, place it over the simmering water, and stir until it is melted.

3. Dip the balls into the melted chocolate until completely covered. Place them back on the baking sheet. When all of the truffles have been coated, place them in the refrigerator and chill until the chocolate is set, about 45 minutes.

INGREDIENTS:

- ½ CUP CREAMY PEANUT BUTTER
- ¼ CUP HONEY
- ¼ TEASPOON FINE SEA SALT
- 4 OZ. DARK CHOCOLATE (55 TO 65 PERCENT), CHOPPED

ALMOND MERINGUE KISSES

YIELD: 24 KISSES / **ACTIVE TIME:** 15 MINUTES / **TOTAL TIME:** 1 HOUR AND 45 MINUTES

Adding a bit of almond to these impossibly delicate meringues will set your heart to racing.

1. Preheat the oven to 250°F and line two baking sheets with parchment paper. Place the egg whites, almond extract, and salt in the work bowl of a stand mixer fitted with the whisk attachment and beat at medium speed with until soft peaks form. Incorporate the sugar 1 tablespoon at a time and beat until the mixture holds stiff peaks.

2. Add the almond flour and fold to incorporate. Spoon the meringue mixture into a piping bag fitted with plain tip and pipe the mixture onto the baking sheets.

3. Place the kisses in the oven and bake until set, about 30 minutes. Turn off the oven and allow the meringues to dry in the oven for 45 minutes. Remove the baking sheets from the oven, gently remove the cookies from the parchment paper, and transfer to wire racks to cool completely before enjoying.

INGREDIENTS:

3	EGG WHITES, AT ROOM TEMPERATURE
1	TEASPOON PURE ALMOND EXTRACT
¼	TEASPOON KOSHER SALT
⅓	CUP SUGAR
1	TABLESPOON FINE ALMOND FLOUR

NOUGAT

YIELD: 24 SERVINGS / **ACTIVE TIME:** 30 MINUTES / **TOTAL TIME:** 1 HOUR AND 30 MINUTES

This is not the candy bar filler that's now associated with the term "nougat." This recipe, which is similar to the torrone that is a traditional part of the Christmas meal in Italy, is a far cry from that mysterious substance.

1. Coat a rimmed baking sheet with nonstick cooking spray. Place the egg whites in the work bowl of a stand mixer fitted with the whisk attachment and beat until frothy. Set aside.

2. Place the sugar, corn syrup, honey, and water in a saucepan fitted with a candy thermometer and bring to a boil over medium-high heat. Cook until the mixture is 300°F.

3. With the mixer running on low, gradually add the hot syrup to the egg whites. When half of the syrup has been incorporated, pour the rest of the hot syrup into the mixture and gradually increase the speed until the mixture is light and frothy. Add the lemon zest, vanilla, salt, and slivered almonds and continue to run the mixer until the mixture has cooled considerably, about 15 to 20 minutes.

4. Pour the mixture onto the baking sheet and let it cool completely before slicing into bars, about 1 hour.

INGREDIENTS:

3	LARGE EGG WHITES
3	CUPS SUGAR
⅓	CUP LIGHT CORN SYRUP
1	CUP HONEY
1	CUP WATER
	ZEST OF 1 LEMON
	SEEDS OF 2 VANILLA BEANS
¾	TEASPOON FINE SEA SALT
1	CUP SLIVERED ALMONDS, TOASTED

JIAN DUI

YIELD: 4 SERVINGS / **ACTIVE TIME:** 1 HOUR / **TOTAL TIME:** 1 HOUR

A crispy and sweet dumpling that is beloved throughout Asia. It can be filled with anything, with peanuts and red bean paste the two overwhelming favorites.

1. Place the peanuts, sugar, and salt in a food processor and pulse until ground. Be careful not to process the mixture too much and make peanut butter. Place the mixture in a small bowl and set aside.

2. Place the sweet rice flour in a separate bowl and make a well in the center. Place the water in a small pot and bring it to a boil. Add the brown sugar, stir until it has dissolved, and then pour the syrup into the well. Stir the mixture until it comes together as a dough.

3. Transfer the dough to a flour-dusted work surface and knead until smooth. The dough needs to be hot, so be careful. Cut the dough into 2 pieces and roll each one into a log. The dough tends to dry quickly, so keep a bowl of water near the work surface and dip your hands into it as necessary. Cut each log into eight pieces and roll each piece into a ball. Cover the pieces with plastic wrap to keep them from drying out.

4. Place a ball in the palm of one hand and use the thumb of your free hand to make a hole in the center of the ball. Fill with 1 teaspoon of the peanut mixture and smooth the dough over the filling. Pinch the seam and twist to remove any excess dough. Roll into a smooth ball, place on a parchment-lined baking sheet, and cover with plastic wrap. Repeat with the remaining balls and filling.

5. Add peanut oil to a Dutch oven until it is 2 inches deep and warm it to 350°F over medium heat. Place the sesame seeds in a shallow bowl. Dip each ball into the bowl of water, shake to remove any excess, and roll them in the sesame seeds until coated.

6. Working in batches of four, drop the dumplings into the hot oil and cook, gently stirring initially, until they float to the surface, about 3 minutes. Push the dumplings to the edge of the Dutch oven and baste them with the hot oil as they cook. Cook for another 3 to 4 minutes and transfer to a paper-towel lined plate. Serving the dumplings warm is preferred, but they are also delicious at room temperature.

INGREDIENTS:

¼ CUP ROASTED PEANUTS, CHOPPED

2½ TABLESPOONS SUGAR

⅛ TEASPOON KOSHER SALT

11.3 OZ. SWEET RICE FLOUR (GLUTINOUS RICE FLOUR), PLUS MORE FOR DUSTING

¾ CUP WATER

5.3 OZ. LIGHT BROWN SUGAR

PEANUT OIL, AS NEEDED

⅓ CUP SESAME SEEDS

CHOCOLATE & WALNUT FUDGE

YIELD: 16 SERVINGS / **ACTIVE TIME:** 15 MINUTES / **TOTAL TIME:** 2 HOURS AND 30 MINUTES

A piece a year may be all you need to get your fill, but it's still a necessity.

1. Preheat the oven to 350°F and line a square, 8-inch baking pan with heavy-duty aluminum foil, making sure the foil extends over the sides. Coat the foil with nonstick cooking spray.

2. Cover a baking sheet with the walnuts, place it in the oven, and toast the walnuts until they are fragrant and lightly browned, about 5 to 7 minutes, until lightly browned. Remove from the oven and set the walnuts aside.

3. Place the chocolate and butter in a heatproof mixing bowl and set aside. Place the sugar in a large saucepan fitted with a candy thermometer and cook over medium heat until it has dissolved and is boiling. Continue to cook, stirring constantly, until the sugar reaches 236°F on a candy thermometer. Carefully pour the sugar over the chocolate-and-butter mixture in the mixing bowl. Whisk until the mixture is smooth and then stir in the toasted walnuts and the vanilla.

4. Spread the fudge in an even layer in the cake pan. Refrigerate the fudge until it is set, about 2 hours. Use the foil to lift the fudge out of the pan and cut it into squares.

INGREDIENTS:

1	CUP CHOPPED WALNUTS
1	LB. QUALITY BITTERSWEET CHOCOLATE, CHOPPED
4	OZ. UNSALTED BUTTER
2	CUPS SUGAR
1	TEASPOON PURE VANILLA EXTRACT

WHITE CHOCOLATE BARK

YIELD: 24 SERVINGS / **ACTIVE TIME**: 10 MINUTES / **TOTAL TIME**: 40 MINUTES

Use absolutely any combination of dried fruits and nuts you'd like, but know that white chocolate and dried cranberries have an enormously powerful connection.

1. Fill a small saucepan with water and bring it to a gentle simmer. Place the white chocolate in heatproof bowl, place it over the simmering water, and stir until it is melted.

2. Line a baking sheet with parchment paper. Pour the melted chocolate onto baking sheet and spread it into an even layer with a rubber spatula, making sure not to spread it too thin.

3. Sprinkle the cranberries and pistachios onto the chocolate and lightly press them down into the chocolate. Place in the refrigerator until set, about 30 minutes.

4. When the chocolate is set, break the bark up into large pieces and serve.

INGREDIENTS:

1   LB. WHITE CHOCOLATE, CHOPPED

½   CUP DRIED CRANBERRIES

½   CUP CHOPPED PISTACHIOS

CHOCOLATE & AVOCADO TRUFFLES

YIELD: 36 TRUFFLES / **ACTIVE TIME:** 10 MINUTES / **TOTAL TIME:** 45 MINUTES

Unorthodox, yes. But avocado's rich, fresh flavor ensures that these treats stick the landing.

1. Fill a small saucepan halfway with water and bring it to a gentle simmer. Place the chocolate chips in a heatproof bowl, place it over the simmering water, and stir until it is melted.

2. Place the avocados, vanilla, and salt in a mixing bowl and stir to combine. Fold in the melted chocolate, cover the bowl, and refrigerate for 30 minutes.

3. Line a baking sheet with parchment paper and place the cocoa powder in a shallow bowl. Form approximately ¾-tablespoon portions of the mixture into balls, roll them in the cocoa powder, and refrigerate until ready to serve.

INGREDIENTS:

1   LB. BEST-QUALITY DARK CHOCOLATE, CHOPPED

     FLESH OF 2 AVOCADOS

2   TEASPOONS PURE VANILLA EXTRACT

½   TEASPOON KOSHER SALT

½   CUP UNSWEETENED COCOA POWDER

CARAMEL APPLES

YIELD: 12 APPLES / **ACTIVE TIME:** 30 MINUTES / **TOTAL TIME:** 4 HOURS

Refrigerating the apples before coating them in the caramel will help you avoid the mealy apple syndrome that so often causes this fun treat to fall short of its promise.

1. Line a large baking sheet with parchment paper and coat it with nonstick cooking spray.

2. Insert the dowels in the bottoms of the apples and push up until they are secure. Place the apples on the baking sheet and chill in the refrigerator for 2 hours.

3. In a medium saucepan fitted with a candy thermometer, combine the butter, brown sugar, corn syrup, and sweetened condensed milk and cook over medium heat, swirling the pan occasionally, until the mixture is, 248°F. Remove the pan from heat and whisk in the vanilla extract.

4. While working quickly, grab the apples by the end of the dowels and dip them into the caramel until evenly coated. Let any excess caramel drip off.

5. Place the apples back on the baking sheet and let them set before enjoying.

INGREDIENTS:

- 12 6-INCH WOODEN DOWELS
- 12 HONEYCRISP APPLES
- 4 OZ. UNSALTED BUTTER
- 14 OZ. LIGHT BROWN SUGAR
- 1 CUP LIGHT CORN SYRUP
- 1 (14 OZ.) CAN OF SWEETENED CONDENSED MILK
- 1 TEASPOON PURE VANILLA EXTRACT

CARAMEL POPCORN

YIELD: 4 SERVINGS / **ACTIVE TIME:** 15 MINUTES / **TOTAL TIME:** 45 MINUTES

Turn a night of sitting at home and streaming into an occasion to remember with this easy-to-perfect popcorn.

1. Pop the bag of popcorn in the microwave and set aside. Line a baking sheet with parchment paper and coat it with nonstick cooking spray.

2. In a large saucepan fitted with a candy thermometer, combine the butter, corn syrup, brown sugar, sugar, and salt and cook over medium heat, swirling the pan occasionally, until the caramel reaches 248°F.

3. Whisk in the vanilla, add the bag of popcorn, and fold the mixture until the caramel is evenly distributed.

4. Transfer the caramel popcorn to the baking sheet and spread it into an even layer. Let cool completely before enjoying.

INGREDIENTS:

1	BAG OF MICROWAVE POPCORN
6	TABLESPOONS UNSALTED BUTTER
⅓	CUP LIGHT CORN SYRUP
½	CUP LIGHT BROWN SUGAR
½	CUP SUGAR
¼	TEASPOON KOSHER SALT
¼	TEASPOON PURE VANILLA EXTRACT

MACADAMIA BRITTLE

YIELD: 24 SERVINGS / **ACTIVE TIME:** 40 MINUTES / **TOTAL TIME:** 2 HOURS AND 30 MINUTES

Brittle is great with any nut, but becomes transcendent with the buttery macadamia. This is great at a holiday party, or as a small gift.

1. Preheat the oven to 350°F. Line a baking sheet with parchment paper and place the macadamia nuts on it. Place in the oven and roast until golden brown and fragrant, about 15 minutes. Remove the nuts from the oven and let them cool for 30 minutes.

2. Place the nuts in a food processor and pulse until roughly chopped.

3. Make sure all of the ingredients are measured out, as you must work quickly once the sugar caramelizes. Place two 18 x 13–inch silicone baking mats on the counter, along with one rolling pin and a cooling rack.

4. In a large saucepan fitted with a candy thermometer, combine the butter, corn syrup, brown sugar, sugar, and salt and cook over medium heat, swirling the pan occasionally, until the caramel reaches 248°F.

5. Remove the pan from heat and carefully whisk in the water and vanilla.

6. Add the baking soda and toasted macadamia nuts and work quickly, whisking the mixture to deflate the bubbling up of the caramel.

7. Pour the mixture over one of the mats, using a rubber spatula to remove all the caramel from the pan. Place the second silicone mat on top. Using the rolling pin, roll the caramel out until it is the length and width of the mats.

8. Carefully transfer the mats to the cooling rack. Allow the brittle to set for at least an hour before breaking it up.

INGREDIENTS:

1½   CUPS MACADAMIA NUTS

1   TABLESPOON UNSALTED BUTTER, SOFTENED

½   CUP LIGHT CORN SYRUP

3.5   OZ. BROWN SUGAR

1   LB. SUGAR

½   TEASPOON KOSHER SALT

½   CUP WATER

½   TEASPOON PURE VANILLA EXTRACT

¾   TEASPOON BAKING SODA

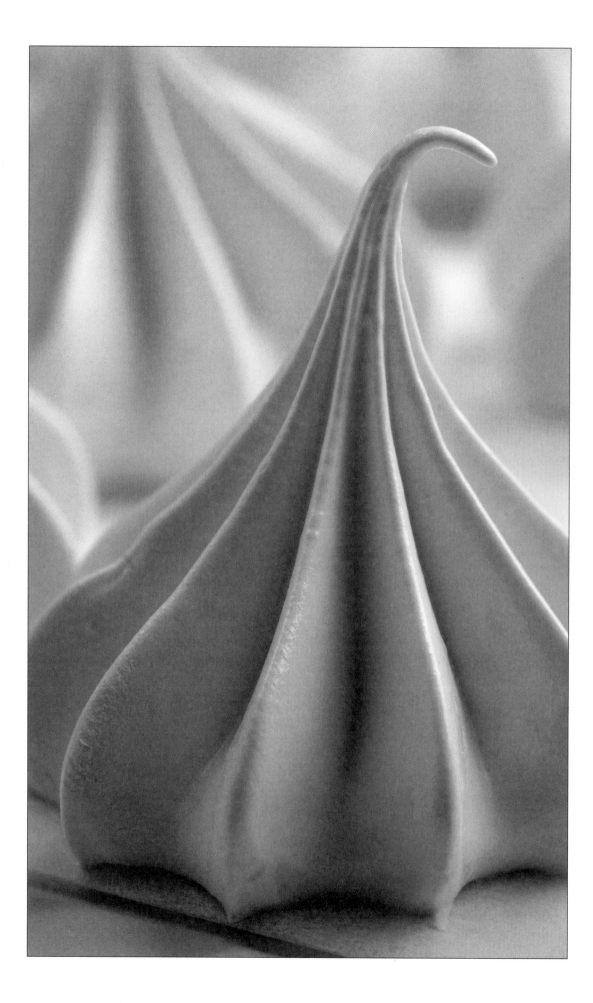

MERINGUE KISSES

YIELD: 50 KISSES / **ACTIVE TIME:** 30 MINUTES / **TOTAL TIME:** 1 HOUR AND 30 MINUTES

You'll savor each one.

1. Preheat the oven to 200°F and line two baking sheets with parchment paper.

2. Fill a small saucepan halfway with water and bring it to a gentle simmer. In the work bowl of a stand mixer, combine the egg whites, sugar, and salt. Place the work bowl over the simmering water and whisk continually until the sugar has dissolved. Remove the bowl from heat and return it to the stand mixer.

3. Fit the mixer with the whisk attachment and whip the mixture on high speed until it holds stiff peaks. If using coloring or vanilla, add it now and whisk to incorporate.

4. Transfer the meringue to a piping bag fit with a round tip.

5. Pipe the meringue onto the baking sheets, leaving about 1 inch between them. Place the sheets in the oven and bake the meringues until they can be pulled off the parchment cleanly and are no longer sticky in the center, about 1 hour. If the meringues need a little longer, crack the oven door and continue cooking. This will prevent the meringues from browning.

6. Remove from the oven and enjoy immediately.

INGREDIENTS:

4   EGG WHITES

7   OZ. SUGAR

     PINCH OF KOSHER SALT

1-2   DROPS OF GEL FOOD COLORING (OPTIONAL)

1   TEASPOON PURE VANILLA EXTRACT (OPTIONAL)

LUQAIMAT

YIELD: 4 SERVINGS / **ACTIVE TIME:** 30 MINUTES / **TOTAL TIME:** 1 HOUR AND 30 MINUTES

This sweet and simple dumpling is typically the reward at the end of a fast during Ramadan.

1. Place the flour, yeast, milk powder, sugar, cardamom, and saffron in a mixing bowl and stir until combined. While working the mixture with your hands, gradually incorporate the water until it comes together as a dough. Cover with a dry kitchen towel and let the dough rest for 1 hour.

2. Add vegetable oil to a Dutch oven until it is 2 inches deep and warm it to 350°F over medium heat. Wet your hands and roll tablespoons of the dough into balls. Carefully set them in the hot oil and fry, while stirring, until they are dark brown, about 3 to 5 minutes. Transfer to a paper towel-lined plate to drain and cool.

3. When all of the dumplings have been cooked, place them in a serving bowl, add the date syrup or honey and the toasted sesame seeds. Toss to coat and serve immediately.

INGREDIENTS:

5	OZ. ALL-PURPOSE FLOUR
½	TEASPOON INSTANT YEAST
½	CUP NONFAT DRY MILK POWDER
2	TABLESPOONS SUGAR
½	TEASPOON CARDAMOM
	PINCH OF SAFFRON
⅓	CUP LUKEWARM WATER (90°F), PLUS MORE AS NEEDED
	VEGETABLE OIL, AS NEEDED
½	CUP DATE SYRUP OR HONEY
1	TABLESPOON SESAME SEEDS, TOASTED

RASPBERRY PÂTE DE FRUIT

YIELD: 6 SERVINGS / **ACTIVE TIME:** 45 MINUTES / **TOTAL TIME:** 3 HOURS

A sweet French gummy that is positively bursting with fresh flavor.

1. Line a 9 x 13–inch baking pan with parchment paper and coat it with nonstick cooking spray.

2. Place the pectin and ¼ cup of the sugar in a mixing bowl and whisk to combine.

3. In a large saucepan fitted with a candy thermometer, combine the raspberry puree and water and warm the mixture over high heat. While whisking continually, gradually add the pectin mixture and bring the mixture to a boil.

4. Once boiling, add 4 cups of the sugar and whisk until dissolved. Lower the heat to medium and cook the mixture until it is 230°F.

5. Remove the pan from heat and carefully pour the mixture into the prepared baking pan. Transfer the pan to a cooling rack and let it sit at room temperature until cool and set, about 2 hours.

6. Dust a cutting board with sugar, transfer the candy onto the board, and cut it into 1-inch squares.

7. Place the remaining sugar in a medium bowl, add the candies, and toss until coated.

INGREDIENTS:

1	OZ. APPLE PECTIN
2	OZ. SUGAR
14.2	OZ. RASPBERRIES, PUREED
28.5	OZ. WATER
6¼	CUPS SUGAR, PLUS MORE AS NEEDED

SMOKED APPLE CRISP

YIELD: 8 TO 10 SERVINGS / **ACTIVE TIME:** 35 MINUTES / **TOTAL TIME:** 2 HOURS AND 30 MINUTES

If you don't have a smoker, that doesn't mean this preparation is out of reach—you can easily turn your gas or charcoal grill into an effective approximation of a smoker. To use a grill to smoke the apples, prepare one side of the grill for indirect heat. To do this, bank the coals to one side of a charcoal grill or leave one of the burners off on a gas grill. When the grill is 300°F, place the soaked wood chips on the coals or in a smoker box for a gas grill. Place the apples over indirect heat, cover the grill, and smoke for 8 to 10 minutes.

1. Soak the wood chips in a bowl of water 1 hour before you are ready to cook the apples.

2. Bring your smoker to 250°F. Place the soaked wood chips in the smoking tray and place the apples in the smoker. Smoke for 8 to 10 minutes. Remove the apples and set aside.

3. Preheat the oven to 350°F and coat a baking pan with nonstick cooking spray. Place the sugar, flour, 2 teaspoons of the cinnamon, oats, brown sugar, baking soda, and baking powder in a mixing bowl and mix by hand until combined. Add the butter and mix until the butter has been incorporated and the mixture is a coarse, crumbly meal.

4. Place the apples in a bowl with the remaining cinnamon, the nutmeg, and half of the crumble. Toss until the apples are evenly coated. Evenly distribute this mixture into a greased baking dish, top with the remaining crumble, and bake until golden brown, about 35 to 45 minutes. Remove from the oven and let the apple crisp cool slightly before serving.

INGREDIENTS:

1	CUP HICKORY OR APPLEWOOD CHIPS
4	LBS. APPLES, SLICED (BALDWIN OR GRANNY SMITH RECOMMENDED)
1	CUP SUGAR
1	CUP ALL-PURPOSE FLOUR
1	TABLESPOON CINNAMON
1	CUP ROLLED OATS
1	CUP BROWN SUGAR
¼	TEASPOON BAKING SODA
¼	TEASPOON BAKING POWDER
4	OZ. UNSALTED BUTTER, AT ROOM TEMPERATURE
1	TEASPOON FRESHLY GRATED NUTMEG

BLUEBERRY & BASIL JAM

YIELD: 3½ CUPS / *ACTIVE TIME:* 10 MINUTES / *TOTAL TIME:* 1 HOUR AND 30 MINUTES

Be sure to lay a few jars of this away for the winter—it'll help on those days when the gray has nearly ground you down.

1. Place all of the ingredients in a large saucepan and bring to a boil over medium-high heat, stirring occasionally.

2. Once the mixture has come to a boil, reduce the heat so that it simmers and cook, stirring frequently, until the mixture has reduced by half and is starting to thicken, about 1 hour. Remove from heat and let it thicken and set as it cools. If the jam is still too thin after 1 hour, continue to simmer until it is the desired consistency.

3. To can this jam, see page 623. If you are not interested in canning it, let cool completely before storing in the refrigerator.

INGREDIENTS:

3   QUARTS OF FRESH
       BLUEBERRIES

       LEAVES FROM 1 BUNCH
       OF FRESH BASIL, FINELY
       CHOPPED

2   TEASPOONS FRESH LEMON
       JUICE

2   CUPS SUGAR

½   CUP WATER

BANANAS FOSTER

YIELD: 6 SERVINGS / **ACTIVE TIME:** 10 MINUTES / **TOTAL TIME:** 10 MINUTES

Boozy, simple, and in possession of unique charm: it should come as no surprise that Bananas Foster originated in New Orleans, at the landmark Brennan's restaurant.

1. Place a large cast-iron skillet over medium-high heat and add the butter and brown sugar. Once the butter and sugar are melted, add the bananas to the pan and cook until they start to caramelize, about 3 minutes. Shake the pan and spoon some of the sauce over the bananas.

2. Remove the pan from heat and add the rum. Using a long match or wand lighter, carefully light the rum on fire. Place the pan back on the heat and shake the pan until the flames go out. Add the cream and stir to incorporate.

3. Divide the bananas and sauce between the serving dishes. Top each portion with ice cream and sprinkle cinnamon over the top.

INGREDIENTS:

8   OZ. UNSALTED BUTTER

1   CUP PACKED LIGHT BROWN SUGAR

6   BANANAS, CUT LENGTHWISE AND HALVED

½   CUP DARK RUM

½   CUP HEAVY CREAM

     VANILLA ICE CREAM (SEE PAGE 516 FOR HOMEMADE), FOR SERVING

     CINNAMON, FOR DUSTING

PEAR & GINGER CRUMBLE

YIELD: 4 SERVINGS / **ACTIVE TIME:** 30 MINUTES / **TOTAL TIME:** 1 HOUR AND 30 MINUTES

The subtle, smooth notes of vanilla that pears are known for are a natural match for the spicy kick of ginger.

1. Preheat the oven to 350°F. Place 1 tablespoon of the butter in a large cast-iron skillet and melt it over medium heat.

2. Trim the tops and bottoms from the pears, cut them into quarters, remove the cores, and cut each quarter in half. Lay the slices in the melted butter. Sprinkle the ginger over the pears, cook until they start to brown, and remove the skillet from heat.

3. Place the flour and brown sugar in a bowl and stir to combine. Cut the remaining butter into slices, add them to the bowl, and use your fingers to work the mixture until comes together as a coarse, crumbly meal. Stir in the rolled oats and then spread the mixture on top of the pears.

4. Put the skillet in the oven and bake until the filling is bubbling and the topping is golden brown, about 25 minutes. Remove the skillet from the oven and let cool for a few minutes before serving with ice cream.

INGREDIENTS:

4.5	OZ. UNSALTED BUTTER, CHILLED
4	PEARS
1	TEASPOON GRATED FRESH GINGER
1	CUP ALL-PURPOSE FLOUR
½	CUP PACKED DARK BROWN SUGAR
½	CUP ROLLED OATS
	VANILLA ICE CREAM (SEE PAGE 516 FOR HOMEMADE), FOR SERVING

GALUSTE CU PRUNE

YIELD: 4 SERVINGS / **ACTIVE TIME:** 30 MINUTES / **TOTAL TIME:** 1 HOUR

A dumpling as beautiful as it is delicious, it's easy to understand how these became the pride of Romania.

1. Place the plums in a small bowl, sprinkle the confectioners' sugar over them, and toss to combine. Set the plums aside.

2. Place the potatoes in a saucepan, cover with water, and bring to a boil. Cook until they are fork-tender, about 20 minutes. Drain the potatoes, place them in a large mixing bowl, and mash until smooth. Add the eggs, flours, and salt and stir until the mixture comes together as a dough.

3. Bring water to a boil in a large saucepan and add the olive oil. Place the butter in a skillet and melt it over medium heat. Add the bread crumbs to the skillet, reduce the heat to low, and cook, stirring frequently, until the bread crumbs are golden brown. Remove from heat, stir in the sugar, and then let the mixture cool completely.

4. Divide the dough into 12 pieces and flatten them to ¼-inch thick. Place one of the sugar-coated plums in the center of each piece, shape the dough around the plum, and gently roll them into balls.

5. Place the dumplings in the boiling water and cook until they rise to the surface, about 4 minutes. Remove them with a strainer and roll them in the bread crumb mixture until completely coated. Place the dumplings on a platter and let cool completely before serving.

INGREDIENTS:

- 3   PLUMS, PITTED AND QUARTERED
- 3   TABLESPOONS CONFECTIONERS' SUGAR
- 1.5   LBS. YUKON GOLD POTATOES, PEELED AND CHOPPED
- 2   EGGS
- 1   CUP ALL-PURPOSE FLOUR
- 3   TABLESPOONS SEMOLINA FLOUR
- ¼   TEASPOON KOSHER SALT
- 1   TABLESPOON EXTRA-VIRGIN OLIVE OIL
- 1.5   OZ. UNSALTED BUTTER
- 2   CUPS BREAD CRUMBS
- 6   TABLESPOONS SUGAR

BAKED APPLES

YIELD: 6 SERVINGS / ACTIVE TIME: 15 MINUTES / TOTAL TIME: 1 HOUR

A sweet-tart, crisp apple such as the Pink Lady is what you'll want to use in this recipe.

1. Preheat the oven to 350°F. Slice the tops off of the apples and set them aside. Use a paring knife to cut out the apples' cores and then scoop out the centers, leaving a ½ inch thick wall inside each apple.

2. Rub the inside and outside of the apples with some of the melted butter. Place the jam and goat cheese in a mixing bowl and stir to combine. Fill the apples' cavities with the mixture, place the tops back on the apples, and set them aside.

3. Coat a baking pan with the remaining butter and then arrange the apples in the pan. Place in the oven and bake until tender, 25 to 30 minutes. Remove from the oven and let cool briefly before serving.

INGREDIENTS:

6   APPLES

3   TABLESPOONS UNSALTED BUTTER, MELTED

6   TABLESPOONS BLACKBERRY JAM

2   OZ. GOAT CHEESE, AT ROOM TEMPERATURE, CUT INTO 6 ROUNDS

GRILLED PEACHES
WITH BOURBON CARAMEL

YIELD: 6 SERVINGS / **ACTIVE TIME:** 20 MINUTES / **TOTAL TIME:** 20 MINUTES

Put on Theo Parrish's "Summertime Is Here," fashion yourself a long cocktail, and then soak up a summer evening outside with this.

1. Preheat your gas or charcoal grill to medium heat (about 425°F). Place the sugar and ¼ cup of bourbon in a small saucepan and cook over medium heat until the sugar has dissolved. Reduce the heat and add the heavy cream, stirring constantly and being careful, as the mixture will splatter. Add the remaining bourbon, the butter, and salt, remove from heat, and pour into a heatproof mixing bowl.

2. When the grill is ready, place the peaches, cut side down, on the grill and cook until the flesh becomes tender and starts to caramelize, about 5 minutes. Turn the peaches over and cook for another 4 to 5 minutes. Place 2 to 3 peach halves in each bowl, drizzle the caramel over them, and top with ice cream.

INGREDIENTS:

½ CUP SUGAR

¼ CUP BOURBON, PLUS 2 TABLESPOONS

¼ CUP HEAVY CREAM, WARMED

1 TABLESPOON UNSALTED BUTTER

1 TEASPOON FINE SEA SALT

6 PEACHES, PITTED AND HALVED

2 PINTS OF VANILLA ICE CREAM (SEE PAGE 516 FOR HOMEMADE), FOR SERVING

PEACH COBBLER

YIELD: 4 TO 6 SERVINGS / **ACTIVE TIME:** 30 MINUTES / **TOTAL TIME:** 1 HOUR

I f you can track down the low-protein White Lily flour that is a staple in Southern kitchens, you'll get the biscuits you've always dreamed of.

1. Preheat the oven to 400°F and place a cast-iron skillet in the oven as it warms. To begin preparations for the biscuits, place the flour, sugar, salt, and baking powder in a mixing bowl and stir to combine. Add the butter and work it into the mixture with a pastry blender. When a crumbly dough forms, add the buttermilk and work the mixture until it comes together as a stiff dough. If the dough is not holding together, incorporate more buttermilk 1 tablespoon at a time until it does.

2. Place the dough on a flour-dusted work surface and pat it out into a 1-inch-thick rectangle. Use a flour-dusted biscuit cutter or mason jar to cut the dough into rounds.

3. To prepare the filling, place the peaches, sugar, and flour in a bowl and stir to combine. The amount of flour you use will depend on how juicy the peaches are; more juice means more flour is required. Remove the skillet from the oven, transfer the filling into the skillet, and bake for 10 minutes.

4. Remove the skillet from the oven and place the biscuits on top of the filling, making sure they are evenly distributed. Sprinkle the cinnamon on top and return the skillet to the oven. Bake until the biscuits are golden brown and the filling is bubbling, about 12 minutes. Make sure not to burn the topping. Remove from the oven, let cool briefly, and serve with Chantilly Cream or ice cream.

INGREDIENTS:

FOR THE BISCUITS

2 CUPS ALL-PURPOSE FLOUR, PLUS MORE AS NEEDED

1 TEASPOON SUGAR

1 TEASPOON FINE SEA SALT

1 TABLESPOON BAKING POWDER

3 OZ. UNSALTED BUTTER, CUT INTO SMALL PIECES

½ CUP BUTTERMILK, PLUS MORE AS NEEDED

FOR THE FILLING

5 PEACHES, PITTED AND SLICED

¼ CUP SUGAR

1-2 TABLESPOONS ALL-PURPOSE FLOUR

1 TEASPOON CINNAMON

CHANTILLY CREAM (SEE PAGE 89), FOR SERVING (OPTIONAL)

VANILLA ICE CREAM (SEE PAGE 516 FOR HOMEMADE), FOR SERVING (OPTIONAL)

STRAWBERRY PRESERVES

YIELD: 2 CUPS / ACTIVE TIME: 30 MINUTES / TOTAL TIME: 2 HOURS AND 30 MINUTES

Because the taste of a hand-picked strawberry is too wonderful to be restricted to the short growing season. And, for those wondering: absolutely any berry can be preserved in this way.

1. Place all of the ingredients in a large saucepan and warm it over low heat, using a wooden spoon to occasionally fold the mixture. Cook until the sugar has dissolved and the strawberries are starting to collapse, about 15 minutes.

2. Remove the pan from heat. If you are canning the preserves, see the sidebar on the opposite page. If you are not going to can the preserves, transfer them to a sterilized mason jar and let them cool at room temperature for 2 hours before enjoying or storing in the refrigerator, where they will keep for up to 1 month.

INGREDIENTS:

1   LB. STRAWBERRIES, HULLED

1   LB. SUGAR

    ZEST AND JUICE OF 1 LEMON

    SEEDS AND POD OF 1 VANILLA BEAN

¼   TEASPOON KOSHER SALT

CANNING 101

Bring a pot of water to a boil. Place your mason jars in the water for 15 to 20 minutes to sterilize them. Do not boil the mason jar lids, as this can prevent them from creating a proper seal when the time comes.

Bring water to a boil in the large canning pot. Fill the sterilized mason jars with whatever you are canning. Place the lids on the jars and secure the bands tightly. Place the jars in the boiling water for 40 minutes. Use a pair of canning tongs to remove the jars from the boiling water and let them cool. As they are cooling, you should hear the classic "ping and pop" sound of the lids creating a seal.

After 6 hours, check the lids. They should have no give and should be suctioned onto the jars. Discard any lids and food that did not seal properly.

CHERRY & WATERMELON SOUP

YIELD: 4 SERVINGS / **ACTIVE TIME:** 20 MINUTES / **TOTAL TIME:** 24 HOURS

Save this one for company, as its brilliant red color and vibrant freshness are sure to impress.

1. Place 1 cup of the watermelon cubes, the kirsch, lime zest, lime juice, and vanilla seeds and pod in a mixing bowl, stir to combine, and chill in the refrigerator for 1 hour.

2. Spread the mixture evenly over a rimmed baking sheet, place in the freezer, and freeze overnight.

3. Place the remaining watermelon, the cherries, and the Riesling in a food processor and puree until smooth. Strain through a fine sieve and place the puree in the refrigerator until ready to serve.

4. Remove the baking tray from the freezer and cut the mixture into cubes. Add these cubes and the Champagne to the puree, ladle the soup into chilled bowls, and enjoy.

INGREDIENTS:

2½   CUPS WATERMELON CUBES

1   TABLESPOON KIRSCH

     ZEST AND JUICE OF 1 LIME

     SEEDS AND POD OF ½ VANILLA BEAN

¾   CUP CHERRIES, PITTED

1   CUP RIESLING

1   CUP CHAMPAGNE

MUDDY BUDDIES

YIELD: 8 TO 10 SERVINGS / **ACTIVE TIME:** 5 MINUTES / **TOTAL TIME:** 50 MINUTES

One of those retro, out-of-a box treats that is irresistible, no matter how refined one's palate has become.

1. Fill a small saucepan halfway with water and bring it to a gentle simmer. Place the chocolate chips and peanut butter in a heatproof bowl and microwave on medium for 30 seconds. Remove from the microwave, add the vanilla, and stir until the mixture is smooth.

2. Place the Chex in a large mixing bowl and pour the peanut butter-and-chocolate mixture over the cereal. Carefully stir until all of the Chex are coated.

3. Place the mixture into a large resealable plastic bag and add the confectioners' sugar. Seal bag and shake until each piece is coated with sugar.

4. Pour the mixture onto a parchment-lined baking sheet. Place the sheet in the refrigerator and chill for 45 minutes before enjoying.

INGREDIENTS:

1   CUP SEMISWEET CHOCOLATE CHIPS

¾   CUP CREAMY PEANUT BUTTER

1   TEASPOON PURE VANILLA EXTRACT

9   CUPS RICE CHEX

1½   CUPS CONFECTIONERS' SUGAR

CHOCOLATE FETTUCCINE

YIELD: 1¼ LBS. / **ACTIVE TIME:** 25 MINUTES / **TOTAL TIME:** 1 HOUR AND 45 MINUTES

Top this with ice cream, Caramel Sauce (see page 103), and/or chopped pecans and you've got the makings of an unforgettable dessert.

1. Combine the flour and cocoa in a mixing bowl and make a well in the center. Add the eggs, water, and olive oil. Using your fingers, gradually start pulling the flour-and-cocoa mixture into the pool and work the mixture until it comes together as a dough, adding more water—1 tablespoon at a time—if the mixture is not coming together.

2. Place the dough on a flour-dusted work surface and knead until it is smooth and elastic, about 8 minutes. If the dough still feels wet, tacky, or sticky, dust it with flour and continue kneading. If it feels too dry and is not completely sticking together, wet your hands with water and continue kneading. The dough has been sufficiently kneaded when it is very smooth and gently pulls back into place when stretched.

3. Cover the dough completely with in plastic wrap and let it rest at room temperature for 1 hour.

4. Unwrap the dough, cut it into thirds, and roll each one out to a thickness that can go through the widest setting on a pasta maker. Run the rolled pieces of dough through the pasta maker, adjusting the setting to reduce the thickness with each pass. When the dough is the desired thickness, roll the sheets up and cut into ¼-inch-wide strips.

5. Dust the cut pasta with cocoa powder and place on a surface lightly dusted with cocoa powder. Let stand for 15 minutes before cooking.

INGREDIENTS:

1½ CUPS ALL-PURPOSE FLOUR, PLUS MORE AS NEEDED

½ CUP COCOA POWDER, PLUS MORE AS NEEDED

3 LARGE EGGS

1 TABLESPOON WATER, PLUS MORE AS NEEDED

1 TABLESPOON EXTRA-VIRGIN OLIVE OIL

CHOCOLATE & COCONUT SOUP
WITH BRÛLÉED BANANAS

YIELD: 4 SERVINGS / ACTIVE TIME: 25 MINUTES / TOTAL TIME: 1 HOUR

When soup serves as the last course, it's got to be unbelievable. This one more than meets that charge.

1. Place the milk, coconut milk, cream, and the vanilla seeds and pod in a saucepan and bring to a simmer over medium heat. Turn off the heat and let the mixture stand for 20 minutes.

2. Cut your bananas on a bias. Dip one side into a dish of sugar and then use a kitchen torch to caramelize the sugar. Set aside.

3. Preheat the oven to 350°F. Remove the outer shell of the coconut and use a spoon to remove the meat. Slice the coconut meat very thin and set aside. In a small saucepan, add the ¾ cup sugar and the water and bring to a boil. Remove the syrup from heat and let stand until cool.

4. When the syrup is cool, dip the coconut slices into the syrup and place on a parchment-lined baking sheet. Place the sheet in the oven and bake until the coconut is golden brown, about 8 minutes. Remove and set aside.

5. After 20 minutes, remove the vanilla pod from the soup and return to a simmer. Turn off the heat, add the chocolate, and stir until the chocolate is melted. Strain the soup through a fine sieve and serve with the bruléed bananas and candied coconut.

INGREDIENTS:

2	CUPS WHOLE MILK
1	(14 OZ.) CAN OF UNSWEETENED COCONUT MILK
1	CUP HEAVY CREAM
	SEEDS AND POD OF 1 VANILLA BEAN
2	BANANAS
¾	CUP SUGAR, PLUS MORE TO TASTE
½	FRESH COCONUT
½	CUP WATER
12	OZ. DARK CHOCOLATE (55 TO 65 PERCENT), CHOPPED

DRINKS

After a particularly great meal, one does not always have the space to enjoy the richness of a cake, the tart sweetness of a fruit pie, the outlandish decadence of an eclair or profiterole, or the all-around perfection of well-made ice cream.

But, still, one needs something to put the cap on a memorable day. Something to soothe and leaven the mind as it muses on all that has passed today and what will come tomorrow.

These preparations are made for such moments. Crafted by some of the world's finest mixologists, they are sure to provide the satisfaction one looks for in a last course, without saddling you with the baggage other desserts come with.

CHOCOLATE MILKSHAKES

YIELD: 4 SERVINGS / **ACTIVE TIME:** 2 MINUTES / **TOTAL TIME:** 2 MINUTES

Of course, you can swap your favorite ice cream in for the chocolate here. Just keep in mind that this may affect how much of the other ingredients you want to include.

1. Place all of the ingredients, other than the garnishes, in a blender and puree until combined.

2. Pour the milkshakes into tall glasses and garnish each one with the Chantilly Cream and chocolate.

INGREDIENTS:

2   PINTS OF CHOCOLATE ICE CREAM (SEE PAGE 515 FOR HOMEMADE)

½   CUP WHOLE MILK

½   TEASPOON FINE SEA SALT

2   TEASPOONS PURE VANILLA EXTRACT

CHANTILLY CREAM (SEE PAGE 89), FOR GARNISH

CHOCOLATE, GRATED, FOR GARNISH

IRISH COFFEE

YIELD: 1 DRINK / **ACTIVE TIME:** 2 MINUTES / **TOTAL TIME:** 2 MINUTES

The rare dessert that makes sense any time of day.

1. Pour the coffee into an Irish Coffee glass and add the sugar. Stir until the sugar has dissolved.

2. Add the whiskey and stir again. Top with Baileys Irish Cream. If you can, layer the Baileys on top rather than stirring it in. Garnish with a dollop of Chantilly Cream.

INGREDIENTS:

½   CUP FRESHLY BREWED
     COFFEE

     DASH OF SUGAR

1   OZ. IRISH WHISKEY

1   OZ. BAILEYS IRISH CREAM

     CHANTILLY CREAM (SEE
     PAGE 89), FOR GARNISH

STRAWBERRY DAIQUIRI

YIELD: 2 SERVINGS / **ACTIVE TIME:** 2 MINUTES / **TOTAL TIME:** 2 MINUTES

Lose the negative associations that have been fostered by restaurants and resorts using pre-packaged mixes—this drink is fun, beautiful, and delicious, the perfect way to roll into a summer weekend.

1. Place all of the ingredients in a blender, puree until smooth, and pour into tall glasses.

INGREDIENTS:

1	LB. FROZEN STRAWBERRIES
½	CUP FRESH LIME JUICE
2	TABLESPOONS SUGAR
1	TABLESPOON HONEY
½	CUP WHITE RUM

MEXICAN HOT CHOCOLATE

YIELD: 4 SERVINGS / **ACTIVE TIME:** 15 MINUTES / **TOTAL TIME:** 15 MINUTES

Incorporating a bit of spice into a simple cup of hot chocolate will wake up more than just the drink. If you desire nothing more than the taste youth accustomed you too, remove the seasonings and add some miniature marshmallows.

1. Place the milk, half-and-half, cinnamon sticks, and chili pepper in a saucepan and warm it over medium-low heat for 5 to 6 minutes, making sure the mixture does not come to a boil. When the mixture starts to steam, remove the cinnamon sticks and chili pepper.

2. Add the sweetened condensed milk and whisk until combined. Add the chocolate chips and cook, stirring occasionally, until they have melted. Stir in the vanilla, nutmeg, and salt.

3. Ladle into warmed mugs and top with Chantilly Cream.

INGREDIENTS:

3	CUPS WHOLE MILK
1	CUP HALF-AND-HALF
3	CINNAMON STICKS
1	RED CHILI PEPPER, STEMMED AND SEEDED
¼	CUP SWEETENED CONDENSED MILK
1.5	LBS. SEMISWEET CHOCOLATE CHIPS
½	TEASPOON PURE VANILLA EXTRACT
1	TEASPOON FRESHLY GRATED NUTMEG
½	TEASPOON FINE SEA SALT
	CHANTILLY CREAM (SEE PAGE 89), FOR GARNISH

PIÑA COLADA

YIELD: 4 SERVINGS / **ACTIVE TIME:** 2 MINUTES / **TOTAL TIME:** 2 MINUTES

If your mix is just not quite hitting the mark, try adding a pinch of fine sea salt to the blender.

1. Place all of the ingredients in a blender, puree until smooth, and pour into tall glasses.

INGREDIENTS:

1   CUP FROZEN PINEAPPLE
    CHUNKS

1   CUP ICE

½   CUP PINEAPPLE JUICE

½   CUP CREAM OF COCONUT

½   CUP WHITE RUM

½   CUP DARK RUM

1   TEASPOON FRESHLY
    GRATED NUTMEG

SGROPPINO PLAGIATO

YIELD: 1 DRINK / **ACTIVE TIME:** 2 MINUTES / **TOTAL TIME:** 2 MINUTES

This twist on the classic Italian cocktail comes via the craft cocktail revolution. If tracking down a bottle of Select Aperitivo proves difficult, substitute Aperol.

1. Place the scoop of sorbet in a goblet and pour in the Select Aperitivo.

2. Slowly pour Prosecco into the goblet and serve.

INGREDIENTS:

1   SCOOP OF STRAWBERRY SORBET (SEE PAGE 556 FOR HOMEMADE)

1¾   OZ. SELECT APERITIVO

PROSECCO, TO TOP

RUM BA BA

Translating the classic French cake into a cocktail will keep you light on your feet.

1. Add all of the ingredients, except for the garnishes, to a cocktail shaker filled with ice and shake vigorously until chilled.

2. Double-strain into a rocks glass filled with ice.

3. Garnish with the passion fruit slice and a sprig of mint.

INGREDIENTS:

1½   OZ. APPLETON ESTATE RUM

1½   OZ. HEAVY CREAM

1   OZ. MONIN ALMOND SYRUP (ORGEAT)

½   OZ. FRESH LEMON JUICE

1¼   OZ. PASSION FRUIT PUREE

2   DASHES OF PEYCHAUD'S BITTERS

1   SLICE OF PASSION FRUIT, FOR GARNISH

1   SPRIG OF FRESH MINT, FOR GARNISH

CAFÉ MOCHA

YIELD: 10 SERVINGS / **ACTIVE TIME**: 10 MINUTES / **TOTAL TIME**: 20 MINUTES

The only reason you need to justify shelling out for an espresso machine.

1. Place the milk, cream, sugar, and espresso in a saucepan and warm it over medium heat.

2. Place the chocolate in a bowl. When the milk mixture is hot, ladle 1 cup of it over the chocolate and whisk until the chocolate is completely melted, adding more of the warm milk mixture if the melted chocolate mixture is too thick.

3. Pour the melted chocolate mixture into the pot of warm milk and whisk to combine. Add the orange zest and salt and stir to combine. Taste and adjust if necessary before pouring into mugs and topping with the Chantilly Cream.

INGREDIENTS:

8	CUPS WHOLE MILK
1	CUP HEAVY CREAM
½	CUP SUGAR, PLUS MORE TO TASTE
½	CUP FRESHLY BREWED ESPRESSO
8	OZ. BITTERSWEET CHOCOLATE, CHOPPED
1	TABLESPOON ORANGE ZEST
½	TEASPOON FINE SEA SALT
	CHANTILLY CREAM (SEE PAGE 89), FOR GARNISH

COCONUT CREAM FLOAT

YIELD: 4 SERVINGS / ACTIVE TIME: 2 MINUTES / TOTAL TIME: 2 MINUTES

The criminally underutilized cream soda lends its talents to this delicious twist on the root beer float.

1. Place ice cream in the bottom of four tall glasses. Sprinkle the nutmeg over the ice cream.

2. Top with the cream soda, ganache, and rum (if desired).

INGREDIENTS:

1   PINT OF COCONUT ICE CREAM (SEE PAGE 520 FOR HOMEMADE)

2   TEASPOONS FRESHLY GRATED NUTMEG

3   (12 OZ.) BOTTLES OF QUALITY CREAM SODA

2   TABLESPOONS CHOCOLATE GANACHE (SEE PAGE 99)

1   TABLESPOON COCONUT RUM (OPTIONAL)

MARATHON MAN

YIELD: 1 DRINK / **ACTIVE TIME:** 2 MINUTES / **TOTAL TIME:** 2 MINUTES

The miniature Snickers bar isn't just there as a wink. It actually binds the numerous strong flavors here together.

1. Add all of the ingredients to a blender along with two large ice cubes and pulverize until there are fine bubbles throughout and all the ice has been thoroughly incorporated.

2. Pour over ice into a rocks glass.

INGREDIENTS:

1	OZ. BOURBON
¾	OZ. KAHLÚA
2	TEASPOONS MONIN ALMOND SYRUP (ORGEAT)
¾	OZ. FRANGELICO
¾	OZ. MOZART DARK CHOCOLATE LIQUEUR
1	TABLESPOON PEANUT BUTTER
1½	OZ. WHOLE MILK
1	MINIATURE SNICKERS BAR

CAKE BOSS

YIELD: 1 DRINK / **ACTIVE TIME:** 2 MINUTES / **TOTAL TIME:** 2 MINUTES

For the most part, it pays to be wary of flavored alcohol. But Pinnacle's cake-flavored option is an eye-opening exception.

1. Place a cocktail glass in the freezer.

2. Add the vodka and chocolate liqueur to a cocktail shaker filled with ice, shake vigorously until chilled, and strain into a chilled cocktail glass.

2. Pour the Baileys over the back of a spoon to float it on top of the cocktail and garnish with the cake crumbs.

INGREDIENTS:

2   OZ. PINNACLE CAKE VODKA

1   OZ. MARIE BRIZARD ROYAL CHOCOLAT LIQUEUR

BAILEYS IRISH CREAM, TO TOP

CAKE CRUMBS, FOR GARNISH

CAMPFIRE S'MORES

YIELD: 1 DRINK / **ACTIVE TIME:** 2 MINUTES / **TOTAL TIME:** 2 MINUTES

If you happen to be able to find one locally, a marshmallow-flavored milk stout will be dynamite here.

1. Place the graham cracker crumbs and chocolate shavings in a Shallow Bowl and stir to combine. Wet the rim of a pint glass and dip it into the mixture.

2. Add the bourbon and crème de cacao to a cocktail shaker filled with ice, shake vigorously until chilled, and strain into the pint glass.

3. Top with the stout and garnish with the toasted marshmallow.

INGREDIENTS:

GRAHAM CRACKER CRUMBS, FOR THE RIM

CHOCOLATE SHAVINGS, FOR THE RIM

1½ OZ. BOURBON

1½ OZ. GIFFARD CRÈME DE CACAO (WHITE)

12 OZ. STOUT, TO TOP

1 TOASTED MARSHMALLOW, FOR GARNISH

GOURMET LEMON

YIELD: 1 DRINK / **ACTIVE TIME:** 2 MINUTES / **TOTAL TIME:** 2 MINUTES

A glorious combination of techniques and crafts result in this glorious, inventive cocktail.

1. Add the tequila, limoncello, lime juice, and bitters to a mixing glass filled with ice, stir until chilled, and strain into the coupe.

2. Top with the Meringue and torch until it is browned.

3. Garnish with the sprig of mint and dehydrated lemon wheel.

INGREDIENTS:

1.5   OZ. SILVER TEQUILA

¾   OZ. LIMONCELLO

¾   OZ. FRESH LIME JUICE

2   DASHES OF LEMON BITTERS

   ITALIAN MERINGUE (SEE PAGE 71), TO TOP

1   SPRIG OF FRESH MINT, FOR GARNISH

1   DEHYDRATED LEMON WHEEL, FOR GARNISH

ELEVATED IRISH COFFEE

YIELD: 1 DRINK / **ACTIVE TIME:** 2 MINUTES / **TOTAL TIME:** 2 MINUTES

Pull this show-stopper out for your next brunch.

1. Fill an Irish Coffee glass with boiling water. When the glass is warm, discard the water.

2. Add the whiskey, syrup, and sherry to the glass and stir to combine.

3. Add the espresso and hot water—reserving room for the cream—and stir to incorporate.

4. Float the cream on top by pouring it over the back of a spoon.

SIMPLE SYRUP

1. Combine the sugar and water in a saucepan and bring to a boil over medium heat, stirring to help the sugar dissolve.

2. When the sugar has dissolved, remove the pan from heat, pour the syrup into a mason jar, and let it cool before using or storing in the refrigerator, where it will keep for up to 1 month.

INGREDIENTS:

- ¾ OZ. BUSHMILLS BLACK BUSH IRISH WHISKEY
- ½ OZ. SIMPLE SYRUP (SEE RECIPE)
- ½ TEASPOON PEDRO XIMÉNEZ SHERRY
- 2 OZ. FRESHLY BREWED MEDIUM-ROAST ESPRESSO

  HOT WATER, TO TOP

  HEAVY CREAM, LIGHTLY WHIPPED, FOR GARNISH

SIMPLE SYRUP

- ½ CUP SUGAR
- ½ CUP WATER

CHOCOLATE BURDOCK MARTINI

YIELD: 1 DRINK / **ACTIVE TIME:** 2 MINUTES / **TOTAL TIME:** 2 MINUTES

An eye-opening introduction to the wonders infused spirits offer. For those wondering, a bar spoon is equivalent to 1 teaspoon.

1. Add all of the ingredients to a cocktail shaker with ice, shake vigorously until chilled, and strain into a coupe containing 1 large block of ice.

BURDOCK & CACAO NIB BRANDY

1. Combine all of the ingredients in a mason jar and let the mixture steep at room temperature for 3 days.

2. Strain and use as desired.

INGREDIENTS:

2	OZ. BURDOCK & CACAO NIB BRANDY (SEE RECIPE)
½	OZ. CHOCOLATE LIQUEUR
2	BAR SPOONS PEDRO XIMÉNEZ SHERRY
1	BAR SPOON MAPLE SYRUP
3	DASHES OF ORANGE BITTERS

BURDOCK & CACAO NIB BRANDY

1	PIECE OF BURDOCK ROOT
⅓	OZ. CACAO NIBS
3	CUPS BRANDY

PEANUT BUTTER CUP MILKSHAKES

YIELD: 4 SERVINGS / **ACTIVE TIME:** 2 MINUTES / **TOTAL TIME:** 2 MINUTES

Setting the bright sweetness of bananas alongside the winning combination of peanut butter and chocolate means that your tastebuds are in for quite a ride.

1. Place all of the ingredients in a blender and puree until smooth.

2. Pour into tall glasses.

INGREDIENTS:

2   PINTS OF CHOCOLATE ICE CREAM (SEE PAGE 515 FOR HOMEMADE)

4   BANANAS, PEELED AND FROZEN

1   CUP CREAMY PEANUT BUTTER

½   CUP WHOLE MILK

6   TABLESPOONS CHOCOLATE GANACHE (SEE PAGE 99)

½   TEASPOON FINE SEA SALT

ARCADIA

YIELD: 1 DRINK / **ACTIVE TIME:** 2 MINUTES / **TOTAL TIME:** 2 MINUTES

This award-winning cocktail was fashioned with the conceit that, if baked, it would turn into a cake.

1. Place all of the ingredients, except for the garnishes, in a cocktail shaker with ice, shake until chilled, and strain into a coupe.

2. Garnish with crushed chocolate and a sprig of fresh mint.

INGREDIENTS:

⅔   OZ. FINLANDIA VODKA

2   BAR SPOONS MIDORI MELON LIQUEUR

2   BAR SPOONS KAHLÚA

⅔   OZ. HEAVY CREAM

1   EGG YOLK

    DARK CHOCOLATE, CRUSHED, FOR GARNISH

1   SPRIG OF FRESH MINT, FOR GARNISH

BRANDY ALEXANDER

YIELD: 1 DRINK / **ACTIVE TIME:** 2 MINUTES / **TOTAL TIME:** 2 MINUTES

A classic after-dinner drink that has experienced a much-deserved revival the past few years. Initially, it featured gin, crème de cacao, and heavy cream, so tip your cap to whoever had the good sense to press on in the face of that slog.

1. Chill a cocktail glass in the freezer.

2. Place the ingredients in a cocktail shaker with ice and shake vigorously until chilled.

3. Strain into the chilled cocktail glass.

INGREDIENTS:

1.5   OZ. BRANDY OR COGNAC

1   OZ. CRÈME DE CACAO

¾   OZ. HEAVY CREAM

DWIGHT'S FRIEND

YIELD: 1 DRINK / **ACTIVE TIME:** 2 MINUTES / **TOTAL TIME:** 2 MINUTES

The orange bitters are the key to keeping this one in line, so don't hesitate to alter the amount you use to get this one tailored to your taste.

1. Place the bourbon, Kahlúa, and bitters in a mixing glass with ice and stir until chilled.

2. Strain over ice into a rocks glass and garnish with the orange twist.

INGREDIENTS:

2 OZ. BOURBON

½ OZ. KAHLÚA

2 DASHES OF ORANGE BITTERS

1 ORANGE TWIST, FOR GARNISH

ICE AGE

YIELD: 1 DRINK / **ACTIVE TIME:** 2 MINUTES / **TOTAL TIME:** 2 MINUTES

For those summer days when a cup of spiked hot coffee just won't do.

1. Add all of the ingredients to a rocks glass filled with ice and stir until chilled.

INGREDIENTS:

SPLASH OF SIMPLE SYRUP
(SEE PAGE 663)

DASH OF PEYCHAUD'S
BITTERS

2   OZ. BOURBON

4   OZ. ICED COFFEE

AT THE MERCY OF INERTIA

YIELD: 1 DRINK / ACTIVE TIME: 2 MINUTES / TOTAL TIME: 2 MINUTES

Regardless of one's stance on desserty drinks, people just have to give into this one. The vanilla extract amplifies those notes in the bourbon, making this a cocktail to savor.

1. Place the bourbon, milk, syrup, and vanilla extract in a cocktail shaker with ice and shake until chilled.

2. Strain into a coupe and top with a dash of nutmeg.

INGREDIENTS:

2   OZ. BOURBON

4   OZ. WHOLE MILK

     DASH OF SIMPLE SYRUP
     (SEE PAGE 663)

2   DROPS OF PURE VANILLA
     EXTRACT

     FRESHLY GRATED NUTMEG,
     FOR GARNISH

ROOT BEER FLOATS

YIELD: 4 SERVINGS / **ACTIVE TIME:** 5 MINUTES / **TOTAL TIME:** 5 MINUTES

The rare uncomplicated piece of America's fabric.

1. Place 2 scoops of ice cream in the bottom of 4 tall glasses.

2. Slowly pour a bottle of root beer into each glass, top with the Chantilly Cream, and serve.

INGREDIENTS:

2 PINTS OF VANILLA ICE CREAM (SEE PAGE 516 FOR HOMEMADE)

4 (12 OZ.) BOTTLES OF QUALITY ROOT BEER

   CHANTILLY CREAM (SEE PAGE 89), FOR GARNISH

GODFATHER

Don't hesitate to tinker with the amount of amaretto used here—you want just enough to temper the Scotch to your liking, and it's very easy for this nutty liqueur to steal the show.

1. Place the ingredients in a mixing glass with ice and stir until chilled.

2. Strain over ice into a rocks glass and garnish with the orange twist.

INGREDIENTS:

2   OZ. BLENDED SCOTCH WHISKY

⅔   OZ. AMARETTO

1   ORANGE TWIST, FOR GARNISH

SNOW BOWL

YIELD: 1 DRINK / **ACTIVE TIME:** 2 MINUTES / **TOTAL TIME:** 2 MINUTES

This beautiful, creamy cocktail was made to star at your holiday party.

1. Place the gin, chocolate liqueur, and crème de menthe in a cocktail shaker with ice and shake until chilled.

2. Strain over ice into a rocks glass and garnish with a dusting of nutmeg.

INGREDIENTS:

- 2 OZ. GIN
- 2 OZ. WHITE CHOCOLATE LIQUEUR

  SPLASH OF WHITE CRÈME DE MENTHE

  FRESHLY GRATED NUTMEG, FOR GARNISH

COOPER'S CAFÉ

YIELD: 1 DRINK / **ACTIVE TIME:** 2 MINUTES / **TOTAL TIME:** 2 MINUTES

A damn fine cup of coffee. If you want to enjoy this on the rocks, top up your glass with Topo Chico.

1. Place the espresso, mezcal, and syrup in a cocktail shaker with ice and shake until chilled.

2. Strain into a Nick & Nora glass and garnish with the strip of orange peel.

CINNAMON SYRUP

1. Place the sugar and water in a saucepan and bring to a boil, stirring to dissolve the sugar.

2. When the sugar has dissolved, add the cinnamon sticks, cook for another minute, and remove the pan from heat. Let it steep for 1 hour.

3. Strain the syrup into a mason jar and let it cool completely before using or storing in the refrigerator, where it will keep for up to 1 month.

INGREDIENTS:

1	OZ. FRESHLY BREWED ESPRESSO
2	OZ. MEZCAL
½	OZ. CINNAMON SYRUP (SEE RECIPE)
1	STRIP OF ORANGE PEEL, FOR GARNISH

CINNAMON SYRUP

1	CUP SUGAR
1	CUP WATER
3	CINNAMON STICKS

WHITE RUSSIAN

YIELD: 1 DRINK / **ACTIVE TIME:** 2 MINUTES / **TOTAL TIME:** 2 MINUTES

As everyone knows, the Coen Brothers' late '90s masterwork, *The Big Lebowski*, breathed considerable life into this creamy cocktail, which had lost its way during the calorie-conscious '80s.

1. Place a few ice cubes in a rocks glass.

2. Add the vodka and Kahlúa and stir until chilled. Top with a generous splash of heavy cream and slowly stir until combined.

INGREDIENTS:

2	OZ. VODKA
1	OZ. KAHLÚA
	HEAVY CREAM, TO TASTE

MUDSLIDE

YIELD: 1 DRINK / **ACTIVE TIME:** 2 MINUTES / **TOTAL TIME:** 2 MINUTES

It remains the apex of decadent and delicious dessert drinks.

1. Place the vodka, liqueurs, ice cream, and ice in a blender and puree to desired consistency.

2. Pour into a cocktail glass and garnish with a dusting of cocoa powder.

INGREDIENTS:

1.5 OZ. VODKA

1.5 OZ. KAHLÚA

1.5 OZ. CREAM LIQUEUR

¾ CUP VANILLA ICE CREAM

½ CUP ICE

COCOA POWDER, FOR GARNISH

CROSSEYED & PAINLESS

YIELD: 1 DRINK / **ACTIVE TIME:** 2 MINUTES / **TOTAL TIME:** 2 MINUTES

Infusing the rum with chipotles turns this twist on a Painkiller into something like spicy ice cream. It's good any time, but particularly at the end of an autumn day.

1. Place the rum, cream of coconut, orange juice, and pineapple juice in a cocktail shaker with crushed ice and shake until chilled.

2. Pour the contents of the shaker into a glass, grate nutmeg over the cocktail, and garnish with the orange slice.

CHIPOTLE RUM

1. Place the rum and chipotle in a mason jar and let the mixture steep at room temperature for 3 hours.

2. Strain and use as desired.

INGREDIENTS:

2   OZ. CHIPOTLE RUM (SEE RECIPE)

1   OZ. CREAM OF COCONUT

1   OZ. ORANGE JUICE

4   OZ. PINEAPPLE JUICE

     FRESHLY GRATED NUTMEG, FOR GARNISH

1   ORANGE SLICE, FOR GARNISH

CHIPOTLE RUM

8   OZ. AGED RUM

1   DRIED CHIPOTLE PEPPER, TORN

MY SILKS AND FINE ARRAY

An underappreciated gem, much like the Julie Covington song that lent its name to this drink.

1. Add all of the ingredients to a cocktail shaker with ice and shake until chilled. Strain into a rocks glass filled with ice.

INGREDIENTS:

1   OZ. VODKA

1   OZ. CHOCOLATE LIQUEUR

1   OZ. KAHLÚA

2   OZ. MILK

CREAMSICLE

YIELD: 1 DRINK / **ACTIVE TIME:** 2 MINUTES / **TOTAL TIME:** 2 MINUTES

The childhood favorite, all grown up.

1. Add all of the ingredients, except for the orange slice, to a blender and puree until smooth.

2. Pour into a glass and garnish with the orange slice.

INGREDIENTS:

1.5 OZ. ORANGE JUICE

1.5 OZ. VODKA

2   SCOOPS OF VANILLA ICE
     CREAM (SEE PAGE 516 FOR
     HOMEMADE)

     SPLASH OF TRIPLE SEC

½   CUP ICE

1   ORANGE SLICE, FOR
     GARNISH

ALL THE HEARTS

YIELD: 1 DRINK / **ACTIVE TIME:** 2 MINUTES / **TOTAL TIME:** 2 MINUTES

Brugal, a Dominican rum, is a reliable and affordable option for this cocktail.

1. Place the rum, Kahlúa, and Irish cream in a cocktail shaker, fill it two-thirds of the way with ice, and shake until chilled.

2. Strain over ice into a rocks, add the dash of crème de menthe, and garnish with the sprig of mint.

INGREDIENTS:

1   OZ. AGED RUM

1   OZ. KAHLÚA

1   OZ. IRISH CREAM

     DASH OF WHITE CRÈME DE MENTHE

1   SPRIG OF FRESH MINT, FOR GARNISH

TOM & JERRY

YIELD: 1 DRINK / **ACTIVE TIME:** 2 MINUTES / **TOTAL TIME:** 2 MINUTES

I f you're one of those who is allergic to even the thought of eggnog, warm a bit of milk with the cinnamon stick and swap it in.

1. Place the syrup, rum, brandy and warm eggnog in an Irish coffee glass and stir to combine.

2. Garnish with the cinnamon stick.

INGREDIENTS:

1   OZ. SIMPLE SYRUP (SEE PAGE 663)

1   OZ. DARK RUM

1   OZ. BRANDY

2   OZ. EGGNOG, WARMED

1   CINNAMON STICK, FOR GARNISH

GRASSHOPPER

YIELD: 1 DRINK / **ACTIVE TIME:** 2 MINUTES / **TOTAL TIME:** 2 MINUTES

O f all of the contributions New Orleans has made to the cocktail world, this may be the most impressive. No matter where one stands on that debate, they have to admit it's at least the most handsome.

1. Chill a cocktail glass in the freezer.

2. Place the ingredients in a cocktail shaker, fill it two-thirds of the way with ice, and shake until chilled.

3. Strain into the chilled glass.

INGREDIENTS:

1   OZ. GREEN CRÈME DE MENTHE

1   OZ. WHITE CRÈME DE CACAO

1   OZ. HEAVY CREAM

INDUSTRY INSIDERS

*A*fter working your way through this book, you may be feeling pretty confident in your ability to crank out praise-worthy confections. Cocky, even.

But there is always another level above, no matter how good you get.

These folks are proof of just that. From the genius that is required to master specialties like hypoallergenic or gluten-free baking to the uncompromising devotion one needs to master French pastry, these folks have ascended to the top of the sweets game, and have been kind enough to share a few of the secrets and recipes that powered this climb.

SWEET ANNIE'S OF MAINE

Manchester, ME

Annie of Sweet Annie's of Maine is of the firm belief that cupcakes and cake should both taste and look incredible. That extends to all forms of treats, from wedding cakes to birthday cakes or "I deserve it" cakes. Based out of her home kitchen in Manchester, Maine, Annie seeks to use only the freshest local ingredients she can find. Occasionally, she grows produce herself, using canned rhubarb for cakes, mint for mint chocolate chip cupcakes, and of course, wild Maine blueberries.

KEY LIME PIE CUPCAKES

YIELD: 24 CUPCAKES / **ACTIVE TIME:** 1 HOUR / **TOTAL TIME:** 24 HOURS

These light and fluffy cupcakes have the perfect balance of tart and sweet.

1. Prepare the cream cheese filling at least a day in advance so that it has time to harden in the fridge. To do this, beat the softened cream cheese in a large bowl until smooth, add the sweetened condensed milk, and then slowly add the lime juice to avoid splattering.

2. To prepare the crust, completely crush the graham crackers in a large resealable bag with a rolling pin. Place crumbs in a large bowl and add the sugar, mixing to incorporate. Next, add the melted butter and mix until you've achieved a graham cracker paste. Prepare a large, 24-cup muffin tin with cupcake liners and spoon the graham cracker paste into each one until evenly divided. Press the graham cracker crumbs down in each well to form a crust.

3. To make the cupcakes, combine the flour, baking powder, and salt in a medium bowl. Whisk together for 20 seconds with a fork. In a large bowl, add the granulated sugar and softened butter. Beat on low with a stand or handheld mixer, adding the eggs, vegetable oil, and sour cream. Once smooth, alternate adding the flour mixture with the milk and lime juice until the flour and liquid have all been incorporated. Using an ice cream scoop, fill each muffin tin well nearly completely full and bake at 325°F for 15 to 17 minutes.

4. Once baked, remove from the oven and let the cupcakes cool for 15 minutes before removing from the tin. The cake is still cooking the first few minutes after it comes out and it is fragile until completely cooled. Please note that the center of the cupcakes will seem uncooked and won't be firm to the touch; this is normal. Once the cupcake centers are cored in the next step, you will be left with a perfectly baked cupcake. If you were to bake the cupcakes until the centers were firm, the outer part that remains after coring would be too dry.

5. Core the cooled cupcakes with a cupcake corer (or a spoon, but you'll get a cleaner core with the corer), and fill with the cream cheese filling, placing it either in a pastry bag or a large resealable bag with a hole cut on one of the bottom corners.

INGREDIENTS:

FOR THE FILLING

8   OZ. CREAM CHEESE, SOFTENED

1   (14 OZ.) CAN OF SWEETENED CONDENSED MILK

⅔   CUP FRESH LIME JUICE

FOR THE GRAHAM CRACKER CRUST

2   (4.8 OZ.) PACKAGES OF GRAHAM CRACKERS

2   TABLESPOONS SUGAR

8   OZ. UNSALTED BUTTER, MELTED

FOR THE CUPCAKES

12.5 OZ. ALL-PURPOSE FLOUR

5   TEASPOONS BAKING POWDER

1   TEASPOON FINE SEA SALT

10.5 OZ. SUGAR

4   OZ. UNSALTED BUTTER, SOFTENED

4   EGGS

½   CUP VEGETABLE OIL

½   CUP SOUR CREAM

⅔   CUP WHOLE MILK, AT ROOM TEMPERATURE

⅔   CUP FRESH LIME JUICE, AT ROOM TEMPERATURE

Continued . . .

6. To make the buttercream, gradually add the confectioners' sugar to the softened butter in a stand mixer while beating on low. If it's too messy, alternate adding the confectioners' sugar with the lime juice, or simply add the lime juice after the confectioners' sugar if the sugar is not flying out of the bowl. Using a zester, zest the lime, mixing the buttercream on low so that the lime zest is evenly distributed. If you'd like to tint the buttercream, add the tiniest amount of green gel food coloring until a delicate lime green has been achieved.

7. Spread the buttercream over the cooled core and filled cupcakes with a knife, or use a pastry bag and a piping tip. At the very end, I like to top the cupcakes with clear sugar crystals.

8. Refrigerate any leftovers. They will keep for roughly 3 to 4 days if they are stored in an airtight container.

INGREDIENTS:

FOR THE LIME BUTTERCREAM

1   LB. CONFECTIONERS' SUGAR

8   OZ. UNSALTED BUTTER, SOFTENED

¼   CUP FRESH LIME JUICE

     ZEST OF 1 LIME

1-2   DROPS OF GREEN GEL FOOD COLORING (OPTIONAL)

CAKELOVE

Alexandria, VA

CakeLove was started to share founder Warren Brown's love of food. Warren's goal is to bring people together through cake, and he has a unique business model to accomplish that. After years of running a chain of shops, CakeLove moved away from brick and mortar stores and now sells cake in a jar online. The concept might sound odd, but Warren developed a creative way to bring customers their own personal layer of cake. The cakes come in a variety of flavors and make it easier for customers who want an easy way to carry cupcakes. CakeLove now has two product lines, including family-sized cake jars from Don't Forget Cake! and the multigrain energy snacks Spark Bites.

WET BREAD PUDDING WITH APPLES

YIELD: 8 TO 10 SERVINGS / **ACTIVE TIME:** 20 MINUTES / **TOTAL TIME:** 50 MINUTES

Warren Brown: "These days at home I tend to bake with whatever I have on hand. Nearly all of the desserts I make are spur of the moment affairs, more for the distraction than anything else. Dessert that calls for exotic ingredients or rarities I save for work at the bakery. But bread pudding, that's one we can have just about any time! And, it's a family affair. With all four of us home a lot of the time, there's not much room for claiming the kitchen as 'my domain' anymore. My kids want to be in the mix just as much as me.

What I like the most about bread pudding is how soft and moist and squishy it is, all while served just under whatever temperature qualifies as piping hot. Desserts served hot not only offer a different texture and mouthfeel, you often don't need as much sugar! The heat works its magic and throws flavor far and wide across the palate, especially if you enjoy the first spoonful within minutes of emerging from the oven.

With this recipe I keep the sugar at ½ cup, but you could cut that in half if you want. Use the preserves unless you just hate stone fruits—the addition gives the whole dish a second layer of composition that feels floral on the nose, without tasting like rosewater. The addition of water may seem odd for a rich dish, but it helps to lighten things a bit, especially with the addition of the butter which, like the preserves, is helpful to set up the background, this time for texture.

The apples are really nice in this dish. Keep the dice small enough so they'll bake through and keep pace with the bread. That's easily done as it's only about 2 cups worth from four small apples, a few of which were wrinkly and only good for peeling and baking off in a wet pool of eggy, milky madness. Any firm fleshed type will work; I used Envy apples because they taste so good.

Cardamom? Yeah, that may violate the 'no exotic elements' rule for some, but in my kitchen, there's always cardamom. It's not used much, but when it is, it's just lovely."

---

1. Preheat the oven to 325°F.

2. Combine the milk, water, and preserves in a two-quart saucepan and bring to a simmer over medium heat. Immediately remove from the heat and set aside.

3. Slice the bread into ¾-inch slices. It's not recommended to use very old bread that is brittle or will fall apart into bread crumbs.

4. Stir to combine the eggs, vanilla, and spices in a large bowl. Add the bread slices and toss until the bread is heavily coated and nearly all of the egg is absorbed. This might take about 2 minutes.

5. Peel and dice the apples and add to the bowl with the egg-coated bread. Toss lightly to combine.

INGREDIENTS:

2	CUPS WHOLE MILK
¾	CUP WATER
1	TABLESPOON PEACH PRESERVES
1	BAGUETTE
4	LARGE EGGS
1-2	TEASPOONS PURE VANILLA EXTRACT
¼	TEASPOON CINNAMON, PLUS MORE TO TASTE
5-8	GRAINS OF CARDAMOM, CRUSHED (OPTIONAL)

Continued . . .

6. Rub a light layer of unsalted butter onto the interior of a two-quart casserole dish—across the bottom and all the way up the sides. Then add the turbinado sugar and a shake of cinnamon and rock the dish back and forth to coat the butter well. Pour off any extra spiced-sugar and reserve for topping off the bread pudding.

7. Gently transfer the bread one slice at a time to the casserole dish, decoratively lining them in a standing position. Add a few fingers full of apples between each slice of bread and work your way around the dish. Broken pieces of bread work just as well. Fill the center with bread and apples.

8. Gently ladle in about half of the milk mixture. It should be come up to just about one inch below the bottom rim of the casserole dish. Sprinkle on some of the reserved spiced-sugar.

9. Place on a parchment-lined baking sheet and cook, covered, for about 25 minutes. Then, add another ladle or two of the milk mixture and continue to cook uncovered. If no lid is available, then just leave uncovered the whole bake time. You'll have about 1½ cups of the milk mixture leftover, which makes for a great accompaniment when serving.

10. The casserole will be finished when the milk mixture bubbles on the edges. Watch it carefully, as it tends to drip over the sides and can burn easily. A temperature check will easily be over 180°F but check it if you want to be sure about how well the eggs have cooked. Remove from the oven and let cool for a few minutes before serving in bowls with a ladle of the milk-sauce for anyone who likes it.

TIP: When it comes to cardamom, you have choices that can be a bit confusing and involved. But when it comes to baking, it's a such a delicate and delicious spice where just a pinch goes a long way that it can easily become your secret ingredient if you haven't yet experimented with it. Ground is OK, but the flavor is in the oils which, of course, evaporate in store bought ground spices. Decorticated is convenient, but hard to find. Those seeds are typically pulled from green pods, the standard type for baking. Whole green pods are tricky to use—crack it in a mortar and pestle, pull out the seeds which are black when they're in the best condition, or kind of tan brown when in so-so condition, weaker in flavor but still usable. Discard the green husk and then crush the seeds in the mortar and pestle. Don't use black cardamom pods with baking, the flavor is not the same.

INGREDIENTS:

- 2.5 OZ. UNSALTED BUTTER, PLUS MORE AS NEEDED
- ½ CUP SUGAR, PLUS MORE FOR DUSTING
- 1 TABLESPOON TURBINADO SUGAR

  DASH OF FINE SEA SALT
- 2 CUPS DICED APPLES

BAMBAM BAKERY

Portland, ME

BamBam is a dedicated 100 percent gluten-free facility. That means it's celiac friendly and there is no risk of cross-contamination. Some say that eating gluten free is fad diet but many non-celiacs benefit from a gluten-free diet for many different health reasons. Some people just eat gluten free because they feel a lot better. BamBam provides delicious gluten-free treats in either case. Owner Tina Cromwell says that

"The best part of this job is when kids come in and they are told that they can have anything in the store. When people ask 'Do you have anything that's gluten free?' We get to say 'Yes! Everything.'" BamBam doesn't claim to be a health food store. What they try to do is provide treats that taste as good as their gluten counterparts and dream up new delights to accommodate dietary needs.

GLUTEN-FREE SPICY CHOCOLATE COOKIES

YIELD: 12 COOKIES / **ACTIVE TIME:** 35 MINUTES / **TOTAL TIME:** 1 HOUR AND 45 MINUTES

Get the best of both worlds with the spicy cayenne and the sweet chocolate. These delicious cookies are dairy-, nut-, and soy-free.

1. Preheat oven to 325°F.

2. Mix the flour, cocoa powder, xanthan gum, baking soda, cinnamon, and cayenne pepper together in a bowl and set aside.

3. Mix the eggs, sugar, canola oil, and vanilla extract in a stand mixer until well combined.

4. Add the dry ingredients. Mix on low for 5 minutes, then fold in the chocolate chips.

5. Let dough chill for 1 hour in the refrigerator.

6. Scoop the dough into 1.5-oz. balls and place on cookie sheet.

7. Bake for 12 minutes.

INGREDIENTS:

- 3.2 OZ. GLUTEN-FREE ALL-PURPOSE FLOUR
- 2.6 OZ. COCOA POWDER
- ½ TEASPOON XANTHAN GUM (IF MISSING FROM ALL-PURPOSE FLOUR)
- 1 TEASPOON BAKING SODA
- 2 TEASPOONS CINNAMON
- ½ TEASPOON CAYENNE PEPPER
- 2 LARGE EGGS
- 7 OZ. SUGAR
- ½ CUP CANOLA OIL
- 1 TABLESPOON PURE VANILLA EXTRACT
- 1 CUP CHOCOLATE CHIPS (DAIRY- OR SOY-FREE IF DESIRED)

GLUTEN-FREE COCONUT BREAD

YIELD: 1 LOAF / **ACTIVE TIME:** 20 MINUTES / **TOTAL TIME:** 1 HOUR AND 50 MINUTES

Gluten-free recipes like this one benefit from a blend of flours so you can get the taste and texture just right.

1. Preheat oven to 325°F. Coat a standard loaf pan with nonstick cooking spray.

2. Lightly toast the coconut for about 5 minutes. Let cool.

3. Mix together the flours, tapioca starch, xanthan gum, baking powder, baking soda, and salt. Set aside.

4. Mix the sugars, canola oil, vanilla and coconut extracts, and coconut milk in a stand mixer. Add eggs one at a time until combined.

5. Add in dry ingredients and let mix for 5 minutes, then fold in toasted coconut. Mix together.

6. Fill bread pan with batter to about three-quarters of the way full. Any leftover batter makes great cupcakes!

7. Top the loaf with untoasted coconut flakes for decoration.

8. Bake for 1 hour and 20 minutes.

9. Let cool in pan for 10 minutes and then turn out onto cooling rack. Let the bread cool completely before enjoying.

TIP: If you're using the coconut bread for strawberry shortcake, slice the coconut bread, brush with olive oil, and broil until toasted. Macerate strawberries with a splash of vanilla and sugar. Top with choice of whipped cream (dairy-free, if desired).

INGREDIENTS:

8.4	OZ. WHITE RICE FLOUR
3.2	OZ. SORGHUM FLOUR
3.2	OZ. TAPIOCA STARCH
½	TEASPOON XANTHAN GUM
1½	TEASPOONS BAKING POWDER
1	TEASPOON BAKING SODA
¾	TEASPOON KOSHER SALT
7	OZ. SUGAR
3.5	OZ. BROWN SUGAR
¾	CUP CANOLA OIL
1½	CUPS UNSWEETENED COCONUT MILK
1	TEASPOON VANILLA EXTRACT
1	TEASPOON COCONUT EXTRACT
4	EGGS
1	CUP SWEETENED COCONUT FLAKES

TEATOTALLER

Somersworth, NH

Twice named "Best of New Hampshire" in *New Hampshire Magazine*, Teatotaller is best described as a queer, hipster oasis of tea, coffee, and pastry goodness. Teatotaller is a café, teahouse, bakery, and venue located in Historic Downtown Somersworth, New Hampshire. Drawing inspiration from flavors around the world, Teatotaller's kitchen makes everything from scratch—loose-leaf tea blends, hand-crafted tea and espresso drinks, and pastries for any palate. Teatotaller has garnered attention for its cheeky billboards, vibrant venue, and eccentric flavors, including being named "Most Instagrammable Restaurant in America" by *Food Network Magazine.* Emmet Soldati opened Teatotaller to create vibrancy in his one-road downtown, just one block away from his childhood lemonade stand.

GINGER MOLASSES COOKIES

YIELD: 15 COOKIES / **ACTIVE TIME:** 30 MINUTES / **TOTAL TIME:** 1 HOUR

These delicious cookies are dairy-free.

1. Preheat oven to 325°F.

2. To begin preparations for the cookies, cream the margarine and sugar with an electric mixer.

3. In a separate bowl, mix together the remaining dry ingredients.

4. Add eggs and molasses into electric mixer. Slowly add the dry ingredient mixture in and mix until it forms a dough.

5. Roll dough into 1-oz. balls and then roll in a bowl of sugar. Place on a parchment lined baking sheet with plenty of room between each ball.

6. Chill in the refrigerator for 15 minutes.

7. Bake 12 minutes, turning the baking sheet halfway through. The cookies should be spread out with cracks. Even if center looks slightly wet, remove from the oven because the cookies will finish baking on a wire rack. Let cool completely and then transfer to the refrigerator.

8. To prepare the filling, place all of the ingredients in a mixing bowl and whip until combined.

9. Place 1 tablespoon of cream filling between two cookies, bottom side in, and gently twist and press together until cream gets to edge. Chill until ready to serve.

INGREDIENTS:

FOR THE COOKIES

3.2	OZ. MARGARINE
7.7	OZ. SUGAR, PLUS MORE AS NEEDED
6.7	OZ. BROWN SUGAR
11.6	OZ. ALL-PURPOSE FLOUR
2	TEASPOONS BAKING SODA
½	TEASPOON FINE SEA SALT
1	TEASPOON GROUND GINGER
1	TEASPOON CINNAMON
2	EGGS
2.5	OZ. MOLASSES

FOR THE CREAM FILLING

7	OZ. FLUFF
8.8	OZ. CONFECTIONERS' SUGAR
5.3	OZ. MARGARINE
2.1	OZ. COCONUT OIL
1	TABLESPOON COCONUT MILK

LEMON POLENTA CAKE

YIELD: 1 CAKE / **ACTIVE TIME:** 15 MINUTES / **TOTAL TIME:** 1 HOUR AND 30 MINUTES

This simple lemon polenta cake is sure to become a family favorite.

1. Preheat oven to 325°F.

2. Beat together the oil and sugar until fluffy.

3. In a separate bowl, combine the dry ingredients and add to the sugar mixture, alternating with the eggs.

4. Add the lemon zest to the mixture.

5. Cut a circle of parchment paper to the size of an 8" or 9" springform pan. Spray the pan with nonstick cooking spray and place the parchment paper on the bottom.

6. Pour the batter into the pan and bake for 50 minutes, turning the pan halfway through. Bake until a cake tester inserted into the center comes out clean. Remove and let cool before serving.

INGREDIENTS:

7	OZ. COCONUT OIL OR BUTTER
7	OZ. SUGAR
7	OZ. ALMOND FLOUR
3.5	OZ. POLENTA OR CORNMEAL
1½	TEASPOONS BAKING POWDER
3	EGGS
	ZEST OF 2 LEMONS

MO'PWEEZE BAKERY

Denville, NJ

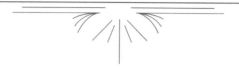

Mo'Pweeze Bakery is vegan friendly, kosher, and allergen free. Coming from a family of five with a wide range of allergies, Christine Allen began her quest for allergen-free baked goods after her son was diagnosed with over 35 food allergies. In an interview with the Elijah-Alavi Foundation, Christine detailed her struggles while trying to find a birthday cake for her kids. "I tried to find a cake, and no one could accommodate those food allergies. I remember a baker saying to me, 'Do you want me to make a cake out of air?'. 'How can I eliminate 12 food allergens? You need eggs, and you need butter and gluten.' So I decided to make my sister's banana bread recipe and eliminated the food allergens. I served it at their birthday party, and everyone loved it. No one knew the difference. That is when I realized I was on to something. That is how my business, Mo'Pweeze Bakery, came about. That is actually what the kids said, when they had their first cupcake, they said 'Mo' pweeze.'"

Christine wanted to not only accommodate her own child but other families with similar experiences as well. All products at Mo'Pweeze are free of the top ten allergens and animal products, and the bakery is adept at meeting special orders for custom treats and cakes for other dietary needs. "I figured if I could give my children this joy, why not spread that love to other families. I had this vision of what I wanted my bakery to be. I wanted my bakery to be where kids with all these restrictions could come in and know that anything in this safe place is something that they could have. That in itself is a reward. To have parents come in and say this is the first time that they have been able to come into a place and be able to choose or touch anything without thinking that it could have gluten, or nuts, or other allergens. Knowing that I can provide treats, cakes, and safe baked goods is a blessing and a dream come true."

RED VELVET VEGAN CUPCAKES

YIELD: 16 CUPCAKES / **ACTIVE TIME:** 1 HOUR AND 5 MINUTES / **TOTAL TIME:** 1 HOUR AND 25 MINUTES

These classic cupcakes are vegan and allergen friendly so everyone can enjoy! Pair these with a vegan cream cheese frosting.

1. Preheat the oven to 350°F.

2. Make buttermilk by combining 1¼ cups plant-based milk with 2 tablespoons lemon juice. Place the vegan buttermilk the refrigerator.

3. Combine the dry ingredients in a stand mixer and mix on low.

4. Add in remaining ingredients and mix thoroughly. Add the vegan buttermilk as desired, making sure that the batter is mixed thoroughly.

5. Pour the batter evenly into a greased or lined cupcake tin.

6. Bake for 20 minutes, or until a cake tester inserted into the center of each cupcake comes out clean. When done, let cool, then decorate.

INGREDIENTS:

1¼ CUPS PLANT-BASED MILK

2 TABLESPOONS FRESH LEMON JUICE

15 OZ. ALL-PURPOSE FLOUR

1¼ TEASPOONS BAKING SODA

1¼ TEASPOONS FINE SEA SALT

15.75 OZ. SUGAR

1¼ TEASPOONS COCOA POWDER

1½ CUPS CANOLA OIL

¾ CUP APPLE SAUCE OR EGG REPLACER

1¼ TEASPOONS WHITE VINEGAR

1¼ TEASPOONS PURE VANILLA EXTRACT

2 TABLESPOONS WATER

RED FOOD COLORING, TO TASTE

WORLD-FAMOUS CINNAMON DONUTS

YIELD: 12 DONUTS / **ACTIVE TIME:** 20 MINUTES / **TOTAL TIME:** 40 MINUTES

Many desserts trumpet their own fame—few back it up like these doughnuts from Mo'Pweeze.

1. Preheat the oven to 350°F.

2. Combine the dry ingredients in a stand mixer and mix well.

3. Slowly add the wet ingredients and mix until all ingredients are fully incorporated.

4. Butter the donut pans and spoon the batter in. Bake for 9 to 11 minutes or until done.

5. Remove from oven and cool donuts on baking tray, then coat in granulated sugar and cinnamon.

INGREDIENTS:

1	CUP MO'PWEEZE FLOUR
3.5	OZ. SUGAR
1½	TEASPOONS BAKING POWDER
½	TEASPOON FINE SEA SALT
¾	TEASPOON CINNAMON
½	CUP PLANT-BASED MILK
½	TEASPOON APPLE CIDER VINEGAR
1	TEASPOON PURE VANILLA EXTRACT
1	TABLESPOON APPLESAUCE
¼	CUP VEGAN BUTTER

SUGAR BAKESHOP

Charleston, SC

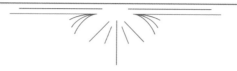

Lost in all the talk of Charleston's rapidly growing foodie scene is its rich baking legacy, which has existed as long as the city itself. And few bakeries, in Charleston or otherwise, carry that legacy as elegantly as Sugar Bakeshop. Sugar Bakeshop is coziness incarnated—nuzzled in at 59½ Cannon Street, you would be forgiven for underestimating the bakery's prowess. But the bite-sized pastries in this small space have made waves well outside of Charleston, having merited the bakery's inclusion on *Travel + Leisure*'s "Best Bakeries in America" list in 2013. "Our original goal was to be a neighborhood bakeshop," says co-owner Bill Bowick. "We're proud we have achieved that. What we didn't expect was attention on a more national level. But we're equally proud of both of those achievements."

Bill and David's path to baking was anything but direct. While originally from the South, both men began their careers as architects in New York City. Bill knew how to bake from his family of "from scratch" bakers; David from his own sweet tooth and his grandmother's beloved apple pie. Says David, "It wasn't until I met Bill that I embraced the idea of baking as a creative and visual process. The idea of consuming this culinary item you've created is so satisfying. You can't eat a building!"

A spontaneous subway conversation made all the difference in their lives. Bill and David fell in love and immediately began planning the beginnings of Sugar Bakeshop. They moved to Charleston, spent some time in London and then returned home to South Carolina. All along, the plan was to open a bakery that would be woven into the fabric of the community. Bill and David accomplished that goal by embracing locally grown ingredients—in some cases, grown literally on the premises. Their rooftop garden is home to herbs like mint, lemongrass, and rosemary, plus two beehives that produce honey used and sold in-store. "People may say buying an herb at the grocery store is easy, but I can tell you that growing mint is actually easier than a trip to the store. It's not that hard. And tending your overgrown mint bed next to your neighbor's garden is a great way to build community. And it's a great way to live your life. Because of our efforts with these things, I think Charlestonians view us not as just a brand, or a purveyor of baked goods, but as friends and allies in building community."

In this way, Sugar is the embodiment of Charleston's baking scene—even if its founders did spend their formative years in the Big Apple!

IN THEIR OWN WORDS:
BILL BOWICK AND DAVID BOUFFARD

Who inspired you to bake? Who inspires you now?

Bill: My mom, grandmother, and aunts. They expressed their love through baking for others. That's what David and I do for others now. From that perspective, I guess you could say our customers inspire us now. We're baking for them, figuring out what baked treats bring them joy and taking pleasure in that.

I would also say Lee Bailey. He was a fellow Southerner who approached the culinary arts as a lifestyle. He assembled delightful concoctions using his heritage, knowledge of French cooking, and his noggin. He's a bit forgotten now, but I reference his books often. A small note: when I first moved to New York, he happened to have a loft in the same building where I lived near Union Square. I had some happy interactions with him and he was gracious enough to sign one of his books for me.

David: I was inspired by my family bakers including my two sisters . . . and especially by Bill!

What is your golden rule of baking?

Use the best and the freshest ingredients available and never over-mix. In architecture school, we were taught to "keep a light hand" in sketching. We keep that phrase in mind when baking. Don't overwork it.

What does Sugar Bakeshop represent to you?

Sugar Bakeshop is the manifestation of an attitude and a philosophy. The design and brand of the shop reflect honesty, simplicity and purity of design, in both ingredients and method of baking. Our shop's name is actually a double entendre. Sugar is our primary ingredient. It is pure. Elemental. But it is also a term of endearment. What Southerner (of a certain age) didn't grow up and hear an elder use the term "sugar" as a term of affection? It is the perfect

embodiment of our shop: baked items, evocative of love and affection, translate to love and confection.

What is your favorite thing to bake? Why? Least favorite thing to bake? Why?

We love to bake tartlets—the yield of the simple dough recipe is plentiful, reliable, and easy to make. It complements available ingredients for fillings, which provide punchy bursts of flavor in your mouth when paired with the buttery crust. Our least favorite is anything fussy and complicated. As any modernist architect would say—less is more.

What are your most popular items?

Our miniature tartlets are always a crowd-pleaser—especially the lemon tarts. We vary the tarts seasonally, so you may find heirloom pumpkin tarts in the fall, and strawberry rhubarb in the spring. But everyone loves a pie. Our focus on freshness means we don't sell pie by the slice. Pies are made to order only—baked just for the customer.

What nonessential items should every baker have?

A fluted pastry wheel is a fine tool to have on hand. It helps make basket weave piecrusts even more beautiful. We also use a marble cutting board that we chill in the refrigerator before preparing pie dough. Piecrusts are best when worked cold, and a chilled board gives you a leg up there.

What book(s) go on your required reading list for bakers?

I find Nick Malgieri's *The Modern Baker* to be a thorough and handy reference for bakers. Also, *The Fannie Farmer Cookbook*. Don't laugh! Vintage cookbooks were written when many people didn't have ready access to ingredients or modern cooking. These books have practical knowledge, including substitutions, variations with available ingredients, and general wisdom passed from generation to generation on how to make your baking a success.

What outlets/periodicals/newspapers do you read or consult regularly, if any?

The New York Times, Cook's Illustrated, Food & Wine, Bon Appetit, Lucky Peach, Kitchen52, Martha Stewart, and Kinfolk.

Tell me about your most memorable collaboration with another chef.

Well . . . we married each other!

Who inspires you? Do you follow any cooking shows or chefs? If so, which is your favorite?

Bill: I sometimes watch The Great British Bake Off. It's classy and full of smart feedback from the judges. Otherwise, Ruth Reichl—her career is less about hype and more about authenticity and the relationship between food and our everyday lives. Oh, and I love old footage of Julia Child.

Where did you learn to cook?

Bill: I learned to cook over the phone from NYC to points south—conversations with my mom, grandmother, aunts. My first internship as an architect was with an old school fellow who imparted some sage advice. He said that some people expend a lot of time on marketing. He felt that if one does good, quality work, people respond to it. That advice has served me well in both my careers.

David: I've always enjoyed cooking, but didn't get into baking until I met Bill—so I would have to say I apprenticed with Bill. My love of numbers, formulas, and chemistry has propelled me to the front line of our bakery. I have literally hijacked the oven and kicked my mentor out of the kitchen!

Bill: It's true! Over time our roles have shifted in our shop. Now, David and other bakers in our shop do most of the actually baking. Now I am more interested in the menu and what kinds of things we're actually baking as well as the presentation of our baked goods. Baking is such a visual pursuit.

SUGAR'S LEMON MERINGUE PIE

YIELD: 8 SERVINGS / **ACTIVE TIME:** 1 HOUR / **TOTAL TIME:** 1 HOUR AND 25 MINUTES

A simple classic, you can't go wrong with lemon meringue. Just be careful—it's so well known that mistakes are easily noticed!

1. Begin by making your pie dough. Heat oven to 425°F and cut butter into small pieces. Keep the butter slices in the freezer.

2. Mix the flour and salt in a food processor. Add shortening and pulse until they are in small pieces. Add your sliced butter, mixing until small, pea-sized pieces form. Gradually add water and mix until combined. Finish mixing by hand, making sure not to over-mix.

3. Form the pie dough into a ball, wrap in plastic wrap and refrigerate for 1 hour.

4. After 1 hour, flatten the dough into a 6-inch disc. Roll it out over a large sheet to ¼-inch thick.

5. Line a 9-inch pie pan with the dough and pierce with fork. Brush pie dough with egg wash and bake until slightly brown. Remove from oven and set aside.

6. In a medium saucepan, combine cornstarch, flour, sugar, and salt. Mix well. Gradually add water, stirring until smooth.

7. Over medium heat, bring the mixture to a boil, stirring occasionally for approximately 20 minutes or until thick and set-up. Remove from heat.

8. Quickly stir some of the hot mixture into the egg yolks. Then, add egg yolk mixture back to saucepan and return to heat. Stir in lemon juice, lemon zest, and butter.

9. Remove filling from saucepan and allow to cool. Pour into your baked pie shell.

10. Heat your oven to 400°F.

11. Using a handheld mixer, beat the egg whites, cream of tartar, and salt together until the mixture has stiffened. Gradually add sugar and continue to beat until well dissolved and very stiff.

INGREDIENTS:

FOR THE PIECRUST DOUGH

3	OZ. UNSALTED BUTTER
6.25	OZ. ALL-PURPOSE FLOUR
¼	TEASPOON FINE SEA SALT
2	TABLESPOONS LEAF LARD (USE SHORTENING IF LEAF LARD IS NOT AVAILABLE)
2½	TABLESPOONS COLD WATER
1	EGG, BEATEN, FOR EGG WASH

FOR THE FILLING

¼	CUP CORNSTARCH
¼	CUP ALL-PURPOSE FLOUR
1¾	CUPS SUGAR
¼	TEASPOON FINE SEA SALT
2	CUPS WATER
4	EGG YOLKS, SLIGHTLY BEATEN
½	CUP FRESH LEMON JUICE
1½	TABLESPOONS LEMON ZEST
1	OZ. UNSALTED BUTTER

Continued . . .

12. Gently fold in fresh lemon juice. Spread the meringue over the lemon filling to top edge of piecrust, using a large spoon or spatula to create swirled peaks.

13. Bake for 6 to 8 minutes, until meringue is light brown at peaks. Let the pie cool completely before serving.

INGREDIENTS:

FOR THE MERINGUE

4	EGG WHITES
½	TEASPOON CREAM OF TARTAR
	PINCH OF FINE SEA SALT
½	CUP SUGAR
1	TEASPOON FRESH LEMON JUICE

LEMON TARTS

YIELD: 24 TARTS / **ACTIVE TIME:** 20 MINUTES / **TOTAL TIME:** 1 HOUR

These bite-sized treats are a year-round favorites. The simple dough and lemon filling topped with confectioners' sugar work for both rustic outings and elegant events.

1. To prepare the dough, place the butter and cream cheese in the mixing bowl of a stand mixer and beat until just combined. Place flour and confectioners' sugar in a separate bowl and whisk to combine. Add the dry mixture to the butter-and-cream cheese mixture and beat until the dough just holds together. Work the mixture with your hands until it is smooth and homogenous.

2. Spoon approximately 1 tablespoon of dough into the wells an ungreased miniature tart pan. Using your fingers, press down on the dough spread it to fill the wells. Set the pan aside and preheat the oven to 350°F.

3. To prepare the filling, combine the sugar and flour in the work bowl of a stand mixer fitted with the whisk attachment. Add the eggs and beat until incorporated, scraping down the work bowl as needed. Add the lemon zest and juice and beat until incorporated.

4. Fill the tart shells with the filling, place the tarts in the oven, and bake until the shells are golden brown, about 20 minutes. Remove and let cool in the pan for 15 minutes.

5. Run a knife around the edge of each tart, remove them from the wells, dust with confectioners' sugar, and serve.

TIP: Add blueberries or raspberries to lemon filling for a delicious fruit-filled variation!

INGREDIENTS:

FOR THE DOUGH

6	OZ. UNSALTED BUTTER, SOFTENED
3	OZ. CREAM CHEESE, SOFTENED
7.5	OZ. ALL-PURPOSE FLOUR
2	OZ. CONFECTIONERS' SUGAR

FOR THE FILLING

2	CUPS SUGAR
5	TABLESPOONS ALL-PURPOSE FLOUR
4	EGGS
	ZEST AND JUICE OF 2 LEMONS
	CONFECTIONERS' SUGAR, FOR DUSTING

LIL'S CAFE

Kittery, ME

Envisioned by a restauranteur, three bakers, an event planner, a tea expert, and a coffee nut, Lil's Café is the beating heart of the small business community in downtown Kittery, Maine. Lil's began to take shape with the idea of doughnuts and improving Wallingford Square. Locals wanted a place to meet friends, eat great food, and return to time and time again. They got that place in Lil's. Featuring a wide array of products from crullers to baked goods and breads, the café has brought the town to life and draws in a steady stream of customers with its welcoming and creative atmosphere.

CRULLERS

YIELD: 96 CRULLERS / **ACTIVE TIME:** 1 HOUR / **TOTAL TIME:** 1 HOUR AND 15 MINUTES

These delicious crullers will make your morning. The crispy outside, soft interior, and delicious glaze are the perfect way to start your day off with a smile.

1. Place the flour in a bowl. Combine the sugar and salt in a separate bowl.

2. Crack the eggs into a measuring cup with the vanilla paste and vanilla extract.

3. Place the butter and water in a large pot. Bring the butter and water to a boil. Once boiling, pour the sugar and salt into the liquids and stir to combine. Return to a boil.

4. Add the flour to the boiling liquids, reduce heat to low, and cook, stirring constantly until the batter begins to cook to the bottom of the pot, about 10 minutes.

5. Transfer the batter to a stand mixer fitted with the paddle attachment. Beat the batter on low speed until steam no longer rises from the bowl and the exterior of the mixing bowl is cool enough to touch.

6. Gradually pour the eggs into the mixer while it is running on low speed. Mix until batter is fully homogenous. Raise mixer speed to medium-high and beat for 1 to 2 minutes.

7. Transfer batter to a piping bag fitted with a star tip. Pipe crullers onto greased or parchment-lined baking sheets. Chill the piped crullers in the refrigerator for 10 minutes.

8. In a large pot, heat several inches of canola oil in a large pot to 350°F. Add 1 to 2 crullers to the pot at a time, face up. Fry on the first side for 3 minutes. Flip the crullers in the oil. Fry upside down for 3 minutes. Flip the crullers again. Fry for an additional 1½ minutes.

9. Remove from oil and transfer to a wire rack to cool. Glaze with desired icing and serve.

INGREDIENTS:

10.6	OZ. ALL-PURPOSE FLOUR
3.7	OZ. SUGAR
1	TEASPOON (SCANT) KOSHER SALT
6	LARGE EGGS
¾	TEASPOON VANILLA PASTE
⅓	TEASPOON PURE VANILLA EXTRACT
8	OZ. UNSALTED BUTTER
2	CUPS WATER
	CANOLA OIL, AS NEEDED

SWEET LIFE PATISSERIE

Eugene, OR

Sisters Cheryl and Catherine Reinhart have always been bakers at heart—the issue has never been "what," but "where." Before they opened Sweet Life, Catherine had been working in local bakeries, practicing with wedding cake decoration, while Cheryl worked primarily in restaurants, baking whenever possible. Says Cheryl, "We wanted to work for ourselves and we owned a house together. We thought, 'Why not convert our one-car garage into a certified kitchen and make wedding cakes?' So that's what we did." Both women kept their other jobs for the first year, attending shows and marketing to restaurants in order to build a base. Before long, Sweet Life had earned a reputation as a go-to place for celebratory desserts.

The Reinharts have truly embraced this identity, even describing the bakery's essence as "a party every day, where everyone in the community can celebrate special occasions." And while the bakery has since moved out of the garage, this personal touch is what keeps Sweet Life so in touch with the community. That, and their eagerness to accept and promote different kinds of diets. "We were doing gluten-free and egg- and dairy-free desserts long before it caught on in the mainstream." Why? "Because the customers asked." This wasn't an easy transition—Cheryl and Sarah knew they wanted to keep their original recipes, but they wanted everyone to feel comfortable at Sweet Life. That

meant a lot of experimentation. "We didn't think it was possible until someone gave us a really good egg- and dairy-free chocolate cake recipe and we were sold on the idea. We kept at it until we felt our vegan and gluten-free dessert options were delicious for everyone."

Part of this can be attributed to Eugene, Oregon, where the bakery can be found. "Eugene is famous for its many alternative lifestyles, including dietary ones," says Cheryl. But different diets have only become more prominent since they expanded their menu, and the experimenting can be fun, if trying. Cheryl admits, "There are some desserts that just don't taste good when translated with certain dietary restrictions, and we just don't do them." In other words, quality is always the most important thing.

The treats at Sweet Life have resonated outside of the Eugene area, earning the bakery a place on *Buzzfeed's* "23 Bakeries You Need to Visit Before You Die" list. Still, the Rein-hart sisters take more pride in their partnership than anything else. "More than being a chef, I think running a successful business as sisters has been a journey that we're both proud of. We've learned a lot from each other and I feel like we have a huge community that supports us and we support them by giving a lot of people meaningful work in a supportive environment."

IN THEIR OWN WORDS:
CATHERINE AND CHERYL REINHART

How and when did you get your start baking?

We both started baking and cooking when we were young kids. Both of our grandmas and our mother were amazing cooks and made cakes, cookies and pies from scratch. We were immersed in a culture of home cooking and baking, so for us it was just natural to join in with the baking.

Who inspired you to bake? Who inspires you now?

When we started baking professionally, we were inspired by French pastry chefs and their beautiful creations. Our scratch baking roots provided inspiration as well. Today, we find inspiration from many sources, including the locavore movement, our employees, and the wealth of food culture that has blossomed everywhere around us.

What is your golden rule(s) of baking?

We attempt to achieve the perfect balance of flavors and textures by combining complementary elements in our desserts.

What is your favorite thing to bake? Why? Least favorite thing to bake? Why?

My favorite is our passionfruit tart with fresh raspberries. We start with a shortbread shell, fill it with passionfruit curd, top with fresh organic local raspberries, glazed with apricot glaze. Why? Because, well, it's so delicious! Least favorite: Gluten-free cakes. Why? Because it's so tricky to get the texture just right.

What are your most popular items?

Our Chocolate Orgasm Cake is one of our customers' all-time favorites. It's a chocolate cake, filled with vanilla custard and chocolate mousse, and topped with blood orange buttercream. A few other favorites are: the Josephine (our version of a Napoleon, it's a crispy puff pastry shell filled with vanilla custard and served with an organic raspberry puree); pumpkin cookies with brown sugar frosting; black bottom cupcakes (chocolate cake with a baked cheesecake top and milk chocolate chips) and cheesecake (we do all kinds of different cheesecakes and the customers love them all!).

What nonessential items should every baker have?

My favorite nonessential items are cool stencils for making fancy shaped designs on top of cakes.

What book(s) go on your required reading list for bakers?

There are so many options nowadays. I recommend experimenting with recipes that sound good to you and modifying them as needed whether it's adding darker chocolate or more salt to a recipe. As far as acquiring skills, libraries and the internet have a wealth of knowledge. Just Google what you want to know and you'll find hundreds of "how-to" resources.

Tell us about your favorite part of collaborating on a recipe.

What is really interesting to us is collaborating with our bakers. They all come with some experience and creativity so when we want to come up with a new dessert or an exciting flavor combination, we love to brainstorm together to make the perfect dessert.

Where did you learn to cook? Please tell me about your education and/or apprenticeships.

Mostly it was on the job. As mentioned before, we grew up in a family that loved food and cooking, so it's in our blood. We spent time in all sorts of kitchens from a galley on a crab processor in Alaska, to a homey bakery to a high-end restaurant in Eugene, Oregon. As for learning how to bake, we still continue to improve our recipes and refine our techniques. It's an ongoing education.

SWEET LIFE'S PUMPKIN PIE

YIELD: 10-INCH PIE / **ACTIVE TIME:** 45 MINUTES / **TOTAL TIME:** 2 HOURS

This comforting seasonal classic gets an added touch of color and flavor from the addition of molasses.

1. Preheat the oven to 350°F. Combine all of the ingredients, except for the piecrust, and mix until evenly incorporated.

2. Pour approximately 5 cups of the filling into unbaked pie shell.

3. Bake for 30 minutes at 350°F, then 30 to 40 minutes at 275°F. Pie should be firm and jiggle only slightly. The center should not be sticky, cracked, or dry looking. Remove and let cool completely before serving.

INGREDIENTS:

2	CUPS PUMPKIN PUREE
¾	CUP SUGAR
½	TABLESPOON MOLASSES
½	TEASPOON FINE SEA SALT
¾	CUP HEAVY CREAM
¾	CUP MILK
2	EGGS
2	TEASPOONS PURE VANILLA EXTRACT
½	TEASPOON FRESHLY GRATED NUTMEG
½	TEASPOON GROUND GINGER
½	TEASPOON ALLSPICE
1	PERFECT PIECRUST (SEE PAGE 46)

BLOOD ORANGE CHEESECAKE

YIELD: 6 TO 8 SERVINGS / **ACTIVE TIME:** 1 HOUR / **TOTAL TIME:** 24 HOURS

This decadent and rich cheesecake is sure to impress.

1. Preheat the oven to 350°F. To begin preparations for the crust, place the butter and sugar in the work bowl of a stand mixer fitted with the paddle attachment. Beat at medium speed until the mixture is light and fluffy. Add the remaining ingredients and beat until incorporated. Press the mixture into a 9-inch springform pan.

2. Place the pan in the oven and bake for 30 minutes. Remove and let cool. Lower the oven temperature to 300°F.

3. Wipe out the work bowl of the stand mixer. To begin preparations for the filling, add the cream cheese and 1 cup of the sugar to the work bowl and beat at medium speed until combined. Incorporate the eggs one at a time, scraping down the work bowl after each has been incorporated. Add the blood orange compound, beat until incorporated, and pour the mixture into the crust.

4. Place the cheesecake in the oven and bake until the edges are set and the center jiggles slightly, about 1 hour. Turn off the oven and leave the cheesecake in the cooling oven for 1 hour.

5. Remove the cheesecake from the oven and preheat the oven to 300°F. Place the sour cream and the remaining sugar in a mixing bowl and stir to combine. Spread this mixture over the top of the cheesecake, return it to the oven, and bake for another 20 minutes. Remove the cheesecake from the oven and let it cool until just warm. Cover with plastic wrap and place in the refrigerator overnight.

6. Remove the cheesecake from the refrigerator and let come to room temperature. To prepare the ganache, place the chocolate chips and butter in a mixing bowl and set aside. Place the cream and sugar in a saucepan and bring to a boil over medium heat, stirring. When the sugar has dissolved, pour the mixture over the chocolate and butter and let stand for 5 minutes.

7. Stir the ganache until it is smooth and then spread it over the top of the cheesecake. Let the chocolate set for 10 minutes before serving.

INGREDIENTS:

FOR THE CRUST

4	OZ. UNSALTED BUTTER, MELTED
7	OZ. SUGAR
1½	TABLESPOONS WATER
⅓	CUP COCOA POWDER
1½	CUPS ALL-PURPOSE FLOUR

FOR THE FILLING

4½	CUPS CREAM CHEESE, SOFTENED
1⅓	CUPS SUGAR
4	EGGS
2	TABLESPOONS BLOOD ORANGE COMPOUND
2	CUPS SOUR CREAM

FOR THE GANACHE

1⅓	CUPS BITTERSWEET CHOCOLATE CHIPS
1.5	OZ. UNSALTED BUTTER
1⅓	CUPS HEAVY CREAM
3	TABLESPOONS SUGAR

SWEET LIFE'S STRAWBERRY RHUBARB PIE

YIELD: 1 PIE / *ACTIVE TIME:* 45 MINUTES / **TOTAL TIME:** 2 HOURS

Sweet strawberries, sour rhubarb, and plenty of brown sugar combine to make a winning version of this classic dessert.

1. Preheat oven to 350°F.

2. Combine water, lemon juice, 1 cup of brown sugar, starches, and tapioca in a bowl. Pour over rhubarb and mix.

3. Heat over low until starches are clear and thick. Add strawberries. Cool.

4. Combine flour, oats, and the remaining brown sugar in mixer.

5. Chop cold butter into 1-inch cubes and add to dry mix. Mix until butter is mostly broken down and crumbles begin to come together. Avoid a floury, dry-looking mixture, as that will create a dry, non-crispy topping. The topping should be uniformly moist-looking and hold together when pressed lightly.

6. Pour filling into pie shell and top with the crumble. Bake for 50 minutes to 1 hour. Remove and let cool before serving.

INGREDIENTS:

⅓	CUP WATER
2	TABLESPOONS FRESH LEMON JUICE
1	CUP BROWN SUGAR, PLUS ½ CUP
2	TABLESPOONS ARROWROOT POWDER
1½	TABLESPOONS CORNSTARCH
2½	TABLESPOONS INSTANT TAPIOCA
6¾	CUPS STRAWBERRIES, HULLED AND QUARTERED
4½	CUPS RHUBARB, CHOPPED IN ½-INCH SLICES
1	PERFECT PIECRUST (SEE PAGE 46)
½	CUP ALL-PURPOSE FLOUR
⅔	CUP REGULAR OATS
3	OZ. UNSALTED BUTTER, CHILLED

THE SWEETERY

Anderson, SC

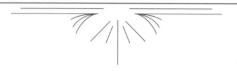

When asked to describe what The Sweetery represents to her, owner Jane Jaharian has a specific answer in mind: "A child that never grows up." It is an apt description; the bakery has endured for over 30 years and barely aged a day. And though her son Ryan has indeed grown up, he hasn't strayed far—the mom-and-son duo work together in the bakery to bring sweetness to South Carolina. A lifelong Anderson resident, Jane set out to help working mothers—baking homemade cakes for them to bring home after a long day so as not to "take precious time away from their families." Once people began tasting her cakes, though, word began to spread. Today,

Jane is not only a master baker but also the president of the South Carolina Specialty Food Organization, where she helps local farmers and retailers expand their businesses. As a bakery, The Sweetery doesn't overcomplicate things. In true Southern fashion, simple ingredients and traditional flavors are the bakery's hallmarks. "I read a lot about cooking foods, techniques, ingredients and recipes from all generations—and also get a lot from the Food Network!" For Jane and the team, the proudest moments come from happy customers. And with The Sweetery's output, those moments occur every day.

IN HER OWN WORDS:
JANE JAHARIAN

How and when did you get your start baking?

I began baking pizza and pies—both sweet and savory—when I was 13 years old.

Who inspired you to bake? Who inspires you now?

From an early age, I think all Southern women, or homemakers in general, are inspired by the satisfaction of seeing people enjoy food they've prepared. My Sweetery customers inspire me now!

What is your golden rule(s) of baking?

Use quality ingredients.

What is your favorite thing to bake? Why? Least favorite thing to bake? Why?

Favorite: A special holiday cake—it doesn't matter what kind. Least favorite—a recipe that leaves something out.

What are your most popular items?

Strawberry Cake, Brownies & Crème, and Tomato Pies are our bestsellers.

What book(s) go on your required reading list for bakers?

I have several baking books I refer back to from time to time, to list just some would be an injustice.

What outlets/periodicals/newspapers do you read or consult regularly, if any?

I like *Bake Magazine*, and the Retail Baker's Association also puts out good newsletters.

Tell me about your most memorable collaboration with another chef.

There have been many, but Paula Dean and I once had a conversation on Southern food that was like talking recipes with an old friend.

Where did you learn to cook?

I've always had a love of cooking and am self-taught through years of practice.

What is your favorite thing about The Sweetery?

The feeling of being a part of your community. When I was growing up in Anderson, we had our own town baker; when he retired, he began working part-time in The Sweetery, and was kind enough to pass some of his special recipes to us. This continuing of community traditions is very special to me.

THE SWEETERY'S PECAN PIE

YIELD: 8 SERVINGS / **ACTIVE TIME:** 20 MINUTES / **TOTAL TIME:** 1 HOUR AND 5 MINUTES

This 30-year-old recipe of a classic Southern dish belongs in every bakery, no matter the location.

1. Preheat the oven to 350°F.

2. Combine all of the ingredients, except for the piecrust, in a large bowl.

3. Roll the piecrust into a 12-inch circle on a lightly floured surface. Fit the dough over a greased 9-inch pie dish. Trim the edges, leaving a 1-inch overhang. Crimp the edges. Refrigerate the dough for another 15 minutes.

4. Pour filling in crust and bake for 45 to 50 minutes. Remove and let the pie cool before serving.

INGREDIENTS:

1	CUP LIGHT CORN SYRUP
1	CUP FIRMLY PACKED DARK BROWN SUGAR
3	EGGS, LIGHTLY BEATEN
⅓	CUP UNSALTED BUTTER, MELTED
½	TEASPOON FINE SEA SALT
1	CUP PECANS
1	PERFECT PIECRUST (SEE PAGE 46)

FLOUR BAKERY

Boston and Cambridge, MA

It's nearly impossible to talk about the New England baking scene without going on a tangent about Flour Bakery + Café, Joanne Chang's highly acclaimed chain. Chang, a true culinary star, has been featured or reviewed in too many publications to count—from *Zagat* to *Food & Wine* to dozens of Boston outlets. In 2007, she beat celebrity chef Bobby Flay on *Food Network*'s "Throwdown with Bobby Flay," besting his sticky bun with her own now-famous recipe. And she won the James Beard Foundation's award for Outstanding Baker in 2016. In other words: Joanne Chang is a busy woman.

Incredibly, all of this could have never happened had Chang ignored her gut. After graduating from Harvard with a degree in Applied Math and Economics, she began her career as a management consultant at The Monitor Group in Cambridge. Thus began two years of spreadsheets and meetings that never quite suited Chang, despite the respect she held for her bosses. And so, she began applying for work at Boston's top restaurants. Chef Lydia Shire gave her a start at the bottom of the totem pole at Biba, where she worked for a year before leaving to work with Rick Katz at his bakery in Newton Center. Before long, Chang was working at Payard Patisserie with legendary pastry chef Francois Payard.

"He was the stereotypical French chef. He yelled a lot in French and English, threw things at times, was such a perfectionist." I spent a year with him working from 4 a.m. to 7 p.m., 6 days a week. I'm not exaggerating. We all worked this hard—it was sort of like boot camp. Of course, I learned so much! But I also realized that no one can work those hours and stay sharp and strong. It was while I was in NYC that I started thinking about opening a bakery of my own. I had loved working with Rick and all of the personal touches we were able to give our customers, and I dreamed of opening a place back in Boston in which we would make everything from scratch and we would give the best service ever. We would be like the bakery version of Cheers."

Chang realized her dream in 2000, opening the first Flour Bakery + Café in Boston's South End. She has soared since then, but the bakeries' collective mission statement has remained unchanged: "total unwavering commitment to excellence in every way." The aforementioned sticky buns are perhaps the best in the country, but everything baked at Flour is reliably delicious and fresh—so much, in fact, that you may have to prepare for a (well worth it) line!

Today, Chang owns seven Flour locations in addition to their "Breadquarters" (where Flour's offices and baking classes can be found) and Myers + Chang, a sit-down restaurant she operates with chef Karen Akunowicz and co-owns with her husband, Chris Myers. If this all sounds like too much, don't worry; Chang has been so successful at every level that it's fair to wonder if she's just getting started.

FLOUR'S FAMOUS BANANA BREAD

YIELD: 19-INCH LOAF / **ACTIVE TIME:** 45 MINUTES / **TOTAL TIME:** 2 HOURS

Joanne Chang: "I remember grocery shopping with my mom and toting home large bags of overripe bananas when we found them on special for ten cents a pound. My mom would encourage my brother, my dad, and me to 'have a banana!' every time we were near the kitchen. My brother and I began to avoid the kitchen for fear of being accosted by Mom and her banana entreaties. In time, I developed this banana bread as a protection device for us."

1. Position a rack in the center of the oven and heat the oven to 325°F. Butter a 9 x 5–inch loaf pan.

2. In a bowl, sift together the flour, baking soda, cinnamon, and salt. Set aside.

3. Using a stand mixer fitted with the whip attachment or a handheld mixer, beat together the sugar and eggs on medium speed for about 5 minutes, or until light and fluffy. (If you use a handheld mixer, this same step will take about 8 minutes.)

4. On low speed, slowly drizzle in the oil. Don't pour the oil in all at once. Add it slowly so it has time to incorporate into the eggs and doesn't deflate the air you have just beaten into the batter. Adding it should take about 1 minute. Add the bananas, crème fraîche, and vanilla and continue to mix on low speed just until combined.

5. Using a rubber spatula, fold in the flour mixture and the nuts just until thoroughly combined. No flour streaks should be visible, and the nuts should be evenly distributed. Pour the batter into the prepared loaf pan and smooth the top.

6. Bake for 1 to 1¼ hours, or until golden brown on top and the center springs back when you press it. If your finger sinks when you poke the bread, it needs to bake a little longer. Let cool in the pan on a wire rack for at least 30 minutes, and then pop it out of the pan to finish cooling.

7. The banana bread can be stored tightly wrapped in plastic wrap at room temperature for up to 3 days. Or, it can be well wrapped in plastic wrap and frozen for up to 2 weeks; thaw overnight at room temperature for serving

INGREDIENTS:

1½	CUPS UNBLEACHED ALL-PURPOSE FLOUR
1	TEASPOON BAKING SODA
¼	TEASPOON GROUND CINNAMON
½	TEASPOON KOSHER SALT
1	CUP PLUS 2 TABLESPOONS SUGAR
2	EGGS
½	CUP CANOLA OIL
3½	VERY RIPE, MEDIUM BANANAS, PEELED AND MASHED (1 CUP MASHED)
2	TABLESPOONS CRÈME FRAÎCHE OR SOUR CREAM
1	TEASPOON PURE VANILLA EXTRACT
¾	CUP WALNUT HALVES, TOASTED AND CHOPPED

KOUIGN-AMANN

YIELD: 12 SMALL CAKES / **ACTIVE TIME:** 2 HOURS / **TOTAL TIME:** 5½ HOURS

❝ A specialty of Brittany, the small, rich kouign-amann, literally "butter cake," is possibly the most extraordinary pastry of all time. Imagine a flaky croissant–type pastry filled with layers of butter and sugar, and then more butter and sugar, and baked until the sugar caramelizes into a marvelously sticky, crispy coating. The first time I had one—in Paris, of course—I knew I had to make it at Flour. It remains for me the most delicious pastry I've ever eaten. Nicole, our executive pastry chef, spent hours perfecting the recipe to make sure it has the right balance of sugar to butter to dough, and then tweaked it so that it could be baked in a muffin tin rather than ring molds. Read through the recipe a few times to make sure you understand the directions. If you've made laminated doughs of any kind before (puff pastry, croissant), you'll have no problem with this one. If you haven't, it is not difficult to make, but you'll need to familiarize yourself with the simple technique of folding and turning the dough, explained in the recipe. These small cakes are more of an after-party treat or decadent breakfast than an opulent plated dessert, although if you were to serve them with some ice cream and berries, I guarantee that you would be showered with compliments."

1. In the stand mixer, mix together the yeast and 1 cup tepid water until the yeast dissolves. Add the flour, salt, and 1 tablespoon melted butter and mix on low speed for 3 to 4 minutes, or until the dough comes together and is smooth. (If the dough is too wet, add 2 to 3 tablespoons flour; if it is too dry, add 2 to 3 teaspoons of water.) The dough should be soft and supple and should come away from the sides of the bowl when the mixer is on. To make the dough by hand, in a medium bowl, dissolve the yeast in 1 cup water as directed and stir in the flour, salt, and melted butter with a wooden spoon until incorporated. Then turn the dough out onto a floured worksurface and knead by hand for 8 to 10 minutes, or until the dough is soft, smooth, and supple.

2. Transfer the dough to the baking sheet and cover with plastic wrap. Leave in a warm place for 1 hour to allow the dough to proof. Then transfer the dough to the fridge and leave it for another hour.

3. Transfer the dough from the fridge to a generously floured work surface. Roll it into a rectangle about 16 inches wide and 10 in from top to bottom. With your fingers, press or smear the room-temperature butter directly over the right half of the dough, spreading it in a thin, even layer to cover the entire right half. Fold the left half of the dough over the butter and press down to seal the butter between the dough layers. Turn the dough 90 degrees clockwise so that the rectangle is about 10 inches wide and 8 inches top to bottom, and generously flour the underside and top of the dough.

INGREDIENTS:

1⅛ TEASPOONS ACTIVE DRY YEAST, OR 3 TEASPOONS FRESH CAKE YEAST

13.75 OZ. ALL-PURPOSE FLOUR

1¼ TEASPOONS KOSHER SALT

8 OZ. UNSALTED BUTTER, SOFTENED; PLUS 1 TABLESPOON, MELTED

10.5 OZ. SUGAR, PLUS MORE FOR ROLLING AND COATING

4. Press the dough down evenly with the palms of your hands, flattening it out before you start to roll it out. Slowly begin rolling the dough from side to side into a rectangle about 24 inches wide and 12 inches from top to bottom. The dough might be a little sticky, so, again, be sure to flour the dough and the work surface as needed to prevent the rolling pin from sticking. Using the bench scraper or a knife, lightly score the rectangle vertically into thirds. Each third will be about 8 inches wide and 12 inches from top to bottom. Brush any loose flour off the dough. Lift the right third of the dough and flip it over onto the middle third. Then lift the left third of the dough and flip it on top of the middle and right thirds (like folding a business letter). Your dough should now be about 8 inches wide, 12 inches from top to bottom, and about 1½ inches thick. Rotate the dough clockwise 90 degrees; it will now be 12 inches wide and 8 inches from top to bottom, with the folded seam on top. The process of folding in thirds and rotating is called turning the dough.

5. Repeat the process once more, patiently and slowly roll the dough into a long rectangle, flipping it upside down as needed as you roll it back and forth, and then fold the dough into thirds. The dough will be a bit tougher to roll out and a bit more elastic.

6. Return the dough to the baking sheet and cover it completely with plastic wrap, tucking the plastic wrap under the dough as if you are tucking it into bed. Refrigerate the dough for about 30 minutes. This will relax the dough so that you'll be able to roll it out again and give it more turns. Don't leave the dough in the fridge much longer than 30 minutes, or the butter will harden too much and it won't roll out properly.

7. Remove the dough from the refrigerator and place it on a well-floured work sur-face with a long side of the rectangle facing you and the seam on top. Again, roll the dough into a rectangle about 24 inches wide and 12 inches from top to bottom. Sprinkle ½ cup (100 g) of the sugar over the dough and use the rolling pin to gently press it in. Give the dough another fold into thirds and turn as directed previously. The sugar may spill out a bit. That's okay, just scoop it back in.

8. Once again roll the dough into a rectangle 24 inches wide and 12 inches from top to bottom. Sprinkle the remaining sugar over the dough and use the rolling pin to press the sugar gently into the dough. Give the dough one last fold into thirds and turn. Return the dough to the baking sheet, cover again with plastic wrap, and refrigerate for another 30 minutes.

9. Meanwhile, liberally butter the cups of the muffin tin and set aside.

10. Remove the dough from the refrigerator. Sprinkle your work surface generously with sugar, place the dough on the sugar, and sprinkle

the top with more sugar. Roll the dough into a long rectangle 24 inches wide and 8 inches from top to bottom. The sugar will make the dough gritty and sticky, but it will also make the dough easier to roll out. Using a chef's knife, cut the dough in half lengthwise. You should have two strips of dough, each 24 inches wide and 4 inches from top to bottom. Cut each strip into six 4-inch squares.

11. Working with one square at a time, fold the corners of the square into the center and press down so they stick in place. Shape and cup the dough into a little circle, and press the bottom and the top into more sugar so that the entire pastry is evenly coated with sugar. Place the dough circle, folded side up, into a cup of the prepared muffin tin. It will just barely fit. Repeat with the remaining squares. Cover the tin with plastic wrap and let the cakes proof in a warm place (78 to 82°F is ideal) for 1 hour to 1 hour and 20 minutes, or until the dough has puffed up.

12. About 20 minutes before you are ready to bake, preheat the oven to 400°F and place a rack in the center of the oven.

13. When the dough is ready, place the muffin tin in the oven, reduce the heat to 325°F, and bake for 30 to 40 minutes, or until the cakes are golden brown. Remove the cakes from the oven and let them cool just until you can handle them, then gently pry them out of the muffin tin onto a wire rack and leave them to cool upside down. They are extremely sticky and will stick to the muffin tin if you don't pop them out while they are still warm. Let cool completely before serving.

SUGAREE'S BAKERY

New Albany, MS

Every state in the South has its own baking tradition, each wonderful in its own right. That said, you could do a lot worse than Mississippi, where recipes are often passed down through generations of at-home bakers. And if you are in Mississippi, it's hard to do much better than Sugaree's, where owner Mary Jennifer Russell has been creating delicious goodies for the masses since 1997.

Of course, Mary began baking much earlier than 1997. Her education began at 7 years old, learning from her first and most important teacher: her mother. Mary says, "She was that mom who made thirty different candies and baked goods every year to give as Christmas gifts to all of our teachers, church friends, and family. I loved getting a free pass on our normally early bedtime to stay up late every night in December to help her!" This background led Mary to revisit baking after bouncing around pharmaceutical sales jobs after graduation. While the jobs may have bored her, the connections she made went a long way toward getting Sugaree's off the ground. "I borrowed a calligraphy book from the library, handwrote a price list and took samples to all the downtown merchants, teachers' lounges, and local business break rooms. Orders slowly started coming in. When I finally got another part-time contract pharmaceutical sales job, it was approved in the interview stage that I could use my entire $300 monthly expense account to purchase my own cakes and give them to the doctors' offices—and that's exactly what I did for the next three years, which helped spread my footprint to all of North Mississippi."

The enterprise grew from local to wholesale before Mary opened her first brick-and-mortar space in New Albany. And while she still does most of her business wholesale, Sugaree's remains a staple in the community, evoking the "childhood memories of growing up with a master baker in your life" and staying true to the traditional flavors of the Deep South. Her mastery of this difficult balance is what earned Mary the 2017 award for Mississippi SBA Small Business Person of the Year—and what's kept customers coming back for more over the last two years.

CHOCOLATE MERINGUE PIE

YIELD: 8 SERVINGS / **ACTIVE TIME:** 25 MINUTES / **TOTAL TIME:** 2 HOURS

This Southern classic proves that you don't need to love lemons to enjoy a nice meringue pie.

1. Grease a pie plate with nonstick cooking spray and preheat the oven to 375°F. To begin preparations for the crust, combine the flour, salt, butter, and lard in a mixing bowl and work the mixture with a pastry cutter until the mixture is a collection of clumps that are approximately the size of sunflower seeds.

2. Add the ice water 2 tablespoons at a time and work the mixture with the pastry cutter until it comes together as a dough. Make sure you work quickly to avoid overworking the dough.

3. Place the dough between two pieces of parchment paper and roll it out to fit the pie plate. Place it in the pie plate, trim any excess, and crimp the edge of the crust. Place the crust in the freezer for 10 minutes.

4. Combine the heavy cream and egg yolk. Remove the crust from the freezer and brush it with the egg wash. Poke holes all over the bottom and sides of the crust, place it in the oven, and bake for 10 minutes.

5. Check the dough to see if it is puffing up. If it is, remove from the oven and poke more holes in the dough. Return to the oven and bake until the crust is just starting to turn golden brown, about 20 minutes. Remove from the oven and let the crust cool.

6. To begin preparations for the filling, place the flour, cocoa powder, salt, and sugar in a mixing bowl and whisk to combine. Set the mixture aside.

7. Place the water and egg yolks in a separate bowl, whisk to combine, and then strain this mixture into the evaporated milk. Add the dry mixture and whisk to combine.

8. Strain the filling into a medium saucepan and bring to a boil over medium heat, stirring constantly.

9. Remove the pan from heat, stir in the vanilla and butter, and beat at medium speed with a handheld mixer fitted with the paddle attachment until smooth. Cover the saucepan and set it aside.

INGREDIENTS:

FOR THE CRUST

10	OZ. CAKE FLOUR
½	TEASPOON FINE SEA SALT
2	OZ. UNSALTED BUTTER, FROZEN AND GRATED
2.1	OZ. LARD
¼	CUP ICE WATER
1	TABLESPOON HEAVY CREAM
1	EGG YOLK

FOR THE FILLING

5	TABLESPOONS CAKE FLOUR
½	CUP SIFTED COCOA POWDER
⅛	TEASPOON FINE SEA SALT
15.75	OZ. SUGAR
¾	CUP WATER
5	LARGE EGG YOLKS
1¾	CUPS EVAPORATED MILK
2½	TEASPOONS PURE VANILLA EXTRACT
1.25	OZ. UNSALTED BUTTER, CUT INTO SMALL PIECES

FOR THE MERINGUE

1½	EGG WHITES, AT ROOM TEMPERATURE
½	TEASPOON CREAM OF TARTAR
8.75	OZ. SUGAR

Continued . . .

10. Preheat the oven to 325°F. To prepare the meringue, place the egg whites and cream of tartar in the work bowl of a stand mixer fitted with the whisk attachment and beat at high speed until frothy. With the mixer running, gradually incorporate the sugar and beat until the meringue holds stiff peaks.

11. Pour the filling into the crust and top with the meringue, piling it high in the shape of a beehive. Use a spoon to lift the meringue into peaks.

12. Place the pie in the oven and bake until a few cracks form in the meringue, about 45 minutes. Remove from the oven and let cool before serving.

SWISS BAKERY

Vancouver, British Columbia, CA

Michael Siu

Swiss Bakery is home to the frissant. Following the rise of the croissant-doughnut called the cronut, father and daughter Michael and Annette Siu created the frissant, which features a croissant dough in a doughnut shape that is deep-fried and filled with cream. The name is a mix of "fritter" and "croissant." While Swiss Bakery has been in business for more than 20 years, Michael and Annette knew the frissant was a game-changer for the company when customers started lining up down the street before the shop was open to get the pastry.

SWISS BAKERY'S FRISSANTS

YIELD: 8 FRISSANTS / **ACTIVE TIME:** 2 HOURS / **TOTAL TIME:** 5 HOURS AND 30 MINUTES

Skip the cronut line in your city and just make them yourself with this "frissant," a pastry that is as visually stunning as it is delicious. Experiment with fillings and toppings to determine your favorite flavor.

1. Combine all ingredients aside from the 4 oz. butter in a mixer with a dough hook. Mix on slow speed for about 5 minutes. The dough should look underdeveloped.

2. Remove the dough from mixer and flatten onto sheet tray. Cover with plastic wrap and place in the freezer for 1 hour.

3. Place your roll-in butter into a large resealable bag and use your rolling pin to flatten the butter, filling the edges of the bag as much as possible. Make sure the butter is pliable and you can easily poke a finger into it. The butter should not be melted.

4. Remove the dough from the freezer and place onto a sparingly floured surface. Roll the dough out with a rolling pin so that it can envelope the pliable butter.

5. Remove the butter from the resealable bag and place onto one side of the dough.

6. Fold the dough over so that the butter is fully blanketed and enclosed by the dough.

7. Roll out dough and give it one single fold, then let it rest in the fridge for 30 minutes.

8. Remove the dough from the fridge and roll it out. Give it one double-fold, then let rest it in the fridge for 30 minutes. When the 30 minutes are up, repeat this step one more time.

9. Remove dough from fridge and flour surface sparingly. Roll the dough out so that it is about 5 millimeters thick.

10. Cut out frissants and place onto a greased parchment paper. Proof in a warm area until the frissant has at least doubled in size. That will take at least an hour at around 84°F.

11. Pour grapeseed oil into a large pot to prepare to fry the frissants. Use a candy thermometer to figure out when oil is heated to 360°F.

INGREDIENTS:

15	OZ. BREAD FLOUR
3¼	TABLESPOONS SUGAR
¾	TEASPOON FINE SEA SALT
2¼	TABLESPOONS FRESH YEAST
⅔	TABLESPOON EGG
4	OZ. UNSALTED BUTTER, PLUS 1⅓ TEASPOONS
¾	CUP WATER
	GRAPESEED OIL, AS NEEDED

Continued . . .

12. Place up to 4 frissants into the hot oil. Try not to overcrowd the pan as it will lower the oil temperature. Flip when one of the sides is golden brown.

13. Prepare a tray with paper towels to drain the frissants after frying. Using a slotted spoon, remove from oil and place onto the prepared tray to drain the oil. Cool for at least 15 minutes, then roll each side in cinnamon-sugar to coat.

14. Inject cream or jam into the frissants by poking 4 holes from the top.

15. Glaze the top with fondant, ganache, or confectioners' sugar to finish.

CONVERSION TABLE

WEIGHTS

1 oz. = 28 grams

2 oz. = 57 grams

4 oz. (¼ lb.) = 113 grams

8 oz. (½ lb.) = 227 grams

16 oz. (1 lb.) = 454 grams

VOLUME MEASURES

⅛ teaspoon = 0.6 ml

¼ teaspoon = 1.23 ml

½ teaspoon = 2.5 ml

1 teaspoon = 5 ml

1 tablespoon (3 teaspoons) = ½ fluid oz. = 15 ml

2 tablespoons = 1 fluid oz. = 29.5 ml

¼ cup (4 tablespoons) = 2 fluid oz. = 59 ml

⅓ cup (5 ⅓ tablespoons) = 2.7 fluid oz. = 80 ml

½ cup (8 tablespoons) = 4 fluid oz. = 120 ml

⅔ cup (10 ⅔ tablespoons) = 5.4 fluid oz. = 160 ml

¾ cup (12 tablespoons) = 6 fluid oz. = 180 ml

1 cup (16 tablespoons) = 8 fluid oz. = 240 ml

TEMPERATURE EQUIVALENTS

°F	°C	Gas Mark
225	110	¼
250	130	½
275	140	1
300	150	2
325	170	3
350	180	4
375	190	5
400	200	6
425	220	7
450	230	8
475	240	9
500	250	10

LENGTH MEASURES

1/16 inch = 1.6 mm

⅛ inch = 3 mm

¼ inch = 1.35 mm

½ inch = 1.25 cm

¾ inch = 2 cm

1 inch = 2.5 cm

IMAGE CREDITS

INDEX

LLOYD J. H

ARRISS *Pies*

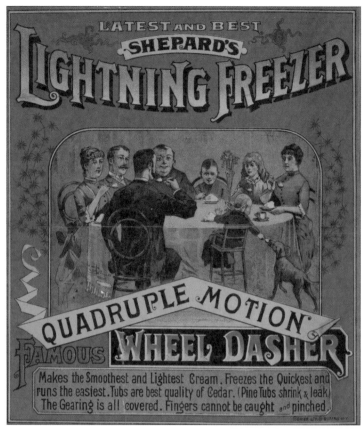

ABOUT CIDER MILL PRESS BOOK PUBLISHERS

Good ideas ripen with time. From seed to harvest, Cider Mill Press brings fine reading, information, and entertainment together between the covers of its creatively crafted books. Our Cider Mill bears fruit twice a year, publishing a new crop of titles each spring and fall.

"Where Good Books Are Ready for Press"

Visit us online at

cidermillpress.com

or write to us at

PO Box 454
12 Spring St.
Kennebunkport, Maine 04046